THE EMPIRE STRIKES BACK?
The Impact of Imperialism on Britain from the Mid-Nineteenth Century

ANDREW THOMPSON

PEARSON
Longman

Harlow, England • London • New York • Boston • San Francisco • Toronto
Sydney • Tokyo • Singapore • Hong Kong • Seoul • Taipei • New Delhi
Cape Town • Madrid • Mexico City • Amsterdam • Munich • Paris • Milan

PEARSON EDUCATION LIMITED

Edinburgh Gate
Harlow CM20 2JE
United Kingdom
Tel: +44 (0)1279 623623
Fax: +44 (0)1279 431059
Website: www.pearsoned.co.uk

_____

First edition published in Great Britain in 2005

© Pearson Education Limited 2005

The right of Andrew Thompson to be identified as author
of this work has been asserted by him in accordance
with the Copyright, Designs and Patents Act 1988.

ISBN 0 582 43829 2

British Library Cataloguing in Publication Data
A CIP catalogue record for this book can be obtained from the British Library

Library of Congress Cataloging-in-Publication Data
Thompson, Andrew, 1968–
    The empire strikes back? : the impact of imperialism on Britain from the mid-nineteenth
century / Andrew Thompson.—1st ed.
      p. cm.
    Includes bibliographical references and index.
    ISBN 0-582-43829-2 (pbk.)
    1. Great Britain—Colonies—Public opinion—History. 2. Public opinion—Great
Britain—History. 3. Imperialism—Economic aspects—Great Britain—History. 4. Great
Britain—Colonial influence—History. 5. Nationalism—Great Britain—History. I. Title.

JV1011.T46 2005
941.08—dc22

                2004060192

10 9 8 7 6 5 4 3 2 1
09 08 07 06 05

Set by 35 in 11/13.5pt Columbus
Printed and bound in Malaysia (CTP-PJB)

The Publishers' policy is to use paper manufactured from sustainable forests.

For Sarah

CONTENTS

LIST OF TABLES

LIST OF FIGURES

ACKNOWLEDGEMENTS

I am fortunate to have benefited from the advice of several colleagues with complementary research specialisms. Particular thanks go to Simon Green for his advice on Victorian religion (and for his helpful suggestions about the project as a whole); Rhonda Semple and Robert Bickers on missionaries; Jon Hyslop, Jeremy Krikler and Alan Fowler on organised labour; Sian Nicholas on the BBC; Jon Lawrence and Miles Taylor on domestic politics; Edward Spiers on the Victorian army; Kent Fedorowich and Marjory Harper on migration; Peter Cain, Mike Collins, Ranald Michie and Gary Magee on the economy; Bill Jones, Mrs H. M. Lay and Glyn Roberts on the Ballarat goldfields and Alice Cornwell; Sarah Crellin on public architecture; Donal Lowry on Irish Unionism; Gilbert Millat and Jean Francois Gournay on comparisons with France, and Benedikt Stuchtey on comparisons with Germany; and Owen Hartley on the post-war era. My father-in-law, Norman Lenton, kindly provided material on the cinema and shared his recollections of several of the films mentioned in Chapter 4. Baroness Shreela Flather relayed the fascinating story of the building of the Memorial Gates on Hyde Park Corner, which mark the Asian and Afro-Caribbean soldiers who fought alongside Britain in the two world wars, while Nigel Rigby and Robert Blyth at the National Maritime Museum, Anthony Tibbles at the Merseyside Maritime Museum and Gareth Griffiths at the Bristol Empire and Commonwealth Museum helped me to make sense of contemporary representations of empire. Liz Boyce at the Empire and Commonwealth museum, Catriona Finlayson at the British Library and Alison Bomford at the National Gallery provided visitor surveys, press cuttings and other material. Neil Plummer and Chris Senior at the Brotherton Library in the University of Leeds responded cheerfully to my endless requests for books. And Heather McCallum, Casey Mein, Christina Wipf Perry and Melanie Carter at Pearson Education commissioned this project and steered it through to publication. I am grateful to them all.

Several people were kind enough to read the manuscript. Richard Grayson [xi]
commented perceptively on early drafts of several chapters. Saul Dubow
offered typically shrewd and subtle observations in the midst of putting
together his own inaugural lecture. John Darwin, David Eastwood and Brian
Harrison all provided constructive criticism and much needed encouragement in the final stages of writing-up – for many years they have been my
chief source of support; generous with their time, and wise in their counsel.

Finally, special thanks go to two of my colleagues and to my family.
Richard Whiting has been a fertile source of ideas for the economic and
political dimensions of this book, which has also benefited greatly from
David Omissi's wide-ranging historical knowledge and sharp editorial pen.
Every author values the support they receive from their family. My Mum
and Dad have helped me in more ways than I can mention. Annabel and
Tasha had to put up with a tired or absent father for too much of the summer prior to the manuscript's submission. Meanwhile, my wife, Sarah,
watched me develop an unhealthy relationship with my laptop computer
when we should have been spending more time together. More than anyone else, she has motivated and sustained me during the preparation of this
book, and so the dedication is to her.

University of Leeds   A.S.T.
October 2004

PUBLISHER'S
ACKNOWLEDGEMENTS

We are grateful to the following for permission to reproduce copyright material:

Table 1 adapted from *Occupation and Pay in Great Britain* by Guy Routh (1980), reproduced with permission of Palgrave Macmillan; Table 2 adapted from Anthony Givens and Gavin MacKenzie (eds), *Social Class and the Division of Labour: Essays in Honour of Ilya Neustadt* (1983), reproduced with permission of Cambridge University Press; Table 8 from Zig Layton-Henry, *The Politics of Immigration: Race and Race Relations in Postwar Britain* (Blackwell Publishers, 1992), reproduced with permission of Zig Layton-Henry.

We are also grateful to Faber and Faber Ltd and Farrar, Straus & Giroux for permission to reproduce a poem 'Homage to Government' from *Collected Poems* by Phillip Larkin.

Plate 1 The National Archives; Plate 2 Royal Institution of Cornwall, Royal Cornwall Museum; Plates 3 and 5 Getty Images; Plate 4 Corbis; Plates 6 and 7 Punch, Ltd; Plate 9 State Library of New South Wales; Plate 10 The British Library; Plate 11 The Spectator; Plate 12 Carmen Ky.

In some instances we have been unable to trace the owners of copyright material, and we would appreciate any information that would enable us to do so.

PREFACE

This book has grown out of a range of research interests, both long-standing and recently developed. These include the political culture of empire, in particular the languages politicians fashioned to make sense of Britain's imperial involvement and the ideologies that it inspired; the domestic repercussions of the South African War (1899–1902); the doctrine of 'loyalism' in Southern Africa (and, more generally, varieties of 'Britishness' overseas); the workings of the British 'imperial economy' and the transnational networks and identities that underpinned it; and the social consequences of Commonwealth immigration. It has also drawn much from my teaching experience at the University of Leeds, where I have been lucky enough to share my research enthusiasms with a large number of lively and gifted final-year and postgraduate students, several of whom have subsequently become friends.

The book is aimed primarily at an academic audience. It is a study of the 'empire at home', namely, of the impact that the colonies had on Britain rather than the other way round. It does not claim to be comprehensive, and readers will no doubt discover aspects of Britain's domestic history that do not figure in the pages that follow, or do not get the attention they arguably deserve. However, a wide range of private and public life is examined, including 'high' and 'low' culture; women and gender; childhood and youth; politics and government; the economy; and regional and national identities. My treatment of 'imperial Britain' is necessarily, therefore, a detailed one. A shorter book would have been too generalised and would not have illuminated the interplay between domestic, imperial and international influences on Britain's past.

Twenty years ago it would not have been possible to undertake a study of this kind – the historiography was too patchy and perfunctory. Since then, several scholars have developed this research field, in particular John Mackenzie and the many authors in the 'Studies in Imperialism' series

[xiv] published by Manchester University Press. Their labours are acknowledged in the footnotes and text. Yet many aspects of Britain's imperial experience remain under- and unexplored, and so this book is also based on substantial primary research. Some of my archival material has been drawn from related research projects, the results of which are summarised here. Other research was required specifically for this project – in the Post Office archives; organised labour and trade union records; oral history archives; the newspaper and periodical press; and public opinion surveys. For the final chapter I interviewed several people from museums who are thanked below.

The book is a study of the nature of imperial influences on Britain as well as their extent. A vigorous debate on the capacity of the empire to 'strike back' is currently taking place and the pages that follow enter into it. However, they also explore why the empire affected some aspects of Britain's domestic history and not others, and why, when it did make its mark, it did so in complex (and often contradictory) ways. The core thesis of the book is that there are two main barriers to understanding the domestic impact of empire. The first is the failure to recognise how diverse and pluralistic that empire was: it is not sufficient simply to assess the 'amount' of imperialism in Britain; the various types of colony from which imperial influences stemmed, the various channels through which they were filtered, and the various results they produced, are of equal if not greater concern. The second is the failure to recognise how diverse and pluralistic British society was: the sources of contact between 'mother country' and colony extended beyond empire families with a tradition of colonial service to many other parts of British society, which became caught up in overseas expansion to differing extents and in differing ways. Hence it was always highly improbable that a single or monolithic 'imperial culture' would emerge in Britain.

The chapters are arranged so as to convey the range of the empire's repercussions and the plurality of responses it evoked. I have chosen to start with general questions about 'society' – how did people react to the empire; how did the empire shape their lives? – before moving on to more specific questions about the precise nature of the imperial impact on British politics, economics, and regional and national identities. The main body of the book covers the period from the mid-nineteenth to the mid-twentieth centuries. A separate chapter at the end of the book deals more schematically with the 'after-effects' of empire post-1945. Although the period after the Second World War arguably merits a separate book, it is nonetheless significant for this study, partly because it provides a point of comparison

for what has gone before, partly because of the persistent influence of empire when it was in decline and after it had gone, and partly because feelings about today's imperial legacies influence the way we interpret the
empire's impact on our past. The drawing together of the different threads
of discussion in Chapters 1–9 is the purpose of the Afterword.

The working classes have three chapters (of varying length) so that their
imperial experiences could be analysed from various perspectives. There
was not the space for a separate chapter on missionaries: they are discussed
in detail in Chapter 5, and more briefly in Chapter 6. For similar reasons,
the armed forces do not get their own chapter: the navy is briefly examined
in Chapter 7, the army at greater length in Chapters 1 and 8. Conversely,
women and children, whose imperial experiences were until recently under-
explored, have their own (comparative) chapter though they are also
discussed in other parts of the book. None of the chapters is entirely
self-contained and there is plenty of cross-referencing in the text; yet the
chapters are constructed in such a way that they can be read on their own.

ABBREVIATIONS

AHR   *American Historical Review*
ASB   Amalgamated Society of Boilermakers
ASE   Amalgamated Society of Engineers
BCINC   British Committee of the Indian National Congress
BIHR   *Bulletin of the Institute of Historical Research*
BOP   *Boys' Own Paper*
CBH   *Contemporary British History*
CHBE   *Cambridge History of the British Empire*
CID   Committee of Imperial Defence
CIM   China Inland Mission
CMS   Church Missionary Society
CO   Colonial Office
CRA   Congo Reform Association
CSA   Cotton Supply Association
EcHR   *Economic History Review*
EDM   Empire Day Movement
EEC   European Economic Community
EHR   *English Historical Review*
EMB   Empire Marketing Board
GOP   *Girls' Own Paper*
HJ   *Historical Journal*
HWJ   *History Workshop Journal*
ICS   Institute of Commonwealth Studies
IFTWA   International Federation of Textile Workers' Association
IHR   *International History Review*
IPC   Indian Parliamentary Committee
JBS   *Journal of British Studies*
JCH   *Journal of Contemporary History*
JICH   *Journal of Imperial and Commonwealth History*

JMH	*Journal of Modern History*
JSAS	*Journal of South African Studies*
JSS	*Journal of Strategic Studies*
LMS	London Missionary Society
LRB	*London Review of Books*
MAS	*Modern Asian Studies*
MMM	Merseyside Maritime Museum
NMM	National Maritime Museum
NPG	National Portrait Gallery
OHBE	*Oxford History of the British Empire*
P&P	*Past and Present*
PEP	Political and Economic Planning
RCI	Royal Colonial Institute
RTS	Religious Tract Society
SAHJ	*South African Historical Journal*
SPCK	Society for the Promotion of Christian Knowledge
TCBH	*Twentieth Century British History*
TLS	*Times Literary Supplement*
TRHS	*Transactions of the Royal Historical Society*
TUC	Trades Union Congress
VS	*Victorian Studies*
WHR	*Women's History Review*

INTRODUCTION

I

After years of neglect, the empire is everywhere today – in novels, news-papers and museums, on the radio and the television. Indeed, the British appear to be attached to their imperial past like a mooring rope; the further they travel, the more they feel its pull. This book asks why, and explores the part played by the empire in shaping British society, past and present. The main body of the book focuses on the period from the mid-nineteenth to the mid-twentieth centuries – the actual impact of imperialism. The final chapter surveys more schematically the various ways in which the British have tried to come to terms with their imperial history during and after decolonisation – the empire's imagined as well as its actual repercussions. Implicitly, at least, the book raises the question of whether Britain's domes-tic history would have turned out differently had Britain never been a colonial power.[1] My purpose is, however, not to create a virtual history of Britain without its empire, but to write a real history with the empire factored back in.

There is of course a deeply-entrenched view of the national past – the so-called 'Little Englander' school of history – that takes it for granted that Britain evolved in relative isolation. This view has formed a powerful strand of both Left and Right-wing historical thought.[2] The Left's version of 'Little Englandism' has a long pedigree. Beginning with the *laissez-faire* doctrines of the Manchester school, it can be traced through progressive anti-imperialist thinking and a non-interventionist foreign policy to the insular and romantic 'people's history' of the History Workshop movement.[3] On the Right, the notion of the English as an 'island race' has exerted an equally powerful appeal.[4] Successive generations of Conservatives have regarded England as intellectually, religiously and constitutionally, as well as geographically, distinct from Europe – an 'exceptional' country whose

[2] home-grown religion and uniquely venerable polity have assured it of special status.[5] Meanwhile, elements of both the Left and the Right have long
treated imperialism as an 'unpleasant aberration' in British history; an aberration disposed of by decolonisation which reinstated a 'normal' course of
autonomous national development.[6]

The fact that this way of thinking no longer seems so credible may have
much to do with later-twentieth-century political developments.[7] Closer
European integration; devolution in Wales and Scotland (and the accompanying assertion of separate Welsh and Scottish identities); the 'troubles'
in Northern Ireland; and Commonwealth immigration – all these have
undermined the idea that British history is merely the history of England
writ large. Partly in response to these events, a self-consciously revisionist
historiography of the 1980s and 1990s began to offer a more expansive
view of Britain's past. This literature has placed the English alongside and
interacting with the Irish, Scottish and Welsh;[8] it has explored Britain's
relationship with Europe;[9] and, in the realm of Commonwealth-Imperial
history, it has drawn attention to the many manifestations of empire in British
popular culture.[10] My book emerges from this scholarly tradition.

I I

The following chapters address six key questions. First, how did the British
people regard their empire, and how far was it embedded in their lives?
This will require us to look at the imperial involvement of Britain's elites,
and at what the empire meant to ordinary working people – how was it
justified to a wider public? Historians have long argued about the popularity of imperialism: this book goes further by exploring the full range of
pro-imperial sentiment as well as the various types of opposition that overseas expansion provoked.

Second, was the empire a source of economic strength or weakness to
Britain? Here we need to examine the long-term performance of the British
economy and British standards of living. Who gained from Britain's
possession of an empire and, conversely, who paid its price? Producing an
imperial balance sheet is far from easy. The data is either hard to interpret
– for example, on investment; or there has not been enough of it – this is
especially true when exploring the effects of empire on the quality of British entrepreneurship, and the economic repercussions of empire migration.

Third, how far did the experience of empire define British nationhood?
There has recently been a lot of interest in whether the British people's

sense of themselves was rooted in their imperial activities and achievements. Here British identity will be investigated linguistically, via the evolving vocabulary of the English language; institutionally, via the monarchy and the armed forces; demographically, via migrants; and geographically and architecturally, via the shaping of urban landscapes and forms of public architecture. Moreover, we will look at 'imperial Britishness' not only at a national level but within the regions too. How did the United Kingdom's local and regional identities connect and compete with a larger British imperial identity?

Fourth, which of Britain's colonies did 'strike back'? Britain ruled over an empire of bewildering variety and complexity. Did different parts of that empire touch different elements of the population? Was India more (or less) influential than the colonies of settlement? Were dominion influences stronger in the case of South Africa than, say, Australia or New Zealand? Were particular types of influence – cultural, demographic, economic, political – more likely to emerge from one part of the empire than another? Could smaller territories, scattered across the Mediterranean, the West Indies, Africa and the Pacific, make their presence felt in the metropole; and if so, how? A lot of scholarship has concentrated on the Raj. It shows how, in addition to Britain's attempts to 'Westernise' India, there are several ways in which India can be seen to have 'Easternised' Britain. India's cultural and ideological impact on Britain is evident in terms of religion,[11] aesthetic concepts,[12] literary fashions,[13] political philosophy and public doctrine[14] and the position of women in the public sphere.[15] But how far were the empire's settler societies – the neo-Britains – also an integral part of metropolitan culture? Only lately have historians begun to look again at the ties that bound the 'new' world to the 'old'. What we now know about migrant identities,[16] political activism and attitudes,[17] women's imperial involvement,[18] and the ideology of British labour,[19] suggests that the self-governing dominions occupied a prominent place in the British public's imperial imagination.

The fifth area of concern is the range and scale of the imperial impact on Britain. Was the empire's influence all-encompassing, or did much of Britain's history remain untouched by its imperial activities? Is there a danger of exaggerating the imperial factor at the expense of 'domestic' or wider 'international' forces? There are three main schools of thought here. The 'minimalists' argue that the British people were relatively unaffected by the empire and cared little about the colonies.[20] The 'maximalists' argue that the empire was a fundamental and determining influence on Britain's past.[21] And the 'elusivists' argue that the (hidden) history of imperial Britain was

[4]   more a matter of the empire reflecting and reinforcing existing social, economic and political trends than pushing them in new directions.[22]

Sixth, opinion further differs over the nature of imperialism's impact on Britain. Was it a reactionary or progressive force? Joseph Schumpeter insisted on the former. He famously described imperialism as the 'heritage of an autocratic state'.[23] More lately, Britain's empire has been portrayed as patriarchal – infused with the ideals of a landed aristocracy and gentry who aimed to replicate in the colonies the ordered and hierarchical society that they were determined to defend at home. 'On the boundaries of empire', it is said, 'much was revealed about the social structure of Britain itself.'[24] But not everyone sees the colonies as the embodiment of a stable social order. The later-Victorian and Edwardian empire might just as well be portrayed as a force for conflict, not least because it 'injected ideas and assumptions into all layers of British society that were in many ways hostile to, and in tension with, domestic social growths'.[25]

Is it possible that at least some of the effects of empire on Britain were more progressive? Was there, indeed, a link between the empire and 'modernity'? Certainly, early and mid-Victorian evangelicals and utilitarians embraced the empire (especially India) as a laboratory for developing concepts of progress and ideas about social reform,[26] while later-Victorian liberals regarded 'the ability of the English to project and then root themselves successfully all over the world' as perhaps 'the ultimate test of the modernity of Englishness'.[27] Meanwhile, during the inter-war years people in Britain continued to take pride 'in colonialism's record of dispensing modern British values', even as doubt began to spread among the nation's political and literary elite about the empire's civilising claims. And even after 1945 the ongoing project of reworking the imperial vision into a liberal, multi-racial Commonwealth meant that imperial impulses could still be reconciled with progress and democracy.[28] Thus far from being a purely domestic construct, modernity is increasingly understood to have been part of a much wider international (and imperial) formation.[29]

III

The core thesis of this book is that there have been two main barriers to understanding the impact of empire on Britain. The first is the failure to recognise how diverse and pluralistic the empire was. The second is the failure to recognise how diverse and pluralistic Britain was. The chapters that follow reject the idea that most Britons were largely ignorant of or indifferent to the empire; they also reject the idea that Britain was awash with, or saturated by, imperialism. Rather, they argue that the effects of empire on the structure of British society, the development of British institutions and the shaping of British identities were complex and (at times) contradictory.[30] With respect to religion,[31] class structures,[32] women's position in society,[33] or the economy,[34] they show how imperialism compelled change and restrained it, propelled progress and fortified tradition. The underlying reason for this is that, after the mid-nineteenth century, the sources of contact between mother country and colony rapidly multiplied, and, as a result, a range of relationships with the empire developed.[35] Whether they were explorers, traders, settlers, soldiers, missionaries or officials, the people of Britain became caught up in the processes of overseas expansion not only in vastly different but unequal ways. There was never likely to be any single or monolithic 'imperial culture' in Britain, therefore.

Nor was imperialism self-contained; it was always part of a larger imaginative complex. For this reason we must take great care in defining the very terms 'domestic', 'imperial' and 'international'.[36] While some historians may wish to distinguish between influences emanating from within Britain and those from beyond, they are in practice often tricky to disentangle. Take J. A. Hobson, author of the most influential critique of British imperialism. His hostility to the 'new imperialism' had deep philosophical roots. Although appalled by the 'jingo' crowds that took to the streets in Britain during the South African War (1899–1902), Hobson's theory of financial imperialism was much more than a knee-jerk reaction to transient political circumstances. It drew together various strands of his progressive creed which pre-dated the partition of Africa but which took on a new significance in the light of it: an antipathy toward monopoly, privilege and 'unearned wealth'; concerns about underconsumption, social inequality and the growing levels of 'irrationality' in British politics; and anti-Semitism.[37] Thus Hobson's interpretation of the 'new imperialism' needs to be set in the wider context of a domestic debate among liberals as to what 'liberty' really meant, how far the state might intervene to redistribute income and wealth without undermining individual responsibility, and what was to be done to reconcile the working man to the capitalist order.[38]

The issue of British economic 'decline' further illustrates the difficulty of disentangling the 'domestic' from the 'imperial'. The empire has often been blamed for the apparently poor performance of Britain's economy in relation to the USA or Western Europe. It either propped up inefficient and backward 'staple' industries thereby impeding the development of new technologies, or it led to punitively high levels of defence spending thus

[6] starving the domestic economy of necessary investment. However, another possibility would be to present the empire as a 'secondary' rather than 'primary' factor, feeding into a range of 'internal' causes of economic decline. For example, the (real or imagined) existence of an anti-entrepreneurial culture can be blamed on the amateur and gentlemanly codes of a public school system geared toward training people for imperial service rather than business success.[39] Similarly, the way in which successive governments privileged the interests of the financial sector over manufacturing industry can be attributed to the fact that it was the former and not the latter upon which the whole imperial complex was understood to turn.[40] And the failure of the state to play a developmental role can be rationalised in terms of a political and bureaucratic elite whose mentality was forged in the heyday of empire and ill-suited to the task of modernising the post-war economy. In other words, cultural, structural and institutional explanations of decline can all be said to have an 'imperial' component. This suggests that the very act of categorising influences as either internal or external may be artificial. The effects of empire may sometimes have been relatively discrete; however, in certain areas of British public life they were so closely entwined with other influences and impulses as to become thoroughly internalised.[41]

Disentangling the 'imperial' from the 'international' is equally problematic. Public attitudes to empire are a case in point. The dividing line between pride in the empire and pride in Britain's broader position as a world power (of which an imperial role was but one manifestation) is by no means always clear. The monarchy and the military are commonly taken to have been the twin pillars of popular imperial sentiment in later-Victorian and Edwardian Britain. Yet each of these institutions possessed a patriotic appeal irrespective of their connection with the empire. Similarly, the growth of imperial news coverage in the popular press can be too readily accepted as evidence of enthusiasm for empire when a thirst for mere sensationalism may explain the demand for such reporting. Arguably fighting and bloodshed attracted the attention of lower-middle and working-class readers – it mattered little whether such escapades were taking place in Europe, the empire or the wider world.[42]

I V

What is the nature and purpose of this growing historiography of 'imperial Britain'? It is worth reminding ourselves that the past we construct for Britain depends very much on the sort of story we wish to tell.[43] This book will show how there are three 'grand' narratives in British historical writing that the empire has helped bring to the fore: 'difference', 'decline' and 'disintegration'. Some of those who postulate a British *Sonderweg* – a separate path of development, making Britain different from other European powers – have pointed to Britain's unique imperial position to corroborate their claim. Others who see national decline as the main theme of post-war history have lamented the loss of a world-wide empire and its effects on Britain's international standing, or, alternatively, have turned to that empire for an explanation of Britain's economic backwardness and for inflated ideas of its international role.[44] Finally, 'disintegrationists' have presented the (potential) break-up of the Union as a concomitant of decolonisation, for without colonies the United Kingdom was deprived of its *raison d'être*.[45]

We must appreciate that these narratives are in no sense neutral descriptions. Rather they represent readings of the past and as such embody certain ideological assumptions.[46] Why, for example, has there been so little writing on Welsh involvement in the empire? Arguably it is because 'for far too long [historians have] conveniently buried aspects of both Welsh and Imperial history'.[47] Dominated by the ideologies of socialism and nationalism, post-war Welsh politics proved reluctant to integrate colonial activity into Welsh history – similar silences have also been observed in the history of Glasgow.[48] One historian summed up the problem we face when writing about the past with the remark that 'historiography originates as the memory of the state'.[49] This remark would seem particularly apt for studies of 'imperial Britain'. How scholars view the empire's domestic impact will be closely related to their definition of the British nation.

To ask in what ways Britain was constituted through its imperial experience is moreover to pose the thorny problem of whether the empire should engender pride or shame. It has long been insisted that imperial history is not primarily a moral question but a subject for detached and dispassionate scholarship. Yet much of the so-called new imperial history does not seem to have been written in this vein; perhaps it is unrealistic to expect that it ever will be. For better or worse, historians have become more rather than less concerned with judging guilt or innocence, and with distributing praise or blame.[50] Britain's colonial record offers rich pickings here, however unhistorical such an exercise may seem. Certainly, if the reaction to the opening of the British Empire and Commonwealth Museum in Bristol in September 2002 is anything to go by, the empire today thrives 'as an emotional force',[51] its legacy continuing to be conceived in strongly negative and positive terms.[52] On the Right the loss of empire signifies an atrophying of Britain, the end of its exceptional place in the world; or, alternatively, it

[8]   provides a scapegoat for the industrial, technological and educational failures of the post-war period.[53] On the Left some still feel awkward about the part played by the empire in the shaping of conservative patriotism, or hold the imperial legacy responsible for misogyny, racism and chauvinism in the mother country.[54] And since the loss of imperialism's intellectual respectability after 1945, there has been a tendency among Liberals to argue that it was never all that important to the British public anyway. In this sense there have been good and bad 'imperialisms', and 'non-imperialisms' too. On all sides of the debate interpretations have been ideologically charged.

What the empire meant to Britain in the past, and what it means now, is therefore of concern beyond the academy. In explaining the nation's present situation or in forecasting its future, historians, press pundits and politicians have all recently turned to the empire and its legacies for answers. Thus, different perceptions of the importance of the imperial connection have moulded the direction and impact of debates about ethnicity, gender and the constitution. The implication here is that political 'decolonisation' has not necessarily led to a more far-reaching 'de-colonialisation'. On the contrary, despite having divested itself of virtually all of its colonies, Britain is still trying to come to terms with the various aspects of its imperial past, which is a powerful testimony to the empire's continuing capacity 'to shape our future as well as our yesterdays'.[55]

CHAPTER 1

ELITES

Historians who acknowledge the empire as a force in British society tend to argue that it promoted social stability rather than strife. In developing this thesis they put forward four main propositions. The first is that the empire was a powerful reminder to the British peoples of those things that they held in common.[1] The second suggests that the colonies acted as a 'safety-valve' for domestic discontents, releasing (or displacing) tensions that existed in the 'home' society by providing a useful outlet for its more anti-social, restless or eccentric elements.[2] The third interprets imperial ideology as something that underpinned a cohesive idea of the social order, extending the life of hierarchical conceptions of society that would otherwise have fallen prey to the language of class.[3] And the fourth identifies the groups that gained the most from overseas expansion as those that were already dominant in society, the main effect of empire therefore being to protect and prolong the status quo.[4] According to this way of thinking, therefore, it is the governing and privileged classes who were tied most closely to the colonies. Further down the social scale support for imperialism diminished, with the working classes harbouring a more narrow and superficial interest in the empire, if indeed any interest at all.

Chapters 1–4 test these propositions. Their aim is not simply to assess how much empire there was in Britain. Rather they try to move on from what is becoming an increasingly sterile debate between 'postcolonialists' (who maintain that it was prevalent and pervasive) and their critics (who are convinced that its influence has been grossly exaggerated).[5] Thus a key concern of these chapters is the nature of the empire's impact on Britain and the type of effects it had on metropolitan life. They show how British society was exposed to a wide range of imperial influences, and how it, in turn, reacted on concepts of empire. As one scholar aptly puts it: the empire provided an arena in which contrasting and competing social visions and values were contested.[6] These chapters also show how British expansion

[10] affected the lives of ordinary working people almost as much as it did the lives of elites. Significant numbers of those at the base of society were caught up in colonial rule and overseas settlement – partly by being subjected to various forms of imperial publicity and propaganda, but more frequently (and profoundly) through remittances and return migration, through changing patterns of consumption, and through the imperial networks forged among organised labour. Indeed, it is a gross oversimplification to say that the working classes did not know or care about the empire and that it did not touch their lives in any meaningful or tangible way. The reality is infinitely more subtle and complex. The class dimensions to British imperialism were important, although popular imperial discourses were emphatically not the same as those of elites.

Even to elites the empire could represent very different things. If it furnished the aristocracy and landed gentry with an ordered, layered and peaceful vision of society and a defence against modernity, among the professional middle classes it was more likely to be regarded as a mainspring of meritocracy and progress – something that embodied their service ideals. Hence the two main strategies employed by Britain to project its power in India were in many ways based on contradictory conceptions of where social authority ultimately lay. On the one hand, the Raj sought to legitimise itself by conservative appeals to 'traditional' authority; on the other, after the Mutiny it came to place increasing emphasis on good government and administration, delivered by an impartial and trained civil service, untainted by commercial considerations.[7] This was in essence a conflict between an aristocratic view of governance, where authority was hereditary and exercised by men born to rule, and a professional view of governance, where authority was acquired and exercised by men trained to rule. Significantly, Britain's experience of governing India could service either point of view. The same was true of relations between the professional and entrepreneurial segments of the upper middle class; the empire drew these two groups together (through imperial philanthropy), but it also exposed and perhaps exacerbated tensions between them. Well-known for their snobbish anti-capitalism, colonial civil servants saw the empire as a matter of duty and tended to look down on those businessmen or 'box-wallahs' for whom it was a matter of making money.[8] They tended to view British rule as an essentially conservative force concerned to preserve pre-capitalist social and economic systems and to protect peasants from exploitation by merchants and traders.[9] Yet it is important not to forget that there were powerful economic interests – the jute barons of Dundee; the textile manufacturers of Lancashire; and the great shipowners – who were very much a part of the British empire and who were inclined to see capitalism as its [11] *raison d'être.*

This chapter examines in turn these three competing conceptions: an 'empire of privilege' (espoused by the aristocracy and landed gentry); an 'empire of merit' (espoused by the professional middle classes); and an 'empire of profit' (espoused by entrepreneurs). The following three chapters then focus on the lower middle and the working classes in order to assess what the empire meant to them.

An empire of privilege

> To have got the whole Barnacle family together would have been impossible for two reasons. Firstly, because no building could have held all the members and connexions of that illustrious house. Secondly, because wherever there was a square yard of ground in British occupation, under the sun or moon, with a public post upon it, sticking to that post was a Barnacle. No intrepid navigator could plant a flag-staff upon any spot of earth, and take possession of it in the British name, but to that spot of earth, so soon as the discovery was known, the Circumlocution Office sent out a Barnacle and a dispatch-box. Thus the Barnacles were all over the world, in every direction – dispatch boxing the compass.
>
> Charles Dickens, *Little Dorrit,* edited by H. P. Sucksmith
> (Oxford, 1979), Chapter XXXIV: 'A shoal of Barnacles'

The Barnacles were a family of conservative aristocrats, convinced of their right to rule. They carried British justice to the far corners of the globe and died 'at their posts with their drawn salaries in their hands'. Clearly, by the mid-1850s, Charles Dickens felt that they were a sufficiently recognisable slice of society to register with his readers – *Little Dorrit* was a novel that drew deeply on contemporary affairs. Historians have frequently followed in Dickens's footsteps by arguing that the empire perpetuated the privileges of a pre-industrial landed elite. There are, however, several reasons to doubt whether this was really so. We will begin by situating the 'imperial' factor among the many other 'domestic' factors that helped to cushion aristocratic decline. We will then examine in more detail the implications of imperialism for the aristocracy's well-being through a number of biographical case studies.

The British empire could not single-handedly sustain the British aristocracy in the later nineteenth and early twentieth centuries. It was, for

[12]   instance, only one aspect of a continued aristocratic commitment to service
and ceremony that provided an illusion of stability in an increasingly urban
and industrial age.[10] Other aspects of that commitment included involvement in parliamentary politics, the armed services and the home civil service (especially the Foreign Office) and the sponsorship of philanthropic
institutions, universities, and reformist pressure groups. Moreover, ownership of urban property, and the aristocracy's absorption into other economic
sectors, were arguably of far greater importance in prolonging its power.
Although aided and abetted by portfolios of colonial stocks and shares,
economic diversification, and the shift from land to investments, was hardly
specifically imperial. The exploitation of canals and minerals and schemes
of urban development (in the form of estate housing) played a much bigger
part in this process.[11]

Nor could the empire make much difference to one of the fundamental
social changes taking place at this time: the inexorable shift from a society
based on heredity nobility, in which great prestige attached to birth and
land, to a society which attached increasing importance to wealth.[12] To put
things into perspective, it is worth reiterating just how profound were some
of the forces arrayed against the empire. Take the importation of greater
quantities of foreign corn from the mid-1870s, and the agricultural depression of 1873–96. Sir Lewis Namier neatly summed up the effects of overseas competition with his remark that 'the coming of American wheat
has wrought a greater change in the composition of the British House of
Commons than the first or second reform acts'.[13] Technical developments
in transport and storage halved the price of American imports, while wheat
from Russia and India subsequently played almost as great a role in ham-
mering down prices as supplies from the 'new world'.[14] As falling prices for
domestic producers put pressure on rural rents and values, many estates
became unprofitable; thus began a process whereby land ceased to look
like a firm security and considerable acreage found its way on to the market well before 1914. The First World War further damaged Britain's landed
elite. Higher taxation and greatly increased death duties triggered an
avalanche of land sales;[15] and the war brought great human losses to many
landed families with their long military traditions. If one also takes into
account the electoral reforms of 1867, 1884 and 1918,[16] and the centralising tendencies inherent in the Victorian state,[17] then the capacity of the
empire to sustain the aristocracy as a governing class – either in their
localities or in national government – begins to look rather doubtful.

We will now look more closely at the experiences of six peers – the
4th Earl of Carnarvon; the 8th and 9th Earls of Elgin; the 7th Earl of

Aberdeen; Lord Dufferin; and the 5th Marquis of Lansdowne. Although a necessarily small sample, it is important to emphasise that all of these men had a close connection to the empire during its later-Victorian and Edwardian heyday. If the empire was vital to the aristocracy's economic position, social status or self-image as a governing class, these peers should help to show why.

It has been suggested that territorial expansion in the tropics provided government posts to men of high status, and that permanent settlement in the self-governing colonies provided new opportunities for a 'migratory elite'.[18] Let us take each of these points in turn. Did an expanding empire really represent financial salvation for hard-up peers? It should be emphasised that we are talking here mainly of the most prestigious positions at the apex of the imperial bureaucracy – the governorships. Below this level, neither the Indian Civil Service nor the Colonial Civil Service recruited many men from the landed aristocracy or gentry. According to one scholar:

> the real attraction of these proconsular jobs [was that] they lasted longer, and were more lucrative, than being mayor or chairing a royal commission; and they were more prestigious, and often less dangerous than serving as a company director. Indeed most poor and middling members of the landed elite were effectively – if temporarily – doubling their income, and many were also able to enjoy, at someone else's expense, a grander lifestyle than they themselves could afford at home.[19]

Yet while there may be some truth in such claims, they are far too boldly stated. Many incumbents of high office in the colonies spent far more than they saved, and many found themselves out of pocket when they returned home. A study of two hundred British colonial governors, covering the period 1900 to 1960, emphasises that most of these posts were practically untenable without a private income, and that the gift of a governorship to a 'poor' man could be a poisoned chalice rather than a prize. It also shows how the social provenance of the majority of colonial governors was predominantly upper or professional middle class: the aristocracy only monopolised the very top positions.[20]

Turning to the finances of our six peers, it is striking how little the empire seems to have helped. To stave off the effects of the agricultural depression the 4th Earl of Carnarvon, Under-Secretary of the Colonies (1858–9) and Colonial Secretary (1866–7 and 1874–8), began to sell off his estates in the 1880s. Though he channelled some of the proceeds into colonial securities and land, he placed even more emphasis on the potential for developing what remained of his own properties. Neither strategy,

[14]   however, was sufficient to take away his chronic insecurity about the plight of the aristocracy, an insecurity that lasted down to his death in 1890.[21] Nor did the 8th and 9th Earls of Elgin, the former serving as Governor of Jamaica (1842–6), Governor-General of Canada (1847–54) and Viceroy of India (1861–3), the latter as Viceroy of India (1894–9) and Colonial Secretary (1905–8), discover in service abroad a way of resolving the problems of maintaining a heavily encumbered family estate. Their Broomhall seat was economically barely viable and a constant source of concern. Though the income from some of these posts contributed to a reduction of the estate's debt, it was a modest contribution that did little to diminish the family's sense of stringency.[22] Meanwhile Lord Dufferin, Governor-General of Canada (1872–8), found that frequent travelling and lavish entertainment – part of his strategy to cultivate Canadian opinion – quickly ate into his personal fortune, prompting the Duke of Argyll to write in 1873: 'I hear terrible things about your expenditure. People say that you will be entirely ruined. Do not be too Irish, or too Sheridanish: it is an awful combination. Of course everybody is delighted, I hear, with you and yours.'[23] The 5th Marquis of Lansdowne, Governor-General of Canada (1883–7) and Viceroy of India (1888–94), fared better. He was able to live on his official income, to put something by each year and to rent out the family property in London – Lansdowne House – while away from Britain. This was important as little money was recovered from his immense estates in County Kerry in Ireland; they had been a mid-seventeenth-century gift to Sir William Petty for his role in subduing the Irish 'rebels' who resisted England's conquest, and the Land League singled them out for special treatment.[24] What ultimately transformed Lansdowne's finances was not colonial service but the sale of a large portion of his Irish estates and the inheritance of properties in Scotland on his mother's death, both of which made him a rich man.[25] Finally, not only did the 7th Earl of Aberdeen, Governor-General of Canada (1893–8), leave the dominion early – 'his estates needed his supervision and his family income could no longer bear the steady drain of his Canadian office' – he then suffered a further financial blow from his investments in commercial fruit farming and cattle ranching in British Columbia. Having made extensive purchases in the Okanagan valley in the early 1890s (the capital supplied by his estates in the north-east of Scotland), Aberdeen proceeded to run up huge debts, partly through his own naivety and inexperience and his prolonged absences as Governor-General, but also through the follies of his employees, one of whom seemed to be more interested in breaking horses than in the business of ranch management.[26]

If prestigious postings in the colonial bureaucracy are in general unlikely to have restored peers' finances, what about emigration to the settler colonies?

A study of 'gentleman emigrants' to Canada suggests that although they were a social mixture, including the sons of the professional middle and mercantile classes, the aristocracy was well represented.[27] A significant number of these migrants invested in large-scale fruit farming ventures in southern British Columbia. But failures in commercial fruit farming were frequent, and those who went to Canada expecting to live leisurely lives were soon disabused of the idea. After 1914, Canada was never again so attractive to this type of migrant, partly because the capital to finance farming dried up, partly perhaps because the imperial spirit that motivated and sustained migration was damaged, and partly because from 1925 the abolition of primogeniture meant that younger sons were able to stand as equals with respect of the family estate. To be sure, some landowners discovered other destinations, including the White Highlands of Kenya to which an 'immigrant clan of British aristocrats' were drawn by the lure of the country's magnificent game resources.[28] But this was European settlement on a tiny scale. There were only 23,000 Europeans in Kenya by the outbreak of the Second World War, and many of these were 'small men' – demobilised soldiers accounted for much of the increase in the colony's white population after 1914.[29]

It is possible, however, that the true significance of the empire for Britain's landed elite lay beyond the economic sphere in terms of its social prestige and self-image as a governing class. Imperial service was certainly an integral part of aristocratic politics: sixty-five peers held imperial office as governors or ministers between 1885 and 1914,[30] and for some of these men a posting to a colony served as a step up the domestic political ladder.[31] Yet Asquith's ministry marks a watershed here. From then onwards appointments were made on ability rather than birth; few peers by succession were appointed to senior posts; and most peer governors were ennobled on appointment.[32] Even before 1907 imperial service was frequently undertaken with a heavy heart. Peers regretted, and in some cases resented, prolonged separation from their families. Shortly after arriving in Jamaica the 8th Earl of Elgin lost his wife after barely two years of marriage, leaving him a widower with a baby daughter.[33] Urged by the Colonial Office to return to Jamaica after a trip home in 1846, Elgin resolutely refused. He subsequently remarried and took up other overseas postings, but felt constant guilt about the resulting separation from his children and about the responsibilities that this imposed on his second wife. In 1861, Elgin reluctantly accepted the Indian Viceroyalty.[34] Just over a year into his term of office he suffered a heart attack while crossing a dilapidated twig bridge on his way to the remote hill station of Peshawar. He died days later with his wife and youngest daughter at his side.[35] If Elgin's misfortunes

[16] were far from typical, other peers nonetheless lamented the human costs of imperial service. During the 1880s, Lord Dufferin asked to move from the Indian Viceroyalty to a European embassy. He wanted to be closer to his sons and daughters who were now approaching adult age, and felt his wife's health could not much longer stand the Indian climate. He also found his duties increasingly dull.[36] The Indian Viceroyalty did not prove all that congenial to Lord Lansdowne either. He was especially close to his mother and so part of him resented any overseas posting; the climate did not agree with his delicate constitution; and the constant ceremonial duties oppressed him.[37]

Nor could the empire do much to protect that most vital of aristocratic assets – the status and prestige of land. Nostalgia for a rural past and the 'back to the land' movement were key features of later-Victorian England.[38] Yet if the empire did buttress the belief that rural life was healthier than urban living it may, ironically, have been to the detriment of landed authority in Britain. After all, it was the colonies (not the mother country) that offered a free, healthy and spacious environment; only there could the vitality of the British people be restored. This was certainly the message of *Oceana or England and her Colonies*, written by the Tory historian, J. A. Froude, and published to widespread acclaim in 1886. For Froude there was little chance of the nation renewing itself within the confines of the British Isles: 'These islands are small, and are full to overflowing. In the colonies only can we safely multiply, and the people, I think, are awakening to know it.'[39] Breaking in, cultivating and living off the land had previously formed the national character, but metropolitan Britain was now regarded as a modern urban and industrial society and hopelessly degenerate. There were also clear limits to the idealisation of the countryside at this time. English culture in the later nineteenth and early twentieth century is more plausibly presented as aggressively urban and materialist; on closer inspection bucolicism was the ideology not of the majority but of 'highly articulate yet fairly marginal groups'.[40]

How far did the empire enable the aristocracy to forge an alliance with the middle classes to protect property and privilege? This certainly seems to have happened in some of Britain's African colonies. But did the benefits of overseas expansion help to cement an alliance between the middle and upper classes at home? It is said that the gentlemanly ethic formed a tight bond between these groups, that the imperial mission was the 'export version of the gentlemanly order', and that gentlemanly capitalists 'tried to recreate abroad the hierarchy with which they were familiar at home'.[41] Yet British social historians have recently called into question the vulnerability

of the middle classes to the blandishments of a landed elite. They suggest [17]
that the Victorian version of the gentlemanly ideal was much more a bourgeois than an aristocratic invention.[42] The following section supports this
revisionism, arguing that the dominant social force in British imperialism
was more likely to have come from the professional middle than the landed
classes.

An empire of merit

It is widely acknowledged that much of the impetus for imperialism came
from enterprising expatriates – the sort of people that Rudyard Kipling
called 'the doers'. Among this group the professional middle classes were
well-represented: they made a striking and substantial contribution to the
history of British expansion while themselves gaining greatly from the
colonial encounter.[43]

Professional people were the dominant group in terms of recruitment to
the colonial bureaucracy and armed forces. As missionaries, doctors, engineers, journalists and teachers they were highly mobile within a British
imperial world. Key characteristics of professionalism – trained expertise,
disinterested public service and selection by merit, all of which gained ground
rapidly during the first half of the twentieth century[44] – were developed
through involvement in the empire. The growth of professional bodies –
instrumental in the recognition and organisation of professions – had to
take into account the aspirations of members working in Britain's colonies.
And the voluntary activity of the professional middle classes was readily
transferred on to an imperial stage, deepening its sense of purpose and
enhancing its prestige in the process. In these ways and others, the professional middle classes were to develop close connections with the colonies
and to incorporate imperial values and beliefs into their lives.

Admittedly, some of the main factors at work in forging professional
middle-class consciousness belong to the period prior to this study. By the
early nineteenth century industrialisation had loosened the bonds between
the professions and the landed aristocracy, replacing the patron–profession
relationship with the client–profession relationship. As a result service no
longer entailed dependency, and professional ideals were able to diverge
from the ideals of those to whom services were rendered. In addition, the
percentage of professional men with landed origins declined during the
early 1800s, the proportion of recruits with professional fathers increased
and specialised training was given greater emphasis. By the mid-nineteenth

[18] century, therefore, the professions were already important.[45] Nonetheless, during the next hundred years or so, their influence rose still further. Not only did professionals become more numerous, more prosperous and more varied, they successfully strove for improved self-organisation and entrenched their ethos of self-sacrificing service to the community ever more deeply in the public sphere.[46] The empire contributed to each of these achievements, and to the emergence of the professional middle class as a powerful part of British society during the first half of the twentieth century.

To begin with, the empire provided a widening field of employment for an expanding and diversifying professional population. After 1900 the Colonial Civil Service recruited almost fifty per cent of its officials from young men whose fathers worked in one of the professions. Similarly, by far the largest proportion of Indian Civil Service recruits came from the sons of the service class; only for a relatively brief moment after the introduction of competitive entry in 1854 were the aristocracy and landed gentry well represented in the new intake.[47] However, we need to tread carefully here. The men who ran the British empire were surprisingly few, their salaries paid out of the budgets of the colonies themselves, which severely restricted recruitment.[48] Take 1920 and 1946, the peak years in the Colonial Office's recruitment roller coaster: 551 and 1737 people were appointed,[49] and many of these were placed in the technical rather than administrative side of the service[50] and hence were almost as likely to have a business as a professional family background.[51] Alternatively one might look more broadly at the three decades after the First World War. From 1919 to 1930 there were 4,616 recruits to the Colonial Service; during the 1930s, 1,887; and from 1940 to 1950, 7,735: a grand total of 14,238. To put these figures into perspective, it is necessary to refer to Table 1, which shows the size

Table 1   Employment in the higher professions, 1911–51

	1911	1921	1931	1951
Medicine	36,000	38,000	46,000	62,000
Law	26,000	22,000	23,000	27,000
Engineering	25,000	35,000	51,000	138,000
Accountancy	11,000	9,000	16,000	37,000

Source: Adapted from G. Routh, *Occupation and Pay in Great Britain, 1900–79* (Palgrave Macmillan, 1980), p. 13. NB. Engineering includes surveyors, architects and ship-designers.

and growth of selected higher professions in the first half of the twentieth
century.

From a low base of about 1,500 officials in 1899, the size of the
Colonial Service increased considerably to about 10,000 in 1947. Clearly,
however, the total numbers employed by the Colonial Office pale in comparison to those employed in the other major professions. Career opportunities in the Indian Civil Service were more limited still.[52] There were 1,032
ICS men in British India in 1919 and 1,029 in 1938. It would also be a
mistake to think that official jobs in the colonies were always highly sought
after by the professional middle classes. Harsh climates, tropical disease,
poor pay and diverse conditions of employment meant that Major Sir Ralph
Furse, the presiding presence over Colonial Office recruitment, frequently
found it difficult to attract the sort of man he wanted,[53] while ICS applications fell in the early 1920s and again in the early 1930s due to European
anxiety over the policy of Indianisation, the pace of constitutional change
and the financial stringencies imposed by the Government of India.[54]

The colonial bureaucracies did not, then, provide a wealth of new career
opportunities. Yet this may be to miss the point. Expanding education but
relatively inexpensive professions resulted in keen competition for jobs in
Britain. Meanwhile the colonies provided an alternative and attractive field
of employment for a variety of middle-class people, some of whom probably lacked the resources to establish themselves in a profession at home.
This was especially true from the late nineteenth century, but even at the
beginning of our period one can see such factors at work.[55] Take the five
sons of the Irish surgeon, Charles Orpen, who migrated to South Africa
during the 1840s. Joseph Orpen, born on 5 November 1828, and arriving
in Cape Town on 15 December 1846, later recalled:

> My father intended to set us up gradually in farming. Land and stock were
> cheap then, and besides his profession, he had independent means from prop-
> erty in Ireland. Charles [an elder brother who had already migrated] assured us
> that there were many openings for enterprising young fellows in South Africa
> and that professions at Home were overstocked. He gave us a very favourable
> account of the new country, the people and the life, and he was right. South
> Africa has used us well (for the rest of the family joined us subsequently) and we
> have worked well for her . . .[56]

After employment as a land surveyor in the Cape, Joseph Orpen helped to
draw up the Orange Free State's constitution and held various administrative positions in Basutoland, Griqualand West and Southern Rhodesia. From
the Union of South Africa in 1910 until his death at the age of 95 in 1923,

[20] Table 2   Empire–Commonwealth membership of UK professions in the first half of the twentieth century (% of total membership given in brackets)

	1900s	1920s	1940s
Accountants (see below)	399 (6)	1,038 (7)	2,580 (7)
Medics (BMA)	3,828 (18)	5,884 (26)	11,677 (30)
Architects (RIBA)	87 (5)	517 (11)	1,225 (11)
Engineers (ICE and ISE)	1,299 (19)	1,558 (19)	2,099 (21)

Source. Adapted from T. Johnson, 'The State and the Professions: Peculiarities of the British', in A. Giddens and G. Mackenzie (eds), *Social Class and the Division of Labour: Essays in Honour of Ilya Neustadt* (Cambridge University Press, 1983), p. 199.
NB. Accountants includes the Institutes of Chartered Accountants of Scotland, and England and Wales, the Society of Incorporated Accountants and Auditors, the London Association of Accountants, the Institute of Municipal Treasurers and Accountants, the Institute of Cost and Works Accountants, and the Association of International Accountants.

he was a fierce critic of the lack of representation accorded to Coloureds and Africans in the colony's constitution.

As the social and economic systems of the settler colonies developed during the second half of the nineteenth century, so the openings for ambitious young men like Orpen multiplied. It is impossible to be precise about the number of migrant professionals because the statistics are far too slippery. But the empire membership of professional associations provides a proxy. Table 2 underlines the fact that middle-class employment in the colonial bureaucracies is only a part of the picture – the private sector opened up many more professional opportunities.[57]

There is, however, a deeper sense in which the identity of the professional middle classes was invested in imperialism. Neither the shaping of a professional ethos nor the rise of professional organisations can be properly understood without reference to the wider imperial context in which they took place. In the second half of the nineteenth century India, in particular, was a forcing house for the principle of meritocracy and open competition. This is perhaps ironic given the autocratic nature of British rule in the Indian subcontinent. Nonetheless, competitive entry to the Indian Civil Service was introduced in 1853, a full year before the publication of the

Northcote-Trevelyan report on the organisation of the home civil service.
Previously the East India Company's directors had nominated young men
to 'writerships' and prepared them for their Indian careers at a special college – Haileybury. Now all appointments were to be made by examination
alone.[58] As success in this examination guaranteed a competence for life,
the ICS began to enter increasingly into the calculations of professional
men seeking a career for their sons.[59] Moreover, the separation from home
and family, and the difficult working conditions associated with service in
India, meant that these opportunities had a particularly strong appeal to
able young men of more modest middle-class backgrounds prepared to
accept such disadvantages in return for the considerable financial rewards.

How far was the Indian experiment with competitive entry – of which
the civil service commissioners were quick to approve – responsible for
the dissolution of the old official world of patronage, purchase and nepot-
ism in the home civil service? It was not until 1870 that all vacancies
(except in the Foreign Office) were opened to competition and many
people remained sceptical about tests of competency for some time after
1853.[60] It was felt that patronage created group loyalty and encouraged cohesiveness; that ending patronage would disturb powerful private
interests; that the existing methods of appointment discouraged deviancy
and ensured the recruitment and promotion of those who had an interest
in the preservation of 'the system'; and that open competition would
not attract a sufficient number of suitably qualified candidates. At the very
least, the last of these objections was called into question by the Indian
experiment. After 1853 strong links were forged between the ICS and the
public schools and ancient universities – civil service reformers had always
intended that this would be so.[61] In 1866, an inquiry into the efficiency
of the new arrangements reported that it had not been difficult to secure
highly-educated people to fill Indian posts, while the system of 'limited
competition'[62] had proved an unsatisfactory instrument of selection because
in most cases very few candidates were nominated for the vacancies and
those that were tended to be of a low educational standard. In the eyes of
the civil service commissioners, limited competitions were hardly competitions at all.[63]

What was true of the ICS was also true of the Indian army, which was
noticeably more meritocratic than the British army.[64] Although the purchase
of commissions was abolished in 1871, soldiering remained an expensive
occupation in Britain: in 1869 the 'pay' of officers remained almost exactly
what it had been during the reign of William II. The best regiments, in
particular, tended to be guarded by considerations of wealth, social standing

[22] and family connections. India was the exception. Under the East India Company military appointments were disposed of gratis and poverty was if anything a recommendation to the directors' benevolence. After the transfer of authority to the Crown, Indian army pay continued to be higher than that of the British army; and the cost of living was of course much lower in India. Hence it was possible for a relatively poor but able man to live on his salary, and officer recruits to the Indian army were generally from more modest middle-class backgrounds. There were approximately 2,700 officers in the Indian army by the turn of the century,[65] the biggest single source of recruits being sons of existing Indian army officers. The Indian army also thought of itself as attracting (and retaining) more able men than the home army. It was not until the 1880s that the rapid growth of the professions in Britain began to be properly reflected in terms of recruitment to the home army. By the 1920s, the distinction between the two forces had begun to dissolve as British army pay became more competitive and officers received a living wage.

To flesh out this account of the empire's significance for professional development in Britain we now need to look more closely at particular professions. For the first half of our period we shall focus on engineering and the 'exploration' sciences of geography, geology, botany and anthropology. For the period from 1900 to 1945 we shall turn our attention to journalism and the so-called 'colonial' sciences of biology and medicine.

In the case of engineering, the key professional bodies – the Institute of Civil Engineers and the Institute of Structural Engineers – maintained a strong empire membership from the early 1900s through to the 1940s (see Table 2). Engineers had a growing stake in the empire well before then, however.[66] Increasing numbers ventured abroad in search of fame and fortune from as early as the 1840s, pushed by the collapse of 'railway mania' in that decade. Although the first markets for their expertise were in Europe and the USA, these countries were anxious to build industries and infrastructures of their own. It was in imperial territories that British engineers had their greatest impact – Canada, Australia, Egypt, South Africa and India offered a wealth of career opportunities on projects ranging from the mining of minerals, to railway, harbour and canal construction, to bridge and dam building. Many household names were involved: Robert Stephenson, Thomas Brassey and Sanford Fleming to name but a few. Influences flowed in the other direction too. One of the most daring of all Victorian engineers, Isambard Kingdom Brunel, adopted an Egyptian style for his first major work, the Clifton suspension bridge in Bristol, and pioneered the building of the steam-driven, screw-propelled ships that linked

London to Cairo, Calcutta and Sydney; several engineers who worked [23] under him were given important colonial commissions.[67]

India and Egypt contributed powerfully to the promulgation of a professional identity among engineers. A measure of India's importance to the profession is provided by *Engineer* and *Engineering*.[68] Many British engineers who worked in India read and contributed to these journals, while such was the interest in the Raj at home that 'Notes on India' appeared in every issue of *Engineering*. Part of India's fascination lay in the massive scale of its engineering projects and the fact that its topography and climate were much more challenging than those of Britain. Indeed, the scarcity of British officials in India meant that it was easier to supervise the construction of a few big projects rather than many small ones, while political considerations pointed in the same direction: the bigger the project the more it was thought to underscore British authority and power. India also played a vital role in shaping new technologies: knowledge of hydraulic engineering, for example, spread from the Victorian Raj to other lands.[69]

One of these lands was Egypt. In the late nineteenth century the vast majority of Egypt's irrigation engineers were trained in India; conditions in the two countries were similar, so technical skills could be readily transferred. By common consent Egypt's irrigation system was in a poor state of repair before the arrival of this Anglo-Indian hydraulic expertise.[70] To increase the cotton crop and balance the budget, money was pumped into the Department of Public Works, headed by Colin Scott-Moncrieff. He was eager for Egypt's British-controlled administration to take full advantage of its newly-acquired powers,[71] and Milner dubbed him and his men the 'saviours of Egyptian irrigation'.[72] The vital importance of the Nile flood in the yearly cycle of Egyptian life gave British irrigation inspectors a lofty position in the eyes of the Egyptian people too. Their skill in extending and improving the country's canal network, and their honesty in distributing the water equitably between small and large landowners, earned them an enviable reputation at a time when other branches of the British administration were far from popular.[73]

How did all this affect engineers back in Britain? An insight into the domestic end of the imperial axis is provided by the Institute of Electrical Engineers, which had branches in India, Canada and South Africa. As relations between Briton and Boer deteriorated after the Jameson Raid, the IEE formed a volunteer corps in 1897. When hostilities broke out in South Africa in 1899, the War Office willingly accepted their offer of services. The seven officers and forty-eight men – designated the South African Detachment of Electrical Engineers – embarked from Southampton in March

[24]   1900. They did valuable service setting up an electric light field plant in the Orange Free State and in establishing telephone and telegraph communications. All but four arrived back safely in England later that year, when Professor John Perry delivered a stirring presidential address of thanks and praise at the IEE's annual conference.[74]

The links between the Victorian empire and the new sciences of exploration were if anything stronger still. It has even been claimed that it was the people involved in establishing the disciplines of geography, geology, botany and anthropology – scientists, military officers, merchants and financiers – who provided the real impetus for overseas expansion. It was they who pushed hardest for the acquisition of new territory, and they who stood to gain the most from it.[75]

The soldiers, sailors and administrators who served on the Royal Geographical Society's council had few doubts about the importance of geographical knowledge to an expanding imperial state.[76] In Britain, as in France, geography was felt to be an intensely practical discipline. It provided the information that helped officials to demarcate spheres of influence, to negotiate with rivals over territorial acquisition and to identify a colony's resources and how best to exploit them.[77] With the aim of securing official funding for a series of expeditions, the energetic president of the Royal Geographical Society, Sir Roderick Murchison, popularised exploration in the 1850s and 1860s. Meanwhile several Fellows of the Society figured prominently in the history of imperial policy. George Curzon was already an explorer of consequence before becoming Indian Viceroy in 1898. He had acquired detailed knowledge of the countries bordering British India, walking extensively in the Karakoram and Pamir mountains. Elected president of the RGS in 1911, he set about raising money from Indian princes and commercial companies to finance the Society's move to Lowther Lodge.[78] Another future president of the RGS was Thomas Holdich, an experienced military surveyor who was appointed Superintendent of Frontier Surveys in India in the 1890s. Holdich's views on race were particularly strident, even allowing for the period in which they were expressed – he believed that the 'rights of the white man' had to take precedence over those of indigenous peoples, and never tired of saying so.[79] Harry Johnston, another active RGS member, held a succession of posts in the consular service in tropical Africa in the 1880s and 1890s, conducting explorations of Mount Kilimanjaro and Mount Ruwenzori, for which he was awarded the Society's gold medal in 1904.[80] Halford Mackinder, described as 'the scientific counterpart of Kipling', had the RGS to thank for half of his salary as Reader in Geography at Oxford University and for subsidising his climb of Mount Kenya in 1899.

Mackinder's university extension lectures on the 'new geography' – sponsored by the RGS – emphasised that Britain's only salvation as a great power lay in the more extensive imperial economic development.[81] The empire, moreover, influenced the development of the RGS organisationally, especially in the provinces where the formation of a number of new geographical societies at the end of the nineteenth century was partly a response to the commercial possibilities presented by the 'new imperialism'.[82] Manchester led the way. On 21 October 1884, H. M. Stanley, the African explorer brought to public attention by his expedition to find Livingstone in 1871, delivered an address in the city's Free Trade Hall.[83] Stanley argued forcefully that London had no more intrinsic interest in the empire than the provinces and that it was time for the large seaports and manufacturing towns to have their own geographical societies. He described geography as 'a science which may best be called the admonitor to commerce', and stressed its importance in clearing the path for enterprise in Africa, where, he insisted, there were many as yet untapped opportunities for trade.

British overseas expansion also opened up opportunities for geologists. The first director of the Geological Survey of England and Wales, Henry de la Beche, instituted surveys of Canada and India in the 1840s, and of New South Wales, the Cape and Natal in the 1850s,[84] while his successor, Murchison, presided over surveys of the West Indies, Tasmania, Kashmir and two provinces of New Zealand, encouraged the exploitation of colonial minerals and promoted the 'Silurian' classification system.[85] However, the great expansion in university geology from the 1860s – which preceded that of geography – transformed the subject from one concerned with fieldwork and mapping to one concerned with laboratory study, lecturing, examining and textbook writing. As geology became more professional it became more parochial, therefore: heavy teaching workloads and technical specialisation undermined its imperial connections.[86] Botany had a similar experience. During the last quarter of the nineteenth century Kew Gardens was turned from a place for recreation into a scientific institution 'committed to pure research and the imperial economy'.[87] Previously, colonial work had given Kew's botanists an opportunity to extend the reach of their discipline through collecting and disseminating valuable plants, through combating fungal diseases that were the main enemies of agriculture, and through forestry conservation. Yet as botany flourished in university laboratories and colonial departments of agriculture multiplied, so Kew's importance as an imperial institution was eroded.

The empire played no less important a role in defining the discipline of anthropology.[88] Nowadays anthropology tends to pride itself on its role in

[26]   vigorously defending the downtrodden. It was not always so. The first generation of anthropologists were quick to appreciate the political as well as
scientific value of their enquiries. Knowledge of indigenous peoples was
seen as a vital aspect of their control and successive colonial administrations called on anthropologists to supply it.[89] Ethnographical surveys – such
as those conducted by the sinister if fictitious racial theorist, Dr Potter, in
Matthew Kneale's Whitbread-Prize-winning *English Passengers* – were considered especially useful. By the 1860s the main emphasis of such surveys
– which aimed to discover the origins and movements of peoples throughout history – had shifted from comparative linguistic analysis to the physical comparison of racial diversity: phrenology (the science of measuring
heads) was a particularly popular anthropological pastime. Not surprisingly,
in view of the bewildering variety of its population, India had a special
attraction, and photography provided the means of documenting its myriad
castes and communities and of comparing distinct 'racial types'.[90] Official
encouragement of photography from the mid-1850s led to the publication
of work by civil and military officers who had taken it up as a hobby
but found that it could be used politically to convey the horrors of the
Mutiny and the anarchy that had generally prevailed before the East India
Company arrived. The most famous of such works was the monumental
eight-volume history, *The People of India.* Published between 1868 and 1875,
the book contained nearly five hundred mounted prints with detailed
descriptions of its subjects. It was believed that the gathering of this data
would facilitate the administration of the many religious and racial groups
that had come under British rule.

Turning to the twentieth century, the empire's impact on professional
development is powerfully conveyed by the press. There was a plethora of
publications providing news and analysis of imperial affairs. Some were the
organs of a particular lobby or pressure group: the *Colonial Quarterly, India,
The Imperial Colonist, The Empire Review* and *The Round Table*, to name but
a few. Some were targeted at British expatriate communities such as the
Anglo-Indian publications the *Oriental Herald, Overland Mail, Homeward Mail*
and *The Indian Magazine.* Others catered for colonials resident in Britain –
the *Canadian Gazette, South Africa*, the *Australasian Trading World*, the *Canadian Mail, Canadian News* and the *British Australasian.* Parts of the 'mainstream'
newspaper press were also to a degree 'imperialised'.[91] The list of wealthy
newspaper editors compiled by W. D. Rubinstein and H. Perkin for their
'Elites Survey' contains several figures with a specific colonial connection or
a marked interest in Britain's colonies.[92] By the early 1900s these men were
being offered lucrative advertising opportunities by dominion governments

and commercial companies eager to attract more migrants and money from Britain. In order to win these contracts papers had to bring in more cable news. With varying degrees of success, the *Morning Post*, *The Times* and the *Standard* all tried to tap this new source of revenue by expanding their coverage of colonial affairs.[93]

Journalists, meanwhile, moved back and forth between Britain and the neo-Britains with surprising ease. Australians travelled to Fleet Street, pushed by the parochialism of their papers back home (produced for capital city and state markets) and pulled by the career possibilities of British journalism.[94] Some made their home in Britain, others returned to Australia or divided their time between the two countries. British newspapermen were likewise highly mobile: 'metropolitan professionals seeking advancement moved out to the areas of white settlement and then "followed the frontier" as new opportunities presented themselves'.[95] Some were also employed in the offices of dominion newspapers in London. Hence for many journalists the empire was their bread and butter, integral to their career prospects and aspirations.

Twentieth-century science was influenced by the needs of the colonial bureaucracies. Tropical medicine provides an interesting example. Its institutional bases – in London and Liverpool – were outside the existing medical establishment and its main audience was not initially a medical one. While the School of Tropical Medicine at Liverpool became famous for overseas expeditions aimed at improving sanitary conditions and public health, its London counterpart concentrated on training practitioners for the Colonial Medical Services and on providing a long-term solution to sleeping-sickness. Efforts to eradicate tropical disease gave a major stimulus to the biological sciences too. By the 1930s there were almost as many professional entomologists working in the colonies as in Britain, and many entomologists at home were based in institutions devoted almost exclusively to colonial work, such as the Imperial Bureau of Entomology, the Farnham Royal Insect-Parasite 'Zoo' and the Locust Research Centre. Indeed, it was owing to its imperial involvement that the medical profession in general was brought into closer contact with government at this time. Between 1863 and 1939, sixty-seven branches of the British Medical Association were formed in the empire. As well as taking up the grievances of overseas members with colonial governments, the BMA lobbied the India and Colonial Offices – both large employers of overseas doctors – for reforms regarding rank in the military medical services, the inclusion of a chief medical officer in the higher echelons of colonial government, and increased salaries in return for surrendering the right to engage in private practice.[96]

[28]   Like medicine, the development of the nursing profession must be placed in this wider imperial context.[97] The empire's consolidation created a greater demand for nurses, at first to care for British personnel and later to develop health care for local peoples.[98] The Colonial Nursing Association, founded in 1896 by Mabel Piggott, wife of the Attorney-General of Mauritius, acted as a recruiting agency for the Colonial Office; by 1929 it had supplied 2,532 nurses for service overseas, 846 of which were then in post.[99] For several reasons the number of openings was not large; nor did the nursing profession in Britain encourage overseas service – it preferred to keep members at home to fight for improved working conditions. During the 1880s and 1890s, however, there were many good supervisory positions in India and South Africa when such posts were in short supply for qualified women in Britain.

Parts of the nursing profession were adept at manipulating imperial rhetoric for their own domestic agenda. War-time service, in particular, provided opportunities for raising funds, improving training procedures and advancing state recognition and registration.[100] A key figure in this respect was Ethel Fenwick (1857–1947), a pioneer of professional nursing who set up the British Nurses Association in 1887. Confronted by a medical establishment reluctant to recognise the professional status of nursing, she fought hard to improve the public image of nurses and to demonstrate their usefulness to the state.[101] Part of her strategy was to make a link between the BNA and colonial military service. General nursing work in the empire received far less attention: missionary societies seem to have monopolised this sphere, and the BNA, like the Royal College of Nursing, was more concerned to increase the number of qualified nurses in Britain.[102]

So far our argument has focused on how far the empire was responsible for sharpening a sense of identity among the professional middle classes in Britain. There is, however, one crucial respect in which imperialism may have served to extend class cohesion across the British bourgeoisie. Recent social history highlights the role of that characteristic bourgeois institution, the voluntary association, as a unifying force in urban society. If true, it would seem likely that a 'voluntarist imperialism' played directly into this process. Certainly, charity work was enlarged and enlivened by an expanding empire. There were emergency relief funds (for alleviating the suffering caused by periodic Indian famines); war relief funds (late-nineteenth-century colonial conflicts provided the focus for a profusion of philanthropic giving and effort); and emigration funds (run by organisations like the Salvation Army, Barnardos and the Charity Organisation Society). There were also several commemorative charities inspired by figures like General

Gordon and David Livingstone; new charitable institutions formed as a result of royal tours of the colonies; and philanthropic bodies for women in which social reform was justified by imperialist ideas (the Girls Life Brigade, the Church Red Cross Brigade and the Girl Guides). The sums raised by some of these charities are staggering. For example, as the British government did little to care for the dependants of the 22,000 British soldiers who died in South Africa from 1899 to 1902, and the 75,000 soldiers who returned home with serious injuries or diseases, a variety of voluntary bodies sprang up to stand in for the state. Contemporary estimates suggest that approximately £6 million was raised by a network of funds – some city and county based, others organised through the press, others national like the British Red Cross Society, the Soldiers' and Sailors' Families Association and the Lloyd's Patriotic Fund. This figure is equivalent to over £400 million in 2000 prices.[103] Fund-raising on this scale involved an army of middle-class people, and is testimony to the dynamism of provincial philanthropy at the time. Thus if volunteering was built into the lifestyle of Britain's middle classes, and if it did draw together the different elements of the bourgeoisie, the empire's contribution should not be overlooked.

An empire of profit

It was once said that professional people were the 'forgotten middle-class', but thirty years on this remark would seem to be truer of entrepreneurs.[104] Apparently incapable of seizing the cultural and political leadership for which their economic wealth qualified them, the manufacturing classes have all too easily been written off as supine. Even revisionists who argue for a more significant role for businessmen in their localities concede that the wider world – region, nation and empire – was largely tangential to their self-awareness: 'they seem to have done everything locally; if anything, more locally as the [nineteenth] century progressed'.[105] Some did of course develop wider imperial connections. Yet they are seen as a minority for whom the colonies were mere milch cows. Indeed, the view that British manufacturers were simply self-seeking materialists – motivated by prices and profits, bent on acquisition, and lacking in ideals – finds its colonial counterpart in the form of the 'exploitation' of empire by the millocracy of Manchester, the tobacco lords of Glasgow and the jute manufacturers of Dundee. For these hard-pressed sectors of British industry the colonies are thought to have held a particular attraction. Reliance on less exacting, safer and in some cases protected markets allowed them to maintain good growth rates

[30] and to continue to trade internationally at a time when the domestic market was open to all comers and foreign markets were being closed by tariffs.

Was the industrial middle class really this insular and inward-looking? If so, what prevented it from becoming more imperially involved – a strong sense of local belonging or a suspicion of all things aristocratic? Moreover, in the case of those businessmen who did enthuse about the empire, did they see it merely as an opportunity for creating private wealth? And how far were 'soft' colonial markets responsible for sapping their entrepreneurial energies? We will return to some of these questions in Chapter 7. Here the focus is on two business groups that are regarded as having a key stake in the British empire – Lancashire cotton magnates and British shipowners – and on another group – Quaker industrialists – who were among the more wealthy and powerful of British businessmen, and who struggled to reconcile their religious beliefs with their overseas business activities.

Entrepreneurial ideals and Colonial Office recruitment policies were certainly not considered incompatible by Sir Ralph Furse – he valued practical experience and know-how much more than speculative intellect or success in 'bookish' examinations.[106] Thus after 1900 business people were recruited to the Colonial Service in increasing numbers – one in twenty recruits to the administrative arm of the service had a business background, as did almost a fifth of technical and professional recruits.[107] Some business families probably felt that they had a 'stake' in the empire, therefore. Nonetheless, from the perspective of trade statistics, the significance of empire to British business is easily exaggerated. From 1850 to 1914 the empire's share of British exports fluctuated between a quarter and a third – it was bigger for certain staples, in particular pig iron and iron goods and cottons. By the 1920s, 37.2% of British exports went to the empire, and by 1934–8 41.3%. The self-governing dominions were the main markets. They took around a half of all British exports to the empire by 1913–14, and their share further increased during the inter-war years. Yet if some industries (e.g. chemicals and tobacco) monopolised these markets, the majority of producers had to compete on quality and price.[108] Even Scottish whisky firms and English chocolate manufacturers – which actively exploited their British heritage and catered to peculiarly British tastes – did not find colonial consumers to be undemanding or particularly predictable. In fact, there is little evidence to suggest that demographic links, language or cultural attitudes counted for a great deal if the product being sold was not already competitive. This is important. Dominion markets were not usually 'soft' touches; more often, they offered a parallel experience to British business's involvement in the international economy. Bearing this in mind, it is hard to believe that many entrepreneurs allowed themselves to be all that sentimental about the empire, at least that is as far as their business activity is concerned.

The investment habits of the manufacturing classes suggest a degree of insularity. The service sector and the south-east were the major source of imperial investment, whereas provincial manufacturers were more likely to invest in the domestic market.[109] Lancashire cotton merchants and manufacturers, for example, tended to put their profits close to home, either in related businesses (carpet manufacture, machine-making), or in the exploitation of minerals (coal), or in public utilities (local government bonds, joint-stock companies for gas and water supply).[110] When they did send their capital overseas, they preferred foreign to imperial investments – American railways were more popular than Indian ones. To be sure, textile interests in Manchester (and Glasgow) did press for improved transport and railway development in India. Yet they were unwilling to tie up their funds in such projects. Rather the majority of people who invested in Indian guaranteed railways were from the professional middle classes – barristers, clergymen, bankers and retired army officers predominated.[111] Dundee invested more overseas up to the 1920s, mainly because local opportunities did not exist on a large scale. But again the vast bulk of Dundee's money went to America, starting with a steady flow of private investment in the 1860s when Dundonians first became conscious of the immense possibilities of an expanding society like the United States.[112]

There were exceptions. The 'Cable King', Sir John Pender, was a onetime Manchester and Glasgow cotton merchant who built and operated a large share of the world's undersea cables. He was made a fellow of the Imperial Institute and a KCMG in recognition of his services to submarine telegraphy, and died in 1896 leaving a substantial fortune of £337,180.[113] Cecil Rhodes is reported to have declared that 'Pender was "imperialising the map" while I was just feeling my way'. Yet for the most part India seems to have mattered to cotton manufacturers and merchants only in so far as it provided a market for their goods or a source of raw materials.[114] Persistent political lobbying took place on both fronts: first, to maintain an open door to a large but increasingly difficult market; second, to develop Indian cotton supply and reduce the dangers of dependence on the American cotton crop. From the 1850s onwards pragmatism seems to have prevailed, therefore: Cobdenite principles of non-interventionism were dropped, and Lancashire mill-owners looked to the India Office for a variety of commercial concessions.[115]

[32]   All too often Manchester was turned away empty-handed, however. Viceroys and Secretaries of State were contemptuous of what they saw as 'the selfish motives of Cottonopolis'. Take the problem of cotton supply.[116] By the mid-1850s there were several publications discussing the possibility of increasing the supply from India.[117] Yet Sir John Hobhouse, the cabinet member responsible for India, felt that government action was completely unjustified. He attacked Manchester for not investing in India. If they wanted Indian cotton, why did they not guarantee the *ryot* (cultivator) a fixed price for it? Subsequently, the sharp rise in raw cotton prices in the wake of the crop failures of the 1850s prompted the Manchester Chamber of Commerce to establish the Cotton Supply Association (1857) – a pressure group that aimed to encourage cotton cultivation in various parts of the world, with the main emphasis on India. The CSA received 'extensive and impressive financial support' from many who had previously subscribed to the Anti-Corn Law League. Yet it failed to inspire the same 'missionary impulse' as the League.[118] Cotton manufacturers were deterred by the poor quality of Indian cotton, the misplaced belief that India produced vastly more of it than could reach the seaports and the anticipated resumption of American supplies. Notwithstanding the CSA's petitions and deputations, ministers and officials went on expressing their exasperation at Manchester's reluctance to do anything for itself. As Lord Palmerston stated in 1861: 'our manufacturers themselves will do nothing unless directed and pushed on. They are some of the most helpless and short-sighted of men . . . They say they have, for years, been looking to India as a source of supply; but their look seems to have only the first effect of the eyes of the rattlesnake, viz. to paralyse the object looked at.'[119]

The CSA was terminated in 1872. Not until the early 1900s was there sufficient anxiety about raw cotton prices to call forth another organisation. This time the Lancashire cotton lobby received a more sympathetic hearing from government. Persistent problems with the American cotton crop had restricted supplies, and other European governments had begun to develop their colonies. The British Cotton Growing Association, formed in 1902, centred its efforts on Africa rather than India. It was given a Royal Charter, received several government grants and worked closely with the Colonial Office. Its role was to investigate possible sites for colonial cultivation; to provide experts to advise on methods of cultivation; to buy seed and pay for its distribution; and to organise plantations and processing facilities.[120] Criticism of the selfish motives of Lancashire continued, however, only now it was directed toward Lancashire's insistence that taxes on British cotton exports should be matched by a countervailing excise duty on the textile industry in Bombay. In 1905 the imperialist Richard Jebb launched a ferocious attack on the 'exploitative imperialism' of Manchester men. He castigated the countervailing excise duty as 'the new slavery', and pulled no punches in asserting that the Lancashire textile industry had attained its present size only by the forcible restriction of competition in the Indian market.[121]

British shipowners were more successful in shaping imperial policy. Curiously their 'hard-headed and selfish interest in the empire' did not provoke anything like the same degree of criticism. Here three shipping magnates will be considered: Donald Currie of the Union-Castle Line,[122] Sir Alfred Jones of Elder Dempster & Co.,[123] and Sir Thomas Sutherland of the Peninsular and Oriental Steamship Company.[124] Each of their shipping companies portrayed itself as a national enterprise carrying on a public service; each gained enormously from government contracts and other forms of subsidy; each actively supported territorial expansion in Africa and Asia; and each played on public and official anxieties regarding competition from other colonial powers and the safety of the empire. P&O's steamers have even been referred to as the 'flagships of imperialism'. The network of lines created by the company fanned out to all parts of the empire east of Suez. In peacetime life in the colonies was made more palatable by the regular delivery of P&O mails,[125] and by the prospect for civil servants of more frequent journeys home. In wartime the Admiralty turned to P&O for troop transports, for hospital ships and for the movement of supplies.

How did these shipowners view the imperial connection? Donald Currie was the son of a barber; he began his business life with nothing, and died one of the wealthiest men in Britain. He had substantial business interests in southern Africa for over thirty years, tenaciously defending his position as a government mail contractor, appealing for support to those interested in the defence of the Cape routes and emphasising the need for a reliable network of imperial communications. All this seems to have been commercially motivated, however. Currie attached little or no importance to imperial sentiment *per se*. He simply went where the openings were, his goals being restricted to the 'pursuit of personal security, independence, wealth and status'.[126] The same cannot be said of Alfred Jones. Starting his working life in Liverpool as a cabin boy at the age of 14, he also rose to a position of enormous power, wealth and influence, transforming a small firm of shipping agents into a mighty monopoly that controlled not only the shipping of West Africa but many aspects of its trade and economy too. But if Jones was initially inspired by the desire to provide financial security for his family – his father died at an early age – he went on to develop a

[34] grand vision of a British empire in West Africa. Indeed, his biographer claims that he was 'virtually alone, at one time, in seeing in the swamps of the mosquito-ridden coast [of West Africa] the promise of a vast imperial possession'. His 'genuine belief in the virtues of imperialism' seems almost 'impossible to separate from his self-interest in this context'.[127] For example, Jones was a key figure in founding two imperial institutions from which he benefited – the Liverpool School of Tropical Medicine and the British Cotton Growing Association – yet into which he ploughed capital. He also offered his own ships to carry cotton from West Africa to Britain free of charge and provided free passages for the scientific expeditions of Ronald Ross, whose work on the malaria-bearing mosquito won him a Nobel Prize in 1902. Not surprisingly, Jones held Joseph Chamberlain (Colonial Secretary, 1895–1902) in high esteem, and maintained that he had done more for West Africa than any other Colonial Secretary.

Thomas Sutherland is more elusive. After working in P&O's Bombay office in the 1850s he moved to Hong Kong, where he was asked to join the legislative council in recognition of his services to the business community. Brought back to Britain in 1868, he was appointed the company's managing director in 1872 and chairman in 1882, a position he held until 1914. He was a member of the general committee of the China Association (an organisation that lobbied for a British protectorate over the Yangtze valley during the 1890s), and a Liberal, then Liberal Unionist MP, advocating a strong navy and national defences. There is no doubt that Sutherland understood how to turn the imperial connection to his own and his company's advantage. He was sent out to India at the very time when P&O was establishing its monopoly in the opium trade from Bombay – the company kept this business very secret for fear of tarnishing its image. Moreover, under his chairmanship P&O benefited greatly from government mail contracts, from transporting cargoes of food during the Indian famine of 1878 and from the movement of troops during the Egyptian expedition of 1882. But was Sutherland's support for imperialism purely pragmatic? As with so many other businessmen, the surviving evidence is too slender to say.

One group of businessmen whose consciences were troubled by British overseas expansion are the Quakers. George Cadbury (1839–1922) and Joseph Rowntree (1836–1925) owned companies that enjoyed growing markets among emigrants and expatriates in the empire. They also spoke openly about the causes and consequences of British imperialism, as they perceived them. While neither man was an impractical idealist – like every other businessman they calculated profits and counted costs – they both had strong convictions and were concerned to apply their religious principles to commerce.

Joseph Rowntree, the York cocoa manufacturer, was a pioneering industrial and social reformer who did much to improve the working and housing conditions of his employees, to promote adult education and to publicise the cause of temperance.[128] A strong admirer of John Bright, he deplored the power of 'selfish and unscrupulous wealth' that he felt to have been behind the opium trade in China, the Egyptian campaign of 1882 and the South African War of 1899–1902. On setting up the now famous Rowntree trusts in 1904, he expressed a wish that some of the money be used to take control of a newspaper that would prevent the new sensational dailies ('flooding the country on a tide of imperialistic sentimentality') from conquering the English press. The Trustees duly obliged, taking control of the *Northern Echo*, and helping to finance *The Nation*, and two London papers, the *Morning Leader* and the *Star*. Acquiring an interest in the latter attracted much criticism as it was a great betting paper. However, the *Star*'s efforts to expose the evils of the opium traffic, to draw attention to the Congo atrocities and to promote the cause of international arbitration, apparently excused the fact that it gave daily advice on the horses.

Like Rowntree, George Cadbury was a politically active Quaker who was profoundly convinced of the iniquity of the Boer War: 'this war seems the most diabolical that was ever waged. It is so evidently a speculator's war, and no one else can derive any benefit from it.'[129] Cadbury paid for the distribution of nearly three million copies of a pro-Boer pamphlet, financed a special train to ensure the delivery of the anti-war paper, the *Morning Leader*, to Midland cities, and advanced £20,000 for the takeover of the *Daily News* – a journal that had been closely associated with the peace movement until, under E. T. Cook's editorship, it had become pro-Milner. Under its new editor, H. W. Massingham, the *Daily News* opposed the setting up of the concentration camps, the burning of Boer farms and the subsequent use of indentured Chinese labour in the Witwatersrand goldmines. Advertising revenue fell dramatically as a result. But this did not deter Cadbury – far from it. He had already been in the public eye for his refusal to tender for orders of chocolate and cocoa for the British army during the war. Indeed, when Queen Victoria eventually commanded Cadburys to supply plain chocolates as a Christmas present for the troops, he accepted no profit on the order and decided not to place the firm's name on the goods. He was insistent that there was no point having principles unless one was prepared to suffer for them. Aware that this stance was unpopular, and that Cadburys' sales representatives had been hindered by

[36] directors' opposition to the war, he duly supplied them with a stock of pro-Boer literature!

Not long after the war Cadburys became embroiled in another colonial controversy. Newspapers alleged that while pursuing an enlightened policy toward its own workforce, the company had acquiesced in a system of virtual slavery on the cocoa plantations of San Thome and Principe – Portuguese islands off the coast of West Africa in the Gulf of Guinea from which part of its supply of raw material was bought. The whole affair culminated in a week-long libel trial – Cadburys *versus* Standard Newspapers – which George Cadbury won, only to be awarded a mere farthing in damages. The facts are complex but can be briefly summarised thus. Rumours of the appalling conditions of the plantation workers reached W. A. Cadbury (George's nephew) in 1901 and he was asked to look into the matter. Having failed to enlist American support for a boycott of forced labour, he visited Lisbon in the spring of 1903 to urge the Portuguese government to take action. Lisbon's Association of Planters suggested that the British cocoa companies send someone to investigate. In the meantime Cadburys continued to purchase San Thome cocoa. In 1905 Joseph Burtt – a Quaker with an interest in social reform – spent six months visiting over forty plantations and returned to England in April 1906. His report – which made it clear that the workers were effectively if not legally in a state of slavery – was presented to Sir Edward Grey at the Foreign Office and to the Portuguese Colonial Minister and planters. Reforms were promised, and Cadburys agreed to wait a year for their implementation; the Foreign Office advised that the best hope lay in strong protest backed up by the threat of withdrawal rather than an immediate cessation of cocoa purchases. In 1908, W. A. Cadbury and Burtt again visited Angola and the islands – it was at this point that the *Standard* published its attack – only to find that no real reform had been attempted. They returned to England to announce that Cadburys would purchase no more cocoa from these sources.

Historians of Cadburys say that the firm should have acted more quickly and unequivocally. This seems harsh. George Cadbury admitted to having been torn between 'our own feelings which would have led us immediately to give up the use of the cocoa' and 'common sense which clearly showed us that there was no other way of ascertaining facts and bringing the necessary pressure to bear except by continuing as buyers'. He also pointed out that the firm had obtained no financial benefit by buying San Thome cocoa – its chief merit was its uniform quality not its cheapness.[130] In fact, the Cadbury brothers had been in regular correspondence with the Anti-Slavery Society, Aborigines Protection Society and Congo Reform

Association on this very issue. It would seem unlikely that they had anything to hide therefore. As Iolo Williams concludes, the publicity to be
gained from the immediate disuse of San Thome cocoa would probably
have earned them 'a cheap and glittering halo', yet it would not have produced any real reforms.[131]

How, then, did British businessmen regard the empire? Were they driven
outwards simply by private interest and the lure of new markets and raw
materials? Or did they also believe that the acquisition of overseas territory
was a 'moral duty to the rest of humanity'?[132] The above case studies show
just how diverse was Britain's business community. While some entrepreneurs saw the empire only as a commercial proposition, others were quick
to grasp its wider military and strategic imperatives, especially when these
could be exploited for their own ends. While some displayed the sense of
superiority, self-righteousness and missionary zeal frequently associated with
British imperialism, others were more sceptical regarding the relationship
between 'progress' and 'expansion' and more willing to question the moral
and humanitarian aspects of colonial rule.

Moreover, for many businessmen the results of the extension of empire
into Africa and Asia must have been very disappointing. Only very partially, and with some difficulty, were non-European societies pulled into
Britain's economic orbit. Certain sectors of the metropolitan economy clearly
benefited from the annexation of new territory after 1870, while the economic advantages of the settler empire were extolled by several contemporary commentators – the self-governing dominions were said to be
'natural' markets for British industry and 'colonials' the best customers for
Britain in terms of trade per head. The precise nature and extent of these
advantages will be investigated further in Chapter 7. Here it is sufficient
to remind readers that the great days of British industrial superiority were
relatively short-lived. For a brief moment, from the 1850s to the 1870s,
the neo-Britains may have offered 'easy' or 'soft' markets to British business. From the 1880s onwards, however, trade statistics reveal that indigenous and foreign competition was ever more keenly felt. There is no reason
therefore to think that British manufacturers and entrepreneurs as a class
had any particular attachment to an empire which impinged on their lives
to varying degrees and in varied ways. Their response to overseas expansion was consequently less coherent than that of the aristocracy or professional middle class. In that sense, at least, it was more akin to that of the
lower middle and working classes, whose imperial attitudes will be examined next.

CHAPTER 2

THE LOWER MIDDLE CLASS AND THE WORKING CLASS AT HOME

C hapters 2–4 examine what the empire meant to the masses – princip-ally the manual workers and their dependants who constituted at least three-quarters of the British population for almost the entire period under study.[1] In addition, this chapter considers the substantial and increasing number of people who were employed in lower-middle-class occupations as a result of the expansion of public administration.[2]

Historians have not been kind to the lower middle class. The small retailers, schoolteachers, minor officials and clerks who made up much of this segment of society have been mocked for their narrow-minded moral-ism and their social conformity.[3] By the end of the nineteenth century they are said to have abandoned their earlier radical allegiances to become ardent defenders of the status quo.[4] They devoured the 'new' or 'yellow' journalism and the imperial adventure fiction of G. A. Henty and H. Rider Haggard.[5] They were convinced that British military intervention in the Transvaal was just. And they were among the most uncompromising critics of the pro-Boers. Economic marginality, fear of downward mobility and the need for approval from their 'social superiors' prompted them to pro-test their patriotism more vigorously than other sections of society and, in so doing, to assert their respectability.[6]

How far the empire mattered to the working classes is more hotly con-tested. One school of thought says that the British public was steeped in imperial propaganda. The Indian mutiny (1857) witnessed the first major burst of it, which then gradually intensified, reaching a high-water mark with the Wembley Exhibition of 1924. A whole range of media – advertis-ing, exhibitions, fiction, music halls, cinema, radio – helped to instil a sense of imperial purpose in British society.[7] What inspired such activity? Some speculate that imperial propaganda was designed to make the working classes more quiescent and to reconcile them to their place in the existing order.[8] Others assert that such propaganda was a bourgeois strategy for imposing

a 'patriarchal conception of Englishness' on the majority of the population,[9]
or that it was 'part of Tory demagogy's design to content the workers with
an illusion of citizenship'.[10] Others go further in presenting imperialism as
part of the explanation for the Victorian social and political 'equilibrium'.
The lure of empire, it is argued, distracted ordinary working people from
radicalism and socialism, thereby stifling their hopes for democratic change.
From here it is one short step to the 'labour aristocracy' thesis of Marxist
historiography: overseas expansion and captive colonial markets produced
material rewards that allowed (some) skilled workers to be bribed into supporting the status quo, in which they themselves had a sizeable stake.[11]

None of the above arguments has received anything like universal
acceptance. There are those who firmly believe that, for the generality of
English people, the empire never signified anything truly vital in their lives:
'they lived on in their towns and shires, before and during and after the
imperial phase'.[12] It is said that few people were employed by the empire,
few colonials visited Britain and even the material connections that were
there – tea, sugar, tobacco – would not have been readily apparent: the
British had 'the least participatory empire in human history'.[13] There are,
moreover, real problems in reading from imperial propaganda – however
widespread or commercially successful – public acceptance or approval of
the opinions therein expressed.[14] In fact, the increasing amounts of imperial
propaganda directed at the British people from the early twentieth century
may point not to enthusiasm for empire but the very reverse: a deepening
disenchantment with various aspects of colonial rule.[15]

A further strand of enquiry concerns race. There was a tendency for contemporaries to compare the squalor and degradation of Britain's new towns
and cities with the primitive conditions of 'Darkest Africa':

> The English governing classes . . . regarded . . . the non-European native just as
> they had, quite openly, regarded their own labouring classes for many centuries:
> as thoroughly undisciplined, with a tendency to bestial behaviour, consequently
> requiring to be kept in order by force, and by occasional but severe flashes of
> violence.[16]

Yet whether this attitude was characteristic of mid- rather than later-
Victorian society is a moot point. Some suggest that the end of the nineteenth century saw a significant shift in opinion; as race became more an
issue of colour, so racial divisions came increasingly to be seen to exist
between rather than within societies. Others insist that hierarchies of race
and class continued to play off each other throughout our period.[17] Either

[40]   way, it is worth pointing out that, in so far as social vocabularies did draw
on racialised images of the colonial 'other', it was frequently to bypass the
language of class as much as to reinforce it. Hence it was the sub-categories
of the working class – the 'undeserving poor', 'vagabonds', 'dangerous
classes', and the 'residuum' – that tended to be compared to the empire's
indigenous peoples: groups that were deemed a threat not only to the wealthy
and privileged but to the moral health of the rest of the working population.[18]

Here it will be shown how different groups of working people were
exposed to the empire in different ways, and how its meaning and popularity varied accordingly. It will be necessary to distinguish between direct
and indirect forms of 'imperial impact' – instances when people were conscious of empire shaping their lives and instances when they were not.[19] In
terms of the former one might point to emigration and employment. We
can begin to recover the experiences of those who settled in the colonies
by looking at specific aspects of the emigration process – recruitment; 'chain'
or 'bridge' migration; remittances; and return migration. For other working
men and women the value of empire is better understood in terms of jobs.
In the mining towns of Cornwall, the cotton factories of Blackburn and
Oldham, the jute mills of Dundee and the engineering and shipping firms
of Glasgow, there were regional concentrations of people whose livelihoods
depended on one or more of Britain's colonies – as a market, a source of
raw materials, or a competitor industry.

So much for the visible impact of imperialism. What about its less obvious manifestations? We should not downplay forces which shaped people's
lives simply because they were unaware of them. This point is developed
below in the discussions of patterns of consumption and of reading habits;
in each case, we will see how the empire entered into the day-to-day lives
of ordinary working people in ways that they themselves did not perhaps
appreciate, but which were nonetheless significant in terms of the type of
food that they consumed and the type of literature that they favoured.

The lower middle class

The latest work on the lower middle class questions the depth of its imperial commitment. If the youthful men who made up the jingo crowds which
celebrated the relief of Mafeking were infected by a bout of colonial fever,
'in married life there is little to suggest that these [imperial] enthusiasms
endured'.[20] On the contrary, the dominant underpinnings of lower-middle-
class male identity seem to have been emphatically private. Such men asserted

the dignity of domestic life and were instrumental in pioneering a more [41]
compassionate form of marriage.

Yet some parts of the *petite bourgeoisie* were clearly drawn to the empire.
The paternal occupations of early ICS entrants included small farmers, coach-
men, upholsterers and undertakers – they accounted for between a fifth to
a quarter of successful candidates from the 1860s until the early 1870s,
when the Indian examinations became 'more and more a rich man's pre-
rogative'.[21] Meanwhile, in the twentieth century, the bulk of recruits to
the Colonial Service who were not upper-middle-class came from a lower-
middle-class background.[22] Typically their fathers worked as clerks or officials, or as skilled tradesmen or artisans, or as self-employed shopkeepers.[23]
Frank Lloyd, the Balliol-educated son of a shopkeeper, joined the Treasury
department in Nigeria in 1927 in the wake of the general strike.[24] Gerald
Payne, the son of a gentleman's outfitter, and a graduate of Coventry Technical College, joined the accountancy department in Uganda in 1952 and
worked in the colony for the next ten years.[25] Payne's case is interesting
because he represents that significant minority of colonial service recruits
who had more modest educational qualifications.[26]

The evidence of lower-middle-class reading habits also lends weight to
the view that they embraced the empire somewhat more readily than those
below them on the social scale. The prominence of colonial news in the
pages of the *Daily Express* and *Daily Mail* is well known. However, the
reporting of the empire in *Lloyd's Weekly* and the *Weekly Times* suggests that
lower-middle- and working-class perceptions may have differed well before the end of the nineteenth century. Both papers had an important *petit
bourgeois* section to their readership, compared to *Reynolds' Newspaper* which
was targeted mainly at skilled workers. Until the late 1870s they were
noticeably more favourable to imperial expansion than *Reynolds'*. Editorial
coverage concentrated on India, although the settler colonies featured in
their news sections, perhaps reflecting the personal ties that existed between
lower-middle-class readers and family members who had emigrated to
Canada and Australasia.[27] Interestingly, Kennedy Jones, the blunt-talking
Scottish business partner of Alfred Harmsworth, singled out the very same
factor when later explaining the centrality of empire to the editorial policy
of the *Daily Mail*:

> It was the policy on which we worked for the whole of my journalistic career –
> One Flag, One Empire, One Home. We are a single family . . . I have always
> found the British public deeply interested in Imperial affairs. There is a personal
> bond, a domestic tie, but in Foreign affairs these were absent and, provided

there did not happen to be a serious international crisis, it was well-nigh impossible to awaken a lively concern in Continental politics outside a limited circle.[28]

The *Mail* declared itself to be 'independent and Imperial' in its politics,
while its rival, the *Daily Express*, proclaimed its policy to be 'patriotism' and
its party to be 'the British Empire'. Launched in 1896 and 1900 respectively, they were mass-circulation daily papers, priced at half-a-penny and
designed to appeal to the increasingly prosperous and newly-literate lower
middle class. They both sank a large amount of capital into reporting the
Boer War, attacking the corruption and heavy-handedness of Paul Kruger's
government,[29] castigating the treachery of the pro-Boers,[30] praising the courage of British soldiers,[31] sympathising with the grievances of the Uitlanders[32]
and defending Kitchener's military methods.[33] Although we should not jump
to the conclusion that readers agreed with all of the opinions expressed in
these papers, it is hard to believe that Harmsworth and Pearson were not in
a general sense articulating the lower middle classes' approval of Britain's
assertion of its supremacy in South Africa. They were, after all, shrewd entrepreneurs whose success as newspaper proprietors had largely been built
on the basis of knowing their readers well and supplying them with what
they wanted.[34] Having already established that they could produce papers
that were lighter and more digestible than the 'quality' press, the war provided them with an opportunity to prove their respectability and to show
that they could be serious and responsible when the occasion required.[35] It
also helped them to sell advertising space – a major source of newspaper
income – to commercial companies like Bovril that were eager to capitalise
on the conflict and to exploit the anxieties and aspirations of lower-
middle-class consumers.[36]

Other historians go further. They claim that it was young males with a
'status anxiety' problem – students, youths and clerks – who formed the
vengeful crowds that broke up peace meetings and prevented pro-Boers
from gaining a public hearing.[37] They even argue that the jingoism of the
Boer War was an 'intrinsic feature' of lower-middle-class behaviour. Are
they correct? It is worth remembering that it was the very same lower-
middle-class people who provided the backbone of the burgeoning Sunday
school movement and of other Victorian voluntary religious organisations,
and who regularly attended university extension lectures and vocational
evening classes.[38] From the later nineteenth century, such people also
demonstrated their commitment to mainstream and progressive politics
by joining the new constituency organisations of the major parties and by
becoming involved in a range of socialist associations.[39] Nor do the lower

middle classes seem to have been any more susceptible than the working [43] classes to outbursts of anti-Semitism; if anything, quite the reverse.[40]

For a while the Boer War captured the attention and fired the imagination of the *petite bourgeoisie* in Britain. As the *Express* proudly proclaimed on the relief of Mafeking: 'the "Nation of Shopkeepers" has transcended even the glorious days of Wellington and Nelson'.[41] Yet if the new halfpenny press had played a part in making war-time celebrations possible and even respectable,[42] such celebrations were very much a cross-class affair.[43] So much is clear from the testimony of those closest to the working classes, in particular that of the Independent Labour Party. It was adamant that the war had lowered the democratic spirit of the *whole* nation and debased *mass* opinion. In the words of the *Labour Leader*:

> There is something truly pathetic in the spectacle of poor, degraded, underfed wretches cheering themselves hoarse over the victories of their country and then creeping back to their cheerless homes to gain a few hours pestilential sleep to fit them for the toils of the coming day.[44]

'The war spirit', the paper concluded, 'had made easy victims among working people.'[45] The diaries of John Bruce Glasier, the Glasgow-born ILP activist, and Labour party chairman from 1900 to 1903, make the same point.[46] Glasier did not attempt to exempt workers from the violence of the jingo crowds. On the contrary, he regretted how these crowds had drawn all classes together with 'workmen, poor girls and ladies and gentlemen parading the street and looking for pro-Boers'.[47] As Philip Snowden was later to recall: 'I think the jingo spirit was more rampant at this time than during World War One.'[48]

The working classes

Labour historians are rightly sceptical about the effectiveness of imperial publicity and propaganda.[49] They tend to emphasise the autonomy of working-class culture and the difficulty faced by official and outside forces trying to manipulate it.[50] Autonomy does not of course necessarily mean insularity, and the charge that ordinary working people were either ignorant of, or indifferent to, Britain's colonies should not be too readily accepted. However, we need to take more seriously the possibility that working people embraced the empire on their own terms, and not because they were told to do so by their masters.[51]

[44]   Two key points should be stressed. First, that working people read into imperialism what they wanted and then moulded its image to fit their concerns. Second, that their responses to the empire depended on the sphere of their life in which it was encountered. The latter may seem self-evident, but studies of popular attitudes to the colonies tend to concentrate on leisure at the expense of the home and the workplace. However, it was at home and at work that people spent the vast majority of their time, and it is here that the historian encounters what they most cherished – their families and their jobs. The rest of this chapter will explore the working-class home with reference to consumption, reading and migration. The following chapter explores the world of work. Only then will we turn to people's recreation in Chapter 4.

The working-class family performed a vital economic and social function.[52] It provided food and shelter to the dependent young and elderly. It played a major role in the growth of communal solidarity and working-class consciousness.[53] It was a 'potent source of emotion and personal identity', transmitting values between generations.[54] And for many fathers it was a refuge from the workplace – even as the working day shortened, most manual jobs remained highly monotonous.[55] The domestic sphere is therefore crucial to any understanding of working-class attitudes, including those toward the empire.

Historians dispute how far working-class consumers were conscious of where their food came from. One school of thought says that few of those who ate bread made from Canadian wheat, or consumed West Indian sugar, or drank tea from Ceylon were either aware of the fact or cared much about it. What mattered was cost and people were not sentimental about the source of supply.[56] Conversely, it has been claimed that it was at 'the level of daily living that the British were perhaps most conscious of empire',[57] and that there was an 'increased consumer awareness of the empire countries and their products' from the early 1900s.[58] According to one scholar: 'some of the most trivial aspects at one level, most significant at another, of the so-called British national character – a nation of tea drinkers, for example – result from the imperial experience'.[59] Another contends that imperial advertising and 'commodity racism' had a much greater purchase than their scientific counterpart and reached a larger, less class-bound audience.[60] Moreover, and more specifically, the rise of the late-Victorian supermarket and the fortunes of 'chain stores' like Liptons are said to have 'rested largely on the sale of Indian and Ceylonese tea, first packaged on a mass production basis in 1884'.[61]

Certainly, by the end of the nineteenth century several companies were [45] exploiting imperial sentiment in marketing their products at home and abroad.[62] Bovril led the way here. Founded by John Lawson Johnston, a Scotsman who emigrated to Canada in his mid-thirties, Bovril commodified the Boer War, most famously with its map of the route taken by Lord Roberts during his march across South Africa which miraculously spelt the company's name.[63] It also instituted a system of 'Bovril War Cables', using a fleet of khaki-clad bicyclists to bring news of the war to shops in Greater London. That said, it was not until the 1920s that efforts to promote the buying and selling of empire goods eclipsed other strands of imperial propaganda. From this point on there was a marked effort to link, in the mind of the purchaser, consumer goods to the colony that produced them. The two key agencies that sought to bring about this change were the Wembley exhibition of 1924 (see pp. 86–7) and the Empire Marketing Board. The EMB was established in 1926 at the instigation of the then Colonial Secretary, Leo Amery. It was granted over £3 million during its seven-year existence, and conducted a series of high-profile publicity campaigns for colonial goods that included press adverts, empire shopping weeks and eye-catching posters on specially-constructed hoardings.[64] It also set up displays of colonial food at the increasingly popular *Daily Mail* Ideal Home Exhibitions which were attracting almost half a million visitors by 1926.[65] Much of the EMB's publicity material featured particular commodities from named colonies. The British public's attention was drawn to Canadian wheat, New Zealand wool, South African oranges, pineapples from Malaya, tobacco from Nyasaland, sugar from Mauritius, and cocoa from the Gold Coast. The impact on consumer behaviour must not be exaggerated, however. The EMB's budget was a fraction of the estimated annual expenditure on advertising at this time, and most people probably purchased on price anyway – they were simply too poor to be swayed by emotional or ideological considerations.[66]

Another and perhaps more fruitful approach to the idea of 'product imperialism' is to set the purchase of particular colonial products in the context of general consumption patterns among the labouring classes. Take the four examples of meat, tea, cocoa and sugar. Notwithstanding the vast increase in food imports after 1850, the staples of the national diet for the rest of the century were potatoes, bread and tea.[67] Only from the late 1800s did a greater range of cheaper food enter working-class households – the result of rising real wages, widening markets, the beginnings of modern food technology and improvements in retailing. Even then the changes were initially relatively modest. Cakes, biscuits, sweets and, above all, jam became

Figure 1   Image from the Empire Marketing Board's poster campaign
Source: The National Archives

more popular from the 1870s, yet the working-class diet remained deficient in protein and dominated by carbohydrates.[68] Not until the early twentieth century did the consumption of dairy products and fresh meat noticeably increase, although skilled workmen and artisans had been enjoying them well before then; and not until the inter-war years did 'luxury' or 'exotic' produce – canned vegetables and fresh fruit – become more widely available. Indeed, by the outbreak of the Second World War many semi-skilled, unskilled and unemployed people probably still existed on a diet based on bread and potatoes common to the mid-Victorian era.[69]

The consumption of meat provides a useful index of changing diets and of the contribution of imperial trade to this process. Until the 1880s very little foreign meat came into Britain. The few live cattle that were imported were mainly from Portugal and Spain.[70] Consumption of preserved meats – generally poor in quality and taken only because of their cheapness – was more widespread. Considerable quantities of dried or 'Hamburg' beef came from Germany, while from the early 1860s tinned mutton and beef from Australia began to appear on the English market.[71] The latter was not well received, partly because of health scares – the Admiralty had to condemn huge numbers of putrid cans in the 1850s – but mainly because it was so unappetising.[72] As Anthony Trollope commented, most English workmen would have preferred half a pound of English fresh meat to a whole pound of Australian tinned meat.[73] However, aggressive advertising, and the purchase of Australian and Argentine canned meat by Co-operative stores, gradually helped to increase consumer confidence in the product; the price was attractive too. By the First World War canned meat had thus become a staple item of consumption.

Imports of frozen meat – made possible by the introduction of refrigerated holds on steamships – were also greeted with caution as many people feared that it could cause food poisoning.[74] On 2 February 1880, the SS Strathleven arrived in London with the first cargo of Australian beef and mutton,[75] and by the late 1890s lamb from Australia and New Zealand, beef from the Argentine, and pork from the USA were making noticeable inroads into the British market.[76] The sources were not exclusively imperial, and initially imported frozen meat would have appeared only on the kitchen tables of better-off workers.[77] Nonetheless, by 1914 English farmers supplied less than half of the country's total meat, and the quality and variety of the diet of the skilled working classes was beginning to improve as a result of imported foreign – including colonial – meat.[78] In the inter-war period imports of meat from the empire expanded further; by 1937 they were approximately double those from foreign countries.[79]

[48]   Colonisation was also a key factor in the provision of new drinks to the British consumer, in particular cocoa from West Africa and tea from India and Ceylon.[80] Britain's take-off in chocolate consumption came toward the end of the 1860s, stimulated by rising living standards, the temperance movement, the lowering of duty on imported cocoa beans (1853), the pressing out of cocoa butter to make a more digestible drink, and advertising campaigns stressing the purity and nutritional qualities of chocolate powders.[81] The 'great chocolate boom' saw consumption of cocoa rise nearly sixfold.[82] By the 1870s and 1880s it was one of the most popular non-alcoholic beverages among the industrial working classes, drunk at home and in the ubiquitous cocoa rooms and coffee houses that, according to the social commentator Charles Booth, were 'an important factor in the life of the people'.[83] No longer the drink of the leisured classes, chocolate had become an article of mass consumption, 'a favourite of the whole nation, if not of advocates of its dental health'.[84]

The British fondness for tea is of course legendary. Tea was a very popular drink by the 1860s – one enquiry claimed that 99% of poor families drank it,[85] while by the 1870s and 1880s the prominence of tea advertisements in the popular press suggests that it was much in demand. Rising consumption was directly linked to the shift in the international tea trade from China to the Indian subcontinent and from 'foreign' to 'empire' production.[86] Although green Chinese tea predominated at first, it was subsequently displaced by black tea from India and Ceylon which was stronger and so more economical; by 1906, 93% of tea came from these new sources and only 7% from China.[87] Among the most dramatic of acquisitions was Sir Thomas Lipton's 3,000-acre purchase in Ceylon in the early 1890s – this made him the largest estate owner on the island and helped to kick off a plantation boom.[88]

Closely linked to the drinking of tea was the consumption of sugar. Before the First World War sugar showed the most rapid rise in consumption of any foodstuff. To secure supplies the British equalised sugar duties in 1846, placing slave-grown and non-slave-grown sugar on an equal footing and thereby removing special West Indian privileges. They also endeavoured to boost output from their own West Indian colonies by drafting in some 100,000 Asian – especially Indian – indentured labourers. Hence the Anglo-Caribbean sugar industry continued to supply much of Britain's sugar, even if the transition from protectionism to free trade brought its earlier dominance to an end. Moreover, the British made extensive use of indentured colonial labour to develop new sugar plantations in their possessions in Mauritius, Fiji, Queensland and Natal.[89] As Cunningham observes, 'the

tea that was drunk by every adult in Britain was closely tied up with the
possession of empire'.[90]

The contribution of colonial sugar to calorific intake rose from an estimated 2% of total intake in 1800 to approximately 15% a hundred years
later.[91] Sugar was spooned by the British into their heavily-sweetened tea,
and the growing popularity of sweets, cheap jams and sugared pastries among
an urban proletariat further expanded demand. The increased consumption
of jam was especially important. Jam was spread on the bread that continued to form a major part of the working-class diet: it had the advantages
of tasting better (and being cheaper) than butter and of not spoiling without
refrigeration.[92] Meanwhile, as a sweetener in tea, sugar may have increased
workers' readiness to consume otherwise unadorned complex carbohydrates.[93] But how far were the British working classes actually conscious
of sugar's source or its benefits? A penetrating analysis of the place of the
sugar industry in modern history says that this question misses the point.
'Product imperialism' was not a question of customer consciousness but of
the implications of imperial trade for the 'underlying [capitalist] forces in
British society' and 'intra-class struggles for profit'.[94] In the place of more
nutritious (but more expensive) foods, sugar helped to increase workers'
energy output and to spur them to greater effort. W. F. Pavy's 1874 *Treatise on Food and Dietetics* supports this claim. Pavy was a Fellow of the Royal
College of Physicians and a Lecturer in Physiology at Guy's Hospital in
London. His investigations into the health effects of tea noted its 'restora-
tive action', its 'reviving influence when the body was fatigued' and the
way it 'enabled hunger to be better borne'.[95] The real significance of sugar,
therefore, was that it eased the changes between work and rest by providing swifter sensations of fullness or satisfaction and by deadening hunger;
in this way it worked to 'reduce the overall cost of creating and reproducing the metropolitan proletariat'.[96] No wonder the rich and powerful liked
it so much.[97]

The extent to which people could read, what they read and its effect on
their attitudes to empire are questions that do not admit easy answers.[98] As
the working day shortened and disposable income rose, so reading gradually became one of the more significant growth areas of popular leisure.[99]
As early as the 1860s, the French traveller and writer, Alphonse Esquiros,
quoted an acrobat who had fallen on hard times: 'Nowadays, so many magazines, papers, and cheap books are printed, that the workmen have a taste
for reading, and they despise tricks. In proportion as public curiosity is
withdrawn from us, talent dies out, and the profession is degraded.'[100] The

[50] acrobat probably exaggerated. By the mid-nineteenth century, literacy was increasing,[101] but low incomes, long hours of work and cramped living conditions meant that many people probably had neither the money, the time nor the inclination to pick up a book or magazine.

Here we will examine three relatively coherent cultural phases: mid-Victorian; later-Victorian and Edwardian; and inter-war. The majority of mid-Victorian readers preferred easily digestible reading matter – a miscellany of religious works of self-improvement, sentimental and romantic serials, sensational news and scandals, crime and police reports (actual and imaginary) and criminal biographies.[102] It is hard to believe that the empire figured very largely here. To be sure, popular papers like *Reynolds' News*, with a wide readership among the skilled working class, reported on foreign policy and international affairs. However, the focus of such coverage was on countries with failing monarchs or rising liberal and nationalist reform movements – France, Italy and the USA.[103] With the exception of the Indian mutiny (which the paper forthrightly condemned), interest in Asia and Africa was relatively slight and increased only gradually over time – the Ashanti war of 1874, the Afghan war of 1878 and the bombardment of Alexandria in Egypt in 1882 (all opposed) were felt to be worth a mention. In so far as empire was more regularly reported in *Reynolds'* and other working-class newspapers at this time it was largely in terms of self-help and emigration, in particular to Australia. (A regular feature in the paper's advertisements and advice columns, emigration is discussed in more detail below.)[104]

The imperial theme was more prominent in the popular ballads and broadsides which date back to the sixteenth century and experienced something of a revival during the Victorian era.[105] Spoken, sung and sold on the street or in public houses, displayed on poles or posted on walls, and performed in village and music halls, ballads were one of the cheapest and widely-circulated forms of print.[106] Writers of this literature seized on contemporary events and followed them in a way that reflected the tastes of their readers.[107] In doing so, they expressed a great deal about the feelings and experiences of the urban working classes to whom this body of verse belonged. The number of broadsheets published could be phenomenal – there were an estimated 2.5 million copies of a ballad describing the execution of F. G. Manning and his wife Maria in 1849 – and the level of literacy required to read them was not high. They may even have helped people to practise basic reading skills.[108]

Ballads covered a wide range of subjects: childhood and family life, romance, the Royal family, heroic individuals, politics, wars, and crime.

Recent writing suggests that the empire was popular too. The empire is
well represented in a compilation of 1,250 popular song-titles – as in
Winifred Hare's 'Britain's Sons Shall Rule the World'[109] – while a major
new study of imperialism and music claims that 'it was song that brought
the empire into the home'.[110] Of particular importance here is the tradition
of heroic ballads.[111] These projected an image of a righteous nation, justly
and benevolently extending its rule over the globe through the deeds of
individual British men (and a few women), whose solitary exploits provided a source of pride and a model of conduct for the rest of Victorian
society. They often contained rousing choruses and recurring phrases that
could be easily learnt and repeated, of which G. W. Hunt's 'By Jingo' is
perhaps the most striking example.

The ballads gathered by Oxford's Bodleian Library[112] suggest that the
public figures acclaimed in ballads were relatively few and not necessarily
part of the 'establishment' – General Gordon of Khartoum, and the 'lady of
the lamp', Florence Nightingale, are the two most widely mentioned. The
type of heroism celebrated was more typically that of the ordinary soldier
who guarded distant colonial outposts, fought against all the odds and was
sometimes rescued but more often overpowered by the enemy ranged against
him.[113] From the Indian mutiny (1857–8), through the confrontation with
the Zulus (1879), to the struggle against the Boers (1899–1902), the empire's 'small' wars gave rise to a string of ballads that were very much alike
in their emphasis on the savagery, brutality and treachery of non-European
peoples, and the courage and bravery of those sent to fight in far-away
locations. In these colonial war ballads a political message frequently underpinned the sympathy and solidarity expressed for the British tommy. Thus
much of the verse about the Indian mutiny (or, for that matter, the South
African war) was clearly designed to remind the British public and government of the extent of the soldiers' self-sacrifice, and the need to take proper
care of them after they returned home.[114]

Emigration, however, was by far the most common empire-related
subject.[115] While many emigration ballads date from the 1840s and 1850s,
they continued to be published in large numbers for the next three decades.
Australia and Canada were the two main destinations, and the whole range
of emigrants' emotions was given vent. There were ballads on the horrors
of transportation; on shipwrecks and massacres on arrival; on emigrants'
longing for England and the pain of separation from family and friends;
and on the opportunity to make one's fortune (Australian gold-digging was
a common subject in the mid-century), or at least to gain regular work and
enjoy a better diet and climate.

[52]   Imperial ballads continued to circulate into the later-Victorian and Edwardian era. Most famously, Rudyard Kipling's *Barrack-Room Ballads* (1892) seems to have reached a mass audience.[116] More concerned with the empire's peoples than with its philosophy, the *Barrack-Room Ballads* were chorus-based character songs, written to celebrate 'Tommy Atkins', the private British soldier serving in India. Other ballads that Kipling wrote were probably intended for the educated middle classes; his Boer War poems, for example, were more about than for the common soldier. Of these 'The Absent Minded Beggar' is the best known. It was a money-spinner for the *Daily Mail*'s appeal fund for medical aid and other comforts for British troops. Set to a catchy tune by Arthur Sullivan, it was much more sentimental and overtly propagandist than his previous work. It also spawned something of a souvenir industry. Single-page song sheets, illustrated booklets, deluxe and silk edition reproductions of the original manuscript and various handkerchiefs with the verse imprinted on them – all these were rushed into production and sold at prices well beyond the reach of the working classes.[117]

Kipling's verse, however popular, needs to be set in a wider context. What else did working people read in the later-Victorian and Edwardian era? Several contemporary surveys tried to answer this question. One of the more interesting was by John Garrett Leigh, published in 1904 in the *Economic Review*, a quarterly journal issued by the Oxford University branch of the Christian Social Union, an organisation which studied social and economic problems.[118] Leigh's study of popular literature focused on the reading habits of artisans and manual workers in industrial Lancashire. While drawing attention to the long working hours and lack of relaxation time of men in this area – a major constraint on the use of free libraries – he identified six types of publication commonly found in working-class households: books owned, specialised periodicals, novelettes, religious weeklies, weekly papers, and daily papers. In no category would the empire have figured very prominently. The books owned consisted chiefly of the Bible, Bunyan's *Pilgrim's Progress*, Pike's *Guide to Disciples*, Harriet Beecher Stowe's *Uncle Tom's Cabin*[119] and Mrs Henry (Margaret) Wood's temperance story, *Danesbury House*.[120] Some families possessed copies of G. A. Henty's stories of colonial military campaigns, perhaps because they had been awarded to a child as a Sunday-school prize.[121] The specialised periodicals were the increasingly prevalent sporting papers, in particular those concerned with horse-racing.[122] Novelettes for the female reader were primarily escapist fiction – the 'domestic story' of a young woman rising from rags to riches was a favoured formula. Religious weeklies appealed to both sexes; they included sermons,

stories of divine providence and didactic descriptions of crime and criminals. [53]
The weekly Saturday paper[123] provided a synopsis of the week's news, medical and legal advice and serialised fiction – including the imperial adventure novels of Henry Rider Haggard. Finally, the daily papers read by the
working class of Lancashire tended to be the sporting ones.[124]

A recent study of the working-class intelligentsia by and large confirms
Leigh's findings.[125] Drawing on social surveys, library registers, school
records and, above all, memoirs and autobiographies, it argues that working-
class readers were culturally conservative. The books most commonly found
in their homes were the Bible, *Pilgrim's Progress* and *Robinson Crusoe.*
The great works of literature were also firm favourites: Defoe, Swift, Scott,
Dickens and Hardy the most popular novelists; Milton, Wordsworth and
Tennyson the most popular poets; and Shakespeare and Shaw the most
popular dramatists. The working classes, therefore, read little imperial fiction;
on the contrary, an intense localism was reflected in the parochial focus
of much of their literature.[126] In so far as the wider world did figure in
working-class reading matter it tended to be the Holy Land and America
– not Britain's colonies.[127] Nor were working people much influenced by
whatever imperial fiction they did encounter. Those who read chauvinist,
racist and imperialist novels were highly unlikely to have been indoctrinated by doing so. Reading was an empowering act, not something that
established the cultural hegemony of the middle and upper classes: 'most
working people knew little of the Empire and cared less'.[128] Although this
study is a useful corrective to some of the more ambitious claims made for
the role of literature in drumming up popular support for the empire, it
does perhaps run the risk of overstating its case: the empire had a higher
profile in certain categories of working-class reading than is allowed. It
also makes the mistake of taking working-class scepticism about the 'official politics of Empire' for evidence of a lack of knowledge of or interest in
a broader British world.[129]

In 1925 an employee of W. H. Smith wrote to the bookseller's in-house
magazine, *The Newsbasket*, to ask for a list of best-selling authors that branches
could stock without fear of loss or remainders.[130] The list included: 'Light
Fiction', 'Detective and Exciting Stories' and 'Western Stories'. Eleven
authors are mentioned under the first heading, nine under the second and
four under the third.[131] As one would expect, the empire provided the back-
drop, or a narrative thread, for some of the books in the second category.
Henry Rider Haggard's novels drew deeply on his personal knowledge of
South Africa and his fascination with the Swazis and Zulus. They also had
widespread appeal: over 650,000 copies of *King Solomon's Mines* were printed

[54] in the author's lifetime.[132] Edgar Wallace's thrillers and adventure stories – whose popularity with library users is affirmed by Q. D. Leavis's study of inter-war reading habits[133] – had a fair smattering of imperialist fantasy; and William Le Queux's travels in North Africa and the Sudan provided plenty of material for his fiction, especially the spy thrillers. Like Haggard and Wallace, Le Queux's books were popular with working-class library users.[134] On the other hand, there were several other authors in this category for whom the empire was not a major influence. The plots and settings of the swashbuckling historical romances of the Italian-born Rafael Sabatini (1875–1950) came from European history – revolutionary France, medieval Italy and the English civil war; the crime novels of Sax Rohmer (1883–1959), otherwise known as Arthur Ward, owed much to his obsession with ancient Egypt; and the historical romances of Joseph Fletcher (1863–1935) reflected his passion for local history, a subject on which he was a prolific writer.

The works of the first category ('light fiction', or romantic novels) may have had an equally strong if not stronger connection to the empire. It would be easy to assume that this type of fiction focused on domestic and everyday life and eschewed the 'unreal' or the 'exotic'.[135] However, even a cursory acquaintance with the authors listed under this category suggests otherwise. Berta Ruck (1878–1978) and Maud Diver (1867–1945) were born in India, the daughters of army officers; Margaret Peterson (1883–1933) was the daughter of a professor of Sanskrit at Elphinstone College in Bombay and married to a colonial civil servant; Gertrude Page (1873–1922) emigrated to Rhodesia with her husband (a farmer) at the age of 27 and stayed for the rest of her life; and Kathlyn Rhodes (d. 1962) travelled in Egypt after its occupation by the British. With the exception of Ruck,[136] the fiction of all these novelists seems to have been shaped by their colonial experiences. Diver wrote several romantic novels about Anglo-India, instructing her readers in the complexities of the Raj and exploring the 'dangers' of mixed marriages. Peterson's first prize-winning novel – *The Lure of the Little Drum* (1913) – was about a cruel Indian prince who lured a young Englishwoman away from her husband and abandoned her when his desire began to fade. The subject of interracial attraction, again in India, formed the plot of her next book, *Tony Bellew* (1914). Page's romances offered detailed descriptions of Rhodesian life and landscapes, displaying an almost mystical reverence toward the men and women who had settled there.[137] And Rhodes's fifty-odd volumes of fiction, published from 1899 to 1954, included many romances in African desert settings. Moreover, in the case of these 'colonial' women one might speculate that it was the greater time and freedom afforded them by their retinue of domestic servants that gave them the opportunity to write. Meanwhile, of the six authors who had no direct connection to the empire at least two wrote about it. In *Olivia's Experiment* (1901), Cecil Adair (1856–1932), otherwise known as Evelyn Everett-Green, told the story of a young scoundrel who later redeemed himself as a soldier in the Boer War, while the output of the prolific author Dolf Wyllarde – the *nom de plume* of Dorothy Lowndes – included sensitive portrayals of settler life in Jamaica, South Africa and India, and of families split between Britain and its colonies.[138]

Thus as the habit of reading for relaxation increased between the wars,[139] and public library provision expanded,[140] so working-class people were more likely to encounter the empire through the written word. How many did so, and to what effect, is virtually impossible to say. Much of the non-fiction that working people liked to read – for example, the provincial papers and the sporting press – may well have served to reinforce the localist strand of popular culture, while the ubiquitous crime novels – a favourite form of fiction – were more often set within than beyond the British Isles.

There is, of course, another sense in which the empire entered into the English novel. Attention has recently been drawn to the role that an off-stage colonial world played in bourgeois fiction – for example, the work of Jane Austen and Charles Dickens – where issues of empire were not necessarily a part of the plot, but nonetheless present as an inescapable background or an implicit concern.[141] The same would seem to be true of one of the classic and most enduring novels of the British Left, Robert Tressell's *The Ragged Trousered Philanthropists*, first published in 1918. An account of working-class life in Hastings, the book was repeatedly reprinted and achieved huge wartime popularity among Britain's armed forces: one soldier said that among the troops in Burma Tressell's book 'was handed around and read and reread until literally it fell to pieces'.[142] But Tressell was in fact Robert P. Noonan, and this apparently British book actually 'came out of the world of Empire'.[143] Its critique of capitalism stems from Noonan's experience of Johannesburg in the 1890s where he was drawn into socialist politics. Here Noonan saw at first hand the social upheaval and strife that was the by-product of the world's most rapidly growing mining industry.[144] The power of the author's portrayal of Hastings workers' lives may also owe something to his position as an outsider which enabled him to take a more stark and sceptical look at English life and institutions. *The Ragged Trousered Philanthropists* is a further example of how working-class life could be subtly shaped by Britain's colonial connections, albeit in ways of which working people were not necessarily conscious.

[56] There is another sphere of family life in which the empire was all too tangible for many working-class people – emigration. Although not every emigrant was from a labouring background, the proportion with manual occupations was high. Neither did they all move to the empire: short-distance migration (village to village, rural to urban, or inner city to suburb) was more common,[145] while for most of the nineteenth century the most popular destination for those leaving the UK was America.[146] That said, from the 1850s to the 1920s Canada took 2.35 million British emigrants, Australia and New Zealand 1.7 million, and South Africa 671,500. Moreover, by the first decade of the twentieth century the flow to the United States no longer predominated: almost two-thirds of emigrants were destined for British territories, a pattern perpetuated by the introduction of restrictive legislation by the USA in 1921 and 1924, and by the Empire Settlement Act of 1922. Thus whereas prior to 1900 the focus of the British 'diaspora' had been on America, it shifted ever more decisively to the neo-Britains as the twentieth century progressed.[147]

As far back as 1944, the social historian G. M. Trevelyan observed that 'life in little England would have been a very different thing if it had not been at the centre of a great maritime trade and moreover of an Empire'.[148] He went on to argue that the ingrained insularity of the English was finally broken down during Victoria's reign as the imperial penny post (1898) kept people at home in touch with family and friends who had 'gone to the Colonies', and emigrants periodically visited the UK with money in their pockets and 'tales of new lands of equality and self-help'. 'In this very human manner,' Trevelyan noted, 'the middle and lower classes knew quite as much about the Empire as their "betters".'[149] Is it possible, then, that popular imperial feeling may have been 'buttressed' by the colonies of white settlement 'to which legions of workers had migrated'?[150] Certainly, migration now seems to loom larger in studies of the forging of modern British identities.[151]

We know that elite attitudes to emigration changed dramatically during the nineteenth century. The perception of the white colonies as a refuge for a minority or a dump for the anti-social gave way to the belief that colonisation was 'a legitimate source of national pride'.[152] Yet how far was this true of working-class attitudes? While emigration may have been an alternative to the workhouse, it was not always a happy one.[153] The image of the convict ship was deeply embedded in early and mid-Victorian culture. Many emigrant ballads, for instance, were about the misery of those forced to leave England,[154] and the Australian Convict Ship, a museum at St Katherine's Dock near Tower Bridge, provided a vivid reminder of the horrors of transportation – leg irons, the flogging frame and the [57] cat-o'-nine-tails.[155]

From the 1840s attitudes began to change. A study of working-class newspapers suggests that there was a 'decisive transformation' in popular images of Australia during this decade.[156] Viewed with virtual contempt until then, the Australian colonies came to be seen as a land of great opportunity. The colonial reform movement helped to undermine earlier perceptions of Australia as a bastion of reaction and privilege; the working-class press abandoned its call for 'home colonisation' as the main remedy for social distress; and there was an increased level of skilled labour mobility – with the railway boom British engineers ventured overseas to supervise construction projects and frequently took British craftsmen and labourers with them.[157] A more favourable attitude toward emigration thus began to emerge, reflected in the Scottish Romantics' sentimental emigration poetry[158] and in the work of the song-writer and journalist, Charles Mackay (1814–89).[159] Mackay edited and managed the London Illustrated News, and was a key figure in the development of the Victorian periodical industry. His twelve popular songs entitled 'The Emigrants' (published from 1851 to 1855) celebrated the new life promised by emigration to Canada:

> The star of empire glitters in the west.
> Here we had toil and little to reward it,
> And ours shall be the mountain and the forest,
> And boundless prairies ripe with golden grain.[160]

Such verse sounds hopelessly idealistic to today's ear. However, it is worth remembering that emigrants were often 'willing exiles' whose decision to leave Britain was prompted by a quest for self-improvement rather than by outright destitution. Interwoven into the fabric of English, Irish and Scottish life, emigration in the second half of the nineteenth century was increasingly regarded as a step toward greater independence and security – a matter of hope rather than shame.[161]

So much for general observations. To recover the experiences of those who emigrated to the empire we need to delve more deeply into the motives for and mechanics of migration. This can be done by looking at migrant recruitment (publicity, promotion and advertising); information networks forged between so-called 'sending' and 'receiving' communities; remittances received from emigrants; and the various types of return migration.

Notwithstanding music hall entertainment, public festivals and popular fiction, it is likely that most people first came to know about particular

[58] parts of the empire through letters from emigrants. Among the lower classes there was a real hunger for information – on soil type, climate, wage rates, food prices – which influenced both the decision to migrate and the choice of destination.[162] A variety of interested parties diffused this information and from as early as the 1830s a flood of promotional literature poured forth.[163] It was produced and circulated by landowners, newspaper proprietors, clergymen and parish officials, religious and charitable societies, gentry-led emigration committees and, above all, emigration agents.[164] What was the impact of this publicity? How far did it give empire migration a wider currency among the working classes?

One way of tackling these questions is to take a closer look at the work of emigration agents employed by shipping companies and the colonies. Active from the 1840s until the 1920s and stationed throughout the British Isles, these agents – initially newspaper editors, emigrants or first-generation colonials; later war veterans or career civil servants – went into the local community to recruit.[165] They travelled widely in their districts, distributing pamphlets, putting up eye-catching posters, organising agricultural displays at markets and summer shows, conducting lecture tours, making extensive use of the local press and corresponding or meeting with potential migrants. Sometimes they offered cheap passages or other inducements. Migration was, of course, a business and they were frequently accused of peddling false impressions and making fraudulent promises. Yet reasonable limits usually prevailed.[166] Indeed, a leading historian in this field accords professional agents a vital role in the migration process, laying particular emphasis on the importance of their personal contact with migrants.[167]

Another measure of the impact of overseas settlement is provided by the concept of 'chain' or 'bridge' migration. This suggests that the flow of information between sending and receiving communities was crucial. On the one hand, letters from friends and relatives back home were a 'cherished link' – a way of coping with loneliness and dislocation,[168] of confirming the durability of familial groups[169] and of keeping up with metropolitan tastes.[170] On the other, good overseas contacts and an increased awareness of conditions in the destination country were a major stimulus to emigration:[171] they helped to show whether it was feasible and reduced the risks of relocation. Owing to the cost of postage,[172] letter-writing was probably quite restricted at the outset of our period – it was not unknown for unstamped letters to be sent home with some pre-arranged device scrawled on them to denote good news, thereby saving relations the expense of redeeming the mail.[173] Yet by the mid-1860s there are signs that letter-writing was increasing,[174] while by the mid-1870s the Postmaster General could report that the public now attached more importance to speed than to low rates of postage in relation to correspondence with the colonies.[175] By the late 1880s (a decade before the introduction of the Imperial Penny Post),[176] the sending of letters and parcels was regular and widespread.[177] This was no doubt partly a result of the formation in July 1875 of the Postal Union, a single postal territory embracing the great majority of the world's correspondents. Several British colonies subsequently joined the Postal Union, starting with India in 1876.[178] It is not, however, until the 1900s that the Post Office archives give a clear indication of the amount of mail being exchanged between Britain and the various parts of the empire. Tables 3 and 4 offer snapshots of the situation in 1904–5 and 1909–10.[179]

Some relatives of migrants also received remittances. These could be sent as cash or bills of exchange or as money or postal orders; alternatively they could be carried in person (or trusted to an emigrant friend) on a return visit. While remitting money appears to have been a fairly frequent practice among migrants from south-east Europe – those in the USA were capable of saving as much as 60–70% of their monthly earnings for transfer home – much less work has been done on the remittance behaviour of British

Table 3   Mail exchanged by the United Kingdom with the colonies, 1904 and 1909 (measured in 000 lb)[a]

	1904		1909	
	Despatched to	Received from	Despatched to	Received from
India	2,983	582	3,675	818
South Africa	3,764	860	2,513	601
Egypt[b]	390	77	618	139
West Indies[c]	508	87	549	83
Canada/ Newfoundland	1,367	668	5,022	1,362
Australia	1,753	629	2,080	841
New Zealand[d]	771	328	1,103	462

[a] Based on the *51st and 56th Reports of the Postmaster General on the Post Office* (1905, 1910), Appendix B.
[b] The figure for Egypt for 1909 also includes mail to and from Morocco.
[c] The West Indies includes Foreign as well as British territories.
[d] Includes Fiji.

Table 4   Colonial parcels despatched and received in 1904–5 and 1909–10[a]

	1904–5		1909–10	
	Despatched to	Received from	Despatched to	Received from
India	192,368	107,253	277,549	123,656
South Africa	405,279	66,688	244,510	52,220
West Indies	51,730	11,531	56,223	10,655
Australia & New Zealand	121,066	35,362	155,246	47,143
Canada	143,444	63,462	314,731	124,671

[a] Based on the *51st and 56th Reports of the Postmaster General* (1905, 1910), Appendix B.

migrants.[180] Chapter 7 looks at the main transfer mechanisms in greater detail. Remittances to Britain's colonies expanded rapidly after 1870,[181] though sizeable sums of money were sent by New Zealand domestic servants and Canadian agricultural labourers to support their relatives back in Scotland well before then.[182] There were two types of remittance: the one-off payments and pre-paid tickets that financed the voyages of family members, and the more regular payments from sons to parents and from husbands to wives. The second type of payment was made 'to fulfil normative obligations within the family'.[183] Despite the fact that migrants were separated from their relatives by great distances, they appear to have accepted responsibility for aged parents and other dependent relatives back home. Indeed, in some parts of the country it is likely that remittances were sufficiently regular and sizeable to be an integral part of the family budget, and all that stood between financial independence and parish relief. For example, in the case of Irish migrants we know that the public back home saw remittances as one of the immediate benefits of migration – a measure of compensation for the separation of a family member.[184] There are even stories of families being allowed to run up credit in December in anticipation of the Christmas letter home.[185]

Yet it is the Cornish miner-migrants in South Africa about whom we know the most.[186] The Cornish were a highly mobile and skilled workforce that made a significant contribution to the development of hard-rock mining throughout the world. From the 1880s, South Africa was their main destination. There were about 7,000 Cornish mine workers on the Rand by the middle of the 1890s – a quarter of the white mine workforce – and this figure rose to about 10,000 by the beginning of the twentieth century.[187] Some were permanent settlers who took their loved ones with them, but mostly they went alone. The families left behind anxiously awaited the arrival of a regular remittance in the South African mail.[188] By the early 1900s it was thought that every mail was bringing £20,000 to £30,000 for 'the wives and families and the old folks at home'.[189] No surprise, then, that when the Cape mail arrived people would flock into the towns from the surrounding villages to collect their money and the business in local shops boomed.[190] Not all were so fortunate, however. When the 'home pay' did not arrive the county's Board of Guardians were left to pick up the pieces, though they themselves were helped by the charitable work of the several Cornish Associations on the Rand which stepped into the breach with ex-gratia payments.[191] These associations also supported the widows and orphans of Cornishmen killed by mine accidents or by the miners' lung disease phthisis.[192]

Remittances had particularly important consequences for the life of Cornish women. Early marriage coupled with migration resulted in many wives and mothers remaining alone in Cornwall with full responsibility for maintaining the family home.[193] This led to the development of a 'dependency culture', whereby their financial well-being was effectively determined by the prosperity of the Johannesburg gold mines.[194] No wonder South Africa was referred to as 'Greater Cornwall', and Johannesburg as but a suburb of the Duchy. With its constant and all-important flow of money orders the colony was a lifeline for Cornwall until at least the early 1920s. After this, emigration began to dry up as industrial unrest on the Rand, and a growing awareness of the horrendous disabilities caused by phthisis, took the shine off South Africa as a destination.[195]

A further connection between the British at home and overseas was the reverse flow of migrants from the periphery to the metropolitan core – an aspect of migration history about which relatively little has been written.[196] How many migrants came back from the colonies? What impressions of the colonies did they carry with them? Rising colonial incomes and improvements in transport and communications made it possible for as many as 40% of migrants to return.[197] The figure is likely to have varied across the British Isles with the lowest rate among the Irish and the highest among the Cornish.[198] In the case of Scotland there appear to have been more returnees from America than from Australasia or Canada.[199] Whatever the exact number, it is clear that many people came back to Britain from the colonies. According to one recent estimate, 1.1 million people returned from

Figure 2 Cornish miners on the Rand, 1896
Source: Courtesy of Royal Institution of Cornwall, Royal Cornwall Museum

Australia between 1901 and 1915 and nearly 1 million people from New [63]
Zealand between 1853 and 1920.[200]

Migrants could retrace their steps for many reasons. Some probably left Britain with the specific intention of coming back, perhaps to fetch their families or to buy a small farm or shop once they had saved sufficient money. Others possibly became homesick or they may have returned because their families refused to join them. Some came back through desperation or were deported by the colonial authorities after having fallen upon public relief. Others may have been restless or peripatetic individuals – 'birds of passage' – who needed to be constantly moving on. There are even those young single men who returned on the so-called 'romance visit' in search of a wife. Clearly, the impact of returning migrants would have differed from case to case. At one end of the spectrum there were those who were disappointed, disillusioned and discontented. These people can hardly have been a positive advert for the colonies. Take, for example, the family of Gwennie Edmondson. Born in 1912, Gwennie grew up in Accrington in Lancashire. At the age of 15 she emigrated to Australia: it was the slump, father was out of work and some of her relatives had recently returned on a holiday to Britain and stumped up a half of the family's fare. But the relatives had made their money in farming, whereas her father was in the grocery trade and could not find regular employment in New South Wales. As soon as the exchange rate permitted, the family returned. Thus in 1937 Gwennie found herself back in the textile mills.[201] At the other end of the spectrum there were the enthusiasts – returnees who sought to profit from their experience and who preached the virtues of empire emigration. In between these extremes were the majority for whom return was neither an admission of failure nor a sign of success; rather it was something that had rarely been far from their minds. Whatever their motivation, the little we do know about returning migrants (and the increasing number of 'colonials' travelling to London from the late 1880s) strongly suggests that there was far more familiarity between Britain and the neo-Britains than hitherto appreciated.[202] Indeed, at the heart of the migration process were highly developed social networks that extended forward from Britain and backward from the emigrants' destinations, both servicing and creating the substantial population flows within the British World.

CHAPTER 3

THE WORKING CLASS AT WORK

W ork occupied the major part of people's waking time and determined the amount of money at their disposal.[1] The experience of the workplace further influenced standards of health and accommodation, the nature of family life and social and political values.[2] It seems only sensible therefore to ask how conditions of employment and the character of the working environment impinged on popular perceptions of the empire.

For most if not all of our period the trade unions were the main agency of working-class self-betterment, and played a key role in improving the terms of labour for working men. Alongside friendly and co-operative societies, they helped to sustain a vibrant associational culture based on the principles of autonomy and independence. Yet trade unions are usually portrayed as insular and inward-looking.[3] Moreover, even when historians do acknowledge external influences on the British labour movement, these tend to be European and American, not imperial. The exceptions here are the handful of export industries with major markets in the empire, and armament manufacturers that benefited from spending on imperial defence. Workers in these sectors of the economy are said to have appreciated the material benefits of empire and favoured overseas expansion.[4] It is also claimed their managers were more conciliatory: exporting to semi-protected colonial territories was felt to be preferable to embarking on a path of continuous confrontation over large-scale modernisation and integration.[5]

What were the attitudes of British labour toward the use of cheap African and Asian workers? While there are plenty of studies of race as a scientific discourse and an elite theory, workers' racial attitudes have not received the same attention.[6] One view states that while exclusion on the grounds of sex was a policy of the old craft unions,[7] exclusion on the grounds of colour was a property of colonial rather than British labour movements.[8] The workers' 'other' in Britain was the capitalist employer, not the Indian factory hand, African mine worker or Chinese coolie. Only when West

Indian immigrants arrived in Britain in the middle of the twentieth century did this change, the competitive threat posed by these newcomers producing deep rifts in the British working population.[9] Another view suggests that racism became a mass force or ideology toward the end of the nineteenth century. Ideas of backwardness and inferiority, hitherto applied to the lower orders at home, were now redirected toward colonial or subaltern peoples. In this way, the language of racial and of colour difference came to transcend the category of class, thereby reconciling workers to the British empire.[10] Neither view is entirely satisfactory. The first overlooks the connections between British labour at home and British labour overseas. The second ignores evidence of workers' hostility to colonial peoples well before the late 1800s,[11] and exaggerates the empire's capacity to reconcile workers to their place in the existing social order.

Whatever workers' attitudes to colonial peoples, their imperial experiences were mediated through class struggle in Britain. This is shown very clearly by two recent studies of labour relations in the dockyards and the shipping industry where union activity was strongly influenced by wider colonial connections. A strike in the London docks during the South African War (1899–1902) painfully exposed the dilemma of workers whose livelihoods were tied up with the empire.[12] Although the leaders of the dockers' union opposed the war, patriotic demonstrations within the docks were common and overshadowed the marches and protests of the strikers. Indeed, union men soliciting funds for the families of striking dockers found themselves in direct competition with the war relief charities for the widows and orphans of British soldiers.[13] By mid-July, the dispute had 'died with a whimper' as the 'men straggled back to work in dribs and drabs'. In the mercantile marine, meanwhile, there were a growing number of black seamen – at least a few thousand by the 1920s. They were hired in colonial ports at colonial wage levels, and toiled in appalling conditions. It is claimed that the discrimination they suffered was a product of employer-initiated practices. Union race policy, by contrast, was deeply ambivalent.[14] Before 1914 unions resisted the principle of unequal pay for blacks and whites; after 1918 they reluctantly capitulated to employers' racial practices, and rejected overtures from colonial unions that might have provided a basis from which to challenge stratification. There was no inherent antipathy between black and white workers; rather they were ruthlessly pitted against each other in a struggle for jobs. Union leaders are also said to have been more culpable than the rank-and-file: it was they who actively colluded with shipowners in the institution of cheap black labour – the ordinary British seaman apparently knew little of this.[15]

[66]   To learn more about workers' racial attitudes it is necessary to delve down into their experiences of empire. We will do this by looking at the influence of two colonies – Australia and South Africa – on the British labour movement, and by examining two industries in which jobs depended on imperial policy: Lancashire cotton textiles and Dundee jute. While the majority of workers in Britain did not have a material connection to the empire (or certainly not one that they were conscious of), these case studies will show that a significant minority did. They will also show that British workers' political culture owed a good deal to their relationships with other groups of 'British' workers in the wider British world. Hence even those men whose jobs did not depend on imperial policy were not necessarily indifferent to it.

     To return to the dockers. It is not the smaller strike of 1900 but the 'great strike' of 1889 that provides evidence of the imperial consciousness of some British workers.[16] The 1889 strike originated with tea warehouse-men who called for an increase in their pay. They were rapidly joined by stevedores, lightermen and coal porters, totalling well over 100,000 work-ers. However, a joint body of two major dock committees refused to make concessions and port employers followed its lead. Blackleg labour was then imported on a large scale and the strikers' funds soon ran short. Hunger undermined morale; support for the strike wavered. A crisis was reached by the end of August when, suddenly and unexpectedly, Australian labourers made several large contributions to the dockers' funds.

     Across Australia there was a strong fraternal feeling for the British dockers, and a genuine sense of shock among all classes at how poorly they were paid.[17] News of the strike was reported daily in the Melbourne, Sydney and Brisbane press. On 29 August the Brisbane Wharf Labourers' Union sent £150 to the London strike fund, and the Seamen's and Firemen's Union followed suit with a donation of £1,000. The Sydney Wharf labourers gave £5,000. Melbourne and Adelaide then set to work to organise subscriptions of their own. Australian trade unions used various methods to raise money (direct grants, levies and subscription lists), and several gave until it hurt.[18] Football clubs also donated their gate money, and a special fund-raising match was arranged between the teams of the Melbourne Wharf Labourers' Union and the Port Philip Stevedores' Society. A great open-air demonstration in Sydney, at which a crowd of at least 10,000 gathered, raised nearly £1,000.

     For a fortnight the money came pouring in. Australian unions and trade societies provided approximately a third of the £30,000 that Australia gave to the London dockers' total fund of £48,700.[19] The first sums were

particularly important in obviating what would have been a desperate [67]
call for a general strike. In fact, most historians agree that it was the intervention of Australian workers that made the difference between victory
and humiliation for the London dockers. The success of their spectacular
struggle proved a defining episode in the 'new unionism'. An undisciplined
labour force had been brought out on strike, the strike had remained solid
and the dockers' pay demands had been conceded. This exploded the myth
that dockers in Britain were so poverty-stricken and demoralised as to be
incapable of collective action. On the contrary, by the end of the year, the
new Dock, Wharf, Riverside and General Labourers Union had enrolled
30,000 members.

The three key organisers of the strike were Ben Tillett, John Burns and
Tom Mann (1856–1941). Mann supervised the picketing and ensured that
it was conducted peacefully. He went on to serve as a member of the Royal
Commission on Labour (1891–4) and as the president of the Dockers'
Union (1893) and the International Federation of Ship, Dock and River
Workers (1896). However, having reached an impasse with his work in
Britain, and attracted by the youthful vigour of dominion labour movements, Mann left for New Zealand in 1901, moving on to Australia the
following year. The next eight and a half years were a formative period in
his life.[20] For three of these years he organised the Labour party of Victoria,
conducting extensive tours of Western Australia (1904) and Queensland
(1905) on the party's behalf. His findings were reported back home in
articles penned for the *Clarion*. On the formation of the Socialist party of
Victoria in 1906, Mann edited the *Socialist*; subsequently, he helped to
establish the Australasian Socialist Federation in 1908.

Mann's Australian experience, in particular that of two major strikes,
led him to drop the parliamentary socialism he had previously espoused.
The first of these strikes was among the railwaymen on the state-owned
system in Victoria in 1904, when he concluded that nationalisation was no
solution to the problems of organised labour. The second involved the miners
of Broken Hill and the smelting workers of Port Pirie. Threatened with a
huge wage reduction, and subject to harsh work conditions, their unions
took advantage of the state arbitration machinery and the courts to obtain
redress. Yet although the arbitrator found in their favour, the Australian
High Court overturned the main part of the decision. The Liberal–Labour
coalition then ordered the intervention of troops to protect imported black-
legs. The strike that ensued collapsed after sixteen weeks with many workers
left unemployed and some militants imprisoned. Mann had accepted the
job of organiser and felt acute disgust with state socialism as a result. He

[68]   also came to appreciate more acutely the need for sympathetic strikes; if the railwaymen of New South Wales had not kept the trains running, it would have been impossible to send in armed police from Sydney.

Having left the country a state socialist in 1901, Mann returned to Britain in 1910 convinced that revolutionary methods were required if labour was to seize its destiny. In the intervening eight and a half years he had built up a reputation as an energetic agitator and a pioneer of trade union organisation. Ramsay MacDonald, Keir Hardie and Ben Tillett had all visited him in Australia, and Tillett especially had wanted him back. An advocate of 'industrial solidarity' and 'direct action', who had abandoned faith in compulsory conciliation, Mann immediately began spreading his version of the syndicalist doctrine. He published a monthly journal, the *Industrial Syndicalist*, founded the Industrial Syndicalist Education League (1910) and set up Amalgamation Committees in a number of industries. He also established the National Transport Workers Federation, which included both dockers and seamen (though not railway workers).

It was a timely moment for Mann to reappear. The industrial unrest of the pre-First World War years meant that syndicalist ideas had a greater chance of permeating British labour than ever before.[21] (Mann's leadership provided the catalyst for one of these disputes – the strike in the Liverpool docks in 1911.) Syndicalism attracted workers disappointed with the progress of the parliamentary Labour party. Its strongest support came from unofficial trade unionists in the South Wales coalfield; they repudiated state ownership of the mines in favour of ownership by the miners. Admittedly, most unions were intent on retaining their own separate privileges, and not a single industry went over to the notion of 'one industry, one union'. Even so, syndicalism manifested itself in the violence of industrial unrest at this time, in hostility to the existing labour leadership and in the broad basis of strike demands. For this Tom Mann must take some of the credit, or bear some of the responsibility, depending on one's perspective. He had helped to transform syndicalism from what had hitherto been 'a tiny propagandist current' into a militant movement capable of actively challenging capitalist authority by promoting workers' control and direct action at the point of production.[22] Internationally mobile, and with a reputation that extended well beyond Britain, Mann was one of several British labour leaders who were refreshed and revitalised by the industrial battlefields of the colonies.[23]

There were, however, other pathways connecting British and colonial labour. Interaction at the level of policy is discussed in Chapter 6 in the context of domestic politics and social welfare legislation (see pp. 144–6). But it was the international mobility of specific groups of workers – such as

the Cornish miners – that was the main vector of working-class imperial [69]
culture.[24] There was a strong sense of cohesion and solidarity among such
workers, some of whom even belonged to the same trade unions.[25] We will
now explore these connections with particular reference to the Amalgamated
Society of Engineers (ASE) and the South African labour movement. How
far was the latter's commitment to the principle of racial discrimination in
employment supported by the ASE and the Trade Union Congress (TUC)
in Britain?

By the 1840s trade unions had already begun to develop colonial
connections. Some had set up emigration funds as an alternative to tramp
relief and as a safety-valve for surplus labour; others were corresponding
regularly with their colonial 'brethren' for news of the latest job opportunities and prospects overseas.[26] The London Typographical Society is a case
in point. From 1853 to 1857 it kept a minute book of the proceedings of
its committee on emigration. The committee met monthly to advance money
to workers who wished to emigrate to Australia (the advances were paid
back by instalments after arrival); it also received letters from typographical
associations in the Australian colonies regarding the state of trade. Many
workers were assisted in this way, their circumstances being examined in
some detail by the committee.[27]

Later in the nineteenth century trade unions opened branches overseas.[28]
The Amalgamated Society of Engineers is perhaps the most striking
example.[29] Its colonial branches had to send fees and reports to Britain and
their procedures had to conform to British standards; often they were led
by members from the UK. The ASE's journal faithfully reflected the union's
imperial reach. It reported regularly on the passage of labour laws and
the growth of the labour parties in New Zealand and Australia; it also provided up-to-date details of trade conditions and work opportunities in these
colonies and in Canada. Moreover, in South Africa many prominent labour
leaders were ASE members. District committees were formed in the Cape,
Durban and Pretoria, and on the Rand; they had the power to regulate
wages, hours of labour, terms of overtime and piecework. Nor was the ASE
unique. By 1913, the Amalgamated Society of Boilermakers had ten branches
in South Africa, which remitted about £1,000 per annum to a London-
based executive council.[30]

What happened when aspirations to human equality on the part of British labour confronted colonial claims for white workers' privileged access
to the labour market? It has recently been argued that British labour was
not ideologically distinct from 'white' colonial labour, and that from the
1870s an 'imperial working class' was forged through overseas migration,

Table 5   Membership of the Amalgamated Society of Engineers[a]

Year	Home[b]	Colonial	USA	Total
1882		1,281	(not known)	46,131
1899	75,196	2,401	1,576	79,173
1907	101,837	5,209	3,038	110,084
1919	291,073	26,335	3,273	320,681
1929	194,334	25,566	0	220,900

[a] Membership figures taken from the ASE's *Annual Reports* (1865–1920), MSS 259x/4/2/1–4, Modern Records Centre, University of Warwick.
[b] Includes England & Wales, Scotland and Ireland.

trans-national social networks and cultural flows. This imperial working class opposed the use of cheap African and Asian labour by capitalist employers, not on the basis of 'biological racism' but out of an instinct of self-preservation.[31] Its ideology of 'white labourism' (or 'racial socialism') manifested itself very powerfully during the controversy over Chinese indentured labour.[32]

In June 1904 the first Chinese workers arrived in Durban. The ASE had already warned the British government of the 'social and industrial demoralisation' that would result from coloured workers being brought to the dominions.[33] Its response to the use of Chinese labour in South Africa's goldmines was shaped by the views of T. J. Kneebone, a pioneer of trade unionism on the Rand and organising secretary of the Johannesburg branch. From 1903 to 1907, letters from Kneebone featured regularly in the ASE's journal. As early as August 1903 he wrote to the editor about the detrimental effects of indentured labour on the British worker: 'All trade unions recognise the evils that must accrue should the Chinamen come in.'[34] ASE members were warned to 'keep a look out and oppose by all means in their power the introduction of Chinese workers into the South African colonies'.[35] In fact, virtually all of the ASE's arguments against the policy can be traced back to its South African branches. First, and most importantly, there was a sense of betrayal. During the Boer War British workers had been told that victory over the Transvaal would mean more jobs for themselves, not cheap, alien labour and inflated profits for the Randlords.[36] As the organising secretary of the Germiston branch, T. Kennerly, explained:

I, as a colonial, fought in the late war with an honest enthusiasm to make the bounds of freedom greater still, but I have to admit I've been swindled. And what do I now find? It was for our own degradation, for they now tell us we are not wanted. They tell us the Chinese are more controllable, and, if Chamberlain and Milner and his nominees have their way the Chinese will be here in a few months in spite of the overwhelming opposition which they know full well is against them. The people – that is those who, like myself, have decided to make this country their own, and who know the Chinese in other lands – regard them with horror. I appeal to our comrades and brothers to think of it when they give the vote at the next election.[37]

Another key aspect of the case against Chinese workers, which originated in South Africa but was repeated in Britain, was that it was not a necessity but a capitalist ploy to undermine the power of white trade unions in the colony. Again, Kennerly hammered this point home:

Everything is in a shocking bad way in consequence of the vile conspiracy of the capitalistic gang of mineowners, who really curse this country. The same gang who made such a mess of the Jameson raid are now the appointed rulers . . . Their policy is one of plunder and oppression, without any regard to the wishes of the people or the welfare of the country. Hence their altogether blackguard hurry to hustle in slave labour in the shape of the servile Chinese, to the utter degradation of the white population, and, if successful in this their crowning infamy, to the destruction of South Africa as a fit place for a white English artisan.[38]

Following this letter a long leading article in the ASE's journal ('The Heathen Chinese') rebutted the capitalists' argument that cheap labour was essential to turn a profit in the mines. It questioned why capitalists in other parts of the empire had not adopted such a policy, reminding readers that since the 1888 Exclusion Acts the Australians had 'persistently and consistently barred contracting Chinamen'. The answer, it ventured, lay in the fact that whereas Australia was governed democratically, thereby maintaining certain standards of living, in South Africa the mining magnates were frightened of white trade unionism and determined to suppress it.[39]

How far, then, was the ASE's hostility to indentured Chinese workers born of racial prejudice? The ASE's members were certainly encouraged to regard 'John Chinaman' as a threat. How could they hope to compete against men who lived on 6d a day? The fact that the Chinese were not unionised was also often remarked upon, and blamed on the backwardness of Asian society: 'the Chinaman does not conform to the civilised usages of more advanced peoples'.[40] That said, in an increasingly competitive international labour market, the ASE's members were acutely aware of the dangers posed by *any* source of cheap labour: 'we object to the employment of low caste, underpaid, compounded and indentured labour, whether black, white, yellow, copper or any other colour'.[41] It seems likely, therefore, that the fight to obtain separate racial status for British workers was mainly about maintaining standards of living and defending their relatively privileged access to labour markets. Indeed, in their view the protection of British labour was among the key functions of empire, and the use of indentured Chinese workers an affront to their understanding of what that empire stood for. As the editor of the ASE's journal opined: 'our flag is alright, but we must rescue it from the dirt wherein it lies'.[42]

The eagerness of the TUC to pick up this issue in 1904 is also worth noting. Chinese labour galvanised trade councils into action, thirty-seven of which organised public demonstrations and forwarded protest resolutions to the government or local MPs.[43] It was no surprise, therefore, that the TUC president referred to the matter in his address to Congress that year: 'It was not supposed at the commencement of the Boer War that £230,000,000 of your money and more than 20,000 lives would be sacrificed in order that white labour in the Transvaal should be ousted and replaced by yellow slave labour.'[44] TUC opposition culminated in a mass demonstration in Hyde Park on 24 March. Posters were printed, banners erected, musicians hired and several actors employed to dress as Chinamen complete with pigtails.[45] *The Times'* correspondent thought that about 30,000 people were present; the TUC 80,000.[46] Either way, it was a huge gathering – some fourteen platforms were set up for the speakers – that was attended by many respected labour leaders. John Burns declared that 'if the Chinese ordinance was not torn from the statute book it would be the beginning of the end of the British Empire'.[47] Ben Tillett declared that 'once the people of this country were khaki mad, but now they were khaki sad as they contemplated the results of their madness'.[48] And John Clifford declared that slavery could not be introduced in one part of the empire without opening the door for it in every other. It was even suggested that, whatever their race, workers within the empire should be given preference over those outside – a statement cheered by the crowd.[49]

The ASE's and the TUC's engagement with Chinese labour was relatively short-lived, though the intensity of interest should be set against the brevity of its duration. However, South Africa was catapulted back on to the agenda of the British labour movement in 1913–14 when a strike by miners and railwaymen resulted in the Smuts government arresting and deporting nine union leaders.[50] The deportations of February 1914 followed hard on the heels of serious labour unrest the previous year. They created a remarkable wave of unity amongst organised labour: 'the widening of solidarities' increasingly 'seemed more natural within a (white) Empire-wide arena than within, say, a European one'.[51] Naturally, there was keen Cornish interest in South Africa. A dominant figure in the strike was Tom Mathews, the General Secretary of the South African Mine Workers Union. Mathews had studied at the Camborne School of Mines and left for Johannesburg in 1898.[52] Moreover, as recently as September 1913, striking clay-workers in Cornwall had been the beneficiaries of a spontaneous collection by one of Johannesburg's Cornish Associations.[53]

The South African deportees were welcomed at Gravesend by a senior Labour delegation led by Arthur Henderson. Over the next few weeks they spoke at meetings as far apart as Glasgow and Cornwall. All of the major labour journals in Britain reported on their fate and on the progress of the strike more generally.[54] As in 1904, the ASE was quick to express its indignation at the treatment of British workers in South Africa. The executive council unanimously condemned Botha's imposition of martial law, while demanding the recall of the Governor-General, Lord Gladstone, for sanctioning the measure.[55] As for the deportations, they elicited the following response: 'Russianised methods of government in a British colony cannot be tolerated by the Trade Union movement of Britain without a spirited protest if it values its own interests of free speech and liberty to combine.'[56] Thus what had happened on the Rand was seen as setting a dangerous precedent for the resolution of labour disputes in the 'mother country'. Meanwhile, the Amalgamated Society of Boilermakers gave its members a detailed account of the grievances of the South African workers and the brutalities of the government response to their strike.[57] Its general secretary reminded them that the South African mine owners lived mostly in London, and that Botha's action had been hailed with delight by employers' associations in Britain. ASB members were then asked to vote in favour of a levy for 'fair play for their brothers in South Africa', and for the repatriation of the deported leaders. They agreed overwhelmingly, 5,203 in favour and only 770 against.[58]

The rhetoric of the ASE and the ASB resonated with other sections of the British labour movement too. Thirty-two Labour MPs moved an amendment to the Address in February 1914, asking the government to reserve the Indemnity Bill which was before the South African parliament and which contained a provision for the deportation of labour leaders.[59] Two months later the Labour party moved another resolution to maintain the rights of citizens throughout the British empire. Meanwhile, at a public meeting in

[74] London the labour movement wheeled out its big guns, followed by a large demonstration of workers who marched from the Embankment to Hyde Park. Tom Mann then visited South Africa in April 1914. He urged white workers across the Rand to strengthen their existing unions and to organise new ones, and repeatedly expressed the solidarity of British workers with their South African counterparts.[60] Mann also wrote a series of reports on the South African labour movement for the British labour press.[61]

It is surprising, therefore, to find that the high point of the battle of South Africa's mine workers for racial protection – the 1922 Rand Revolt – did not have a bigger impact upon the British labour movement.[62] Certainly, there was no lack of British patriotism in the 1922 strike, and the event must have made something of an impression in Britain – Agatha Christie referred to the industrial situation in South Africa in *The Man in the Brown Suit*, clearly assuming that her readers would be generally aware of what had happened.[63] The lack of a labour response may be the result of Cornish immigration drying up – Afrikaner nationalists were fiercely opposed to it. It may also be because many South African branches of British trade unions had become moribund: the South African Council of the ASB was wound up in 1915, despite an appeal against the decision by its South African members,[64] while the half-hearted efforts of George Kendall (one of the Rand deportees) to organise the Workers' Union in the colony led only to one permanent branch at the Simonstown naval base.[65] Another factor may have been the lock-out by the Engineering and National Employers' Federation which began in March and ended in June. The ASE's energies were totally absorbed by this dispute, and its finances nearly exhausted.[66] Moreover, it is possible that the racial attitudes of South African workers were becoming an embarrassment to some British labour leaders by this time. For example, at the first Commonwealth Labour Conference in September 1924, it was the South African delegate, H. W. Sampson, who was responsible for a bitter duel between the South African Labour Party and the All India Trade Union Congress. Sampson acknowledged that the South African delegation to the International Labour Organisation would be strengthened by the inclusion of 'an intelligent Native', but refused to agree to a request for a straight declaration of principle opposing racial discrimination.[67] Given that the purpose of the conference was to increase co-operation between labour movements in the empire, it was an inauspicious beginning.

The focus of our enquiry now shifts to two particular industries that felt the pulse of imperial policy in India: cotton and jute. The Indian consumer was

vital to the expansion of the Lancashire textile industry. By the mid-
nineteenth century India's absolute superiority to all other markets had
been established, and Britain remained the largest foreign supplier of cotton textiles to India until 1935–6, when it was surpassed by Japan.[68] India
proved an ideal market. First, unlike Europe or China, it used cotton for
the entire clothing of its people; cotton's light and absorbent fabric was
perfectly adapted to a hot and humid climate and to the limited resources
of predominantly agricultural society. Second, Indian demand was an
important counter-cyclical influence: exports to India invariably expanded
during a general boom in trade, yet they often increased in years of widespread economic depression. Third, the growth of the Indian subcontinent's
population progressively extended the market for Lancashire goods and
created an immense aggregate demand.

As the cotton industry could not print the designs or colours favoured
by Indian consumers, it exported its cheaper products to India. Such products were not normally made by the great combined firms of Manchester,
Bolton and Preston, which remained firmly based in their extensive home
trade. Rather there was a high degree of local specialisation within the
Lancashire industry, and it was in the industrial frontier towns of Oldham,
Blackburn and Burnley that the Indian market provided the largest single
source of employment.[69] Oldham, in eastern Lancashire, was the centre of
the spinning of coarse cloths; Blackburn and Burnley, in the north, were
the centre of coarse weaving and produced the shirting, dhotis and other
goods shipped to India.[70] The India trade was especially important to
Blackburn. This was the town that perfected the plain calico power-loom,
an innovation that paved the way for the manufacture of cheap goods
for Indian consumption. Hence the acute depression in the cotton trade
of 1891–3 (partly the result of a shrinkage in Indian demand) afflicted
Blackburn in particular.[71] Similarly, the slump conditions of the 1920s (when
Indian tariffs were raised, and Japanese competition in the Indian market
intensified) were endured longer and more severely by Blackburn than by
other weaving town.[72]

Any threat to the textile industry's largest export market galvanised
it into action. On three separate occasions Lancashire managed to modify
Indian import duties in order to enhance its competitive position – in
1860–2, 1874–9 and 1894–5. The last of these is worth exploring further. Facing a serious financial crisis, the Government of India introduced a
general 5% duty on imports that originally exempted cotton, but was later
extended to include it. To protect Lancashire interests, a countervailing duty
was applied to Indian-produced goods. However, there were complaints

[76] about the working of this countervailing duty, especially from the power-loom weavers of Blackburn who protested vigorously that they had borne the brunt of the changes to fiscal policy which were sapping away the very life of the town.[73] They also warned Manchester MPs, who prior to the election had promised to remedy this 'gross injustice', that they would now see what their promises were worth.[74] Even at the level of the firm, there is reason to believe that the 1894–5 tariff agitation affected employees. A broadsheet issued by the Hartford Mills offers an insight into what the workforce was being told by management at this time. The broadsheet alleged that the Indian import duty was equal to an advance of 16% on weavers' wages, and went on to claim that Indian manufacturers had contrived to evade the countervailing duty.[75] The Government of India eventually granted further concessions: cotton yarn was exempted from all taxes, and import and excise duties were reduced to 3.5%.[76] As one member of the Indian legislative council remarked, it was difficult to argue with 'empty [Lancashire] stomachs'.[77]

Nonetheless, cotton workers' attitudes toward Indian textile workers were complex. Certainly, they were determined to defend their own livelihoods. Yet they were also easily stung by accusations of 'selfish little Lancashire' from governmental officials. The Indian famine relief funds raised by Lancashire workers are a case in point. These seem to have been motivated by more than mere self-interest. Trade union records show that they sprang from a desire on the part of cotton workers to at least *be seen to* be using 'their wealth for the good of others', and not to be lacking in 'fraternal feeling' for workers in India.[78] How far this desire was underpinned by genuine labour solidarity can be explored by looking in more detail at two particular episodes: the delegation of the International Federation of Textile Workers' Association to India in 1926–7,[79] and Gandhi's visit to Lancashire in 1931.

The IFTWA's delegation was concerned about the growth of competition in the Indian market; it was led by Tom Shaw MP and English cotton workers were represented through the firm Hindle and Brothers. Indian support came from leading figures in the Bombay textile workers' organisation – N. M. Joshi, a middle-class Brahmin and social reformer, and his helper R. R. Bakhale. After visiting factories in Bombay, Ahmedabad and Madras, Shaw and his colleagues concluded that wages were 'cruelly' low, housing conditions a 'disgrace' and the lack of education 'shameful'. Yet they did not, as might be expected, say that Indian employers were exploiting their workers, or that labour costs in India were being artificially suppressed to the detriment of Lancashire. In fact, their final report

acknowledged that Indian workers lived much more sparingly than their [77]
European colleagues, and that factory life had in many ways benefited them.
It also firmly rejected the argument of Lancashire mill-owners that unfair
competition from India (in the form of low wages and long hours) was
making it impossible to turn a profit. Indeed, the only real comfort for Lancashire was the report's criticism that Indian mill-owners (and even some
trade union leaders) had grown accustomed to 'fabulous profits', and that
their response to declining trade had therefore been to seek refuge in protective tariffs rather than to accept lower margins and more modest returns.[80]

Four years later the leader of India's most successful unions in Ahmedabad
– Mahatma Gandhi – came to London to discuss the Indian constitution.
The late 1920s and early 1930s were years of particular difficulty for Lancashire's cotton industry:[81] a world recession had led to falling incomes in
India; the Government of India had raised duties on British cotton goods
from 11 to 15%; and Gandhi and the nationalist movement had instigated
a boycott of British exports. In September 1931 Gandhi visited Lancashire
to listen to its concerns and to try to explain his principles of Indian self-
sufficiency.[82] Unemployment was high and many mills were closing, so
the atmosphere was highly charged.[83] In the cotton town of Bolton, for
example, Indian itinerant traders had been accused of 'adding insult to injury'
by hawking cheap textiles from India (although the goods in fact turned
out to be French), and of peddling 'swarajist' (nationalist) propaganda.[84]
Hence the British government was not keen for Gandhi to spend a weekend
in Lancashire, and he was kept away from large cities like Manchester and
Blackburn and provided with a police escort wherever he went.

Gandhi met textile workers at Bolton station, at cotton mills in Springvale
and Darwen and finally at the weaving town of Great Harwood, north-east
of Blackburn. Their reaction was much more positive than might be
expected.[85] Here it is worth recalling how cotton workers, who apparently
stood shoulder to shoulder with manufacturers during debates over Indian
cotton duties,[86] had in fact criticised protection from a distinctly labour
perspective – it was viewed as a class measure, operating in the interests of
Bombay capitalists, the remedy for which was to be found in increased
wages.[87] Indeed, the cotton unions' stance on Indian fiscal affairs obscured
their growing support for constitutional change – as early as 1924, the
Bolton Operative Spinners' Association had supported resolutions calling
for Indian self-government. So while the Manchester Chamber of Commerce's recently formed subcommittee on Indian Fiscal Matters could label
Gandhi 'a deadly enemy',[88] and while many of the mill-owners found him
unreceptive to 'anything they said outside his chosen path',[89] large crowds

[78]   of workers gathered to cheer him.[90] There was little sign of hostility; quite the reverse: women brought their babies to see Gandhi, others pushed themselves forward to shake his hand, and several later remarked that he seemed genuinely moved by what he had seen and heard.

To be sure, Lancashire workers were eager to explain the impact of the boycott on their industry. Gandhi spoke to several unemployed operatives including men with children to support. W. R. Hill, who entered the mill at the age of 12, and who later became Vice-President of the Darwen Weavers' Union, recalled having accused Gandhi of stopping Indians from buying Lancashire cloth and Lancashire workers from making a living. Politely and patiently Gandhi explained that 'the poorest man in Lancashire' was 'a king compared to our wealthiest in India'. Hill acquiesced: 'he was quite correct – even in those days we were better off than the poor peasants.'[91] Gandhi even accepted some of the responsibility for the suffering of Lancashire workers. However, he repeatedly returned to the point that they could fall back on the dole, whereas India's peasants were on the verge of starvation with no such state support. His commitment had to be to 'the largest army of the unemployed in the world'. To make sure this message hit home Gandhi wore his loincloth throughout the visit – a gesture aptly described as 'political dressing'[92] – and frequently spoke with his spinning-wheel at his side.[93] Although some workers may have been sceptical, many accepted his sincerity. In the words of Alice Foley, later awarded an MBE for her work as Secretary of the Bolton & District Weavers' and Winders' Association: 'a few of our hard-headed folks considered him to be a "bit of a fraud": I felt that a saint had mingled with us for a brief moment in time.' Foley was far from alone.[94]

The fortunes of Dundee jute workers were also closely linked to a rival Indian industry – in Calcutta in West Bengal. Jute was one of the earliest cases of an Asiatic product competing directly with a European product – 80% of Indian jute was exported. As Gordon Stewart remarks, 'an industrial giant rose on the banks of the Hooghly to push the metropolitan industry on the banks of the Tay out of international markets, and threatened to overwhelm it even in the British domestic market itself'.[95]

Initially, the development of a low-wage industry in India had a marginal impact on mills in Dundee. Only gradually did it encroach on the cheaper end of the market, lowering prices for jute products and making it difficult for Dundee manufacturers to exploit any rise in demand.[96] The first shocks of competition were felt in the 1860s. Within two decades the Calcutta industry had broken the forty-year monopoly of Dundee in the principal markets for jute sacks and hessian cloth in North and South

Figure 3 Gandhi meets textile workers at Darwen, 1931
Source: Getty Images

[80]   America, Australia and continental Europe.[97] The first few decades of the twentieth century were an especially difficult period as Indian competition became more acute and Dundee's share of the world market continued to decline. Employers' attempts to cut costs resulted in speed-ups and productivity schemes that Scottish workers vehemently resisted. The Dundee labour force reached its peak in 1911 when there were 37,000 jute and flax operatives. By 1924 that figure had been sliced to 35,144 and by 1939 to 26,172. Meanwhile the Calcutta mills employed 339,000 workers at their height in 1928, almost ten times as many as Dundee.

Indian competition forced Dundee to move into finer and more specialised lines of jute manufacture such as linoleum and carpet backings, which brought better prices and so met the higher costs of labour in Scotland. However, as the demand for basic sacking and hessian fell off in the 1930s, Calcutta mills turned to the production of the higher-grade hessian products on which Dundee had been surviving. There was intense pressure on Dundee's markets within Britain with the result that, by the early 1890s, no less than 30% of the city's textile workers were out of a job; by 1931 this figure had increased to 50%.[98]

Hence jute provides an interesting case study of British workers' attitudes to empire. How much pressure could Dundee bring to bear on imperial policy? Although synonymous with jute manufacture, Dundee has been described as the 'neglected Cinderella alongside Lancashire, with the Fairy Godmother, in the shape of the imperial Government, always waving the magic wand on behalf of cotton rather than jute'.[99] Complaints from Dundee were frequent. From the 1890s they were heard regularly in parliament, while repeated deputations were received by the Board of Trade. Here two episodes have been singled out for consideration: the first a visit by Thomas Johnston MP and John Sime (Secretary to the Dundee & District Union of Jute and Flax Workers) to Calcutta in 1926 to enquire into the conditions of Indian jute workers;[100] the second a major parliamentary debate on 2 February 1938, part of a wider political campaign mounted by Dundee employers and employees to force the British government to do something about Calcutta competition.

Johnston and Sime travelled to India on behalf of a joint committee of Dundee trade unions. Their investigation was nothing if not thorough: they interviewed proprietors, managing agents and government officials; they inspected balance-sheets, wage books and shareholders' lists; they looked at workers' accommodation; they spoke at length with co-operative society officials and trade union organisers; and they urged Indian workers to join the Bengal Jute Workers' Association. Their findings were published in a pamphlet entitled 'Exploitation in India'. The timing of the publication is significant in that the biggest threat to Dundee during the 1920s came not from India but from the United States and tariff-protected European producers (such as Germany and Czechoslovakia). Johnston and Sime acknowledged this, noting that jute goods from Calcutta were not in competition with the finer quality goods made by Dundee mills; indeed, for the foreseeable future Calcutta was unlikely to compete for these markets. The authors saw no reason for alarm therefore. Nevertheless, their report foreshadowed many of Dundee's criticisms of the Indian industry and demands for its reform that were expressed in the 1930s. It pointed disapprovingly to the enormous dividends enjoyed by those in Scotland who sunk their capital into Indian jute. It denounced the miserably low wages of the Indian workers, the bribes and fines regularly deducted from those wages and the grievously high prices of food in the mill areas.[101] And its main recommendation was to raise the remuneration, purchasing power and status of Indian jute workers by introducing primary education, by strengthening co-operative societies and by improving labour organisation.

By 1938 the circumstances of the Dundee industry had changed. Exports of jute cloth from Bengal to the UK had increased by 375% between 1928 and 1936. The Unionist MP for Forfarshire went so far as to speak of an 'Asiatic plague' – an uncontrolled flow of Calcutta jute imports which was throwing people out of work in the small burghs of his constituency.[102] Yet none of the region's MPs knew quite where to lay the blame.[103] The Labour member, William McLean Watson, felt that Dundee's troubles originated from the eagerness of the city's financiers, manufacturers and technicians to sink their capital into, and to sell their machinery and expertise to, Bengal.[104] If the Calcutta jute mills continued to refuse to raise wages and restrict working hours, he favoured a total prohibition of Indian exports to Britain. Meanwhile two Conservative MPs, Sir Nairne Sandeman[105] and Florence Horsbrugh, were openly critical of the Calcutta mill-owners – especially the new Indian ones – for breaking the agreement to seal looms and reduce hours. They insisted that it was time for the Board of Trade to introduce tariffs and quotas. The city's Liberal MP, Dingle Foot, blamed Dundee for failing to diversify, though he accepted that the breakdown of the short-time regime in Calcutta was the immediate cause of the current crisis. However, all of these MPs agreed that imperial policy had worked to the advantage of Calcutta rather than Dundee. Dingle Foot drew attention to the irony of the Ottawa tariff pact of 1932, under which British industries were protected from foreign competitors but not from the

[82]   dominions or dependencies. Horsbrugh followed suit, insisting that other parts of empire should not be allowed to undermine industry in Britain.

At the end of the 1938 parliamentary debate Dundee received a big vote of sympathy from other MPs in the Commons. The government's position, however, stayed the same. Board of Trade officials continued to work behind the scenes for an informal agreement between the two industries; beyond that it was felt there was nothing more to be done. Only when India became independent in 1947 did Dundee get the relief that it had been seeking since the 1890s. Yet by then it was too late: the imposition of tariffs on Indian jute goods in the 1950s could not save Dundee.[106]

Conclusion

British trade unions are based on the concept of the limited availability of work. Their whole strategy therefore has been to try to control and confront any changes that might reduce employment – this may be why they appear to be so conservative. At first sight the empire was a way of expanding the amount of available work; an escape from the constraints of the domestic economy. Yet it was also fraught with problems, not least because the supply of labour was potentially much greater, so that unions could easily be undermined. The sense of opportunity represented by colonial markets and colonial employment, and the sense of danger represented by cheap colonial labour, conditioned British workers' responses to the empire. While there was considerable solidarity between 'British' workers at home and 'British' workers overseas – expressed, for example, in labour banners[107] – attitudes to coloured colonial labour were much more ambiguous. They were rarely a reflection of racial prejudice pure and simple. More commonly, workers in Britain were torn between their instincts of self-protection, their humanitarian sympathy for the poor and their class identification with the oppressed. If anything the difficulty of resolving these various impulses increased over time. Even so, the evidence presented in this chapter suggests that, even when their own jobs were under threat, British workers were able to show some concern for the condition of coloured colonial workers and to support some of their political aspirations.

CHAPTER 4

THE WORKING CLASS AT PLAY

Historians who seek to show how the empire permeated all aspects of British life and thought have turned to the realm of popular recreation. With reference to a variety of cultural forms – art, exhibitions, film, music halls and radio – they have argued that imperialism was a 'core ideology' in British society.[1] There is much to commend their work. It gets away from the self-contained critiques of British culture that were for too long the dominant mode of modern British historiography; and it brings out more forcefully than any other branch of scholarship the excitement and sheer spectacle of empire to a generation for whom leisure and entertainment were becoming more widely available.

Yet what the empire meant to the masses cannot simply be read from the words of a music hall song, or the catalogue of an exhibition, or the script for a radio broadcast or film. Such sources may tell us a lot about the forms (and even function) of imperial propaganda; they tell us much less about how it was actually received. Moreover, many working people probably had neither the time nor the money for regular recreation outside the home. The later nineteenth and early twentieth centuries did, of course, witness a reduction in working hours, a rise in average real wages and a consequent expansion of leisure.[2] But it is easy to exaggerate the effects of these changes: for most of the period covered by this book home-based hobbies were much more significant than commercial forms of entertainment.[3] Indeed, from the 1880s increasing amounts of time were given to handicrafts and sporting interests – animal raising, betting, card playing, carpentry and gardening, to name but a few. Such pursuits helped to make the routine of industrial work more bearable and acceptable.[4] It is unlikely that they did much to raise people's imperial awareness, even if some of them were exported to the colonies.[5]

This chapter focuses on exhibitions and the cinema. The first section compares imperial imagery and national perceptions of empire at the Great Exhibition of 1851, the Wembley exhibition of 1924 and the Festival

[84] of Britain of 1951. The second explores a form of entertainment with a broad-based appeal, particularly after 1918. In each case, however, we will encounter head-on the difficulties of gauging popular reactions from complex and fragmentary evidence.

Empire and exhibitions

The visual imagery of empire had a strength and immediacy that the written word often lacked. Advertising, cartoons, maps, paintings and photographs – each of these modes of representation could be found at the huge international exhibitions that proliferated throughout western European cities in the second half of the nineteenth century. How, then, can the historian measure the public reaction to these events? Press reports, descriptive guides, commemorative publications and attendance figures provide some insights, though they tend not to tell us what exhibits caught people's attention and what impressions of them they formed. Beyond that, there is the difficulty of distinguishing between imperialism and its related concepts (monarchism, militarism, racism or patriotism), and between formal colonial expansion and other facets of Britain's international relations.

Exhibitions attracted people from all walks of life. Men and women who were unlikely to experience the empire at first hand were given the opportunity to 'go' to India or Canada or Australia[6] and to 'see' their indigenous peoples, landscapes and produce.[7] Colonised peoples tended to be depicted as 'savages' who needed Europeans to civilise them; the colonies' untapped wealth was advertised; and attention was drawn to the riches that came from overseas rule. Exhibitions may also have been intended to give coherence to the empire by presenting what was arguably a set of bilateral colonial relationships as a unified system.[8]

In the summer and autumn of 1851 just over six million visitors – one-fifth of the entire population of Great Britain – saw the 100,000 exhibits at the Crystal Palace. Designed by Joseph Paxton, and sited in Hyde Park south of the Serpentine, this colossal iron and glass structure was 1,848 ft (563 metres) long, 408 ft (124 metres) broad and 66 ft (20 metres) high. Organised on three storeys, it covered some twenty-six acres and conveyed the impression of almost limitless space.[9] What sort of nation was on display to those who filed through its galleries? And was the exhibition really the barometer of Victorian attitudes as so often claimed?

Above all, the Crystal Palace was a showcase for Britain's manufacturing achievement and the physical power and material wealth produced by the

industrial revolution.[10] Machinery and technology were no longer the 'enemy
of humanity' but the 'handmaiden of progress'; industrial production was
declared beneficial to all.[11] Commodities not countries provided the focus
of displays. One French visitor aptly described the Crystal Palace as 'a
volcano erupting with goods of every kind'. The exhibition, moreover,
was international rather than specifically imperial.[12] Its stated aim was to
'promote and increase the free exchange of raw materials and manufactured
commodities *between all the nations of the earth*'.[13] Only 520 of the total 14,000
exhibitors were colonials, and foreign countries were allocated much more
space than the colonies in the official catalogue.[14]

Britain's colonies were on display, however, even if they were not the
centrepiece of the event.[15] At 30,000 square feet (2,787 square metres),
India's was by far the largest of the colonial pavilions,[16] and the East India
Company clearly intended to impress the public with the magnitude of
India's wealth.[17] Agricultural products, handicrafts, jewellery and rare weap-
onry filled much of the display, though there was also a grand bedstead from
Benares and an ivory throne.[18] The Canadian and Australian pavilions paled
by comparison. Australia, in particular, attracted little attention from visitors
or the press, still struggling perhaps to escape its image as a convict colony
while being criticised in some quarters for its treatment of aborigines.[19]
This may mean that by the mid-nineteenth century India had come to occupy
a special place in the public imagination: *Tallis's History and Description of the
Crystal Palace* waxed lyrical about India 'indisputably standing pre-eminent
out of all Britain's colonial possessions'.[20] Or it may just mean the East India
Company was more energetic and enterprising in organising its display.

Although Indian craft traditions were admired, India's peoples were
disparaged. The Sikhs, for example, were felt to lack 'a ray of intelligence',
while the 'Hindoos' were regarded as 'physically weak' and 'incapable of
manual labour'.[21] The use of foreigners to help define the British did
not rely on the (formal) empire alone, however. The indigenous peoples
displayed in the Ethnological Court (North American 'Red' Indians, South
American Indians and the 'Papuans' of New Guinea) served a similar purpose, as did the exhibits of more 'advanced' nations on the eastern side
of the palace ('Scientific Denmark', 'Learned Sweden' and 'Half-Civilised
Russia').[22] Neither is the impact of such racial stereotypes entirely clear.[23]
Does the fact that they had continually to be repeated cast doubt on their
efficacy? Or does the lack of alternative representations of colonised peoples
mean that they were accepted almost by default?[24] Other uncertainties
surround the number of workers who attended the Great Exhibition (the
'Shilling Days' attracted many people from the labouring classes, yet there

[86] is no way of knowing exactly how many); the impact of exhibits on regular (middle-class) season-ticket holders compared to (working-class) day visitors with only a few hours to take everything in; and the popularity of particular exhibits – the 'machinery in motion' display was supposedly the biggest spectacle, but the claim rests on a limited number of press reports and a handful of memoirs. The full extent of working-class participation is also open to question: almost three hundred local committees were formed across the country, but the (bourgeois) organisers opposed the creation of a Central Working Class Committee.[25] Finally, it is difficult to say how much purchase the radical and socialist press had when arguing that growing economic competition among nations – a major theme of this and subsequent exhibitions – was at the expense of both English and colonial workers.[26]

The Wembley exhibition of 1924 was a much more self-consciously imperial affair.[27] Sited on 216 acres of farmland, this miniature model of the empire had some of the most exotic pavilions ever created at a trade fair. Seventy-eight colonies were represented. There were Burmese dancers, Malayan basket-makers, Ashanti weavers, and Nigerian rice-pounders. India, Canada and Australia all spent lavishly – the Canadian pavilion displayed a life-size statue of the Prince of Wales carved from refrigerated Canadian butter and three-dimensional models of Canadian landscapes made entirely from grain.[28] Wembley's fifteen miles (25 km) of walkways were given imperial names by Rudyard Kipling, and the climax of the event was a great 'pageant of Empire' which involved 12,000 performers. In addition to the exhibits, there was a plethora of published material – leaflets, postcards, posters, programmes, maps, postage stamps, and miniature newspapers. Some 27 million people attended the festival over two years. Most workers could afford the shilling and sixpence entrance fee; it was also open six days a week.

Declaring the festival to be 'an educational work of great national importance', Lord Stevenson, Chairman of the Exhibition Board, expressed the hope that visitors would leave 'with a quickened sense of Imperial achievement'.[29] Meanwhile, the official guide referred to Wembley as the 'Family Party of the British Empire', and described its purpose as:

> To find, in the development and utilization of the raw materials of the Empire, new sources of Imperial wealth. To foster inter-Imperial trade and open fresh world markets for Dominion and home products. To make the different races of the British Empire better known to each other, and to demonstrate to the people of Britain the almost illimitable possibilities of the Dominions, Colonies and Dependencies overseas.[30]

However, beyond recognising the colonial contribution to the war effort, and promoting inter-imperial trade and migration, there were several other possible agendas at work in 1924. The first was that of the constructive imperialists. Their vision of a more self-contained imperial economic system had recently received a big blow with the electorate's rejection of tariff reform. Hence Wembley (and its counterpart, the Empire Marketing Board) has plausibly been presented as an alternative strategy for changing consumer behaviour by propaganda rather than by price manipulation.[31] By the early 1920s there were also signs of a concerted effort to 'repackage' the empire by emphasising its high aims and lofty ideals, by defending it as a force for peace in the world, and by linking it with the British love affair with the countryside and the family. Certainly, many of these themes were prominent in the Prince of Wales's and King George V's speeches at the opening ceremony on 23 April, broadcast by the BBC. Again, however, the exhibition's impact is far from certain. Some scholars draw attention to the fact that Wembley featured prominently in the popular songs of the period;[32] and even sceptics concede that such exhibitions were 'by far the most persuasive vehicles of imperialist propaganda'.[33] Interestingly, Labour's Colonial Secretary, J. H. Thomas, felt that Wembley's pavilions gave to 'millions of humble Britons . . . the opportunity which they would never otherwise get of visiting the Empire'.[34] And yet there are alternative interpretations. Wembley may reflect a concern about the extent of the public's ignorance of the empire, or the failure of previous propaganda to fully persuade people of its value. Or the concept of imperialism may have acquired too many unpleasant connotations in terms of money-making, exploitation and oppression (thus being ripe for reinvention by 1924). Or the carnival atmosphere of Wembley – the amusement park covered nearly fifty acres – may have stood in the way of its 'serious' purpose, so that for many visitors it was no more than a 'refuge from reality'.[35] The evidence does not point us in a definite direction.

Sponsored partly by the Labour government and partly by the Labour-controlled London County Council, the Festival of Britain was also organised six years after a world war, though the similarities arguably end there.[36] The populist politician Herbert Morrison supervised the festival, while the architect Hugh Casson took charge of the design. After a period of wartime gloom and post-war austerity, Britain was in need of a lift, and the gaiety and sparkle of the event caught the public mood. From May to September 1951 over eight million people visited the South Bank, including many who travelled from industrial towns in the Midlands and the north.[37] Yet, unlike Wembley, there was no clear notion of what the festival was

[88] supposed to be.[38] Was it a morale booster and a proclamation to the world that Britain had recovered from the exhausting victory of 1945? Or was its purpose more economic, to persuade people to 'buy British'? Was it a publicity drive for Labour's policies of social and regional regeneration? Or was it a showcase for Casson and his progressive friends in architecture and the arts? And how far was it hijacked by the music establishment who craved a new concert hall to replace the bombed Queen's Hall?

Whatever the Festival of Britain was, its colonial content was slender. Imperial nostalgists may have hoped to rekindle memories of 1924, but it was the welfare state rather than withdrawals from India in 1947 and Palestine in 1947–8 that the Labour government wished to celebrate in 1951. Indeed, colonial exhibits were by and large excluded from the event and banished to another site (the Imperial Institute), partly perhaps for fear of offending American sensibilities, partly because it was doubtful whether the dominions would have wanted to join in.[39] Instead the pavilions at South Bank focused on aspects of 'domestic' British life – the home, school, industry, transport, and countryside. Although the festival was to be a 'national display illustrating the British contribution to civilisation, past, present and future',[40] its catalogues made only passing reference to the Commonwealth.[41] Unlike earlier exhibitions the colonies were not even invited to participate; there were no dominion pavilions and there was no contact with the colonial 'other'. The focus was internal not external,[42] and the different identities celebrated those of the United Kingdom. According to Roy Strong, for instance, the festival's planners failed to look towards Europe and virtually eliminated the Empire-Commonwealth.[43] Science, design and technology were the main subjects; self-sufficiency and modernity the order of the day – remember that the de Havilland Comet, the world's first commercial airliner, had been designed and built only two years before.[44] With Ralph Tubbs's huge aluminium Dome of Discovery[45] and Hidalgo Moya's stunning Skylon, the future forecast in 1951 was a far cry from that of Wembley in 1924.

Empire and cinema

Described as the 'social habit of the age',[46] the cinema went from strength to strength between the wars.[47] In 1914 there were around 3,000 cinemas in Britain; by 1939 almost 5,000. The surge in cinema attendance began in the mid-1920s with the development of 'talkies' and colour. By the 1930s regular visits were the norm[48] and cinema-goers included the urban poor.

A survey of the Carnegie Trust at this time found that 80% of the unemployed watched a film more than once a week, while another inquiry indicated that a third of those who went to the movies had no more than an elementary schooling.

The cinema certainly offered an escape from the drudgery of everyday life. But how far did films stir debate about Britain's imperial role and responsibilities? Some scholars argue that we can never really know what impact the cinema had on people's attitudes.[49] They also insist that audiences were not passive consumers of film,[50] but had a strong sense of what they liked and a sharp eye for what was (or was not) realistic.[51] Other scholars claim that cinema was a 'prime vehicle for the dissemination of an imperial outlook',[52] and a 'powerful influence on the public's views on the Empire'.[53] In their view, cinema provided at least a window on the wider world, while the effect of censorship – implicitly if not explicitly political – was to make it more difficult for film-makers to deal with controversial aspects of Britain's imperial past.

The first major imperial event to be captured on film was Queen Victoria's diamond jubilee.[54] Two years later the Boer War (1899–1902) was covered extensively by newsreel photographers. The war in South Africa created an appetite for documentary film and 'extended cinema's cultural function into the realm of news and propaganda'.[55] There was a huge demand for these films, or 'bioscopes' as they were known. In October 1899 the leading producers R. W. Paul and Charles Urban despatched their cameramen to the front. In Britain, meanwhile, battle scenes were re-enacted since it was not technically possible to film the fighting in South Africa.[56] The films were shown in theatres, music halls and at fairgrounds up and down the country. In 1900 they accounted for approximately 40% of total UK film production. Yet 'the reception of these entertainments is notoriously difficult to assess'.[57] We know that Boer War films 'resulted in a boom for the industry',[58] with the British being portrayed in an idealised fashion and the Boers being depicted as complete villains. Equally, we know that audiences did not like many of the films made in Britain (one such film showed the Boers shelling a Red Cross tent),[59] and that they preferred the more realistic 'topicals', filmed on the spot.[60]

Film-makers were also drawn to the Delhi Durbar of 1911. George V was the only reigning monarch to visit India before 1947, and the great durbar was the high point of his stay. Indeed, it was one of the most lavish spectacles ever mounted by the British Raj. There were 233 camps covering some 25 square miles (65 square km) of land, with 10 square miles (26 square km) of canvas, 60 miles (97 km) of new roads and over 30 miles

[90] (48 km) of railway. Two vast amphitheatres were built, one to hold 100,000 spectators, the other for Indian princes and other notables.[61] The occasion – used to proclaim the transfer of the capital from Calcutta to Delhi (the former seat of the Mughal empire) – was 'almost certainly the biggest newsreel event to date'.[62] The leading documentary film-maker, Charles Urban, owner of the first commercial motion picture colour process, produced an unprecedented two-and-a-half-hour epic of the ceremonies.[63] The film was premiered at the Scala Theatre in London on 2 February 1912 and Urban put on a fantastic show – the stage was based on the Taj Mahal, and music played by an orchestra that included twenty-three Scottish bagpipes. Building on the success of the London run, the film was then sent around Britain in a series of 'road show' presentations. Such was its popularity that in fifteen months it took more than £150,000.[64] Other companies to produce films of the event included W. Butcher and Sons Ltd, Kineto, Gaumont and Warwick.

The Durbar films were a major hit with audiences.[65] Part of their interest may have derived from the so-called 'Gaekwar incident'. The Gaekwar of Baroda failed to follow the correct procedure of bowing before the King and Queen, an offence aggravated by the fact that he was suspected of fomenting anti-British sedition in his state.[66] It was said at the time that many people went to these films simply to see the 'Gaekwar incident', and that audiences in the Empire and Alhambra music halls hissed loudly when he was shown turning his back on the thrones.[67] Aside from this controversy, the importance of Durbar films probably lay in the way they allowed cinema-goers to experience something of the pomp and ceremony of the Raj and the excitement of the Royal Tour.

The impact of the documentary school of film-making, which worked under the EMB's patronage, was much more muted. From 1929 to 1933 documentary films were part of a campaign to sell empire produce in Britain. There were about a hundred of these films in total, some of which were sponsored by official organisations and large commercial firms. They comprised both short, static 'poster' films and more cinematic portrayals of the empire and its products.[68] Some like *Conquest* (1930) were about discovery and exploration (in this case of western Canada), but the majority were about the economic interdependence of Britain and its colonies – *Gold Coast Cocoa* (1930), *Lumber* (1931), *Cargo from Jamaica* and *Song of Ceylon* (both 1933) all fit this description.[69] Their outlet was not via general commercial release; rather they were distributed through schools, film societies and various self-improvement organisations. By far the greatest demand came from schools. While documentary films may have had artistic merit, they did not have widespread appeal. Film-making was only a small part of the

Figure 4   The Delhi Durbar, 1911
Source: © Hulton-Deustch Collection/Corbis

[92]   EMB's budget; there were no facilities for recording sound (hence the decision not to try to penetrate the commercial market); and many of the productions were put together from existing footage and were not new films specially made.[70] Moreover, much of the film unit's money was blown on the ill-fated *One Family*, a heavy-handed fable about the gathering of ingredients for a royal Christmas pudding from the different parts of the empire. Berated by critics, it was generally ignored by commercial exhibitors too.[71]

Were audiences more influenced by feature films? Among its holdings, the National Film and Television Archive lists twenty-three films about colonialism in Africa in the period from 1906 to 1939,[72] while empire-related productions figured in the top fifty British films in 1935 (*Sanders of the River*, ranked 6th), 1936 (*Rhodes of Africa*, ranked 40th; and *Song of Freedom*, 43rd) and 1937 (*Elephant Boy*, ranked 27th; *King Solomon's Mines*, 45th).[73] Some of these films portrayed the empire in a negative light,[74] but the majority were made by people who either actively championed imperialism or at least took it for granted.[75] A leading enthusiast was the Hungarian-born movie mogul Alexander Korda. He was a confirmed Anglophile and one of the most powerful figures in the British film industry during the 1930s,[76] who saw the builders of the British Empire as 'the embodiment of all the most noble traits in the English character and spirit'.[77] He was also quick to grasp that lavish films about the empire could make money.[78] His box-office successes included *Sanders of the River*, *The Drum* (1938) and *The Four Feathers* (1939). Shot on location – in Nigeria, India and Sudan respectively – these movies were made by London Films (1931) and directed and designed by Korda's brothers Zoltan and Vincent.[79] They were about the civil officials and military officers charged with the task of maintaining law and order and dispensing justice in Britain's colonies. Whether it was District Commissioner Sanders keeping the peace among 'savage tribes' in Africa, or Captain Carruthers on the North-West Frontier helping an Indian prince to resist a usurping uncle, or the disgraced lieutenant, Harry Faversham, redeeming himself by rescuing his colleagues (while disguised as an Egyptian) during the 1898 Sudan campaign, the justification for imperialism was consistently presented in terms of the moral superiority of the British. Their authority lay ultimately in their 'character'; a mixture of courage, confidence and charisma that enabled them to exercise power and to gain the respect of the governed.

If Korda was determined to outdo Hollywood, it was the American movie moguls who nonetheless produced the greater proportion of imperial epics.[80] Britain was the biggest market for Hollywood films outside America, and

Hollywood bosses assumed that positive portrayals of the empire were a [93] sure-fire way of pleasing the British public, though they themselves also liked the empire and knew that America liked it too.[81] While American movies paid less attention to historical detail, they put across the imperial message just as strongly. A good example would be the *Lives of a Bengal Lancer* (1935), a rousing action drama set on India's North-West Frontier and made by Paramount. Its director was Henry Hathaway. Born into a showbusiness family in Sacramento in 1908, Hathaway made movies for almost forty years. Like Korda, he was fascinated by the nature of colonial authority:

> The point about Lancer was that in India 400 million people were controlled by 40,000. They were kept in line by discipline. The discipline wasn't in beating down the natives, but in being very disciplined among themselves so that the natives watching it thought: 'Holy Jesus! If they punish themselves so harshly, what will they do to us!'[82]

Another Hollywood imperial adventure film, *Gunga Din* (1939), was made by RKO.[83] Loosely based on a poem by Rudyard Kipling, it was directed by George Stevens. Born in Oakland in 1904, Stevens started out as an assistant cameraman; *Gunga Din* was his first large-scale action movie. It told the story of a native water boy who sacrificed his life to save a British regiment from a revolt by the 'Thuggees', a murderous sect of religious fanatics. The character represented all those millions of Indians who supposedly welcomed and remained loyal to the Raj; he was made a posthumous corporal and buried with full military honours.

The outbreak of the Second World War drew the cycle of 1930s imperial epics to a close. In fighting fascism, British wartime propaganda had contrasted the tyrannies and cruelties of Nazi Germany, Fascist Italy and Imperial Japan with the principles of democracy, self-determination and freedom espoused by the Western Allies and embodied in the 1941 Atlantic Charter. The paternalist imperialism of adventure films became more and more embarrassing to officials in the Ministry of Information as a result. Moreover, this genre of films was known to cause offence within the empire. *Lives of a Bengal Lancer*, for example, had been berated by K. S. Shelvankar of the *Times of India* for shedding 'a spurious, belated lustre on the romanticism of empire', and for circulating 'mischievous fallacies' likely to 'foster self-delusion in one party and hatred in another'.[84] Such concerns led to the postponement of RKO's plan to re-release *Gunga Din* and of MGM's plan for an adaptation of *Kim*.[85]

[94]   Yet the cinema was probably the most potent of the new technologies used to sell the empire to the British public between the wars. Korda's trilogy was certainly successful. If London Films was short of money, it was certainly not the fault of *Sanders of the River*, which, together with another film, grossed £450,000[86] – Paul Robeson's rendition of the canoe song 'Ai-ee-o-go' instantly became a popular hit.[87] Meanwhile *The Drum* grossed £170,000 in the USA alone.[88] Recognising patriotism to be the bedfellow of profit, Korda and the Hollywood producers sought to satisfy audiences, not necessarily to stimulate them.[89] They did not lecture British cinema-goers on the empire's economic or constitutional position; rather they invited them to bask in its glory. *Gunga Din* is a case in point. The film was set in late-nineteenth-century India, a period of relative stability compared to the post-1918 era of Gandhian non-co-operation. Though it cost $1,915,000 – the most expensive production RKO had undertaken – it still broke even.[90] In the view of the company's historians, it was worth every cent.[91] Of course much depended on the quality of the film. Whereas *Gunga Din* was praised for its 'well-balanced mixture of spectacle, comedy, adventure and genuine pathos',[92] *The Sun Never Sets* (1939) was criticised for its confusing script and unlikely story.[93] Neither did the absurdity of Shirley Temple's part in *Wee Willie Winkie* (the sex of Kipling's hero was changed to accommodate her) escape viewers.[94] Even allowing for the uneven quality of imperial epics, however, it would be difficult to deny the British public's enthusiasm for this genre of film.

In fact, it is worth pausing to ask why the onus of proof should always rest on those arguing for rather than against the popularity of imperialism. The inter-war cinema may not provide compelling evidence of the British public's enthusiasm for empire, but it does tentatively point in that direction.[95] While it is surely right to require a firm foundation for the claim that working-class society was pro-empire, should not sceptics be required to produce some equally substantial sources to show that apathy or indifference were the order of the day?[96] To say that studies of the imperial impact of exhibitions, the cinema or other arts have not necessarily proven their point is one thing; but it is a massive (and misleading) leap from there to the conclusion that imperialism's impact on British society was negligible or tangential.

Conclusion

In exploring the empire's significance for the British working classes too much attention has been lavished on leisure at the expense of other, more vital spheres of experience. Arguably, the impact of imperialism was greater [95] in the home and the workplace, where it has left a less ambiguous documentary record.

To take the debate a stage further, we now need to turn away from social class as a conditioner of people's imperial experience to consider two other important variables – gender and age. A growing body of literature has recently emerged on women's and children's attitudes to empire. For some scholars, the empire was a force for women's emancipation; for others, their exploitation. For some, it is best understood as a spur to improved juvenile welfare and to the emergence of more modern conceptions of childhood; others highlight its capacity to disrupt family life, to foster naïve and negative views of other races and, in the case of boys, of women too. The next chapter will enter into these debates.

CHAPTER 5

WOMEN AND CHILDREN

The child of 1930 had an imperial view, whatever his class (it is a massive error to suppose that imperialism was confined to the upper and middle classes; if anything, it was stronger among the working class, and I speak from personal experience of the old raj, where a colonel's imperialism was as nothing compared to the private soldier's). The British child of 1930 thought the Empire was terrific, giving him and his country a status beyond all other nations – and he had the evidence to prove it on a world map that was one-fifth pink.

> G. MacDonald Fraser, *The Hollywood History of the World*
> (Harmondsworth, 1988), p. 137.

I remember that May 24th was Empire Day. We were taught all the patriotic songs and had our hair tied with red, white and blue ribbon. Every child had a flag to wave in honour of 'Our Glorious Empire', as it was called. We sang of our lands and possessions overseas. We sang of 'Deeds of Glory'. We sang, and believed we were the mightiest nation on earth. But how many, I wonder, felt as I did. While all this went on I'm afraid I sang with my mouth only, not from the heart. For I saw only those same high walls and thought to myself, 'We sing of our possessions, while not one of us here owns so much as a flowerpot of earth'.

> Grace Foakes, *Between High Walls: A London Childhood* (1972),
> pp. 18–19.

As the above quotations imply, when imperialism did enter into women's and children's lives it rapidly became entangled in a web of complex considerations – place of residence, education, family situation, occupation and, of course, social class. George MacDonald Fraser was born in 1926, the son of a soldier in the Indian army. He served as an infantryman in India during the 1940s, and later became a full-time author whose many books (including the hugely successful Flashman novels) displayed a [97] strong sense of nostalgia. There is precious little nostalgia in the memoirs of Grace Foakes, however. Born in 1901, the daughter of an East End dockworker, she grew up in poverty in a tenement flat in Wapping, sharing her bedroom with three brothers and a sister. (There may have been as many as fourteen children, but only five survived infancy.) After her mother fell terminally ill, it was left to 14-year-old Grace to look after the home. Her father, a strong trade unionist, was a casualty of the dock strike of 1912; branded an 'agitator' by his employers, he was subsequently black-listed wherever he went.[1] Fraser's and Foakes's personal circumstances were profoundly at odds with each other; so too were their perspectives on empire.

This chapter examines the nature of women's and children's imperial involvement. Until recently historians took it for granted that the empire was an essentially masculine world of soldiers, traders, hunters and administrators and the like. It took a determined effort from feminist scholars to challenge this paradigm and to restore women to 'historical visibility across the field of British imperial history'.[2] Whether as teachers, nurses, missionaries or social reformers, women are now recognised to have played a significant part in making and maintaining the British empire.[3] Meanwhile, much of the scholarship on children's experiences of empire predates this work on gender and imperialism, and belongs to a long-standing (and still vibrant) tradition of social history. Here the accent is as much on class as gender: the empire offered elites the chance of self-esteem and self-fulfilment frequently denied them at home, but it extended few of these advantages to the rest of the population.[4]

What impact, then, did imperialism have on the position and perception of women and children in British society?[5] Several scholars have argued that it was responsible for a sharp division of gender roles: 'manliness and empire confirmed one another, guaranteed one another, enhanced one another, whether in the practical disciplines of commerce and government or in the escape zones of writing, travel and art'.[6] Two main approaches can be identified here. The first focuses on 'heroic myths' of empire as purveyed by juvenile adventure fiction, the later-Victorian and Edwardian public schools and the Boy Scout movement. By the end of the nineteenth century these heroes were usually single and celibate figures who renounced home comforts 'in the cause of duty or in pursuit of a fortune',[7] such as the self-declared 'civilian soldier of the British empire', Alfred Milner, or the sub-imperialist Cecil Rhodes. A second approach explains the prevalence of discourses of imperial masculinity in terms of a later-Victorian

[98] 'flight from domesticity'.[8] It suggests that by the 1880s the drawbacks of domesticity were acutely felt; the empire offered freedom and adventure, the domestic sphere routine, conventionality and constraint. The result was a marked shift in conceptions of manliness away from that of the evangelical Christian gentleman, who prized moral seriousness and rationality, and who believed in the inherent equality of all men, toward the model of the imperial hunter and pioneer who privileged action over thought, and who was convinced that African and Asian peoples were incapable of governing themselves.[9]

Another important issue is whether women's and children's lives were enhanced and enriched by the empire, or whether they were diminished and damaged by it.[10] Interpretations have shifted markedly here. For example, for many years depictions of the British memsahib rarely got beyond her alleged indolence, chauvinism and social snobbery, whereas lately it has been shown just how indispensable these women were in terms of managing homes that, far from being a bastion of domesticity, were in fact the hub of official business and public life.[11] Another subject on which opinion is changing is children's education. For as long as historians saw the state as a malign force in people's lives, interference by imperialists in the educational sphere was interpreted in terms of the imposition of bourgeois social norms, the undermining of the authority of working-class parents, and the instillation of a racist ideology among the nation's young.[12] Yet new studies of compulsory schooling (which was prompted, in part, by concerns over Britain's imperial competitiveness) view the extension of state authority much more positively as a spur to new social services and as a powerful agent for social mobility.[13]

The rest of this chapter explores the above issues with reference to literature, missions and children's education. (Women's philanthropic work and political activism is considered separately in Chapter 6.)

Literature

Some scholars argue that women wrote about the empire in much the same terms as men; they upheld British cultural and racial superiority, and thereby justified imperial rule.[14] Others maintain that women approached the empire differently, and that they used race metaphorically in their fiction in order to explore issues of gender.[15] Moreover, even if they ultimately affirmed imperialist ideology, they were more likely than most men to question its consequences and cost.[16]

This begs the question of how much empire there was in nineteenth- and twentieth-century women's fiction. One response is that even when the empire did not figure in the plot of a book, it was often concealed in the text. Thus it is said that several of Virginia Woolf's novels were 'implicitly concerned' with the prospect of the end of the Anglo-Indian empire and its effects on members of the British upper class.[17] Others are more circumspect.[18] A recent study of George Eliot (1819–80) rejects pro-imperialist readings of her work.[19] Eliot did indeed have limited personal experience of Britain's colonies – two of her stepsons had migrated to Natal, and her investment portfolio contained a fair number of Indian, Australian and South African railway stocks and shares. But the empire was only just beginning to emerge in Victorian consciousness when Eliot was writing, and even when she did address the subject of imperialism in her last novel, *Daniel Deronda* (1876), she did so in a characteristically careful way.[20] The same degree of caution needs to be exercised with regard to other female writers. Two examples must suffice. Christina Rossetti (1830–94) dramatised the Indian mutiny in her poem 'In the Round Tower at Jhansi, 8 June 1857', but she wrote very little on any other matter concerned with the empire and was much better known for her devotional poetry and verse for children.[21] And although the popular writer Edna Lyall (1857–1903) set out her opposition to the Boer War in *The Hinderers: A Story of the Present Time* (1902), it was probably the only occasion on which the recurrent theme of her fiction – the struggle between faith and freedom – was developed in a colonial rather than a domestic context.[22]

Since there is not the space here to discuss the full range of either women's or children's literature, we will focus on two genres: Anglo-Indian women's travel writing and children's periodicals. We will explore the demand for these publications; the impression they made upon their readers; the meaning of empire to their authors; whether female writers perceived the empire differently to men; and how far girls' fiction differed from that written for boys.

The number of British women travelling to India increased considerably in the second half of the nineteenth century, and this in turn increased the supply of and demand for Anglo-Indian women's fiction.[23] By the 1880s publishers' catalogues were full of such travelogues[24] and print-runs were impressive.[25] As much of this material falls into the category of light fiction (principally romance novels), its readership extended well beyond the educated middle classes. Moreover, while only a minority of authors (for example, Maud Diver or Flora Annie Steel) engaged explicitly with the political issues of the day, many more spoke metaphorically or allegorically about

[100]   the Raj.[26] Anglo-Indian travel writing was therefore a crucial channel via which images of the Raj were embedded in metropolitan life.[27]

How far was travel writing implicated in imperial power structures? Some scholars speak of a 'feminine picturesque' by which women writers attempted to domesticate all that was alien or threatening about India, and to provide 'the illusion of permanence' to British rule.[28] They also point to accounts of the Indian mutiny that were full of calls for bloody retribution. Even women with misgivings about British India could fall prey to its racism. Although the author of a late-nineteenth-century critique of the Raj, Christina Bremner was disdainful toward Indians and willingly reproduced 'the colonial stereotype of the childlike if cunning native'.[29] Sara Duncan was not known for her flattering portraits of British bureaucrats in India either. Yet she cruelly mocked Indians for their efforts to imitate English ways.[30]

Not all female writers adopted a straightforwardly colonial voice, however, and at least some of them seem to have been less able than male writers to assert the 'truths' of the Raj without qualification.[31] Nor was race necessarily the main influence on their thinking. Arguably, what shaped the relationship between memsahibs and their domestic servants was social class – whether in India or Britain, servants were felt to be lazy and untrustworthy and generally held in low esteem.[32] What many memsahibs did have in common was a strong sense of India's 'regenerative power'.[33] Life in India was felt to be more real and worthwhile than life back in Britain, where there was a decided deficiency of high aims and ideals. One sees this clearly in the writing of Duncan. Her distaste for the bureaucratic snobbery of the Raj did not prevent her from portraying Anglo-Indians as a dedicated and selfless breed, misunderstood and unappreciated by their fellow countrymen in England.[34] There are echoes of Rudyard Kipling here; for whatever else he was, Kipling was a powerful protagonist of Anglo-Indianism.

So what difference did gender really make? A study of Fanny Parks's pre-Mutiny journal[35] and Harriet Tytler's post-Mutiny memoir[36] presents 'confinement' and 'claustrophobia' as key tropes of Anglo-Indian women's writing, which evinced a greater sense of powerlessness as the century wore on.[37] Conversely, Anglo-Indian women's writing can be construed more positively and progressively, with the Indian woman having served as a 'refractory foil' for the self-constitution of the Western woman. Yet neither of these points of view is borne out by a recent magisterial survey of 'mems' fiction'. It concludes that such writing contained not a trace of the enormous social and legal changes that many British women were experiencing from the 1880s and 1920s. On the contrary, the narrative thrust of memsahibs' novels was to call back the past; the aim of their female hero-ines not emancipation but marriage to 'a good man and true'.[38]

Women's perceptions of the wider imperial world, and of their place in that world, could differ markedly therefore. Ghose sums up the situation best when she argues that there is no single 'female gaze' and no overarching story to be told.[39] Rather what we have here is a diversity of responses to the Raj. Why? Because gender was clearly not the only influence upon women's fiction. What memsahibs wrote was further conditioned by their religious convictions (evangelicals like Mary Carpenter[40] and Mary Sher-wood were inclined to see only degeneracy in Indian religion, and to claim that Hinduism had corrupted Indian society from within);[41] by the period in which they were writing (as Indian nationalism gathered pace, and 'sahib–native' relations became more strained, even Duncan rallied to the Raj's defence);[42] by their beliefs about women's place in society (the more intrepid travellers, like Frances Duberly, admired energetic, determined and independent-minded Indian women such as Her Highness Baiza Bai, widow of the Maharajah of Gwalior);[43] and by their social class (the higher mem-sahibs were up the social scale, the more they were inclined, like Emily Eden, to focus on the privileged and princely dimensions of Indian life). In this sense, Anglo-Indian writing, like so many other types of travel litera-ture, was apt to confirm the preconceptions that its authors already held.

From the mid-nineteenth century children's literature became much more varied.[44] Previously the market was dominated by the burgeoning Sunday-school movement: organisations like the Religious Tract Society (RTS) and the Society for the Promotion of Christian Knowledge (SPCK) published 'healthy' fiction which sought to shield children from the corrupting effects of 'wretched' or secular tracts. Toward the end of the century, how-ever, instruction increasingly gave way to entertainment, and 'an evolving spirit of freedom' entered juvenile fiction.[45] Writers allowed the children in their stories to be themselves – no longer devout, hard-working and well-behaved, but imaginative, independent and constantly in trouble.

Favoured reading was the boys' and girls' story paper and magazine. There were over a dozen of these publications by the early 1880s, and possibly four times that number by the turn of the century, though many were ephemeral, circulating only for short periods of time.[46] In view of their cross-class appeal and strong hold on children's imaginations, juve-nile periodicals are believed to have been the closest thing to a universal literature that England ever had.[47] The firms that produced them were rela-tively few. Up to 1900, in addition to the RTS and SPCK, there were

[102] Cassell's, Charles Fox's Hogarth House, Edwin Brett, Thomas Nelson, and Blackie and Son; after 1900, there was Alfred Harmsworth's Amalgamated Press; and after 1918, D. C. Thomson's. Each of these publishing houses had several papers to their name as well as a stable of writers who fed the appetites of their young readers with a miscellany of escapist fiction.

What influence did this literature have on the attitudes of British boys and girls? Children turned to papers and magazines partly for excitement and entertainment, partly to gain the 'geographical and historical literacy' that the school system frequently failed to provide.[48] If their motivation for reading was complex, so too was their reaction to what they read. Thus, according to one scholar it was middle-class schoolboys – those who could realistically look forward to a career in colonial service – who provided the most receptive audience for imperial fiction; it simply could not have the same relevance for working-class children who rarely ventured far from home.[49] To be set against this claim are the recollections of men like Field-Marshal Montgomery, Harold Macmillan, A. J. P. Taylor and Sir John Harvey-Jones.[50] They seem to show that popular periodical fiction did inculcate an imperial ethos in the minds of successive generations of British boys and girls.[51]

Before pitching further into this debate it is worth asking exactly how much empire there was in children's magazines. Take, for instance, the Barry Ono collection of 'penny dreadfuls' in the British Library. It contains 704 penny part novels and journals.[52] A rudimentary analysis of content (judged by title) points to some 18 publications (2.5% of the total) that refer explicitly to one of Britain's colonies. There is also a more general title, *The Boys of the Empire*, edited by Edwin J. Brett and published from 1888 to 1893.[53] Yet this would be an underestimate as there are certainly publications not listed by the Ono collection that had a strongly imperial focus: *Boys of our Empire*, edited by Howard Spicer, and published by Andrew Melrose (1900–3) was crammed full of such material – adventure stories set in colonial outposts, and a miscellany of empire maps, empire calendars, empire jottings and empire conundrums. There were, moreover, several other titles that would not have referred explicitly to the empire but would nevertheless have had at least some imperial content, most obviously the increasingly popular sub-genre of boys' fiction – the schoolboy story.[54]

That said, there is just as big a danger of exaggerating the amount of space allocated to the empire in boys' periodicals and magazines. The stories from one of the most famous schoolboys' series, Jack Harkaway's tales of adventure,[55] published from the early 1880s, were as likely to be set in Europe or America as they were in colonial territories,[56] while during

the inter-war years such adventures were frequently situated within Britain.[57]
More importantly, even a cursory acquaintance with this literature is sufficient to show that there were many themes to rival the empire in terms of
their popularity with readers. Highwaymen and outlaws; crime (especially
murder); pirates and smugglers; ghosts and apparitions; and sport – all these
had just as high (if not a higher) profile. The titles published by Alfred
Harmsworth's Amalgamated Press are instructive here. *Pluck* (1894–1924)
may have been imperially-oriented, but invasion stories were the staple of
Boys' Friend (1895–1927) and *Boys' Realm* (1902–16);[58] *The Marvel* (1893–
1922) specialised in urban thrillers and in journeys in search of buried
treasure; and the *Union Jack's* (1894–1933) adventure fiction had as many
or more pirates, Redskins and monsters of the deep as it did imperial heroes.

How far, then, did children's literature 'instill . . . an appreciation of the
long years of progress that had turned Britain into the greatest imperial
power', or 'nurture the qualities of courage, justice and fair play that had made
and would keep Britain great'?[59] The discussion here will focus on two
particular publications – the *Boys' Own Paper* (1879–1967)[60] and the *Girls'
Own Paper* (1880–1956). These papers were produced by the Religious
Tract Society and sought to drive out 'unwholesome' literature. They did
not explicitly profess Christianity, but they did try to raise standards of
social behaviour. Thus for the *BOP* and *GOP*, imperial ideology was first
and foremost a vehicle for advancing evangelical values.

Striking claims have been made for their influence.[61] We are told that
the *BOP* 'single-handedly established the mode for children's papers';[62] that
it 'wielded considerable weight in the industry';[63] and that it enjoyed an
'enviable position' in view of its sponsors' funds.[64] The *GOP* was apparently 'even more successful'.[65] 'Undeniably popular in its day',[66] it faced
little competition until the growth of magazines for women in the 1920s
and 1930s.[67] However, when one turns to the social basis of their readership,
doubt and dissent begin to creep in. While some scholars are confident that
the *BOP* was read by working- as well as middle-class boys,[68] others are
less sure, suggesting that its high moral tone, content and cost point to
readers coming from a 'respectable' background – the teenage children of
ordinary labourers preferred 'more thrilling and lurid publications'.[69] Likewise, some say the *GOP* appealed to girls of all social classes,[70] but others
believe that while intended for the working classes it actually reached a
predominantly middle-class readership.[71] Sales figures present further problems. The *BOP* is estimated to have sold around 200,000 copies weekly in
1879, rising to 650,000 in the 1890s, tapering off to around 400,000
copies from 1900 to 1914.[72] Meanwhile the publisher's (unverified) figures

[104] suggest that sales of the *GOP* were approximately 250,000 copies per week in the latter part of the nineteenth century.[73] Yet these sales figures are contested by two recent studies.[74] They may not be a very good proxy for readership anyway: for every copy of a boys' or girls' paper sold at least two or three (possibly more) children may have read it.[75]

How did the *BOP* and *GOP* portray the empire? The *BOP*'s imperial ideology was less militaristic than many of its rivals. The paper rarely glorified colonial conflicts and remained 'conspicuously silent' during the Boer War, which it refused to endorse.[76] However, if the stories of W. H. G. Kingston (1815–80),[77] R. M. Ballantyne (1825–94)[78] and Talbot Baines Read (1852–93) spoke of an empire founded on 'peace and brotherhood' and suffused with evangelical concerns,[79] the same can hardly be said for W. Gordon Stables's 'bombastic strain of imperialism'[80] or G. A. Henty's emphasis on the military and economic aspects of empire.[81] For Stables and Henty, British overseas expansion was less a divinely ordained, humanitarian crusade than a symbol of Britain's military prowess and industrial might. What is clear, therefore, is that a variety of authorial voices characterised this (and other) magazines.[82]

In girls' story papers there was a degree of tension between the ideology of domesticity, which saw the home as the empire in microcosm and a woman's main duties as those of a mother and wife,[83] and the stereotype of the 'imperial pioneering woman'. The former was to be found in the historical and didactic novels written for adolescent girls. Readers of these novels were urged to accept the drawbacks of empire. The 'true woman' had to be able to cope with periods of separation and to be willing to despatch her fiancé or husband to do his duty in colonial wars.[84] The latter was a staple of illustrated feature stories. The heroine of such stories was either a missionary, a nurse or a doctor (representing a new brand of imperial philanthropy), or she was an enterprising emigrant – epitomised by the works of the popular children's author, Bessie Marchant (1862–1941). Marchant wrote over a hundred and fifty colonial adventure stories, many of which were set in Canada, though she herself does not appear to have travelled very far from home.[85] The women in her novels exercised power in dominating their environments; the figure of the capable colonial woman was apparently attractive to girls looking for more excitement in their reading.[86] The successor to Marchant's fiction was the 'empire romance' or 'emigrant story' of the 1920s. Here women enjoyed a new, adventurous way of life in Australian sheep stations, Canadian forests, South African and Rhodesian mining camps and cattle farms. The heroine – a newly-arrived emigrant or a girl born of British parents in the new country – found her male mate in the open, limitless spaces of a frontier society. Migration, in effect, served as a metaphor for movement toward economic, social and sexual freedom.[87]

It must be doubted, therefore, whether girls were willing to accept their maternal role as guardians of the race quite as readily as some of the *GOP*'s writers would have wished.[88] As well as being drawn to the 'imperial pioneering woman', many girls engaged in a good deal of cross-over reading and enjoyed Ballantyne's, Kingston's, Kipling's, Haggard's and Wallace's imperial adventure tales – there were a variety of literary influences to which they were exposed.[89] Moreover, for both boys and girls, the perceived impact of juvenile literature depends on how impressionable young minds were and how much ideological baggage children carry with them into adulthood.[90] There is no way of answering such questions with any degree of certainty. It is vital, then, to set this discussion of children's reading habits alongside their involvement in the missionary movement and their experiences at school to see if any clearer patterns emerge.

Missionaries

Voluntaryism and the Victorians go hand-in-hand. Victorian society was philanthropic; charities proliferated, sometimes standing in for, at other times augmenting the state. From the mid-nineteenth century perhaps the most rapidly growing area of philanthropy was missionary work. The energies and enthusiasms of tens of thousands of men and women were consumed by the cause of spreading the gospel overseas. Indeed, if missionary work was the only index of the vitality and vigour of the Victorian and Edwardian church it would be extremely difficult to talk of 'secularisation' or 'religious decline' in this era, such was the mobilisation of manpower and money that it achieved. As one scholar remarks, 'no church capable of accomplishing so much abroad could be completely effete at home'.[91]

By the end of the century women were leaving Britain in increasing numbers for the mission field. Yet those women who stayed behind were no less important: on their shoulders fell the responsibility of mobilising congregational support, raising the necessary funds and, crucially, recruiting the right sort of personnel.[92] All this was a gigantic task, and female organisers were greatly assisted by an army of juvenile helpers. Few other charities had such success in drawing children into their campaigns.

Like emigration, missionary activity was a crucial conduit of colonial culture. However, like emigration, it was never exclusively imperial, which

[106] poses problems for a study of this kind. To be sure, missionary activity was linked to imperial activity in the public mind. Many missions took place in territories that were a part of the British empire (or about to become so); the vocabulary of some of the best-known missionary pioneers was shot through with imperial idioms and imagery;[93] and there was the lasting legacy of the Mutiny of 1857–8 during which large numbers of Indian Christians and British missionaries had been murdered, as the British press did not tire of reminding its reading public. Nevertheless 'there were no simple connections between this religious expansion and a specifically British influence and Empire overseas'.[94] British missionary activity was international in scope, and many Protestant missionaries saw their mission in a global (not colonial) perspective.

In addition to local government, domestic philanthropy and the nursing and teaching professions, missionary work provided a gateway for women from the private to the public sphere. The starting point here is not the few thousand single women who left Britain to serve overseas in the last two decades of the nineteenth century; long before then an independent sphere of women's missionary work had been carved out by missionary wives.[95] Most churches encouraged recruits to go to the mission field as married men with their families in tow. David Livingstone, of course, is famous for having sent his wife and children back to Britain in 1852 and for having virtually abandoned them for the next five years. He was not typical, however. As early as 1835 missionary wives in India had their own organisation for mobilising support amongst friends and sympathisers back in Britain (the Society for the Propagation of Female Education in the East),[96] while from 1840 onwards the Anglican Church Missionary Society (CMS) 'took up' the widows and daughters of male missionaries, placing them on the society's register and transferring to them the allowance previously received by their husbands or fathers. Take the Williams family, for example. Two brothers, Henry and William, arrived in New Zealand with their wives (Marianne and Jane) in the 1820s and later set up a mission boarding school for Maori girls, Hukarere College in Napier. Jane Williams was widowed in 1877 but lived on there with her three unmarried daughters, all fluent Maori speakers, who taught in the school.[97]

Overseas service in the mission field gave energetic and enterprising middle-class women – including missionary wives – the chance of self-esteem and self-fulfilment that they might well have been denied had they stayed at home.[98] Women missionaries had to develop new skills and to exercise new responsibilities. They also had to cope with extreme climates, alien cultures, physical isolation and material hardships, all of which made their careers extremely challenging. And they were rewarded financially by missionary work: salaries for mission teachers and doctors compared favourably with home-based career opportunities, and applications had to be carefully scrutinised for this reason.[99] In emphasising such outcomes there is perhaps a danger of downplaying the force of religious belief. Nevertheless, as much as we need to take this seriously, it would seem naïve not to look beyond faith and altruism as motivation for the rising numbers of women volunteering for mission work at home and abroad.

There is, of course, a wealth of historiography on the relationship between gender and religion in (early) modern Europe which interprets the greater allegiance shown to the church by women, and the proliferation of women's religious organisations, as a form of self-affirmation – women found security, companionship and careers in religious communities that were by and large denied them elsewhere.[100] So how significant was colonial mission work in relation to these other forms of female religious activity? Clearly overseas missions were far from being the only religious-philanthropic outlet for independent-minded women. Their work as Mildmay deaconesses in the slums of East London was well known and appreciated; they grew in numbers as Bible women, parochial mission women and officers of the Salvation Army; they formed the backbone of the burgeoning Sunday-school movement; they were deeply involved in visiting the homes of the poor and in various fundraising activities (not least the ever popular church bazaar); and they made a significant if largely unrecognised contribution to the life of the churches as clergy wives.[101] According to one historian, 'by the end of the (nineteenth) century most of the church work being performed by lay people was being undertaken by women'.[102]

It seems likely therefore that many women who ventured abroad on missions had first cut their teeth on various evangelical and charitable projects at home. A good example would be that of women preachers. Female revivalists in Australia reactivated the debate on preaching during the last quarter of the nineteenth century. They included two widows from Britain. Mrs Emilia Louise Baeyertz, a Jewish convert to Christianity, left England to live with her sister in Melbourne in the 1860s, and conducted a series of successful missions across Australia from 1878 to 1879 as a prelude to evangelistic campaigns in North America and Britain in 1890–2.[103] Mrs Margaret Hampson toured New Zealand and the south-eastern colonies of Australia from 1881 to 1884, establishing several local Prayer Unions in the process. Yet there were a far larger number of British women preaching at home than there ever were in the empire. Female preachers were particularly active in Methodism.[104] Together with their sisters in the Salvation Army – the 'Hallelujah Lasses', as they were known[105] – they tended to be associated with the holiness movement, a new spirituality which emerged from the Keswick conventions of the 1870s, which laid stress on the faith principle, and which provided the theological sanction for breaking with accustomed female roles.[106]

Meanwhile, within the missionary movement women's influence was tightly constrained. The China Inland Mission (CIM), founded in 1865 by Hudson Taylor, professed to hire Protestant laymen and laywomen on equal terms as itinerant evangelists.[107] Yet although the number of women in its first mission party exceeded that of men, it was more than a decade before women were recruited in significant numbers. Moreover, up to 1910, the CIM's China Council had no female representation and was generally resistant to the employment of female workers. Administrative control at home was entrusted to men, and the CIM's Ladies Association was able to make recommendations only to the London Council. It is a moot point, therefore, how far the CIM changed the climate of thinking about what women missionaries could do.[108] In the denominational societies, where ordained men had leadership roles, women had even less of a say. The Wesleyan Methodists were the first to establish a Ladies' Auxiliary in 1859; they were followed by the Society for the Propagation of the Gospel (SPG) and the Baptist Missionary Society (1866), the LMS (1875) and the CMS (1895). But all of these female missionary bodies enjoyed only limited power.[109]

Perhaps the biggest difficulty, however, in assessing the impact of overseas missions on women in Britain is that of disentangling their imperial and international dimensions.[110] Compare the zenana[111] missions and other forms of outreach to women in India with their counterparts in China.[112] There are many parallels between the two. For the majority of British churches, two levels of mission seem to have applied. There were the educated, complex and relatively sophisticated societies such as India, China and Japan where Britain had its primary duty (and, perhaps, its best opportunity) to elevate and educate indigenous women; then there were the more primitive parts of the world – tropical Africa, the South Seas and the West Indies – whose female populations did not attract anything like the same degree of attention.[113] There were, of course, certain aspects of women's mission work that were specifically Indian (such as the campaign against *suttee*). Yet there were others that were common to both India and China (e.g. opposition to female infanticide), and at least one dimension that was specifically Chinese (the anti-foot-binding crusade).

In India, educational work by women missionaries began as early as the [109]
1820s and 1830s, although it was not until the 1860s that Christian teaching
in high-caste homes was undertaken regularly by missionary wives, and
not until the 1870s that the idea of separate zenana missions caught on.[114]
Women's missionary work among Chinese women came slightly later. The
first unmarried 'lady' missionaries were sent out as an experiment during
the 1850s, and missionary societies began to enrol unmarried women in
the second half of the 1860s. Yet these efforts were severely hampered
until the Chefoo convention (1876) opened the interior to foreign missionaries.[115] By the end of the century female missionaries had reached most of
China's inland provinces. They helped to foster many of the anti-opium
societies that were emerging at this time and to forge links with several
Chinese social reformers.[116] The crucial date in the case of China, however,
is 1911. The revolution of that year ushered in new possibilities for access
to Chinese women and for the expansion of education for Chinese girls.

Despite these differences, the rationale for and forms of women's missionary activity appear to have been remarkably similar in India and China.[117]
In both places male missionaries were prohibited by gender taboos from
engaging in personal contact with indigenous women.[118] In both places
indigenous women were shut away in seclusion, denied the gospel and thus
dependent on female missionaries for their enlightenment and emancipation.
The same squalor, boredom, disease and illiteracy were (supposedly) to be
found among women in Chinese and Indian households.[119] Women in both
societies were regarded as the wives and mothers of potential converts.[120]
And China, like India, was widely viewed as a romantic location that offered
the chance of adventure and advancement in a faraway land.[121]

It should come as no surprise, then, that many of the most ardent advocates of female missionary work came from China.[122] Indeed, the four main
areas of endeavour marked out for female labour in China and India were
virtually identical: orphanages; domestic (or zenana) missions; education and
schools; and medical work. Between 1880 and 1910, China witnessed a
similar shift to that in India away from evangelising toward secular missionary activity.[123] The Indian practice of sending children away from the
mission field to be educated in Britain was common in China, the roots of
the decision being effectively the same – to protect the health and moral
welfare of their offspring and to allow women to spend a greater amount
of time evangelising.[124] And although female missionaries in the CIM
were forced to make greater concessions to Chinese culture (they were,
for instance, expected to wear Chinese dress), they were equally intent on
maintaining racial and cultural barriers.[125]

[110]   Thus it is far from clear that India had a unique claim on British female missionaries. By 1895 the LMS had sent 136 women overseas: 97 of these went to India (71%), but 39 (29%) to China;[126] and by 1899 the CIM had some 287 women in the mission field.[127] To be sure, the Indian zenana initially played a crucial role in developing an ideology that defined the need for women's missions. Yet it was not long before the battlecry against false faiths was extended from Hinduism and Islam to incorporate Buddhism too. For these reasons, it is hard to believe that the mentality of female missionaries in China was fundamentally different from their counterparts in India, or that the empire-based missionary work was in any sense exceptional in terms of its impact on British women.[128]

Many children in Britain would have become aware of their country's imperial role through the juvenile missionary movement, in particular missionary biographies and magazines. These await their historian, but they were a staple of children's reading. We know, for instance, that several biographies of David Livingstone were targeted at a younger audience; some were designed for use in the classroom, others were handed out as prizes by Sunday schools and youth organisations, a practice that continued well into the 1920s.[129] Print-runs of missionary magazines, meanwhile, were among the most impressive of the periodical press. The CMS's *The Church Missionary Juvenile Instructor* was published at a halfpenny from 1842, and sold 700,000 copies per annum by the end of the nineteenth century under its new name *The Children's World*. Another publication, *A Quarterly Token*, published from 1856, and free to Sunday-school subscribers, claimed a circulation of 900,000 copies by this time.[130]

    Each of the major missions had juvenile societies: they were organised by the same people who kept the women's mission movement going. Girls rather than boys appear to have formed the backbone of these societies. Certainly in contemporary literature – for example, Mrs George de Horne Vaizey's *A Houseful of Girls*, published by the Religious Tract Society in 1902 – it was enthusiastic and enterprising girls who dutifully organised bazaars and fetes, paid their yearly mission subscription, attended the lectures of missionaries on home visits, knocked on doors to collect money and distributed tracts. Many were middle-class but at least some were working-class: the poor were more effective when canvassing their own districts. What did children gain from mission work? Stories of missionary heroes and martyrs may have inspired them. The social side of missionary work (especially the summer gatherings) may have added variety and colour to their lives. And mission work may have bolstered their self-esteem and provided opportunities for self-expression. To be weighed against this, however, is the likely monotony of many missionary gatherings; the exploitation of children to solicit funds from their own families and neighbourhoods (much was expected of them here); and, above all, the way their minds may have been prejudiced against non-European peoples.

Many children's missionary societies were attached to Sunday schools. According to the latest research, the majority of Victorian children came into contact with a Sunday school at some point in their lives.[131] They were a powerful educational influence and one of the most carefully organised aspects of local voluntary activity.[132] Up to four-fifths of boys and girls aged 5 to 20 were registered; of these it is estimated that about four-fifths actually attended. How many of these children would have become involved in overseas mission activity? By the 1870s a concerted effort was being made to stop the leakage of young people from Sunday schools (and thus the church) by promoting institutional diversity.[133] One historian claims that missions were central to this process because of their powerful juvenile appeal: 'the lure of the exotic and the heroic was the foreign missionary sugar pill for the domestic missionary instruction in lessons of thrift, self-help, and, above all else, gratitude for the manifold benefits of being English'.[134] This seems doubtful. The main mechanisms for achieving institutional diversity were not juvenile mission associations but other forms of associated auxiliaries – confirmation guilds, music groups, reading classes, football clubs and mutual improvement societies.[135] In the words of one leading historian of religion, 'The elixir of juvenile association was nothing more than an ecclesiastical utopia. Nothing, not institutional integration, not organisational extension, nor even pedagogic revolution had prevented or seemingly could prevent the exodus . . . from Sunday school into spiritual oblivion.'[136]

The role of juvenile missionary associations in forming the cultural and racial attitudes of children is likely to have been complex. Evangelic missionaries did portray African and Asian societies as inferior; yet these societies had to be redeemable – otherwise Christianity was redundant. If only for this reason, missionary propaganda rarely indulged in pseudo-scientific racism. Rather it tended 'to stress the potential for good even within the most apparently benighted human communities', and to take as its premise the possibility that anyone could have their life changed by receiving the gospel.[137] Thus, to say that the juvenile missionary movement raised children's awareness of empire does not mean that it also indoctrinated them in racist or xenophobic imperial values.

[112] Education and youth movements

There are several explanations for the expansion of primary and secondary education after 1870.[138] There was the decline of work for children in industry.[139] There was the importance that politicians attached to creating a responsible and public-spirited citizenry following the second and third Reform Acts of 1867 and 1884.[140] There was the need to develop a skilled and literate workforce if Britain was to compete with Germany, America and Japan.[141] And there was the question of 'social control': fears of hooliganism and law-breaking led the ruling classes to look to the school system to instil discipline among the lower orders.[142] Thus we should not jump to the conclusion that educational reform was prompted by an imperialist agenda. Having said that, there does seem to have been a shift of emphasis in education from an early-to-mid-Victorian concern with religion, obedience and duty to a more explicitly patriotic approach in the later-Victorian era.[143] As concerns grew about racial and physical fitness, so the issue of child welfare was increasingly presented in terms of social efficiency as well as philanthropic duty.[144] How far did the teaching and study of the British empire play a part in this process? Who tried to promote imperial education and to what effect? And what exactly did children learn about the empire through school?

Some schoolchildren were unexpectedly and abruptly brought into contact with the empire through overseas settlement. Most people know something of Dr Barnardo's organised schemes of emigration which saw 28,000 children transported to Canada from 1870 to 1914.[145] What is not so readily recognised is that other pioneer social reformers, such as the feminist Maria Rye and the staunch revivalist Annie MacPherson, had been sending children from London to Canada from the late 1860s, albeit on a smaller scale.[146] Under Maria Rye's programme 5,000 children emigrated. MacPherson's work grew steadily from small beginnings (she took a party of a hundred boys to Canada in 1870) to about 12,000 children in total; the scale of the work was deliberately curtailed so that the children were more effectively supervised. Not only did these two women remove children from the workhouses, they also took them out of the reformatory and industrial schools. Reformatory schools housed actual offenders – juvenile criminals between the ages of 7 and 16; industrial schools were intended to deal with children found begging, wandering homeless or left destitute, and considered to be in danger of slipping into crime. No information on the number of reformatory schools could be tracked down, but the number of industrial schools, founded in the larger towns, grew steeply from 1,668 in 1864 to 22,000 in 1898.[147] An Act of 1891 empowered these schools to emigrate any child detained or 'licensed out'; the consent of the Home Secretary was required.[148] Industrial schools all over Britain encouraged the assisted migration of suitable inmates through charitable or governmental agencies. Liverpool Education Authority implemented the policy most extensively; by 1914 it had sent 1,200 children to Canada.[149]

The crux of the debate, however, regarding empire and education rests on the content of the curriculum and the nature of the teaching materials used in the classroom. We should begin with school attendance. Up to the early 1900s this was poor and irregular.[150] Not until ten years after W. E. Forster's 1870 Act was it compulsory for children up to the age of 13 to go to school.[151] Even then cities that provided a mechanism for securing regular attendance were unusual; most Local School Boards sought ways to evade the law.[152] It was also difficult to persuade many working-class parents to send their children to school.[153] For most of the nineteenth century they remained reliant on their labour – in rural areas it was not unusual for schools to close during harvest.[154] Another disincentive was the need to pay school fees; only from 1891 did elementary education become free.[155] Although the price of schooling had been steadily decreasing during the previous decade, average attendance in London was well below 80%. It did not rise above this figure until the mid 1890s. By 1904 it had increased to 88%.[156]

What were children taught? Certainly, there was no shortage of lobbying for more time and effort to be devoted to the study of the empire in British schools.[157] Toward the end of the nineteenth century, the Conservative MP, Sir Howard Vincent, and the extra-parliamentary pressure group, the Navy League, were busy disseminating school maps splashed with red ink and crammed full of facts about the empire's economic worth. Likewise, the League of Empire regarded education as a key aspect of its battle for imperial unity. The League was formed in 1901 as a pen-pal club for children in Britain and its colonies. It later became a clearing centre for information on imperial education and a link between Whitehall and the empire's educational bodies. However, the League's calls for the mutual recognition of teaching certificates, and the exchange of teachers and inspectors, were greeted cautiously. Nor was there much enthusiasm for such centralising measures as the closer integration of curricula, nomenclature and official statistics, though a conference in 1911 did pave the way for the establishment of the Imperial Union of Teachers in 1913.

The other main body to play a part in the campaign for imperial education was the Royal Colonial Institute (RCI). From 1910 the RCI sponsored lantern slide lectures for schoolchildren, and employed a fiery orator,

[114]   W. Herbert Garrison, to wax lyrical about the empire to audiences up and down the country.[158] Garrison was eventually dropped, the emphasis of the RCI's efforts having shifted to the realm of higher education. However, from 1916 the Institute's chairman, Sir Charles Lucas, previously the first head of the Colonial Office's Dominions Department, again sought to persuade children of the benefits of empire.[159] Lucas was vexed by the new tendency in history teaching to downplay national rivalries and animosities, and expressed his frustrations at the Historical Association's annual general meeting that year.[160] He then asked the Board of Education to make the study of imperial history compulsory at teacher training colleges, and to inject more imperial content into the curriculum of all relevant subjects. He gave a series of lectures to a study circle of London County Council teachers in 1921 on the subject of European trusteeship in Africa in which he emphasised their responsibility to educate pupils to accept the nation's imperial responsibilities.[161]

What was the effect of all this propagandising? How far was the curriculum adjusted to take account of the gathering pace of territorial expansion? Scrutiny of the codes issued by the Education Department lends weight to the view that education was to a degree imperialised.[162] A string of suggestions poured forth: the incorporation of military drill in the elementary code of 1871, supplemented by a course of physical training for the upper departments of elementary schools in 1902; the directive to school inspectors 'to excite interest in the Colonial and Foreign Possessions of the British Crown' (1872); the inclusion of information on Britain's colonies and dependencies in geography teaching for Standard VI pupils (1882); and an 'alternative' geography syllabus for upper standard pupils that placed special emphasis on the imperial link (1890). Note should also be taken of the Department of Education's guidelines for elementary teachers. In 1905 these stated that pupils needed to be 'taught how the British nation grew up, and how the mother country in her turn has founded daughter countries beyond the seas'. This theme was continued in the new 1914 edition of the handbook. It stated that, as their study of history progressed, pupils should 'gain knowledge of the government of the country, the growth of free institutions, the expansion of the Empire, and the establishment of our free position amongst nations'. The 1923, 1927 and 1937 editions basically repeated these sentiments, while adding that the empire should be made a selected subject for geography courses.[163] And so on.

Several factors, however, made it difficult to implement these codes and manuals. The system of payment by results, introduced in 1862 and not abandoned until 1898, had a constricting effect on both the school

curriculum and teacher initiative.[164] It put a premium on the so-called [115]
'3Rs' and religious knowledge. Prescribed subjects were reading, writing
and arithmetic; with needlework for girls, and drawing for boys. Many
working-class parents appear to have been entirely satisfied with these
limited objectives: their reason for sending children to school was to secure
basic literacy, and they were neither financially nor perhaps culturally
equipped to take anything other than a narrow view of formal education.[165]
In addition to the prescribed subjects, schools could provide up to two 'class'
and 'special' subjects, taught to pupils in standards IV to VI. History and
geography (the two disciplines most likely to have an imperial bent) were
given such status in 1867 and 1875 respectively. Yet only a fifth of
elementary schools taught history in 1889, while three-quarters taught
geography. The Board of Education, moreover, frequently met with resistance from local authorities. LEAs did not wish to see their classrooms
converted into pulpits. They also faced practical problems in introducing
educational reforms (imperial or otherwise) because of a crowded curriculum; excessive class sizes; a lack of trained staff (and consequent reliance
upon pupil teachers); and their cost. Meanwhile within the Board there
were doubts as to whether primary schoolchildren were capable of grasp-
ing complicated notions of imperial relationships. More seriously still,
the National Union of Teachers jealously guarded the autonomy of the
individual teacher.[166]

Even when reforms were introduced we need to be careful before
imputing to them an imperial rationale. Take the case of military drill,
included in the school curriculum from the late 1860s. It was intended to
teach the habits of obedience and discipline, and to help diminish crime,
raise productivity and eradicate pauperism. Toward the end of the 1880s –
at the height of the so-called 'new' imperialism' – drill became an established
part of the curriculum. However, it was in the process of being broadened
into a much wider (and more liberal) programme of physical exercises and
training. Hence when the enthusiastic imperialist, the Earl of Meath, founder
and president of the Lads' Drill Association, tried to get the London School
Board to reinstate military drill during the Boer War he was instantly
rebuffed. The Board responded that many military exercises were not
suitable for boys.[167]

There is, then, a problem with the study of codes and regulations. 'To
take the strictures of the inspectors, the provisions of the Revised Code and
the advice given in books on teaching method at their face is to conjure
up a picture of well-disciplined children conforming to the norms of the
Victorian middle classes.'[168] The reality of the classroom may have been far

removed. Ideally, what we need to do is to examine education from the point of view of those providing or experiencing it – though this is no easy task. Here we will consider teachers' attitudes; the content of school textbooks; and children's recollections of their schooling. It will be seen that our knowledge of the world of the schoolteacher is very patchy, while studies of the impact of teaching materials are fraught with difficulty. However, oral history archives do shed light on children's responses to what was probably the most explicit appeal to juvenile imperial sentiment – Empire Day.

Notwithstanding what has already been said about the NUT, there are signs that some parts of the teaching profession were eager to bring the empire into the classroom. In London Board schools many teachers were raised to believe in British superiority;[169] those who went through teacher training colleges were actively encouraged to take imperial education more seriously.[170] An example of one such teacher would be Louisa Walker, headmistress of the Fleet Road School in London, who was inspired by the Boer War to write songs to celebrate the courage of British soldiers fighting in South Africa.[171] In the early twentieth century there were also several teacher exchange schemes run by the League of Empire, the (Anglican) Fellowship of the Maple Leaf and the Canadian imperialist Fred Ney, though they operated on a fairly small scale.[172] Meanwhile, some educational reformers embraced the empire. The ILP activist Margaret McMillan (1860–1931) happily harnessed post-Boer War anxieties about the health of the British race in order to draw attention to her lifelong concern – the welfare of working-class children, particularly whilst they were at elementary school.[173] And feminist schoolteachers in London discovered in the language of imperialism a useful tool for protecting their position as professionals. Having accepted the argument for separate spheres in education – single-sex schooling and the expansion of domestic subjects for girls – it was then possible for them to argue that only female teaching staff could provide the appropriate schooling for future mothers of the empire.[174] In these ways, Edwardian socialists and feminists willingly exploited empire in an effort to effect meaningful social change. Having said that, we need to know much more about the teaching profession before we can properly assess its role in disseminating (or resisting) imperial ideals.

Fortunately more research has been done on school texts. After the 1870 Act there was an expanding market for educational publications; Blackie's, Longman, Macmillan and the Oxford and Cambridge University presses were among the first to try to tap it by developing series of books for the Board schools.[175] A survey of over two hundred and fifty school history textbooks is the best place to begin here.[176] The majority of these texts were the work of teachers, academics and clergymen. From the mid-nineteenth century, they began to include more material on Britain's empire – in 1856, the SPCK's *History of England* declared that Englishmen could 'hardly help feeling proud when they look on this little island home of ours, and remember that it holds sceptre over so large a portion of the earth's surface'.[177] India rather than Africa held pride of place. There were frequent mentions of the 'Black Hole' of Calcutta (1756), the first Afghan war (1838–42) and the Mutiny (1857), though not until the twentieth century were whole chapters devoted to the Raj and its achievements in uplifting the Indian population.[178] At best, the authors of these works tended to approach the history of the extra-European world through European (or British) eyes – exploration; military conquest; settlement and economic penetration were the main tropes. At worst, they denigrated the empire's subject peoples through a variety of stereotypes that proved resistant to change.[179] Yet the more bigoted and jingoistic publications were not necessarily the most popular.[180] Moreover, the teaching of empire history remained a fringe activity in the majority of schools throughout our period. By the 1920s the main growth in the curriculum came from 'modern' European history – this was at the instigation of the Board of Education, and clearly a result of the First World War.[181]

How much of what they read in textbooks did children accept or remember? Some historians lament the damaging effects of such propaganda on young minds.[182] Others are more circumspect.[183] More recently this debate has been re-focused on a particular type of school publishing – the elementary classroom reader. These were used to practise reading skills through the medium of English literature, history and geography. By the mid-nineteenth century religious material was being pared down in favour of more secular subjects designed to adjust children to the requirements of the 'machine' or 'industrial' age.[184] During the later-Victorian and Edwardian era there was a further shift from the idea of the 'struggle for freedom' as the core of national identity to the idea of the English having a special place in the world by virtue of their superior moral and physical qualities.[185] In this way, the elementary classroom is said to have helped to spread imperialist ideology.[186]

One of the merits of studying readers is that we can be confident that they were widely used. But whether they had a deep or lasting impact on pupils is not so clear.[187] Oral testimony and autobiographies suggest that working-class schoolchildren were not always receptive to their nationalist and racist messages.[188] In particular, such recollections show how 'contradictions between the rhetoric of imperialism and the daily reality

[118]   of class discrimination and inequality' meant that some pupils resisted a conservative, ethnic sense of national identity.[189] A variety of agencies fostered this resistance. Socialist schoolteachers (who 'increasingly infiltrated the state education system from the 1890s onwards'), trade unions and (some) working-class parents all opposed the inculcation of imperialism and militarism in schools.[190]

Thus it is difficult to get to grips with the perspective of teachers and the experience of pupils. Yet it is possible to gain more direct insights into the impact of imperial propaganda in schools by examining the evidence from oral history archives regarding Empire Day.[191] Celebrated on Queen Victoria's birthday (24 May), the idea of Empire Day was first mooted in 1896 by Reginald Brabazon, the 12th Earl of Meath (1841–1929),[192] though not until 1903–4 did it catch on.[193] It was Meath's intention to use Empire Day to educate schoolchildren about the importance of the empire and their duties toward it. A philanthropist before he became an imperialist, Meath's efforts to improve working-class education can be traced back to the 1870s and his work with the Girls' and Young Men's Friendly Societies; he subsequently sponsored several child welfare bills in the House of Lords. Until 1913, Meath bankrolled the Empire Day Movement (EDM) to the tune of £5,000 per annum. In the early 1920s he handed it over to the RCI. The British government did not officially endorse Empire Day until the recruitment crisis of 1916.

Whereas the membership of many youth movements (Boys' Brigade, Church Lads' Brigade, Boys' Life Brigade, Boy Scouts, Girl Guides) may not have extended much beyond the lower middle and skilled working class,[194] Empire Day had the potential to reach all schoolchildren. According to the EDM's own (and probably inflated) figures,[195] 12,544 out of a total of 20,451 elementary schools marked Empire Day in 1907. In Blackburn, for example, it was enthusiastically celebrated, headmasters tending 'to write more about Empire day than about any other topic except the school inspector's report or the curriculum'.[196] Four years later, 10,000 children paraded in columns a thousand strong in London.[197] By 1919, when 27,323 schools participated in the event, only two Welsh and three English LEAs were refusing to sanction it. The Meath archives also make it clear that Empire Day was promoted by a wide range of newspapers (national and provincial), and by various public bodies like the Church Army, Salvation Army, League of Empire, RCI, Boy Scouts, Girl Guides and Women's Institute.[198] Between the wars the WI was particularly important, its branches heavily involved in the spread of Empire Day festivities at the grass-roots level.[199]

Figure 5   Children at High Middleton School, Empire Day, 23 May 1913
Source: Getty Images

[120]   People's recollections of Empire Day suggest that it was a firm fixture of the school calendar until at least the mid-1940s. For some children it appears to have been among the most memorable of their experiences at school. What happened on this special day? Music was a major part of the proceedings. In the words of a female weaver from Lancashire, 'we used to sing our heads off' on 24 May.[200] Empire Day hymns and the 'Empire Catechism' (one King, one Fleet, one Empire) could be practised for weeks beforehand.[201] Another key aspect of celebrations was marching, parading and the saluting of the flag. Activities normally took place in the school playground. Yet sometimes several schools in an area joined together to put on a grand pageant or festival for the benefit of the local community. On such occasions, children donned costumes (invariably to represent the 'mother country' and her various colonies), climbed aboard floats, processed through the streets and assembled at a central venue to hear an address from a local dignitary on the duties of citizenship. An element of civic pride was often involved. Take the county of Yorkshire, for example, never lacking in intra-regional rivalry. When the town of Batley staged its Empire Day pageant in 1907 – 3,500 children from elementary schools took part, and an estimated 10,000–12,000 adults were present – an explicit comparison was drawn with the (larger) Sheffield pageant of the same year. The occasion was also used to raise a substantial sum for a hospital extension fund.[202]

Not all children appreciated Empire Day. Ian White from West Houghton in Lancashire remembered the event without any affection. Dressed up in African or Indian garb, carrying a packet of tea, a lump of coal or some other product to represent the colony in question, he and his classmates assembled in the school hall and sang various songs: 'It just didn't appeal to me, Empire Day and stuff like that.'[203] Other people's recollections are more positive. Doris Joll from Burnley spoke of 'right enjoying' the day, mainly because of the opportunity it provided for 'showing myself off in a way'.[204] This, of course, raises the tricky question of what Empire Day actually signified for the children who celebrated it? One scholar claims that the spectacle of the occasion 'brought alive in a vivid and emotional way the meaning of Empire'.[205] While not wishing to deny that this may have been true for some pupils, it seems to me an oversimplification. To begin with, it ignores the way in which a significant number of schoolteachers appear not to have co-operated with their heads in marking the event; for that matter head teachers themselves could be lukewarm. In 1938, Miss 'O' at Grange Junior School decided to get her children to do some painting to fill the time: 'Anyway, I don't care. We get a holiday this afternoon and that's the best of Empire day celebrations.'[206] It may also be significant that teachers' journals, *The Schoolmaster* and the *Women Teachers' Chronicle*, hardly ever reported Empire Day, even in the year of the Wembley exhibition.[207] Moreover, there are signs of suspicion from teachers whose political convictions sat uncomfortably with the type of militaristic sentiment that could be expressed on 24 May. An English teacher from Bramford Senior Area School in Suffolk, an ardent Communist, refused to set an empire essay or prepare an Empire Day lesson when requested to do so by her head teacher. She said that she did not see why England should have more empire than other nations and that she did not agree with the event.[208] Another Communist, Nan McMillan, recollected that at her first teaching post in Battersea, the head, 'a good labour woman', had put a map of the empire on the wall and 'not pulled any punches' in telling the children how Britain 'got its hands on the bits painted red'. This attack on Empire Day did not, however, please the local council and, under sustained pressure to say what a good thing the empire was, the head eventually 'broke down'.[209]

Even teachers who were not hostile to Empire Day recognised that its popularity stemmed in part from the fact that it released their charges from ordinary lessons. Mr X at Grange Junior School told his pupils in 1938, 'Now you are having a holiday this afternoon and I expect you will forget all about the empire and think of your holiday.'[210] At other schools it was the practice to spend the afternoon playing organised games.[211] In fact, many of the mentions of Empire Day in oral history records follow on from mentions of other types of leisure activity – playing in the streets or fields, mushroom picking, Maypole dancing, seaside holidays and weddings.[212] For many children, therefore, the meaning of 24 May may not have derived from its patriotic and imperial content but from its status as a public holiday. Indeed, when a newspaper interviewed people about the event in 1923, all six respondents argued in favour of making it a day free from work.[213] For others, who were able to see beyond the excitement and spectacle, the meaning of Empire Day could still be rather vague.[214] Lena Gee was able to recall all fifteen lines of the Empire Day poem word for word. However, when asked what it was all about, she replied: 'But I forgot what Empire Day were for. It was something to with . . . I mean the flag. Something to do with the monarchy isn't it, it must be.'[215] Isabella Curle likewise struggled to grasp the significance of the event: 'we used to have our little flags, what is the meaning of Empire day.'[216]

None of this is to deny that Empire Day, or some of the other educational activities mentioned above, heightened the imperial sensibilities of British schoolchildren. Even if the formal inclusion of empire in the school

[122] syllabus was patchy and did not always ensure the desired outcome in terms of personal belief and conduct, there is no concealing the contrast between late-Victorian and present-day schools in terms of their attitude to Britain's imperial role. That said, it is questionable whether schools much extended children's knowledge of the empire, the intricacies of its government, or the complexities of its peoples.[217] Thus Elvy Morton recalled her arrival in Britain from the small Caribbean island of Nevis in 1959:

> Well, I got so annoyed one day, I call for two pounds of everything on this stall, and then walk away, you know, because I was really annoyed that these things could happen, when you've been taught everything about England, and England knew nothing about you. We had the Union Jack, we flew the flag, we had Empire day, 24th May. We had Prince Charles' birthday. We had every-thing that's going. We knew everything about England. And yet they know nothing about us.[218]

In so far as education did help to foster a sense of pride in the British em-pire, it does not appear to have been very deep-rooted or well-informed.

Conclusion

This chapter has explored what the empire meant to women and children in Britain. Through literature, missionary societies and schools an aware-ness of Britain's imperial role was raised. But the level of that awareness and the precise attitudes that resulted are not open to easy generalisations. In fact, what is striking is just how many and varied were women's and children's experiences of empire, and just how difficult it is to decipher from any of the above case studies whether their lives were enhanced and enriched or damaged and diminished by it. This is primarily because gender and age were manifestly not the only determinants of people's responses to imperialism: social class and regional origin were key factors too. Indeed, it is the interplay between these variables that probably best accounts for women's and children's imperial involvement. What we know about literature, missionary work and education suggests that rather than taking 'gender', 'age', 'class' and 'region' to be fixed and separating categories of experience, they are better seen as fluid and mutually reinforc-ing. Sometimes they exposed women and children to the empire in ways that were subtly or even significantly different to men and adults – women working in the zenana missions and child migrants would be cases in point. But sometimes they did not – the imperial ideology to be found in juvenile periodicals and school texts strongly resembles that of certain types of adventure fiction targeted at adults, while the home-based mission work that middle-class women did was no doubt similar to that of the men – they were just more willing to do it and probably better at it. It is for this reason that, while women and children have been singled out for separate consideration in this chapter, they have not been lost sight of in other parts of the book.[219]

CHAPTER 6

DOMESTIC POLITICS

S tudies of 'imperial Britain' have focused overwhelmingly on the social and economic sphere. Cultural historians and literary scholars have energetically explored representations of the empire in the arts and the mass media, while economic historians have evaluated its benefits and costs. The former tend to argue that imperialism was fundamental to Britain's past and central to the British peoples' self-perception. Many of the latter much more modestly appraise the empire's domestic impact, and play down its contribution to the nation's economic development and well-being. Yet if the historiography has grown rapidly, it has also become somewhat lop-sided. The repercussions of overseas expansion for some key aspects of British public life remain largely unmapped. Chief perhaps among these is the political culture of the modern British state.

It is not that domestic politics has been entirely neglected. In 1981 Jack Gallagher's Ford Lectures presented the empire as a negative factor in party and parliamentary debate.[1] According to Gallagher, the acquisition of territory was mainly discussed within Whitehall and among a policy-making elite (or official mind). The average backbench MP and ordinary voter did not care much about what happened in the empire. In so far as they did, it was mainly to insist that it did not eat up scarce resources more profitably used in Britain. To be sure, particular groups of politicians did, from time to time, take up colonial issues with greater passion and vigour. Yet they did so for largely partisan reasons: political enthusiasm for empire was skin-deep, motivated by party advantage and factional rivalry rather than by any serious or sustained ideological commitment.

This interpretation has lately come in for a good deal of implied criticism. Several scholars now emphasise the reflexive impact of empire on British politics. In the realm of political theory the empire is seen to have been significant in terms of Dilke's, Froude's and Seeley's concept of a 'Greater

Britain', the two Mills', Fitzjames Stephen's and Maine's reflections on
the problems of governing India, and, more generally, British liberalism's
encounter with Asia.[2] It is also understood to have impinged on parliament
– mid-Victorian debates about parliamentary reform were conducted with
one eye on the constitutional experiences of Australia and the West Indies.[3]
Above all, there has been a greater emphasis on how the empire became
tangled up with the development of party structures. The late-Victorian
Conservative party's appeal to cross-class loyalty had strong imperial
resonances (alongside and interacting with its increased identification with
Unionism),[4] while a younger generation of Edwardian Conservatives was
inspired by the doctrine of 'constructive imperialism' – a doctrine that was
responsible for more than a decade of civil war (and fragmentation) in the
Unionist party.[5] Between the wars, parts of the Labour party appropriated
from Radical Liberals their anti-imperialist position, though the marriage
between that and the statist strand of socialism was not unproblematic.[6]
The Conservatives meanwhile returned to imperial preference.[7]

   This chapter considers the capacity of the empire to strike back on the
British political scene. But rather than move from ministry to ministry, or
run through the central figures of this story (this would have been too long-
winded, and have risked obscuring more general patterns), it pursues a
series of questions regarding imperial influences on domestic politics. In
what circumstances could the colonies command the attention of politicians
in Britain? What type of values did imperialists usher into the domestic
political arena? How far did Britain's role and responsibilities as an imperial
power alter attitudes towards its own government? These questions are
examined under three headings: the machinery of government and constitutional reform; political culture; and conceptions of the state. The central
contention of the chapter is that from the mid-nineteenth to the mid-
twentieth centuries the empire was part of what it meant to be a British
politician, and a key aspect of the mental framework of many ministers and
MPs. This was partly because governing the colonies involved difficult
decisions about the allocation of resources, the use of force and the devolution and transfer of power – decisions that politicians could scarcely ignore.
More than that, however, the empire was a spur to theoretical reflection
and a significant source of new ideas: it gave politicians in Britain something to draw upon. J. A. Hobson, of course, took the view that imperialism
debased and corrupted British public life. This chapter advances a different
line of argument, namely that the empire helped to underpin the consolidation of a liberal constitutional state in Britain.

[126] The machinery of government and constitutional reform

The consequences of the gathering pace of territorial expansion for Whitehall were at first 'surprisingly small'.[8] There were several reasons why this was so. For most of the nineteenth century communication with the colonies was difficult and slow. Much of the business of governing the empire had to be devolved to the 'men-on-the spot' – diplomats, proconsuls, army officers and the like. Added to this, and in an effort to cut the cost of administration, the nineteenth century saw a big shift toward the devolution of power in the colonies of white settlement. Many decisions that had previously been taken in Whitehall were now to be taken locally by a new generation of colonial politicians. Finally, until the end of the century there was little need for government to think about intervening in colonial economies: as the first power to industrialise, Britain's lead over its rivals was sufficient for trade to be left to look after itself. It was not until the 1920s that the empire began to make greater bureaucratic demands. Britain then became more pro-active in managing Anglo-Dominion relations, and it acquired new administrative responsibilities in the Middle East in Palestine, Transjordan and Mesopotamia (Iraq) in the form of the League of Nations Mandates.

The Colonial Office was among the smallest departments of state; indeed, in the eyes of many contemporaries it was no more than a 'political backwater'.[9] One official described it thus: 'a sleepy and humdrum office, where important work was no doubt done, but simply because it had got to be done, where there seemed no enthusiasm, no *esprit de corps*, and no encouragement for individual exertion'.[10] The volume of business grew, but there was no corresponding increase in the size of its staff; the work of officials thus rapidly fell into arrears.[11] Here the lack of co-operation from other departments did not help. While only major colonial policy decisions required cabinet approval, many minor questions had to be referred to the War Office, Foreign Office and Treasury, and their responses tended to be tardy or unhelpful.[12] No surprise, then, that when the ambitious and energetic Joseph Chamberlain became Colonial Secretary in 1895 he immediately set out to transform the administrative capabilities of his department. Yet Chamberlain was thwarted by an obstructive and parsimonious Treasury and by a lack of support from cabinet colleagues.[13] He found that the CO's machinery was not up to the task of revitalising the West Indian sugar economies or fostering inter-imperial trade.[14] Admittedly, after his departure the number of CO employees did rise – in 1903 it was 113; in

1925, 431; and in 1947, 1,139. In other ways the department continued to struggle and suffer, however.[15] Its technical and scientific functions expanded,[16] but even with the passage of the Colonial Development Act (1929) the funds provided by the Treasury remained modest and the CO's approach piecemeal. By the late 1930s, the department remained underfunded and wanting in vision, amateur in the way it selected development projects and incapable of initiating new ones of its own.[17]

At first sight the empire's impact on parliament appears to have been correspondingly small. There was nothing like the annual debate on the Indian Estimates to empty the chamber of the Commons.[18] MP apathy was partly to blame. There were also several institutional impediments to a thorough debate of colonial questions – the careful control exercised by party managers; the colonies' lack of direct representation at Westminster; the frequent transfer of officials between colonies to prevent them from identifying too closely with any single territory; and the financial self-sufficiency of the Raj which meant that MPs were not required to sanction Indian expenditure.[19] This is not the end of the story, however. There may be other ways in which the British parliament owed something to the nation's colonial experience, not least in terms of constitutional reform.

Several British parliamentarians formulated their views on citizenship in the light of what they already knew about the operation of colonial constitutions. This should not surprise us. The world of policy-making at home was intimately connected to the political worlds of the colonies by informal channels of private influence, by patronage and clientage and by the lobbying of various pressure groups, publicists and writers. Colony and metropole thus formed part of a larger system of 'imperial politics' in which arguments and precedents circulated freely, facilitated by the more rapid movement of migrants and developments in press communication.[20] For example, when the issue of parliamentary reform resurfaced in Britain in the 1860s it was partly in response to the establishment of representative assemblies and the extension of the franchise in Australia and Jamaica: 'the constitutional settlement which emerged in the colonies in the 1850s [extended suffrage, with the executive retaining the legislative and fiscal initiative] was precisely the balance struck in Britain itself as a result of the Second Reform Act'.[21]

John Bright was a particularly firm believer in 'the common destinies of Englishmen across the empire',[22] and adamant that what was good enough for the overseas settler was good enough for those who stayed at home:

[128] Why an Englishman if he goes to the Cape, he can vote; if he goes farther to Australia, to the nascent empires of the New World, he can there vote; if he goes to the Canadian federation, he can there vote; and if he goes to those grandest colonies of England not dependent on the English crown . . . there can give his free and independent vote. (Loud cheers) It is only in his own country, on his own soil, where he was born, the very soil which he has enriched with his labour and with the sweat of his brow, that he is denied this right which in every other community of Englishmen in the world would be freely accorded to him (Much cheering).[23]

Bright's opponents invoked colonial experience too. Friends of the Jamaican Governor, Edward Eyre, grimly predicted that the move toward democracy in the West Indies would unleash similar horrors at home, while the leader of the 'cave of Adullam', the Whig-Liberal Robert Lowe, drew deeply on his personal knowledge of Australia, where he had lived for eight years, to argue against the extension of the borough franchise. As a member of the Legislative Council of New South Wales in the 1840s, Lowe had actually supported the lowering of the property qualification for the vote: 'I wish to give all classes power to make each dependent on the other so that they may work for the common good.'[24] However he had not supported either household or universal suffrage, and had rejected the idea that the colonies were in any sense a constitutional model for England. In the new societies of Australia and New Zealand, where 'progress' was the guiding political principle, he accepted that constitutions would be framed with one eye to the future. In the mother country, meanwhile, the watchword was 'stability' and this explained why the narrow base of the 1832 constitution had to be maintained. More than that, Lowe became convinced of the evils resulting from democracy in Australia:

> As the polypus takes its colour from the rock to which it affixes itself, so do the members of this House take their character from the constituencies. If you lower the character of the constituencies, you lower the character of the representatives, and you lower the character of this House. I do not want to say anything disagreeable, but if you want to see the result of democratic constituencies, you will find them in all the assemblies of Australia, and in all the assemblies of North America.[25]

Nor was the 1867 Reform Act unique. The fight for women's suffrage in Britain was galvanised by the Boer War and inspired by the achievements of colonial feminists. The war in South Africa stirred into life a number of women's movements;[26] it also intensified suffragette militancy.[27] In order to avoid the accusation that this was a capitalists' conflict, imperial propagandists had made the fight for Uitlanders' political rights the centrepiece of their justification for military intervention.[28] The irony was not lost on British feminists who insisted that if force was to be exercised on behalf of expatriate mine workers, it might equally be expended for a comparable domestic goal (women's rights).[29]

White women in New Zealand and Australia (who gained the vote in 1893 and 1902 respectively) 'took particular pride in their ability to offer British women a lead'.[30] The best-known example is probably that of the renowned Melbourne activist, Vida Goldstein, who arrived in Britain in March 1911 determined to help her 'beleaguered English sisters'.[31] She urged members of the Women's Social and Political Union to remain militant, warned them against dissipating their energies in other causes and praised the bravery of her imprisoned comrades.[32] The same year Australian and New Zealand women living in London formed the Women Voters' Committee, subsequently known as the British Dominions Woman Suffrage Union. It aimed to advance the women's movement across the empire, and to act as a link between feminist and suffrage groups in Britain and the self-governing colonies.[33]

Yet there were also limits to how far politicians in Britain were willing to draw on colonial experience. Constitutional schemes of the federal variety, implemented extensively and successfully across the empire, were invariably rejected as an option for the United Kingdom.[34] The first home rule bill is a case in point. When drafting this measure Gladstone assembled copies of the constitutions of the self-governing colonies, paying particular attention to the Canada Acts of 1840 and 1867.[35] What was the Liberal leader hoping to learn? Canada's constitution was of course federal, but legislative devolution in Scotland, England or Wales was not seriously contemplated in 1886.[36] Rather Gladstone's chief concern was how much devolved power to give to a separate Irish parliament. The cautious and qualified proposal presented to the House of Commons seems to have been based on his reading of the Canadian legislation, its carefully delineated relationship between Ottawa and the provincial capitals, and the degree of control exercised by the federal parliament over local 'home ruling' assemblies.[37] Indeed, such was Gladstone's desire to conserve as well as reform that, as Morley later remarked, the provincial legislatures of the Canadian system 'had more unfettered powers' than the proposed Irish legislature.[38] In the Irish case certain 'reserved powers' were specified (defence, foreign and fiscal policy) – thus the Canadian model was adopted but the details of the bill were particular to Ireland.

[130]   Nevertheless, Gladstone tried to persuade Queen Victoria of the wisdom of timely constitutional concessions to Ireland by directing her attention to their earlier success in the Canadian context:

> Nothing can be more improbable than that Mr Gladstone should ever be called upon to advise Your Majesty as a Minister with reference to the subject known as Home Rule in Ireland . . . On this subject, as on some others, lessons have been learned during the past half century. The self-government now practised in Canada, and generally viewed as safe if not wholly unexceptionable was regarded, in the first years of Mr Gladstone's Parliamentary life, as a thing fatal to the unity of the Empire.[39]

Victoria was not to be moved. Neither was a majority of MPs. Whigs and Radicals joined the Tories in blocking the bill and bringing down the government. The constitutional expertise the British had amassed in the colonies was not to be drawn upon to resolve problems of Irish governance.[40]

Empire: virtue or vice?

For a century or more the empire has been blamed for debasing British politics. Colonial rule is said to have imported attitudes and values into Britain that were inimical to the growth of a modern democracy. At the start of the twentieth century J. A. Hobson railed against the fact that the south of England was 'richly sprinkled' with a class of retired colonial soldiers and officials, 'men openly contemptuous of democracy, devoted to material luxury, social display, and the shallower arts of intellectual life . . . the wealthier among them discover political ambitions, introducing into our Houses of Parliament the coarsest and most selfish spirit of "Imperialism"'.[41] Thirty or so years later, yet in a similar vein, the New Zealand born political cartoonist David Low (1891–1963) took great delight in deriding the xenophobic and racist, if by then largely irrelevant, attitudes of that archetypal imperialist, Colonel Blimp.[42] A recent study of later-Victorian and Edwardian political culture ploughs a similar furrow:

> imperial visions injected a powerful strain of hierarchy, militarism, 'frontier mentality', administrative rationality, and masculine civic virtue into British political culture, at a time when domestic political forces were running in quite the opposite direction towards egalitarianism, 'progressivism', consumerism, popular democracy, feminism and women's rights.[43]

Is it fair, then, to characterise imperialist ideology as essentially anti-democratic? Clearly, this question could be tackled in a variety of ways. Here three lines of enquiry will be opened up: the consequences for domestic British politics of cases of colonial oppression and settler rapacity; the impact of repatriated colonial administrators on parliamentary and party politics; and whether there were any other facets of imperial politics (beyond officialdom) that were more participatory or progressive.

During times of colonial crisis – the Morant Bay rebellion in Jamaica (1865), the Anglo-Indian protest against Lord Ripon's Ilbert Bill (1883) and the Amritsar massacre (1919) – surely the British people must have been tempted to drop any pretence at inclusiveness, liberalism and tolerance, and to rally behind those who were prepared to 'save the Empire', if necessary by a show of armed force? Certainly, this is often the conclusion drawn from the Governor Eyre controversy, an event that brought to the forefront of British politics the nature of colonial rule and the relationship between white settlers and black subjects. Eyre responded swiftly and brutally to the march of four hundred African Caribbeans on the courthouse of the small town of Morant Bay in Jamaica in October 1865. During a month-long period of martial law, people were shot, hanged and flogged, and many houses were razed.[44] Jamaica's white planters praised Eyre for his handling of the situation. Yet the severity of his measures caused the British government to suspend him and to set up a Royal Commission to inquire into his conduct. The Victorian intelligentsia was split down the middle by the episode.[45] A Jamaica Committee led by John Stuart Mill and backed by such luminaries as John Bright, Charles Darwin, Frederic Harrison, Thomas Huxley, and Herbert Spencer, organised a campaign to privately prosecute Eyre, while an Eyre Defence Committee, supported by Thomas Carlyle, John Ruskin, Alfred Tennyson, Charles Kingsley and Charles Dickens, established a fund to pay the Governor's legal expenses. Opinion in the country was also deeply divided. From the outset, abolitionist, missionary and dissenting groups – known collectively as 'Exeter Hall' – bombarded the Colonial Office with petitions and memorials and staged numerous mass meetings. Eyre's figure was even burnt in effigy by a large gathering of working-class radicals at Clerkenwell Green in London. Eyre's supporters came mainly from clergymen, peers and members of the armed forces. Their case was made at a 'welcome home' dinner, in the pamphlet and periodical press, and at various provincial societies. They raised a significant sum of money (rumoured to be over £10,000) on the Governor's behalf.

[132]   The view that black people were inherently inferior to whites is said to have gained a much wider currency as a result of the Eyre controversy.[46] Such an interpretation has already been questioned in Chapter 3. Here it is worth pointing out that although the Jamaica Committee's four legal actions failed, Eyre was nonetheless forced into premature retirement, turned down for several government posts and deprived of the patronage and perks to which other ex-governors had grown accustomed – even the debate on his legal expenses in 1872 was enough to bring previous passions back to the boil.[47] Of course, martial law continued to be invoked in the colonies and a string of other massacres littered Britain's remaining imperial record. Yet this may be to miss the point. In 1865 Eyre's opponents were worried about authoritarian and arbitrary methods of government seeping back from colony to mother country – this was why the debate focused as much (or more) on the uses and abuses of martial law as on rival theories of race. The same fear helped to persuade the British government to replace the old regime of rule by the planter class with a more direct form of government from London. At first sight this looks like a throwback to the past. But the decision actually held out some hope for black Jamaicans in so far as it curbed the powers of the island's 'plantocracy'. In the words of Niall Ferguson, 'the liberalism of the centre' had prevailed over 'the racism of the periphery'.[48] Indeed, in following years the cry of 'democracy in danger' continued to have considerable political purchase during moments of colonial crisis.[49]

The determination and skill with which Anglo-Indians mobilised metropolitan opinion against the Ilbert Bill (1883–4) looks like another example of imperialists riding roughshod over the principle of racial equality (enshrined in the royal proclamation of 1858). Ripon's bill was a statutory amendment to the Criminal Procedure Code whereby Indian judges and magistrates in country areas (the *mofussil*) would be given the power to try British offenders in criminal cases. It became the focus of a 'White Mutiny' – a heady cocktail of racial and sexual fears, which fed on memories of 1857 and engulfed India's community of English businessmen, planters and professionals. In India, a European and Anglo-Indian Defence Association was formed. It staged protest meetings, threatened boycotts and even tried to get army volunteers to resign. Meanwhile in London several newspapers and reviews clubbed together to stop the liberal Viceroy in his tracks.[50] Chief among these were *The Times, Telegraph, Morning Post, Standard*, and *Spectator*. *The Times* spearheaded the anti-bill agitation. Advised by J. C. Macgregor, a Calcutta barrister who was thoroughly opposed to the measure,[51] the paper argued that indigenous Indians were incapable of

THE JAMAICA QUESTION.

WHITE PLANTER. "AM NOT *I* A MAN AND BROTHER, TOO, MR. STIGGINS?".

Figure 6 'The Jamaica Question', *Punch*, 23 December 1865
Source: © Punch, Ltd

[134] shouldering the responsibility that the bill entailed; that British prestige would be irreparably damaged; that Europeans (especially planter families) would be increasingly harassed; and that there was simply no necessity for change.

In the end the Anglo-Indian 'jingoes', as Ripon called them, got their way. The Ilbert Bill was emasculated: Europeans were to have the right to be tried by juries at least half of whose members were themselves European.[52] Yet victory had not been achieved without a fight. Several pro-bill publications – the *Daily News*, the *Echo*, *Reynolds' News*, the *Weekly Times*, the *Pall Mall Gazette* and the *Contemporary Review* – rallied round Ripon. They argued for a more sympathetic approach on the part of the Government of India to the 'native population', and they affirmed the ability of Indians to participate in their own administration. They also reported on the meetings that were organised by John Bright and other Liberal MPs to back the bill. Such expressions of support certainly stiffened Ripon's resolve.[53] Moreover, the anti-bill agitation was very much a press affair. Only a handful of Tory MPs raised the matter at Westminster and the response from the Tory party caucus was likewise lacklustre.[54] In so far as opinion in the rest of the country was caught up in the Ilbert Bill controversy, there is little evidence to suggest that it sided with Anglo-India. On the contrary, an emissary sent by the Anglo-Indian Defence Association – F. T. Atkins – to arouse British engineering and railway employees against the bill proved a complete failure: 'at his most important meeting in Edinburgh, a motion was carried unanimously against him'![55]

To a large extent Ripon had himself to blame for what happened in 1883–4. He was too far ahead of Anglo-Indian opinion, and he failed to properly brief his cabinet colleagues on the details of the bill, to take sufficient care in its drafting and to have it properly debated in parliament – the latter, in particular, 'created a political vacuum' for the pro-bill press to exploit.[56] In Ripon's defence, he was not the only person to have underestimated the strength of Anglo-Indian feeling. Charles Hobhouse had twenty-six years of ICS experience but wrongly predicted that the racial passions aroused by the bill were 'so much froth' and would soon subside once it became law.[57] Other pro-bill periodicals, however, showed greater perspicacity, regretting that Ripon had thrust the measure on Anglo-India at a moment when he was engaged 'in the gigantic and difficult task of introducing local government reform'.[58] There were also those who supported the liberalisation of municipal government but opposed the Ilbert Bill because they felt that only a handful of anglicised Indian civil servants – the so-called 'Bengali Babus' – stood to gain.[59] Understood in this way,

1883–4 was not so much a crossroads in the history of the Raj, whereby [135] colour-blind justice was rejected in favour of a racially-segregated colonial state, as a poorly judged and badly timed albeit well-intentioned reform.

The British reaction to the massacre of an unarmed crowd gathered in the Punjab city of Amritsar on 13 April 1919 adds further weight to my argument. The irascible Brigadier-General Reginald Dyer had issued a pro-clamation banning such meetings. He ordered his men of the Indian army to fire on some 20,000 civilians and ex-soldiers without first demanding that they disperse. The firing continued for a full ten minutes. Official figures recorded 379 deaths and over 1,200 wounded; Indian estimates were much higher. The British government moved quickly to disavow Dyer's actions and he was forced to resign. Again Anglo-Indian opinion was inflamed, and sections of the metropolitan press, a minority of MPs and a majority of peers protested against Dyer's 'punishment'. They argued that Dyer had 'saved India' by the 'splendid severity' of his actions only to be abandoned by craven and cowardly politicians at Westminster.[60] A defence (or 'Scape-goat') fund was set up by the editor of the *Morning Post* newspaper, Howell Gwynne. Within a few weeks almost £15,000 had been collected, and the final total reached £26,317. Dyer was presented with a golden sword as 'Defender of the Empire'.

The wider political context for the defence of Dyer is the build-up of 'diehard' Tory sentiment during 1919 to 1922. Diehards were exercised by the notion of 'imperial weakness' – the feeling that the empire was living on borrowed time.[61] They believed Britain to have 'providentially sanctioned imperial obligations',[62] and they insisted that challenges to colonial author-ity had to be resisted, whether in Ireland, Egypt or India. Their 'finest hour' was the removal from office of Edwin Montagu. He was replaced as Secre-tary of State for India by the Conservative, Viscount Peel, who lost no time in pouring cold water on a scheme for the Indianisation of the army. (Diehard MPs had been incensed by Montagu's rather tactless remarks in the House of Commons on 8 July 1920.[63]) But what was the extent of public support for Dyer? His defenders were a somewhat disparate group made up of retired Anglo-Indian officials and servicemen, military members of the army council, Ulster Unionists and a few right-wing newspapers. The Dyer fund drew donations from a wider range of people, though the manual workers and schoolchildren who parted with their pennies were predominantly Anglo-Indian – working-class opinion in Britain was less sympathetic. The Labour party conference at Scarborough in 1920 passed a resolution denouncing the actions of British officers in the Punjab, and calling for the repeal of all repressive legislation. There was a real fear among

THE ANGLO-INDIAN MUTINY.

(A BAD EXAMPLE TO THE ELEPHANT!)

Figure 7   'The Anglo-Indian Mutiny', *Punch*, 15 December 1883
Source: © Punch, Ltd

delegates of labour unrest at home meeting with similar treatment. As the [137]
Manchester Guardian commented, 'General Dyer's more thorough supporters
by no means intend to stop at India . . . After India, Ireland. After Ireland,
British workmen on strike.'[64]

Other elements of the anti-Dyer camp took their stand on the British
government's obligation to maintain a single standard of justice across the
British empire.[65] For Winston Churchill this was the 'most frightful of all
spectacles'. Britain had shown 'the strength of civilisation without its mercy'
and the episode stood in 'singular and sinister isolation' in the modern
history of its empire. In fact, after the First World War politicians across
the political spectrum seem to have been much more willing to question
the use of the army. A mixture of war fatigue, post-war fears about the
brutalisation of society (connected to urban rioting and industrial unrest)
and new myths of British 'peaceableness' all heightened the determination
to curb militarism within the British state.[66] There was, in particular, a growing doubt about the role of 'overwhelming force' in the maintenance of
imperial rule, and a sense that idealistic notions of a 'civilising mission' were
incompatible with the bloody suppression of colonial unrest. Thus there is
a real danger of exaggerating the significance of Diehardism, which was a
minority if passionately held view. Ranged against it was a phalanx of much
more liberal and progressive sentiment, put on its guard by the possibility
that government and society had become inured to violence during the
carnage and slaughter of the war years.

Can the authoritarian, hyper-masculine and militaristic mentality of
imperialists be more clearly perceived in the attitudes of overseas officials?
Again we should take care before jumping to conclusions: 'the same class
structure that produced this imperial governing elite was responsible for
producing the bankers, clerics, government ministers and civil servants
that found employment at home'.[67] To assess how far officials from the
far-flung corners of the empire may have influenced (or infected) political
life at home we will focus on the service ideologies of two groups – the
South African 'Kindergarten' and the Indian Civil Service. The Kindergarten
spearheaded Milner's reconstruction programme and occupied key positions in the bureaucracy of what was becoming an increasingly racially-
segregated state. The ICS was frequently criticised for its arrogance and
assumption of (racial) superiority. In 1908 the Liberal statesman and Indian
Secretary of State, John Morley, went so far as to complain that it was a
service soaked in self-esteem, 'hard, persistent, mechanical, and a good many
other things beside, which I'd rather not write down'.[68] If one wanted to

[138] find proof of imperialism's anti-democratic tendencies what better place to look?

Milner's men were mostly young Oxford graduates, recruited by the High Commissioner to help rebuild the economies (and societies) of the two former Dutch Republics. They stayed on after the restoration of self-government in 1906 to work for the goal of a united South Africa, loyal to the empire and flying the British flag. Subsequently they organised the Round Table movement to achieve greater unity for the empire as a whole. They included Robert Brand, a financier and managing director of Lazard Brothers; Lionel Curtis, the constitutional expert and Beit Lecturer in Colonial History at Oxford; Geoffrey Dawson, editor of the Johannesburg *Star* (1905–10) and *The Times* from 1911; Patrick Duncan, Governor-General of South Africa from 1937 to 1943; Richard Feetham, the Johannesburg lawyer and town clerk; Philip Kerr, later private secretary to Lloyd George (1916–21) and ambassador to the United States (1939–40); Dougal Malcolm, a future director of the British South Africa Company; and Hugh Wyndham, private secretary to Milner who subsequently took up farming on the Vaal river. In the words of the Kindergarten's historian, its members were 'looked upon by some during World War I and the post-war years as a cabal of considerable power'.[69] They operated behind the scenes. They had the ear of powerful people in government and the press. Their activities were funded (secretly) by the Rhodes Trust. Worst of all, they were arguably the father of the 'Cliveden Set', that collection of well-heeled, well-connected individuals who supposedly controlled British foreign policy from a country house in Berkshire during the 1930s.[70]

On closer inspection, however, the Kindergarten does not seem to have wielded all that much influence over Edwardian affairs,[71] or even to have followed Milner's precepts as closely as one might expect. New work on the construction of a white South African identity after the Boer War emphasises just how far the Kindergarten departed from Milner's policies after he left South Africa in 1905.[72] Recognising a chauvinistic sense of Britishness to be unworkable, Milner's acolytes worked hard to cultivate a more open, tolerant and inclusive South African patriotism, which could then provide the basis for broader political loyalties. This rethinking of the relationship between Britons and Boers had a practical side in terms of the introduction of scientific and technical expertise into agricultural policy, and the planning and co-ordination of railway development. It was also expressed culturally, not least in terms of the proclaimed virtues of Cape Dutch architecture and the new literary interest in the so-called 'cult' or 'romance' of the veldt. Indeed, it was only after Milner returned to England that the

Kindergarten became fully receptive to their South African environment.
Their love of intrigue may never have left them, yet their enduring legacy
was to have promoted a broader (white) South African identity 'founded
on the principles of compromise and conciliation' – an identity that was
integral to the merger of the Unionist and South African parties after 1921,
and that was not expunged from South African politics until the Second
World War.[73]

The mentality of the mandarins who served the Raj was similarly complex. It depended on their background in Britain and their subsequent
experiences in India. Two main schools of thought have been identified:
the 'Gospel of Uplift' and the 'Cult of Friendship'.[74] The first stemmed from
an evangelical ethic. Indians were sunk in sin, their poverty the result of
indolence and ignorance; it was the ICS's responsibility to convert them to
English norms. The second stemmed from humanism and the belief that
personal relations were the highest human good; it deplored Anglo-Indian
racism and insisted that it was the ICS's responsibility to reconcile Indians
to British rule. To be sure, the relative strength of these two service ideologies – 'assimilation' and 'preservation' – varied over time. They were also
opposite ends of a spectrum: the majority of officials did not espouse views
that were so clear-cut. The key point, however, is that by no means all ICS
officials adopted an air of patronising and paternalistic superiority toward
Indian society and culture.

Particularly interesting here are the 'mavericks' and 'misfits' – the ICS
produced more than it cared to admit[75] – whose careers were brought to a
premature end as a result of the unconventional views they held. One such
figure is William Wedderburn. Passed over for a judgeship of the Bombay
High Court in 1885, he resigned two years later and returned to England
to become the Liberal MP for Banffshire in 1892. He was a key figure in
the formation of the British Committee of the Indian National Congress in
July 1889.[76] The BCINC's chief protagonists were drawn from the ranks
of retired Indian civil servants. In addition to Wedderburn there was Alan
Octavian Hume, a committed reformer who reached the rank of Secretary
of Revenue, Agriculture and Commerce only to be demoted after Lord Lytton
abolished his department in 1879 (he subsequently resigned); Sir Henry
Cotton, who ended his career as Chief Commissioner of Assam from 1896
and was induced into early retirement in 1902 by Curzon's offer of a KCSI
(Knight Commander in the Most Exalted Order of the Star of India); and
C. J. O'Donnell, a critic of Curzon who retired from the ICS in 1900 and
went on to become a Liberal MP (1906–10). All had been proponents
of radical policies while in India. Back in Britain they tried to place the

[140] (moderate) nationalist view of Indian affairs before politicians and the public. To this end, they championed greater Indian political participation; the Indianisation of the ICS; the extension of agricultural credit through co-operative banks; and the rights of Indian immigrants in the Transvaal and Natal. They also called for the reduction of government land tax, and for the 'proper' control of military policy on India's North-West frontier.

In 1893 the BCINC set up an Indian Parliamentary Committee (IPC). For much of its history this body was frustrated by the irregular and restricted nature of debate on India in the British parliament. However, having been reconstituted in 1906 with a membership of 192 MPs (the active core was far smaller), the IPC's persistence finally paid off in 1908–10 during a controversy surrounding the deportation of nine Bengali subjects accused of terrorism.[77] Not even the India Office was able to stand in its way. The IPC joined hands with Frederick Mackarness MP – a barrister who had taken up the cause of Indian civil liberties – to draw attention to the methods being used by the Government of India to combat political extremism, in particular suspension of the judicial process and restrictions placed on public meetings and the press. It sent a protest memorial to the Prime Minister signed by 146 MPs. Watching this 'pretty heavy gale' blow up among his parliamentary colleagues, the Secretary of State, John Morley, lost patience with his Viceroy, Lord Minto, and told him that the sentences were outrageous and would have to be quashed. The deportees were released in February 1910. The BCINC and its retired ICS officials had been the catalyst for this extraordinary campaign.

It would be wrong, however, to judge the political repercussions of imperialism solely in terms of expatriate communities or colonial officials. There are other dimensions of imperial politics that were more progressive. The later-Victorian and Edwardian years saw the emergence of an extra-parliamentary movement comprising the Emigration Committee of the Royal Colonial Institute, the Navy League, the Primrose League, the Tariff Reform League, and the Victoria League – groups which not only put the empire at the centre of their political creed but paved the way for a more open, lively and participatory form of politics. Key to understanding this point is an appreciation of what was happening to the party caucuses, or mass party organisations, at this time.[78] Rather than ushering in a new phase of democratic politics, they actually fashioned a more controlled and structured political environment dominated by the provincial urban bourgeoisie. The failure of the party caucuses to absorb growing concerns about the empire provided much of the impetus for the proliferation of imperial pressure groups at the turn of the century. Several of these pioneered new types of political agitation and new techniques of political mobilisation.[79] Take, for example, the Tariff Reform League. Its local branches covered the length and breadth of the country, and they took up the cause of working-class parliamentary candidates more enthusiastically than any other part of the Edwardian Unionist party – such were the funds at the League's disposal that party managers saw it as a direct threat. The same dynamism and capacity to innovate characterised the Empire Crusade of 1929–31. The power of the popular press and a raft of novel campaigning and fund-raising techniques were harnessed to Beaverbrook's lifelong passion – complete free trade within the empire in agriculture as well as manufacturing.[80]

Many imperialists, therefore, far from fighting shy of popular politics actually adopted an evangelical, crusading approach to their causes, breathing new life into old methods (pamphleteering, stumping, sandwich-board men), exploiting new technologies (the new journalism, the gramophone, the cinematograph), and displaying a sharp eye for the striking gesture (Arthur Pearson's 'fiscal parrot show' organised through the offices of the *Daily Express* is my particular favourite). In other words, imperial campaigning struck deep roots into civil society and embraced areas of the nation's political life that the conventional party caucuses were struggling to reach. This does not mean that imperialists mobilised huge numbers of ordinary working-class people – but who else other than the Chartists, trade unionists (and perhaps the temperance activists) did? Rather it means that the many different causes that imperialists championed appealed across class, gender and (sometimes) party lines, and that they made a significant contribution to the reconstitution of the 'low' political sphere in later-Victorian and Edwardian Britain.

Of particular note here is the way in which, in Britain as in Germany, various imperial societies broadened the social basis of politics by involving many more women.[81] Some of these societies were run by and for women – the Victoria League, the Girls' Friendly Society and the various emigration groups. Others, including the Navy League and the Tariff Reform League, formed women's auxiliaries affiliated to the male-dominated parent body but constantly trying to widen the scope of their work. Either way, they are testimony to just how deeply embedded imperialism became in the lives of many upper-middle-class and aristocratic women.[82] Two good examples are Violet Brooke-Hunt and Lady Louisa Knightley. Driven by a mixture of religious conscience and imperial sympathy both women displayed formidable energy and organisational talents. They certainly did

[142] not look to men to take the lead. Neither did they fight shy of platform appearances. Brooke-Hunt earned the respect of the male leadership of the tariff reform campaign (no easy task). Knightley rose rapidly through the ranks of the Primrose League and established herself as a key player in the Edwardian migration movement.[83] To that extent, they challenged the practical and ideological constraints placed on women's activism and acclimatised at least some men to women's participation in politics.

So much for the 'lady imperialists', some of whom supported the campaign for women's suffrage, some of whom did not. Imperialist ideologies were also articulated for explicitly feminist purposes.[84] 'Lady imperialists' were predominantly concerned with the self-governing dominions, but for 'imperial feminists' the non-white empire loomed large. India, in particular, occupied a privileged position in feminist thought, galvanising pro-suffrage women into new forms of political activity.[85] For many years upper-class women had embraced their special mission to the downtrodden and the poor in Britain. From the 1860s this domestic mission was then extended to the 'Indian woman' who was regarded as passive and helpless and utterly dependent on her British sisters for emancipation. Mary Carpenter took up the cause of Indian girls' education and lobbied against child marriage, while Josephine Butler campaigned for the repeal of the Contagious Diseases Acts, first in England and later in India. Where Carpenter and Butler led the way, other feminist groups followed. In fact, well into the twentieth century figures like Nancy Astor and Eleanor Rathbone continued to champion the rights of Indian women and to take responsibility for their welfare.[86] According to recent writing, the main motive behind this apparently selfless concern for the suffering Indian female was actually to show British women's fitness for political rights and to secure their own inclusion in the British state.

A neglected aspect of women's politics is their anti-imperial involvement. Critics of empire have long fascinated historians, yet there are few studies of women's place in anti-colonial movements. One historian once referred to their 'increasing prominence' in the campaign against the South African War, but there has been no systematic analysis of their role.[87] Several prominent women protested against this conflict – Catherine Courtney, Isabella Ford, Katharine Bruce Glasier, Alice Stopford Green, Emmeline Pankhurst, Ellen Robinson and, most famously, Emily Hobhouse. Meanwhile, the South African Conciliation Committee relied on a large group of lesser-known female helpers, especially in the London area. The Women's Liberal Federation also frequently debated the war. Initially it argued for the justice of British military intervention. By 1901, however, it had passed a resolution denouncing the British government's demand for unconditional surrender [143] by a majority of three to one.[88] Some of these criticisms were fuelled by women's religious beliefs (especially the Quakers), some by humanitarian concerns (especially for the Boer women and children in the camps), some by political ideology (pacifist and Irish nationalist), and some by personal connection (family and husbands who opposed the war).

The Congo Reform campaign owed much to the courage and persistence of one particular woman – Alice Harris – and to her husband the Reverend John Harris.[89] Together they had worked for the Congo Bololo mission since 1896. Having been harassed and intimidated by officials of the Anglo-Belgian Indian Rubber Company, they returned to Britain on furlough in 1905 with photographs of mutilated bodies of Africans taken by Alice (including one of a child's severed hand and foot). They immediately set about mobilising support for the Congo Reform Association by embarking on a national speaking tour, targeted mainly at the churches. Their 'atrocity meetings' drew public attention to King Leopold's sanctioning of slavery, and to the exploitation of African labour by the various concessionaire companies that accompanied the growth of the Belgian rubber industry from the mid-1890s. They were incredibly successful. Approximately two dozen CRA auxiliaries were formed, stretching the length of the country from Plymouth to Edinburgh. Nineteen of these survived to stir up local interest in the Congo over several years. It was the swan song of the nonconformist conscience in Britain.

Between the wars the sources of inspiration for women's anti-colonial activism, much of which was now centred on tropical Africa, gradually began to shift.[90] Humanitarians and abolitionists like Ruth Fry and Anna Graves were joined by a new generation of female ethical socialists (Rita Hinden, Winifred Holtby, Vera Britain, Diana Stock and Ellen Wilkinson MP); by a group of women who fell under the spell of Mahatma Gandhi (Muriel Lester and Madeleine Slade in India; Charlotte Despard in Britain);[91] by the small British Communist Party in which women had a strong voice (the 1927 International Women's Day celebrations centred on the necessity of defeating British imperialism);[92] and by a handful of black women activists (Una Marson, Eslanda Goode Robeson, Amy Ashwood Garvey) resident in Britain in the 1930s. Influenced by the First World War, and inspired by Edwardian feminism, these middle- and upper-class women visited the colonies, formed societies and worked closely with black male activists. It is claimed that they helped 'to bring a more critical perspective on race and imperial issues on to the agenda of the "chattering classes" of the 1930s'. They had far less interest in colonial women's

[144] welfare than Edwardian imperial feminists. Nonetheless, their gender was arguably significant in so far as it may have helped them to sympathise with the downtrodden and oppressed.[93]

Welfare policy was another way in which progressive ideas were transferred from the colonies to Britain. Hobson thought that imperialism and social reform were 'an inherent opposition of policy involving contradictory methods and processes of government'.[94] Yet this view required him to define 'imperialism' narrowly as territorial rule in the tropics. In reality, the advance of public welfare and the growth of the empire were in several respects mutually reinforcing. From the early 1900s, Liberal and Tory imperialists recognised the need for a healthy and expanding home population if Britain's imperial supremacy was to be maintained.[95] By harmonising the fiscal system of colonial and metropolitan economies, Joseph Chamberlain and the tariff reformers planned to generate the revenue required for social reforms. Others looked toward emigration as a solution to domestic difficulties; it was hoped that schemes of rural resettlement would rescue those living in urban squalor and expand markets for British exports, especially if migrants were kept within the empire rather than 'lost' to foreign lands.

Colonial precedents in social reform were important too.[96] In 1896 the future British Prime Minister, H. H. Asquith, described New Zealand as 'a laboratory in which political and social experiments are every day being made for the information and instruction of the older countries of the world'.[97] Liberalism flourished in New Zealand from 1891 to 1912 as the machinery of government was expanded to tackle the socio-economic problems of the day.[98] The colony prided itself on the progress it had made,[99] in particular in the realm of old age pensions and compulsory arbitration. Australia's attractions have already been referred to in the context of changing working-class attitudes to emigration (pp. 56–7) and will be explored further in the next chapter (pp. 156–8). Suffice to say that a variety of factors gave rise to the notion of Australia as a 'working man's paradise': the absence of workhouses; the provision of state-funded education; the protection afforded to employees; a relatively large sector of public workers; and tariff protection – although the pull of each of these varied considerably over time.[100] Labour legislation was an aspect of Australian public policy in which there was an ongoing interest; the British Trade Boards Act (1909) – which established boards of employers, employees and government nominees in order to fix wages in certain 'sweated' industries – was directly influenced by Australian precedent. Advocates of state

action in Britain borrowed the idea of wages boards from the colony of
Victoria and pored over the Victorian evidence in an effort to master their
subject. According to one scholar, the Trade Boards Act 'represented the
most explicit attempt to imitate a colonial example'.[101]

There were also special bonds between the British and colonial labour
movements.[102] These have already been explored in the South African
context (pp. 69–74), but the 'Britishness' of labour activists in Canada,
Australia and New Zealand needs to be emphasised as well. Many originated from Britain. They read British labour journals. They corresponded
with British labour leaders. They even returned home to renew the roots of
their radicalism.[103] Yet they firmly believed that the 'mother country' had
something to learn from them. Take Australia's donations to the London
dock strike in 1889. They were partly motivated by sympathy with British
kin, partly by pride in Australia's prosperity and democratic egalitarianism,
and partly by pleasure in 'role reversal' – the following year a new silk
banner showed a grateful English worker shaking hands with his Australian brother.[104]

British labour leaders, meanwhile, were determined that Britain should
not fall behind the self-governing colonies. Thus Philip Snowden rejected
the idea that Britain's heavier spending commitments invalidated New
Zealand precedents: 'we as an old established country should be able to
do what is impossible for a new country . . . to undertake.'[105] Dominion
visitors to London helped disseminate developments in colonial welfare
policy (the New Zealand Agent-General, William Pember Reeves, was a
key figure in this respect), yet it was the visits of British labour leaders to
the colonies that probably mattered most. The Webbs' journey to Australia
and New Zealand is of interest here. Sidney was intrigued by the way the
Australian colonies – 'an adult Anglo-Saxon Democracy' – had adopted
manhood suffrage, vote by ballot, payment of MPs and the like, without
any of the negative political consequences associated with such measures in
America: 'No wonder that we continue to ignore Australia – it might teach
us too much.'[106] For Beatrice it was New Zealand that had the stronger
appeal: 'taken all in all if I had to bring up a family outside of Great Britain
I would choose New Zealand as its home'.[107] Two years prior to the Webbs'
arrival in 1898 the first wages boards had been established in Victoria,
while New Zealand had recently enacted the Industrial Conciliation and
Arbitration Act (1894), a piece of legislation in which they took a particular
interest in view of their campaign for state regulation in this field. How
much the Webbs' 'conversion' to liberal imperialism owed to their Antipodean experiences is a moot point – political opportunism was responsible

[146]   too (see below).[108] Moreover, the main impulse to the growth of public welfare in Britain was undeniably domestic. Pressure from the professional classes; middle-class self-interest and religious scruples; the call of voluntary societies for targeted measures of state intervention; and threats to working-class respectability – these are the primary explanations of mounting social expenditure from the late nineteenth century.[109] That said, the Webbs' concern for social reform should not be divorced from their knowledge of what was happening in the colonial world. Nor were they alone. John Burns, H. H. Champion, Will Crooks, Ben Tillett, Tom Mann, Ramsay MacDonald and Keir Hardie – all these figures visited the dominions in the early twentieth century. Part of their reason for making these journeys was to promote wider working-class co-operation; Tillett, especially, looked to the British labour movement to develop a 'true imperial consciousness'.[110] Moreover, British socialists and labour leaders were clearly convinced that these experiments in social democracy had something to teach them about solving the social and economic problems of modern capitalism in Britain.[111]

Conceptions of the state

Party electioneering, pressure group and press activity, debates on the constitution, the development of social welfare, and the *Weltanschauung* of ministers and officials – in each of these spheres the effects of the empire on the British political scene are now being taken more seriously. Yet there has been relatively little reflection on how politicians formulated their views about the empire. Why did it get under the skin of some but not others? The final section of this chapter will argue that a belief in government was as important as a belief in the empire *per se*. From the 1860s onwards, the imperatives of imperial expansion and consolidation conspired not only to promote a wider conception of the role of the British state, but to pinpoint policy areas where increased activity was required and even to suggest the form it might take.

This is not to deny that there were other factors conditioning politicians' imperial attitudes. Those born in the colonies but who later resettled in Britain did not easily forget their roots. Canada, for example, produced three of parliament's most committed imperialists. *Vanity Fair*'s 'Member for Greater Britain', Sir Horatio Gilbert Parker, heralded from Ontario where his mother's family had strong connections with the United Empire Loyalists. Perhaps more famous now for his best-selling historical novels (many of which had a colonial setting), Gilbert Parker spearheaded the pro-Milner

propaganda body, the Imperial South Africa Association.[112] Max Aitken (Lord
Beaverbrook) was born in New Brunswick, a Maritime province which
'looked naturally to the old country' (Halifax to Liverpool was one of the
great sea routes).[113] Aitken's desire to strengthen the bonds of empire drew
him to the fight for tariff reform. Even the Tory leader and Prime Minister,
Andrew Bonar Law, regarded as an intensely practical businessman, was
not immune to the appeal of imperial sentiment. Having returned to Scotland
from New Brunswick, he subsequently made his money in the Glasgow
iron trade. Yet according to his latest biographer Canada 'was always close
to Bonar Law's heart': 'he wished with all sincerity that [it] should remain
joined by spiritual as well as economic and imperial links to Britain'.[114]

Politicians previously employed as colonial administrators naturally tended
to spend more of their time thinking about imperial problems. James Mill
will be considered below. Here two further examples must suffice. Neither
became an MP, though both men stood unsuccessfully for parliament –
they were part of the politically active intelligentsia rather than professional
politicians. The authoritarian liberal, James Fitzjames Stephen, was the
legal member of the Viceroy's Council in India from 1869 to 1872, and
then returned to England determined to defend the Raj: 'I do not envy the
Englishman whose heart does not beat high as he looks at the scarred and
shattered walls of Delhi or at the union jack flying from the fort at Lahore.'[115]
Stephen saw the use of force as necessary to the creation of a civilised social
order in India and firmly believed in the superiority of the British as the
'conquering race'. Leonard Woolf's spell in Ceylon (1904–12) had a rather
different effect. Entering the colony as an imperialist, he left the service
disaffected and disillusioned – the interests of the metropolitan economy
and local settlers seemed consistently to have been placed before those
of the 'native' population. He later became secretary of the Labour party's
Advisory Committee on Imperial Questions, 'a radical lobby advocating
gradual but far-reaching reform leading to self-government'.[116]

Visits to the colonies could be influential too. Salisbury's travels in South
Africa, Australia and New Zealand in 1851–3 helped to persuade him of
the necessity of responsible government for the settler colonies.[117] Dilke
and Rosebery returned from the dominions in 1866–7 and 1883–4,
respectively, infused with grand ideas of imperial union. The ten months
spent by the Irish nationalist, John Redmond, in Australia and New Zealand in 1883 instilled in him 'a new and enduring appreciation of the difficulties that confronted Irish immigrants in a colonial context'; they also
helped him to raise nearly £15,000 for the National League.[118] Keir Hardie's
(1907) and Ramsay MacDonald's (1909) visits to India laid the foundations

[148] for their subsequent interest in Indian problems and their support of the moderate wing of Congress,[119] while the publication of Ramsay Muir's *The Making of British India 1756–1858* (1915) was preceded by a lecture tour of the subcontinent the previous year.[120] Harold Wilson's journey to see his family in Western Australia in 1926 certainly made a lasting impression. He was only 10, but returned to school in Milnsbridge near Huddersfield to regale teachers and classmates with stories of his adventures. In the view of one of his biographers, 'it is possible to believe Wilson's later claim that his sympathy for the Commonwealth idea began with his early experience in Australia'.[121] R. A. Butler and Stanley Baldwin saw parts of the empire in 1926–7. Rab took in India, Australia, Canada and New Zealand, and was persuaded of the strength of the ties binding together an Anglophile political elite, the necessity for some form of imperial protection and that Britain's future lay in the Commonwealth rather than Europe.[122] Baldwin was the first serving Prime Minister to travel to an overseas dominion – Canada. The trip reinforced his Seeleyite conception of the empire; India was secondary to Baldwin's imperial outlook and would hardly have attracted his attention had it not been such a divisive issue from 1929 to 1935.[123] This was not true of H. N. Brailsford, however. He was a 'staunch advocate of Indian liberation', but wrote surprisingly little about the Raj before 1930. It was only after a visit to India during the civil disobedience of that year that Brailsford became convinced that the time was ripe for self-government and took up the role of spokesman for the nationalist cause.[124]

Education may also explain some politicians' imperial involvement. A large proportion of Tory 'diehards' were educated at public school, in particular at Eton where Edmund Warre (headmaster, 1884–1905) strove to cultivate a sense of patriotic and imperial duty. Another important institution was Haileybury College. Founded by the East India Company in 1806, and reopened as a public school in the 1860s, Haileybury was imbued with the tradition of imperial service. It supplied many ICS recruits and was closely involved with St John's College in Agra.[125] The 'imperial-ist ardour' of the young Attlee owed something to the atmosphere at Haileybury.[126] Attlee later recalled a map hung on the school wall with large portions painted red: 'it was an intoxicating vision for a young boy'.[127] The universities were important, too. For Cambridge undergraduates, Sir John Seeley's famous 'Expansion of England' lectures (1881–2) caused a great stir. Stanley Baldwin, Austen Chamberlain and Leo Maxse all fell under Seeley's spell. At Oxford the influence of the imperial connection was, if anything, even stronger.[128] All Souls College earned a reputation as

'the spiritual home of the British empire'. A 'Rhodes–Milner group' was [149]
clearly identifiable in the college – they even celebrated an All Souls gaudy
in Johannesburg in 1907.[129]

Yet while it would clearly be foolish to ignore these various personal
influences – birth, occupation, travel and education – either separately or
in combination, they are not in themselves a sufficient explanation of
why such a diverse body of politicians became imperially involved. More
fundamentally, the empire affected how the British chose to govern themselves. It did so by providing a spur to theoretical reflection on the proper
powers and purposes of the British state. In the nineteenth century,
non-interventionist liberal government faced some of its most serious and
sustained challenges from the empire, both theoretically in terms of the
'imperial political economy' evolved by protectionist Tories, and practically
in terms of how state-managed schemes of labour and investment from post-
emancipation West Indies and post-Mutiny India worked their way back to
Britain via Ireland during Lord Salisbury's administration of 1895–1902.[130]
At the end of our period similar processes were still at work. Hence debates
about planning and development during the Second World War need to
be set in their wider colonial context: 'the important role being projected
for the state in Britain's post-war reconstruction was matched, and even
surpassed, by expectations of a re-born, reinvigorated colonial state'.[131] And
the decline of public ownership after 1945 is at least partly to be explained
in terms of the downfall of the empire overseas. As Britain divested itself
of its colonies, so the state began to lose much of its authority and 'the
mystique of the detached public servant' was thereby discredited.[132]

Here it is vital to appreciate that imperialism gave rise not to one but
several interventionist ideologies: utilitarian-imperial, constructive-imperial
and social(ist)-imperial – the latter hardly a single doctrine, but a composite
of Fabian-style welfare-paternalism, Mosleyite protectionism and the white
colonial labourism explored in Chapter 3.[133] Two aspects of these ideologies merit further consideration: the part they played in forging the British
state's identity, and the part they played in delineating its boundaries.

Let us take the issue of identity first. The British state has been described
as the child as well as the parent of the empire: 'the grandeurs and servitudes
of empire were of its very essence; and the same grandeurs and servitudes
inevitably shaped the identity it claimed to embody.'[134] This so-called 'Whig
Imperialist' vision was based on the notion of the British as a uniquely
global and freedom-loving people; it is said to have shaped the mentality
of the entire political class, Left as well as Right. Politicians imagined the
British state not just as a piece of territory or a framework of administration,

[150]   but as a genuine community of people tied together by common sentiments and traditions, a shared sense of purpose and a collective memory. Such an understanding of the state can be traced back at least as far as Sir John Seeley's *Expansion of England* lectures: 'men should conceive themselves as belonging, and belonging in such an intimate and momentous union, to a corporation which is not simply the family'.[135] Seeley's 'corporation' comprised not only the British Isles but a wider Britannic 'federation': 'our Empire is not an Empire at all in the ordinary sense of the word. It does not consist of a congeries of nations held together by force, but in the main one nation, as much as if it were no Empire but an ordinary state.'[136]

What is interesting about this 'imperial whiggism' is that it had multiple political expressions. It was, of course, at the heart of the ideology of the constructive imperialists for whom tariff reform was as much a question of national character as it was of national wealth. It was an important source of workers' political culture, too. Their ideology of 'white labourism' was premised on a strong sense of solidarity among skilled labour at home and abroad, in particular their shared interest in maintaining the so-called 'colour bar' – a special racial status for whites. Such was the stance taken by William Royce Stapleton, Labour MP from 1918 to 1924.[137] Stapleton left England for South Africa in 1876 having accepted a free passage and three-year labour contract from the Cape Colony. He was employed to train and supervise African labour laying a railway line from East London to Queenstown. At the end of his contract he went into the construction business, eventually establishing a permanent base in England but shuttling back and forth to manage projects in South Africa until the outbreak of the Boer War. His South African experience led him initially to stand as a Conservative parliamentary candidate; he defected to Labour in 1918, dropping his support for tariffs while continuing to support the policy of segregation, especially in the sphere of labour. Royce had little sympathy for the internationalism and egalitarianism of some of his parliamentary colleagues, and was a stout defender of Milner's record as Colonial Secretary. In 1922 he became the first chairman of the Labour party's Commonwealth Group. Two years later, during a debate on the treatment of Chinese workers on the Pacific island of Nauru, he gave full vent to his feelings:

> It seems to me that the nigger or the Chinaman is looked upon as somebody who ought to be preserved, while we intend to take no care of our own people. We import Chinese into this country, they enter into competition with our own people, and they are a source of trouble to our social order. We are quite unconscious of what is going on under our nose.

Not long after this intervention, Ramsay MacDonald offered Royce the Governorship of Tasmania, though he died before he could accept the post. Far from being foisted on them by their capitalist 'superiors', therefore, loyalist and imperialist values would seem to have emanated from within the ranks of British workers.

As well as helping to forge the identity of the British state, the empire influenced and informed debates on advancing state power. Take, for example, John Stuart Mill. His justification of empire was based on the concept of 'tutelage' or 'parentage': Britain was in India to facilitate its transition to a higher stage of civilisation and to prepare Indians for representative institutions. The argument for presently denying Indians such political rights was exactly the same as it was for the propertyless, the uneducated and women at home: they were not in a sufficiently advanced state.[138] And yet recent writing on Mill's political thought detects influences flowing in the opposite direction. In particular, Mill's enthusiastic advocacy of land reform in Britain has been linked to his Indian administrative experience. To build a peasant economy in India, Mill observed, the English had overcome their superstitions about private property and the state. Revenue assessments were made directly with individual cultivators or with village authorities that then dealt with the peasants themselves.[139] Though Mill's views on this subject were formulated as early as the 1840s, he was later influenced by Henry Maine's *Village-Communities in the East and West*, published in 1871. Mill's efforts to lessen aristocratic control of land in Britain – especially his work with the Land Tenure Reform Association – owed much to his Indian experience and to his reading of Maine.[140] Together they led him to an appreciation of the village community 'as a seemingly ancient and stable element in Indian society', and of the advantages of peasant proprietorship over great estates. This, in turn, gave Mill the confidence to challenge the antiquity and universality of domestic feudal property rights. Britain had once had village communities like those in India, and what she had once possessed could now be restored.

Later in the nineteenth century, parallels can be drawn between New Liberal arguments for government action in the domestic and the imperial spheres.[141] Progressives justified state intervention at home in terms of enhancing individual liberty. Similarly, their cardinal test of colonial state activity was whether it served to further the freedoms of subject peoples, or whether it merely exploited them and retarded their self-development.[142] Hence the Fabian Society embraced the empire (albeit opportunistically) as a vehicle for socialist planning. Specifically, George Bernard Shaw and the Webbs looked to the imperial ideal to help advance their notion of a

[152] 'national minimum' – a country-wide standard of living below which no imperially-minded government could afford to allow its citizens to fall. They also argued in favour of wresting the South African goldmines from the hands of speculators and financiers (whom they held responsible for the outbreak of hostilities) and bringing them into public ownership.[143]

Oswald Mosley (Labour MP, 1926 to 1931) was another figure in the labour movement who tried to harness imperial ideas to his developing political vision. From the mid-1920s Mosley wished to realise the empire's latent wealth. He saw in the colonies a way of insulating the home market from the instabilities of the world economy and the immense power of American industry.[144] His goal was an autarchic Commonwealth bloc that recognised the necessity of state power over the capitalist economy. In practice this meant that government was to take responsibility for planning, allocating and regulating trade through a combination of credit controls, tariffs and import boards.[145] Royce's 'social-imperialism' was of a different hue. Whereas Mosley abandoned free trade in favour of his own rather idiosyncratic version of protection,[146] Royce travelled in the opposite direction. He fought (as a Tory) on a tariff reform platform in 1910, but proclaimed himself a free trader as a Labour candidate in 1923. However, Royce's lifelong concern with national and social efficiency was clearly Milnerite in inspiration, and led him to support state-controlled housing schemes, land reform, the expansion of education and public works – all as a contribution to post-war reconstruction. Meanwhile, his South African experience may explain why he was prepared to advocate public owner-ship of coal mining and railways but not of any other sector of British industry.

Above all, however, it was fiscal forms of state power that were most responsive to what was happening in the empire. The whole edifice of the nineteenth century 'fiscal constitution' was at first sustained and subsequently sunk by Britain's colonial relationships.[147] The Victorian state passed on the costs of central government not only to the localities but to the colonies too. But by the later nineteenth century this process of devolving expend-iture to its supposed beneficiaries started to falter. This was partly because of concerns for peace and stability: the transfer of colonial tax revenues to Britain was an open goal to nationalists looking to exploit popular griev-ances. It was also a consequence of the South African War, the bill for which had put huge pressure on the national finances and stretched the existing Peelite and Gladstonian fiscal system to its limits. In this way, the task of subjugating the two Boer Republics was to force a reassessment of the entire structure of government revenue.

One solution to this emerging financial crisis was to raise more money [153] through customs duties. This was the preferred method of the construc- tive imperialists who more than any other group of British politicians were intent on expanding the fiscal forms of state power. They looked specific- ally to preferential tariffs to consolidate Britain's colonial relationships and to forge stable and permanent markets for metropolitan and dominion producers. Under free trade, they argued, the United Kingdom had been turned into a cosmopolitan clearing-house for money and goods, while the resources of the empire had been shamefully neglected. What was required was creative and dynamic government – the antithesis of Salisbury's quietist domestic policy and cautious negativism in foreign affairs – and the active implementation of policies aimed at enhancing imperial unity. Constructive imperialists were especially critical of free traders' search for immediate profits. They insisted that the state had a duty to act on behalf of wider communal rather than narrowly individual interests.[148] Government was to be guided not by a philosophy of *laissez-faire* but by *vouloir-faire* (the will to act) and *savoir-faire* (the knowledge to act).[149] Contemporary international developments were an influence on their thinking: state-building in Europe and the expansion of frontiers in Russia and the USA seemed to show the necessity of organising on a larger scale.[150] Social Darwinist theory and evolutionary thought were important too, at least in so far as they sug- gested that states on the old scale of magnitude were insignificant, unsafe and essentially obsolete, or at least destined to become so. Finally, German historical economics, which inspired many of the members of the Com- patriots Club – the intellectual powerhouse of constructive imperialism – confirmed the empire as the only resource base 'which could match the territorial and material advantages of Britain's major rivals'.[151] For all of these reasons new fiscal powers (in the form of preferential tariffs) were felt to be essential: only then would it be possible to make a reality of Seeley's vision of a 'Greater Britain'.

Conclusion

Politicians' views on the empire were conditioned by a variety of (poten- tially conflicting) concerns. The desire for low taxation through economies in public spending had to be weighed against the need to maintain Britain's position and prestige as a world power. Moralistic and humanitarian con- siderations vied with moves to open new markets and expand interna- tional trade. The empire, moreover, could climb rapidly up the political

[154] agenda when it was yoked to 'wider if more diffuse domestic anxieties and discontents'.[152] Precisely how these concerns played with different types of politician depended, to an extent, on their own personal upbringing and experiences. It also depended on their beliefs about the appropriate size and scope of the British state. As we have seen, the languages involved in defining the purpose of the state were themselves shot through with imperial idioms and imperatives. India was not unimportant here, and there was no one attitude or approach to imperial power. Nevertheless, for much of our period the concept of a 'British world' did tend to dominate debate. It evoked a range of emotions and responses from across the social and political spectrum. Implicitly, at least, many of these responses were racialised – the Aboriginal Australians, New Zealand Maori and Canadian Innuit were rarely mentioned by the ideologues of this global imperial identity. Yet Britain's 'manifest destiny' to rule non-European peoples was not nearly as pervasive or prominent a political discourse as often assumed. For sure, domestic politics was never impervious to what was happening in the dependent empire, especially when it involved the sanctioning of martial law and the use of armed force. During the Morant Bay uprising, the Ilbert Bill controversy and the Amritsar massacre the empire did 'strike back' on the British political scene. Even on these occasions, however, there is little evidence to suggest that the harsher and more militaristic side of colonial rule constituted a serious or sustained threat to liberal and progressive values or to widening political participation in Britain. Indeed, in the fashioning of a more democratic political culture, the empire arguably proved as much of a friend as a foe.

CHAPTER 7

METROPOLITAN ECONOMICS

This chapter pursues two related lines of enquiry, one regarding the empire's effects on the distribution of wealth within Britain, the other regarding its significance for the long-term performance of the British economy. In the first place the question of who benefited from the possession of an overseas empire has long exercised historians and it is fundamental to this study. What economic opportunities did Britain's older settler colonies or newly-acquired tropical dependencies offer to entrepreneurs, investors and migrants? How far did the British consumer benefit from cheaper colonial sources of supply? Conversely, how big was the bill for imperial defence and (just as importantly) who footed it? A second strand of enquiry concerns the growth and diversification of the British economy. Was imperial expansion a source of strength or weakness to Britain, either in terms of finance or trade? Some scholars see the empire as the motor for the most dynamic element of the British economy – the service sector; others see it as a welcome refuge for British business from the pressures of international competition. Thus it is important to look at the British economy from several overlapping perspectives. The first section of this chapter examines the movement of people – migration is a factor frequently overlooked in the balance sheet of empire debates. The second and third sections turn to the movement of money and goods; the former the subject of a large and complex body of historiography, the latter referred to widely in the literature, yet mainly in terms of trade flows (much less has been said about the behaviour of colonial consumers or the nature of empire markets). The final section of the chapter considers the cost of the empire's defence requirements, and balances this against the colonies' contribution to Britain's military effort during the First World War.

At several points this book has questioned the view that the empire had a negligible influence on Britain's domestic history. But what follows offers qualified support for the 'minimal impact' thesis by showing that Britain's

[156] economic position was neither substantially improved nor materially weakened by the possession of an overseas empire. It will be argued that while imperialism may have had vast economic consequences for the extra-European world, it did not fundamentally change Britain's own economy. Only in times of crisis was the idea of a closed imperial economy seriously entertained; for most of our period Britain was confident in its ability to compete as an industrial and financial power on the world stage.[1] To that extent, the 'minimal impact' thesis is not without its merits. The mistake has been to apply the same framework of analysis to the empire's effects on British society and politics.

Migrants

Although migration was woven into the fabric of British life, the empire's significance as a region of labour mobility must not be exaggerated: many people migrated beyond its boundaries in pursuit of their economic, social and personal goals.[2] That said, the opportunity to emigrate was probably among the biggest benefits of empire; and it was a benefit available to all classes of society, not just elites.[3] Of the 9.7 million who migrated from Britain from 1853 to 1920, 2.3 million went to Canada, 1.7 million to Australia and New Zealand, and 671,500 to South Africa.

A leading historian of empire migration maintains that it was inspired by the vision of 'building Britain's greatness o'er the foam'.[4] Indeed, several scholars depict the colonies as societies with familiar cultural values to which people from Britain felt they could more easily transfer.[5] There was also a remarkable freedom of entry to the British imperial world; only the sick, the criminal, the politically dangerous and those likely to become a public charge were refused.[6] In the later nineteenth century about a third of migrants chose colonial territories over the United States; from 1901 to 1910, the proportion increased to about a half. It was as high as four-fifths shortly after the end of the Second World War, although the total number of migrants had declined significantly by then.[7]

For mid-Victorian migrants, Canada was the most popular destination – Australia struggled to escape its image as a 'convict colony' and, along with New Zealand, suffered from the fact that it took longer and cost more to get there. Later-Victorian migrants ventured further afield. The termination of transportation to the eastern Australian colonies; the Antipodean gold strikes; the opening of the Suez Canal; and the state subsidies offered by the governments of New Zealand, Queensland and South Australia – all these helped would-be migrants to widen their horizons.[8] Thus well before the United States' imposition of immigration quotas in 1921, and the financial support provided by the Empire Settlement Act from 1922, the percentage of people leaving Britain for America rather than the empire was already falling. In 1920, 90,811 people chose the USA (26% of total migration); 134,079 Canada (38%); 29,019 South Africa (8%); 49,357 Australasia (14%); and 49,545 'other places' (14%). By 1935–8, 82.7% of the 103,860 emigrants leaving Britain were heading for the empire.[9]

Migrants were drawn from all echelons of British society. The 'labouring poor' took advantage of various forms of private emigration aid, trade-union subsidies and labour contracts.[10] They also received charitable help from a plethora of emigration societies. The Salvation Army led the way here. In pursuit of its goal of rehabilitating the 'submerged tenth' of the British population, the SA became the largest emigration agency in the British empire, selecting colonists, supervising their relocation and securing them work. By 1930 it had helped some 200,000 working-class men and women to migrate, the vast majority going to Canada. Skilled workers, meanwhile, made their own way to the colonies, increasingly with the benefit of a remittance from a friend or relative who was already there. In Australia, the building of reservoirs, roads, railways and bridges put the skills of English workers in general at a premium, while copper smelting and gold-mining relied specifically on the technical knowledge and experience of migrants from Cornwall and Wales.[11] In addition, there was a surge of career migrants – bureaucrats, missionaries, bankers, accountants, journalists, nurses, doctors, planters, policemen and the like. As Chapter 1 showed, the empire opened up opportunities for a variety of official and professional employment. The structural shift that occurred in the dominions' economies from the early 1900s, and the resulting diversification of their labour needs, made them highly attractive destinations to the urban middle classes in Britain.[12]

The social and economic advantages of empire migration were multiple. Real wages and rates of owner-occupation were higher in Australia and New Zealand than the UK, their climates were better, infant mortality was considerably lower, and there was probably the prospect of greater self-esteem.[13] Those who got in at the start of colonial expansion had a particularly good chance of bettering their position by emigration. For example, many people of humble origin who left Britain for New Zealand before 1870 became substantial rural property owners; they made up for their lack of capital with years of labour.[14] Nor was migration to the empire simply a bid for a better standard of living. It was often 'an assertion of individual freedom, a search for dignity and worth'.[15] Here it is worth recalling that,

[158] by the 1850s, five out of six Australian colonies had developed the secret ballot, more than ten years before it was introduced in the UK; universal manhood suffrage was established in Australia and New Zealand fifty years before it was established in Britain; New Zealand women gained the vote in 1893, a generation before their British sisters; and schools in the Australian colony of Victoria were 'secular, compulsory and free' well before their counterparts back home.[16] Yet notwithstanding these attractions, overseas migration was not always a positive experience,[17] and it continues to resist inclusion in imperial balance sheets – the complexity of motivations, the variety of destinations and the sheer range of possible repercussions all stand in the way of generalisations about the 'migrant experience'.

There is, however, a neglected aspect of the migration process that can be more readily quantified – remittances or 'migrapounds'. These are one-off and regular payments made by migrants to friends and relatives back home. No historian has yet published accurate figures for personal remittances to the British Isles.[18] By drawing on the Post Office archives and the Postmaster-General's *Annual Reports*, it is possible to piece together these private flows of capital from the colonies for the period from the mid-1850s until the outbreak of the First World War, after which the *Annual Reports* become *Commercial Reports* and no longer contain the necessary information.[19]

The main mechanism for such transfers was the money order. The first financial service supplied by the Post Office, money orders allowed for small amounts of cash to be sent through the mail. They were organised by the Money Order Office (1838), a separate and specialised department that had its origins in an officially sanctioned private business carried on from the late eighteenth century.[20] The office grew rapidly, and a limited overseas service was introduced in 1856 as a result of the Crimean War.[21] At the end of the decade orders were for the first time exchanged between Britain and Canada;[22] they then spread rapidly to many other parts of the empire.[23] By 1873, the money order service was in full operation between the United Kingdom and the majority of its colonies, India and Ceylon being the last to be added in that year.[24] In 1868, the first money order agreement was signed with a foreign country (Switzerland). Not until 1871, however, are colonial and foreign money orders accounted for separately in the Post Office's records.

For many years money orders were unreliable: numerous cases of incomplete addresses led to unnecessary delays and correspondence before payment could be made. A new application form introduced in 1873 improved their transmission. The number and value of money orders grew rapidly from this point. The year 1902 recorded the largest increase on

record: 19% in number and 23% in value, though some of this increase can
be put down to the end of the South African War and the resumption of
the service from the Transvaal.

In addition to money orders there was the postal note or order, introduced in 1881 by the Liberal politician and Postmaster-General, Henry
Fawcett.[25] Intended as a cheaper and simpler means of transmitting small
sums of money, postal orders were charged at a lower rate. They could be
cashed by the bearer on sight and made for varying amounts by affixing
the necessary postage stamps to the face of the order.[26] The postal order
service proved an immediate success: 4.5 million inland orders were purchased in 1882, 20 million in 1885 and nearly 90 million in 1900.[27] By
1905 the service extended throughout the empire;[28] Australia and Canada
organised their own systems, which were in effect an expansion of the
British. From 1900 to 1910, the value of postal orders from the colonies to
Britain grew annually at 8.5%. The figure would probably have been higher
but for the lack of publicity given to the scheme in the UK; the difficulties
involved in replenishing the colonies' stock of orders from London; and
the Post Office's initial failure to consult the colonial Postmasters-General
on their design.

There was a major injection of private capital into the British economy
from the colonies and foreign countries in the form of money and postal
orders. Figure 8 tracks the annual volumes of money orders received by the
UK from some of the major remitting countries in the decades prior to the

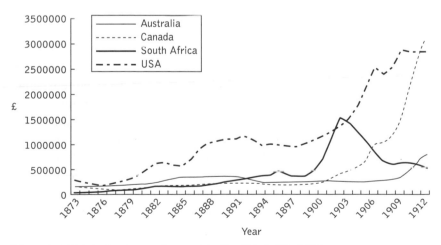

Figure 8   Value of money orders sent to the UK, 1873–1913
Source: Raw data taken from the *Postmaster General's Annual Reports*.

[160] First World War. The main sources of colonial remittances were Canada, South Africa, India, Australia and New Zealand. Canada always topped the table; the ranking of the others varied over time. The United States was by far the biggest sender of foreign money orders, partly reflecting the sheer number of British emigrants who went there, partly their tendency to send 'migrapounds' to relatives at home for their passage across the Atlantic.[29] In addition to the USA, foreign money orders were sent from France, Germany, Belgium, Holland, Egypt, Austria, Russia, Italy and Switzerland, roughly in that order of importance.

From the mid-1850s until the end of the 1870s the number of money orders received from the colonies was significantly larger than the number received from foreign countries. The gap then began to close. During the 1880s a higher rate of growth was achieved by money orders issued in foreign countries: 11% (by value) compared to 8% for the colonies. In 1886–7, foreign countries for the first time exceeded the colonies in terms of the number and value of money orders sent to the United Kingdom: 462,287 foreign orders (worth £1,210,620), compared to 301,739 colonial orders (worth £1,108,169). The balance remained in favour of foreign countries until 1912–13, when colonial remittances were valued by the Post Office at £5,188,000 and foreign at £4,570,000. This may have been the beginning of a new trend because the following year colonial money orders again exceeded those from foreign countries: £5,450,000 as against £4,672,000. Unfortunately the data then stops.

Tables A–E (see Appendix) show that the total value of colonial money orders was slightly higher than that of foreign money orders. It is important to set these figures in context. The £19,112,145 remitted from the colonies from 1856 to 1914 is equivalent to approximately 5% of total customs revenue collected during these years, while the £2,929,397 remitted in 1909–10 is equivalent to approximately 10% of that year's customs revenue. These are considerable sums of money. The true picture is, however, somewhat more complex for we need to take account of the number and value of orders issued in the UK and sent abroad. Interestingly, the outflow to foreign countries was consistently higher than the outflow to the colonies. From 1901 to 1910, £6.6 million of money orders left the United Kingdom for the colonies. The figure for foreign countries was over double this amount at £13.8 million. Colonial money orders to the UK during this decade amounted to £26,447,255, while those coming from foreign countries amounted to £28,246,896. This leaves a net (positive) balance of £19.8 million in the case of the colonies, and £14.5 million in the case of foreign countries. It is vital, therefore, to look at the movement of money orders in both directions. Not only was the total sum of money [161] privately remitted by the colonies somewhat higher than that remitted by foreign countries, the colonies appear to have siphoned off less private capital than foreign countries from the United Kingdom.

What was the impact of postal and telegraph orders? From 1895 to 1914, £105.5 million worth of postal orders were issued in the colonies and paid in the United Kingdom.[30] Technically speaking, the Imperial Postal Order Service was not inaugurated until 1 October 1904, though Malta and Gibraltar (under direct control of the Post Office) remitted money in this way from 1882, and sizeable sums of cash were sent back to Britain as postal orders from South Africa from 1901 to 1903. Postal orders were not exchanged between Britain and foreign countries. The sums remitted by telegraph orders were far smaller: they totalled only £1,470,795 for the years 1900–10. Business did not even commence with Canada and the United States until 1 January 1910, and proposals for extending the service to India, Ceylon, South Africa, Australia and New Zealand were still under consideration in 1913–14.[31] For present purposes telegraph orders can be discounted.[32]

The Post Office was a key mechanism for transferring private capital from the colonies back to Britain. Migrants who sent money or postal orders to their families in the UK did so because they had 'made good' and enjoyed relatively high standards of living. Hence remittances lend weight to the view that empire migration was economically advantageous to Britain. Yet was it any more advantageous than migration to foreign lands? The amount of colonial capital remitted to Britain was greater than that from foreign countries; the gap, however, closed over time. Table E (Appendix) records a balance of £249, 677 in the colonies' favour. But this is for 1873 when the money order service had just begun. Table C shows the rapid expansion of remittances from foreign countries during the next three decades. Of course, the real point of comparison is the United States – the only 'foreign' recipient of large numbers of migrants from Britain. The USA remitted £27.3 million worth of money orders to the UK from 1880 to 1914, and this equates to 65% of foreign money orders during these years. It seems likely, therefore, that the US migrant was remitting to Britain roughly equivalent sums of money to the colonial migrant; there was certainly no marked disparity. Similarly, if one looks at other aspects of the migration process – the resulting rise in living standards; the supply of foodstuffs to the UK; and export demand for the products of British industry – it is difficult to claim that empire migration did much more to foster British economic growth than migration from Britain to the United

[162] States. This point will be underscored when we examine the behaviour of colonial consumers below.

Money

To assess the empire's impact on the British economy, historians have compared the yield on money invested at home, in foreign countries and in the colonies. They are, however, deeply divided as to what type of capital flows need to be taken into account, how such flows are best measured, and what store can be put by the results.

Before pitching into the detail of this debate, it would seem sensible to outline my own argument. This is that, on average, across our period, the financial gains to be made from the empire were not significantly greater than those to be made from investing in the UK or in other markets overseas. Moreover, these gains were largely confined to particular groups of people in particular parts of the country – especially the professional and rentier classes of south-east England.

The place to start is Davis and Huttenback's study of 'portfolio finance'– bonds and shares passing through the City of London, and of the profitability of a sample of just under five hundred British companies operating at home, in the empire and the rest of the world. The British economy saw a marked rise in overseas investment from 1865 to 1914. Only a quarter of all capital issues found their way to the empire, however. Australia received significant sums of money during the 1880s, as did Canada prior to the First World War. Over the period as a whole, India, too, attracted a steady flow of funds.[33] The main 'foreign' recipients of British finance were the United States and South America (especially Argentina), the 'non-empire' category accounting for some 40% of all capital issues. Between the early 1860s and the early 1880s the empire yielded higher rates of return than either domestic or foreign business. It then became less lucrative (with domestic enterprise generally outperforming British companies operating overseas), until after the turn of the century it regained approximate parity with domestic and international investments (a situation which continued until 1914).[34]

Davis and Huttenback deny that overseas investment was a drain on the British economy: industry at home attracted significant sums of capital, a variety of enterprises were funded, and borrowing rates were competitive for British producers. Others share their scepticism and argue that there is little evidence to support the proposition that banks prejudiced domestic

industrial development by opting for 'easy' empire investments instead: 'what [163]
was lacking was not so much capital as manufacturers urgently demanding
it'.[35] This was because family-owned British firms (of which there were
many) tended to raise capital either by reinvesting profits or through a range
of informal and local sources of supply; they did not need to rely on the
London Stock Exchange to fund their enterprises. Why, then, did funds
flow out of Britain at such prodigious rates? Answer: because the country
was increasingly wealthy.[36] This is not to deny that British banks exhibited
a strong preference for overdraft facilities and short-term credits. Yet they
were not indifferent to the requirements of British industry. The commercial banking sector was determined to minimise the costs of loan monitoring and to maintain a high degree of liquidity; this is partly why it was able
to avoid the sort of banking failures that would have threatened industrial
and commercial stability.[37]

Davis and Huttenback do seem, however, to neglect three of the economic advantages of empire (emigration, direct investment and government
bonds), and to manipulate their time frame so as to exclude the real gains
that accrued to Britain from its privileged access to the foodstuffs, raw
materials and manpower of the dominions during the First World War.
The difficulty of incorporating emigration into imperial balance sheets has
already been noted. But the lack of consideration given to direct forms
of capital export – British controlled firms operating abroad – is harder to
excuse. Many of these firms generated high profits. They also showed an
increasing interest in imperial opportunities. To be sure, British multinationals were much more likely to invest in colonial production, or to establish colonial manufacturing plants, between the wars when local producers
increasingly sheltered behind tariff barriers, export licences were refused to
non-essential commodities, and competition from the colonies intensified.[38]
Yet several British companies had travelled down this road well before then;
in fact, it is estimated that up to a third of the value of British international
investment was 'direct' rather than 'portfolio' before 1914. There is also
a difficulty with excluding bonds: they formed a sizeable percentage of capital
issues, and 'imperial' bonds (approximately 40% of the total) significantly
outperformed British government securities over the period 1870 to 1913.

What happened to investment after 1914? The empire certainly became
a more important outlet for British capital – for example, from 1918 to
1931 colonial stocks replaced railway bonds as the main type of security
issued in London.[39] Owing to the absence of colonial default after 1931
the country may also have gained from concentration on empire lending in
the longer term.[40] Equally, it must be emphasised that these colonial stocks

[164] were a bigger proportion of a diminished whole, for in real terms the sum invested abroad was half that during the corresponding period before 1914, while the income from overseas investment was falling.[41]

Michael Edelstein's figures make imperial investment look somewhat more attractive. He has studied the returns from paper assets traded on the London Stock Exchange by sampling 566 securities quoted in the *Investor's Monthly Manual* from 1870 to 1913. Edelstein's supporters believe his methodology of relying on market valuations to be superior to that of relying on contemporary accounting practice; they also argue that his sample is more representative.[42] Edelstein's critics complain that the prices of securities printed in the *IMM* provide only a proxy for actual rates of return whereas Davis and Huttenback look at realised rates of return. We need not get drawn into this dispute. For our purposes two things are significant about Edelstein's study. First, that although it reveals a higher yield on investments outside the UK (by a margin of around 1.58%), the overall gap between overseas and domestic securities is not large.[43] Second, the 'imperial' component of Edelstein's funds can only be disaggregated for a small sub-set of securities (including railways, banks and social overhead capital) on which returns appear to have been below those of foreign securities but on a par with those of domestic securities for most of the years in question. It is hard, therefore, to make a convincing case for the superiority of colonial over either domestic or foreign investment using Davis and Huttenback's or Edelstein's research – neither would seem to justify such a position.

This does not mean that particular groups of investors did not favour the empire. Manufacturers tended to favour domestic investments while the empire proved popular with elite social groups – peers, gentlemen, financiers, merchants – who lived in London and the Home Counties and had plenty of spare capital. This elite enjoyed the benefits of various forms of imperial subsidy without having to pay the cost of imperial defence, which fell disproportionately on the middle-class taxpayer. Imperial investments also appealed to the increasingly prosperous professional classes.[44] Take, for example, the Indian railways, which attracted significant sums of capital during the nineteenth century.[45] The Government of India's 5% guarantee on railway securities proved popular with the well-to-do middle class in whose hands a great deal of Victorian wealth was concentrated.[46] Widows, barristers, clergymen, spinsters, bankers and retired army officers were all significant subscribers: 'the guarantee at once provided for the needs of this class of investor and enabled India to acquire capital for its railways at relatively low rates'.[47] These, then, were cautious investors who wanted security as much as high rates of return.

The empire enticed the speculative investor too.[48] The dominions drew the funds of wealthy people willing to take a risk on private stocks in mining and urban development.[49] Mining markets, in particular, had few equals as an arena for speculation. From 1894 to 1902 the mining sector took around one-third of new overseas capital issues, securing a yearly average of £20 million. A substantial slice of the money was raised through informal networks of personal contact, family and education: 'the capital market financed the known and the social web the unknown'.[50] The most famous case is that of the South African gold stocks – the so-called 'Kaffirs' – demand for which skyrocketed during 1894–5, so much so that they were traded on provincial exchanges in Britain.[51] The prices quoted for these mining securities fluctuated sharply;[52] fraudulent promoters abounded, and not even the emergence of mining consultancies and the professional mining engineer did much to reduce the risk for investors, who may have been more vulnerable to market manipulation in 1914 than in the 1890s.[53] The British lost as much as $150 million in Canadian mining ventures between 1890 and 1914,[54] while only a tiny number of the five hundred or so Western Australian goldmines paid dividends.[55]

A fascinating figure here is Alice Cornwell, a.k.a. 'Queen Midas' or 'Madam Midas', a mining prospector and financial entrepreneur who emigrated from Essex to Australia as a young girl and married a 70-year-old blacksmith at the age of 21.[56] The marriage survived for five years and there was a child – a boy. Alice was forced to give up custody of her son when she joined her father in mine management in the Ballarat goldfields; the majority of women in Ballarat at this time were either housewives or domestic servants. This truly remarkable woman owned and managed the Midas and Speedwell mines. The Midas mine, situated north-west of Ballarat, is recorded as having owed much to 'the courage and enterprise of Miss Cornwell' (in the Jubilee year it produced one of Australia's largest nuggets of gold, weighing 617oz). The Speedwell mine was among the larger producers in the northern section of the Ballarat East goldfield, purchased by Cornwell on behalf of a syndicate in 1883. Her particular skill was to see that the successful mining of gold required the effective amalgamation of local areas of mining property together with long continuity of mine management. To this end she regularly returned to England to raise capital for her business ventures. It was not uncommon for Australian mining ventures to be floated wholly or partly in London. Mining company promotion held out the prospect of huge speculative profits for those in the know, and Cornwell rose rapidly in this world to become the London representative of the British Australasian Mining Investment Company, formed for the

[166] purpose of developing mining properties throughout Australia. It was a prestigious position – the board included the Tasmanian Agent-General, E. N. C. Braddon. He was forced to withdraw, however, as the Tasmanian premier and parliament grew uneasy about encouraging speculation. Neither did they like the fact that Cornwell's new company planned to take over several of the mines that she owned. Cornwell later returned to England to live as a wealthy property speculator. She died in 1932.

The market in mining securities was not the only form of speculation. Faced by Lloyd George's 'People's budget', the British landed elite was lured by the Canadian property boom of the Edwardian era – a boom sustained by rising agricultural prices in world markets and by the opening up of low-cost farming land and mineral deposits.[57] Lord Esher extolled the merits of investing in real estate in the dominion to King George V: 'income retained there did not have to pay any tax in Britain, while Canada itself did not impose income taxes or death duties'.[58] As he wrote, the rapid development of Saskatchewan, Alberta and Manitoba was providing the scope for an astonishing level of speculation in urban property and agricultural land with acre after acre being pegged out and sold at grossly inflated prices. British newspapers willingly supplied their readers with news of these 'opportunities': 'as a key publicity tool, the press was used by unscrupulous promoters to sell pups to gullible punters, with the connivance of editors and journalists'.[59]

Prized by particular types of investor, the empire was perhaps even more important to the commercial strategy of certain banks and other types of financial institution. Imperialism's impact on the City as a whole has recently been emphasised: given the lack of industrial demand at home, it was natural for institutional investors to look abroad for outlets for their surplus capital.[60] Yet we also need to consider corporate histories. Here I have selected Barclays Bank and Standard Life (a life assurance and pension company), both of which sourced a lot of their business in the empire.[61] Though not necessarily representative of the service sector as a whole, they were major players in their respective fields and illustrate the type of connections that could develop between the colonies and British finance.

Barclays pursued a policy of overseas expansion between the wars. It focused on the British empire rather than on continental Europe, and played a key role in the establishment of a commercial banking structure to serve the colonies. A series of acquisitions led eventually to the formation in 1925 of Barclays Bank Dominion, Colonial and Overseas, a merger of the Colonial Bank (active in the West Indies), the Anglo-Egyptian Bank and the National Bank of South Africa. Barclays DCO, as it came to be known, had total assets of nearly £69 million – about one-fifth of the group's [167] domestic balance sheet. It was opposed by the Governor of the Bank of England, Montagu Norman (1871–1950), who feared the destabilisation of British banking through unnecessary overseas entanglements. However, thanks to the perseverance and skill of Frederick Goodenough (1866– 1934), DCO proved Barclay's most profitable large trade investment. Goodenough was born in Calcutta, the son of an East India merchant. He was appointed to the board of Barclays in 1913 and became its chairman in 1917. He also served on the India Council from 1918 to 1930 and founded London House (1930), a hall of residence for dominion students visiting Britain. A staunch imperialist, Goodenough firmly believed in the policy of empire development through cheap inter-imperial finance, fixed imperial exchange rates and the extension of banking organisation to the colonies.[62] His ambition of an imperial trading bloc was unrealistic, but his concentration on empire banking resources in the 1930s and 1940s was actually quite shrewd. He saw that domestic banking business could be successfully combined with an overseas branch network and that this, in turn, could help to offset Britain's increasing dependence on American financial support – something which Goodenough and other Barclays directors found distasteful.

Standard Life was a pillar of the British life assurance establishment. It opened offices all over the world, many of which supported Scottish expatriate communities involved in the engineering, construction and oil industries. By the early twentieth century one-third of the company's new business came from Britain, a further third from professionals in the British empire and the remainder from a miscellany of 'foreign' countries (including Hungary, Argentina, Uruguay, China and Egypt). It was Standard Life's Manager, William Thomson, who pressed for life cover for emigrants. He was quick to appreciate the security they craved. To this end, a new company was created in 1845, Colonial Standard Life.[63] Four areas were earmarked for operation: Australia, North America, Ceylon and the West Indies. The first Colonial Life policy was issued to George Smith, a 28-year-old merchant in Ceylon, on 6 November 1846. Though progress in India and Ceylon was initially slow, by the mid-1850s the company's agents in Madras and Colombo were producing much new business, and by the 1870s the Calcutta branch had outstripped all other overseas branches. Yet there was a marked reluctance to insure Indian lives and to employ Indians as agents. The company thus faced growing competition from newly established Indian life offices; only its monopoly of business from Anglo-Indian civil servants and service personnel kept it going.

[168] Standard Life also had premiums to invest. When the company restructured its portfolio in the 1870s it was attracted by Indian and colonial government securities and by colonial property markets and municipal bonds.[64] Salaried staffs in India and Canada facilitated this shift in investment strategy by monitoring trends in these economies and gauging prospective investment yields. At first, however, Standard Life turned to Australia and New Zealand. In 1881, it took £20,000 of debenture stock from the recently reconstructed New Zealand and Australian Land Company, followed by two large advances on the security of freehold property in New South Wales and Queensland in 1883. Many of these loans were to sheep farmers, with sureties provided by partners in Scottish Borders textile mills who had switched to buying wool from Australian and New Zealand producers. Not until the financial crises of the mid-1890s, which brought the Australian land boom to an end, did Standard Life look further afield. Thereafter it favoured Canadian municipal bonds and high-yielding urban and farm mortgage transactions; they, in turn, stimulated new life assurance business in Canada from 1913–14.[65]

The empire figured prominently in the calculations of particular types of investor and financial firm, therefore. Yet if the frame of reference is the service sector as a whole, the empire's importance must not be exaggerated. It was the international rather than specifically imperial reach of banking, shipping and insurance that helped to bolster Britain's GNP and thereby to offset Britain's relative industrial decline. Moreover, chronologically, 'the dominance of London as the empire's financial centre was limited': it reached its apogee between 1860 and 1890 but thereafter the City's position was much less secure.[66]

Markets

Britain signed the Anglo-French Treaty in 1860 in an effort to encourage freer intra-European trade. Thereafter falling prices and profits led continental states to erect tariff barriers. Britain had to decide whether to turn to imperial markets to try to sustain its industrial lead.[67] There were certainly those who enthused about the potential of these markets. As it transpired, however, the empire's share of Britain's overseas trade did not increase markedly before 1914. If we consider British trade in its entirety 'the headway made by the empire remained very modest' – 25.4% of total commerce in 1854–7 and 27.5% in 1909–13.[68] Admittedly, these aggregate figures conceal emerging trends. There was a big growth in 'temperate' foodstuffs from Canada and Australasia; imports from India were decreasing appreciably, while those from the British West Indies were falling as a consequence of the decline of the sugar trade. There was also a drop in the proportion of total exports from Britain to the empire made up of textiles, compensated for by a rise in the export of metallurgical goods. Yet notwithstanding these new developments it is clear that, up to the First World War, Britain was more reliant on American and European than it was on imperial trade.

Commercial ties with the colonies grew stronger between the wars and particularly after the slump of 1931, though the overall context was one of declining international trade. By the late 1920s 32.9% of Britain's imports came from the empire; by 1934–8 41.2%. Over the same period the proportion of exports to the empire grew from 37.2% to 41.3%, mostly due to increased trade with the self-governing dominions – India's share of British exports decreased, while exports to the tropical African colonies rose marginally. In July–August 1932 representatives of the British and colonial governments met in Ottawa to discuss trade policy.[69] The outcome of these negotiations was a series of bilateral tariff agreements that only partially fulfilled Britain's aim of (further) shifting trade from non-empire to empire channels. Ottawa demonstrated that each part of the empire was intent upon protecting its own special interests. Dominion politicians were adept at extracting concessions for rural export staples in the British market while conceding the minimum to British manufactured goods in the setting of tariffs.[70] It must be remembered that Australia, Canada and South Africa were all striving to develop their own infant industries at this time; in so far as preferential tariffs were adopted it was to raise them against foreign goods rather than to lower them against British ones. British politicians, for their part, were understandably reluctant to expose themselves to the charge of raising the cost of living for consumers, or of sacrificing the future of British farming to dominion agriculture. Moreover, throughout the 1930s they continued to negotiate trade treaties with non-imperial suppliers (including Denmark, Germany and Argentina).[71]

Despite this, the empire is frequently blamed for Britain's twentieth-century (relative) industrial decline. First, it is held responsible for a lack of commitment on the part of successive governments to manufacturing. By the end of the nineteenth century the needs of finance and industry are said to have bifurcated as the empire became crucial for one but not the other.[72] Where one stands on this issue depends partly on whether one accepts that the capital sent abroad after 1850 would have been better ploughed back into Britain's domestic economy. This is a complex debate, touched upon above, and not to be resolved here.[73] Suffice to say that it is far from being

[170] a universal view that industrial growth in Britain was held back for want of adequate funds. Second, an unhealthy dependence on 'soft', 'sheltered' or 'easy' empire markets is held responsible for the competitive weaknesses of British industry and its reluctance to move out of older staple types of production. It is this 'soft market thesis' – the idea that British industry's reliance on empire markets obstructed its efficiency and growth – that I wish to pursue further. Though something of a received wisdom, it is a 'wisdom' that largely belongs to the realm of assumption and speculation. Few scholars have taken the time or trouble to study the behaviour of colonial consumers or to compare the performance of British industry in empire markets to that of indigenous and foreign producers.[74]

Definitions are clearly important here. A 'soft' market could be taken to exhibit the following characteristics: (a) a cultural or sentimental preference for British goods; (b) little or no need to adjust products to local tastes; (c) guaranteed and predictable levels of demand; and (d) low levels of local or foreign competition. On this basis, I shall argue that the empire did not 'featherbed' British industry, and that the colonies were not life-rafts into which British manufacturers could effortlessly escape when faced by intensifying international competition. Put simply, consumer behaviour in the self-governing dominions – the fastest-growing empire markets, and the ones most likely to have displayed a tendency to 'buy British' – was shaped more by price, income and quality than it was by sentiment or preference. The journalist and writer of humorous verse, William Thomas Goodge, hinted at as much in his poem *The Australian*, written at the turn of the twentieth century:

> His clothes are West of England tweed;
> His boots are from the Strand;
> The bike which he propels with speed
> Was made in Yankeeland.
> He drinks a glass of Belgian gin,
> Jamaica rum, perchance,
> And strikes the 'best Virginia' in
> A pipe that's 'made in France'.
> He looks at his imported watch to see the time of day,
> And hurries, for he wants to see a new imported play.
> The lamp is made in Germany that lights him on his way;
> He's a patriotic thoroughbred Australian![75]

Dominion trade statistics lend weight to Goodge's observation that the colonial consumer was prepared to shop around in search of the most fashionable (and competitively priced) products of the day. Broadly speaking, these statistics show that before 1914 per capita expenditure on British goods in the dominions did not match that on exports from outside the empire; that the proportion of the average colonial consumer's income spent on British products did not increase significantly over time; and that the rate at which these markets absorbed British exports did not match the rate at which they absorbed foreign exports (especially those from Germany and the USA).[76] Neither was this a consequence of different countries specialising in different products, for when per capita growth rates on 'competitive' exports are compared, the relatively faster rates achieved by Britain's main competitors are retained.

Company histories further reveal that pro-British sentiment on the part of the colonial consumer counted for little if the product being sold was not already competitive.[77] Indeed, when a preference for British products did exist, British manufacturers had actively to exploit it; arguably this was an act of entrepreneurship in itself. This is not to say that there were no branches of British industry that benefited from a degree of 'softness' in empire markets. Chemicals and tobacco enjoyed privileged access to colonial consumers, the former as a result of formal international agreements dividing the world into spheres of commercial influence, the latter as a result of mergers and amalgamations for the purpose of jointly exploiting markets overseas. These industries were not typical, however, and strong export performance to the dominions was more likely to reflect sound or even innovative business practice than an attempt to eschew competition encountered in other parts of the world. Thus, dominion markets were not an easy ride: British producers took them for granted at their peril.

Did India provide a better bolt-hole for British industry?[78] After all, Britain supplied some 85% of India's imports in 1870, 70% in 1890 and 66% in 1913.[79] Foreign competitors – Germany, Belgium and later Japan – struggled to make inroads into the Indian market, and Britain was generally able to defend its dominant position. Admittedly, the UK's share of Indian imports declined more steeply during the inter-war years: it was approximately 45% in 1928–9, and 30% in 1938. Yet on the eve of the Second World War, India remained Britain's largest single market for exports of general machinery and chemicals; the second largest market for electrical goods; and the third largest market for iron and steel goods.[80]

Clearly, 'softness' in the Indian market is unlikely to have been a matter of cultural preference on the part of the consumer (the Anglo-Indian community was not sufficiently large for this to be true). The key question is that of political power. Take, for example, the concessions granted by the

[172]   Government of India to British contractors and suppliers of capital equipment.[81] Before 1914 tenders for contracts to supply the Indian public sector were submitted for the consideration of the India Office in London, a situation that favoured British manufacturers, especially of iron and steel products, railway equipment and machinery for government workshops and mines. A case in point would be the huge orders for Indian railways. These sustained the first major expansion of British exports to the subcontinent from 1875 to 1885, with materials for the guaranteed lines sourced overwhelmingly from the UK.[82]

Did British business become cocooned in a colonial economy that took away the need for technological innovation and organisational reform? A leading economic historian of India argues that the effect of official favouritism was not sufficiently strong to give British interests the power to fight off domestic and foreign rivals, and that the securing of private business interests was always a marginal part of the Government of India's imperial commitment anyway.[83] The Lancashire cotton industry bears this out – here the scope for commercial concessions was severely restricted by the requirements of official finance and by the need to retain indigenous support for colonial rule. Tariffs were a particularly valuable source of income, especially after the First World War; expenditure was increasing, and the Montagu-Chelmsford reforms (1919) handed the land tax over to provincial administrations.[84] The result was a rapid rise in import duties during the 1920s and 1930s when newly-established Tariffs Boards granted protection to various Indian industries. They did not pursue a policy of long-term integrated protection, but several existing branches of Indian manufacturing benefited from their decisions (cotton textiles, iron and steel, paper, salt, sericulture) while others (matches, rubber manufactures, hydrogenated vegetable oils, paper) were set up as a result of the changes they made.[85]

Yet the favourable position enjoyed by British business in India does not have to be explained by a pro-British bias on the part of government officials. For example, having been trained in England and Scotland, the majority of the engineers who supervised railway construction in India were much more familiar with and thus inclined to favour British-made goods. Some even visited UK suppliers prior to their departure to approve designs and to place provisional orders for equipment.[86] To be sure, their tendency to buy British was reinforced by the minimal tariffs on imported railway goods.[87] Failure to obtain protection stifled the manufacture of locomotives and rolling stock in Indian railway workshops – between 1865 and 1941 a mere 700 locomotives were produced in India, while some 12,000 were exported to the subcontinent by British firms.[88] Nonetheless, the advantage enjoyed by the British railway industry in selling to India stemmed in part [173] from the involvement of British engineers in Indian railway construction: it was they who forged the trans-national social networks that reduced the costs of international transactions and that helped British firms to operate overseas.

After the First World War control of government expenditure was progressively handed from London to New Delhi, and purchasing policy gradually came to favour Indian over British suppliers. The initial steps were taken in 1919 when an official report recommended the establishment of a purchasing agency in India, and in 1924, when new rules encouraged the purchase of local products 'so far as is consistent with economy and efficiency'. In the following year provincial governments were given full discretion over the purchase of all stores, while in 1928 a new system was adopted whereby the bulk of stores were to be obtained by rupee tenders in India and not sterling tender in London. Stores purchase officers were told that, in comparing goods of equal price, preference was to be given first to Indian-produced articles, second to articles wholly or partially manufactured in India, and third to stock held in India. If goods were of adequate quality, the cheaper article was to be preferred even if it was of lower quality.[89] The total value of stores purchased in India was modest, but such purchases proved important for certain sectors of Indian industry – by 1939 over a quarter of all railway stores and almost a half of the value of stores for state railways were bought from indigenous firms.[90] The new department also encouraged the manufacture of articles not previously made in India, thus widening the range of indigenous products.[91]

What about those British manufacturers who did not benefit from government contracts or who did not supply the colonial state? One of their strengths was that they were actually quite skilled in identifying the specialised needs of the Indian market and in coping with its cyclical fluctuations.[92] Certainly, John Lean & Sons of Glasgow, a firm of muslin weavers, did not find its main market in India undemanding. Leans constantly changed product design to meet the latest Indian fashions in pattern and style. Up until the 1880s, when the telegraph came into more regular use, news travelled slowly from India to Scotland. This often left the company with a long run of goods for which there was reduced demand. Thus volatility and uncertainty were the chief characteristics of this branch of the Indian trade; a mixture of enthusiasm, hard work, caution and common sense was needed to overcome them.[93]

In other branches of trade, foreign competition posed the biggest challenge. Belgian steel; German woollen manufactures, household utensils, iron

[174]   nails, pillars, girders and bridge works; Japanese silks; and various types of tubes and fittings from the United States – in each of these areas Britain's market share was contracting by the early twentieth century.[94] While competition in India may not have been as intense as in foreign markets, there was enough of it to guard against complacency,[95] and it increased over time. Indeed, such was the concern about foreign competition, the boycott of British goods and increasing tariffs that several British multinationals looked toward local production between the wars.[96] The soap-maker Unilever manufactured its first consignment of Indian soap in Bombay in 1934.[97] Other famous names to build or take over manufacturing and packing plant in India at this time include the British American Tobacco Company, Brooke Bond and Metal Box.[98] More than half the British subsidiary manufacturing companies prominent in India in the early 1970s had made sizeable investments in the subcontinent before independence.[99]

Textile machinery offers another interesting case study.[100] From their inception in the 1850s, India's cotton mills looked to the British textile machine-making industry to supply their equipment needs.[101] Indian mill owners relied heavily on Lancashire technicians and fitters to install plant, train operatives and oversee production runs. Even when the Government of India introduced a more discriminating tariff policy textile machinery continued to enjoy special treatment.[102] Did this near-monopoly of the Indian market breed complacency? It seems unlikely. From 1893 to 1939 India accounted for a third or more of total exports of textile machinery on only five occasions (1915, 1921, 1922, 1923, 1932); it averaged 23.75%.[103] Hence the British industry had to exploit many other markets, principally those of continental Europe, Russia and Japan. These markets are not commonly viewed as 'easy' or 'soft'; on the contrary, by 1900 British firms in these regions faced strong US competition.[104] Even in the Indian market British firms worked hard to secure orders; marketing representatives regularly visited Bombay to promote products, and many directors went out to India to familiarise themselves with local conditions and to establish local contacts.

In summary, then, it was not the nature of empire markets but the manner in which British producers catered for and competed in them that ensured export success. It was not easy to use state power to protect British producers against indigenous or foreign competition in the colonies. Nor did pro-British sentiment among emigrants and expatriates give any clear or compelling advantage to manufacturers in Britain. (There was also active hostility to British goods during the *swadeshi* movement in India in the early 1900s and the cotton boycott of the early 1930s.) The empire was not a 'safe haven', a 'bolt-hole' or a 'retreat' for most branches of British [175] industry. Rather, it provided a parallel experience to Britain's participation in the international economy: products competed on quality and price, and producers who thought otherwise were in most instances to be sorely disappointed.

Military expenditure

For some historians the empire was no more than a 'psychological crutch' – a 'world power fantasy' that resulted in strategic over-extension.[105] After 1870, we are told, Britain locked herself into an imperial world role that she lacked the resources to sustain. As a result, British power was slowly but surely drained away. Is this fair? The crucial issue here is that of Britain's defence spending and whether it was disproportionately high. It has been argued that Britain maintained two defence establishments – one for home defence, the second for imperial protection – while recovering only the most meagre proportion of the total cost from the colonies.[106] In this way, the costs of imperial defence 'practically wiped out the additional returns derived by British investors from sending their capital to the colonies rather than keeping it at home'.[107] Indeed, 'on any plausible hypothesis about the shares of income appropriated as taxes and used to defray expenditure on defence' it is said that Britain was right at the top of international league tables from 1860 to 1914'.[108]

Yet closer inspection of British defence expenditure, in particular in relation to that of other Western European powers, seems to suggest that it was not artificially inflated by the empire. Those who see the empire as a defence burden on Britain tend not to take account of the fact that in Germany a lot of revenue was raised by the states (rather than by central government); that European states borrowed heavily on the money markets which deferred the cost of payment for armaments; that conscription on the Continent was costly (in terms of the income forgone by those conscripted); and that Britain enjoyed relatively higher standards of living which meant it could afford to spend more. Thus the gap between defence spending in Britain, Germany and France was probably far narrower than frequently assumed: 'on the face of it, there seems to be no real substance to the case that British defence cost more, in relative terms, than that of its direct European rivals'.[109] On this basis, it has even been asserted that 'if it was not exactly an empire "on the cheap", it can hardly be portrayed as a crushing burden'.[110]

The debate about strategic over-extension is not simply about the reliability of evidence on defence spending, however. Other issues are at stake, especially those regarding the funding and function of British naval supremacy, and the benefits derived from the empire during the First (and Second) World Wars. These will now be considered in turn.

Before trying to apportion defence costs between Britain and its colonies we need to ask who or what the navy existed to defend. As naval historians make clear, supremacy at sea was not merely a matter of protecting the far-flung parts of the empire. The navy had many other responsibilities. It had to keep the shipping lanes open to international commerce in the event of war (crucial given Britain's dependence on imported foodstuffs); to clamp down on privateering during peacetime; to suppress the slave trade; and, of course, to defend the British Isles. Nor were Britain's most significant international trade routes necessarily imperial: 'Britain could live without trading with most of its empire. It could not live without trade with the United States and South America.'[111] There is therefore no simple equation between naval supremacy and imperial defence, a point that is underscored when looking at defence from the colonial perspective. Britain's colonies faced varied military threats but they were generally more secure than the mother country. A large proportion of Canada's trade, for instance, went overland to the United States, while Australia and New Zealand were largely self-sufficient in terms of foodstuffs and did not face the same fear of famine in the event of an international conflict.[112]

It is also doubtful whether the different parts of the empire could rely upon the navy to the same extent. The whole drift of British naval policy in the decade prior to the First World War – the scrapping of obsolete vessels, the policy of concentration, the preponderance of battleships over cruisers – was toward shoring up the defence of the British Isles rather than the wider British world.[113] To be sure, the Admiralty had a perfectly rational (and perhaps reasonable) justification for these measures. It centred on the concept of the decisive naval battle. Defence planners worked on the assumption that the outcome of any future war would be determined by a grand showdown between the world's major naval powers. Ultimately, the security of the dominions depended on the Royal Navy emerging victorious from such a decisive encounter; the more the navy's ships were dissipated, the less likely victory would be.[114] This rarefied strategic thinking did not allay the growing insecurity felt by Australia and New Zealand, however; nor did their statesmen take much comfort from the insurance policy of the Anglo-Japanese alliance. Thus in negotiations about imperial defence costs it may well be the case that

Britain received about as much as it could bargain for.[115] As the senior [177]
partner in the empire, it was bound to bear the greater share of defence if
only because the junior partners calculated that the navy was not equally
available to them.

Finally, there is the matter of the colonies' military contribution to the
First World War. How far do 'the distinct wartime benefits of empire' over-
shadow its costs during peacetime?[116] One scholar estimates that military
expenditure might have been 10% higher without the colonies' support
and British wartime deaths 30% higher without colonial troops. Certainly,
the combat role performed by the colonies must not be underestimated.
In 1914, Canada, Australia and New Zealand together mobilised some 1.2
million men; 14% of Canada's and Australia's male population saw service
overseas and 20% of New Zealand's. The British Expeditionary Force was
further strengthened by two infantry divisions of Indian sepoys who fought
and died in many of the major battles on the Western front. On top of this
Britain benefited from a steady supply of vital foodstuffs and raw materials
(Canadian wheat 'stood between Britain and starvation in 1917') and artil-
lery shells.[117] While it is likely that the dominions would eventually have
been drawn into hostilities had they not been a part of the empire (for
similar reasons to the United States), neither they nor India would have
mobilised their troops so quickly. There is also the incalculable psychological boost that the British enjoyed by knowing that the 'mother
country' and its colonies stood shoulder-to-shoulder from 1914 to 1918.
On the tide of this wartime imperial co-operation it is even possible to float
the idea of a 'reverse subsidy', namely that the colonies relieved the British
of wartime military expenditure and did more than could reasonably have
been expected of them to aid British home defence.

Conclusions

This chapter has sought to provide a more rounded picture of the metropolitan economics of empire than that currently on offer. In evaluating
whether the empire was a benefit or burden to the British economy it
has reviewed existing debates on foreign capital flows, naval defence and
imperial security. It has also drawn migration and trade into the discussion
by presenting new material on migrant remittances, and by offering new
perspectives on the behaviour of colonial consumers, the nature of empire
markets and the competitiveness of British industry. In general it has
argued that, for better or worse, Britain's economic situation after 1850

[178]   was the outcome of its pursuit of a world role and of the fact that it clung
tenaciously to the concept of 'comparative advantage'.

The empire does not seem to have had an economic logic of its own.[118]
Britain was a global power and the empire of itself could not provide the
basis for a comprehensive commercial or financial system. This was undeniably the case in the later-Victorian and Edwardian era, yet it remained
true after the First World War. Only at times of crisis – especially after
1929 – was it possible to regard the empire as an essential prop to the
British economy. For most of our period Britain's imperial role simply
reflected the strength of its world trading and financial position.[119] This
conclusion is, moreover, corroborated by what happened after 1945 when
the British economy faced many problems, but the empire was not one of
them.[120] Decolonisation did not, as anticipated, have major consequences
for investment and trade: the cost of imports was not significantly raised;
markets for exports did not significantly diminish; and income obtained
from overseas assets did not significantly fall. We need to look elsewhere to
explain the country's apparent economic 'failure' in the 1950s and 1960s.

Finally, the chapter reiterates the difficulty of disentangling imperial from
international influences on the British economy – whether in terms of the
repercussions of overseas migration, the relative rates of return on empire
and non-empire investments, the nature of imperial *versus* foreign markets
or the percentage of Britain's defence expenditure attributable to specifically imperial rather than wider international strategic commitments.[121]
In so far as commercial, financial or defensive ties with the colonies can
be separated from those with foreign countries, it has shown how these
two external sources of influence on the British economy frequently ran in
tandem. Britain's 'imperial economy' reflected and reinforced a deepening
involvement in international finance and trade; it did not stand apart
from it. Hence, although the empire's economic impact was not 'entirely
negligible',[122] neither was it decisive.

CHAPTER 8

THE FORGING OF BRITISH
IDENTITIES

Historians of Britain and its empire have long been concerned with identity formation, whether in terms of social class, region or gender. Yet the interest they have shown in the forging of a 'British' identity is relatively recent,[1] prompted in part by its apparent unravelling during the last twenty years or so.[2] In exploring the rise and fall of 'Britishness' over time, some scholars see the empire as an arena in which what were felt to be key national characteristics – a capacity for commerce, the spirit of exploration and discovery, and an aptitude for political organisation – were acted out and further proven.[3] Others argue that pride in the empire helped the British people to transcend their internal divisions: by acquiring colonies in Africa and Asia, the English, Welsh, Scots and, somewhat more ambiguously, the Irish, came into protracted contact with an array of colonial 'others' against which the national character could be more sharply defined.[4]

This chapter questions whether the empire's impact on British identities was as positive or significant as the above interpretation implies. It explores several aspects of the nation's public life not yet touched upon in this book. These include the vocabulary of the English language and its borrowings from 'foreign' tongues; the relationship between the empire and the built environment; public perceptions of groups of indigenous colonial peoples who visited the 'mother country'; imperial influences on the nation's institutional life, as reflected by the development of the monarchy and the army; and the repercussions of imperial expansion for internal relations within the United Kingdom. At the outset, it must be acknowledged that the forging of a British identity is a slippery subject, and that these strands of identity can provide only a proxy for national consciousness. Indeed, different types of evidence – architectural, cultural, demographic, institutional and linguistic – can point to contradictory conclusions. We must tread carefully therefore.

[180] Language

Words reflect their times.[5] Some societies try to avoid the use of foreign terms, but the English have welcomed them and a significant proportion of our vocabulary derives from other vernaculars.[6] Trade and travel have led to the borrowing of new words; so too has contact with foreign peoples through warfare, conquest and colonisation. The Boer War catapulted several South African words into the English language – *mafficking, concentration camp, kop* and *pom-pom* among them – while phrases popular among dominion troops fighting on the veldt – 'back chat', 'skoff', 'skrim shanker'[7] – were readily adopted by the British soldier.[8] However, by far the greatest intermingling took place between English and the languages of India – Bengali, Hindi, Persian and Urdu; some directly, some via Portuguese and some as hybrids and adaptations. Among the most easily recognisable borrowings are: *bungalow, cashmere, caste, chintz, chits, chutneys, coolie, cummerbund, curries, Delhi belly, dhobis, dinghy, dungarees, guru, gymkhana, juggernaut, kedgeree, khaki, loot, mogul, polo, pucka, pundit, punkhas, puttee, pyjamas, shampoo, thug, toddy, tom-tom,* and *veranda* – all pretty well naturalised and self-explanatory, and all to be found in the *Oxford English Dictionary*. Other Indian words include *blighty* ('one's home country', from the Hindi word 'bilayati' meaning 'foreign', whence 'British'); *black hole* (from the Black Hole of Calcutta); *punch* (derived from the Hindu 'panch' – or five – referring to the drink's ingredients); and *tickety-boo* (correct or satisfactory, probably from the Hindi 'thik hai' meaning 'all right'). During the eighteenth century such expressions belonged to the small European speech community in India and to East India Company officials in London.[9] Not until the mid-nineteenth century was there a marked rise in the number of words of Indian origin entering everyday English usage. As more people were employed in the civil and military services, more correspondence was exchanged between Anglo-Indians and their relatives at home, and more news of India appeared in the Victorian media, so Anglo-Indian terminology was adopted to a far greater extent than hitherto. Such was the richness of 'Indian English' that in 1886 Arthur Burnell and Henry Yule were able to compile a hefty Anglo-Indian dictionary, the *Hobson-Jobson* as it became known.[10] Even as these words were being written there was a flurry of correspondence in *The Times* from old India 'hands' as to the precise derivation of the word 'Doolally'.[11] While loan-words from India may not match those borrowed over a much longer course of time from continental Europe,[12] they easily outnumber those borrowed from elsewhere in Asia (China, Indonesia, Japan), or from Africa or the 'New World'. They are testimony to a persistent Anglo-Indian influence upon our national culture.

Urban landscapes[13]

John Ruskin said that people should be able to read a nation's character in its public buildings, while one of the twentieth century's leading architectural historians insisted that it was impossible to design without a sense of history.[14] If architecture can be inscribed with such meanings, to what extent has it been used to convey Britain's imperial heritage? There are certainly examples of major British buildings that merit the description 'imperial'. One might point to the India Office (1863–8) in Whitehall with its magnificent Durbar Court designed by Matthew Digby Wyatt (architect to the East India Company and first Slade Professor of Architecture at Cambridge) and George Gilbert Scott (Professor of Architecture at the Royal Academy).[15] Then there is the (late) Imperial Institute (1887–93) in South Kensington designed by Thomas Collcutt and built with money raised by public subscription following Queen Victoria's Golden Jubilee. In the City of London, the Institute of Chartered Accountants (1888–93) boasts a frieze sculpted by W. H. Thornycroft with figures representing a Parsi merchant, a South African gold-digger, a 'loyal' Canadian wheat-farmer and an Australian sheep-farmer.[16] Beyond the capital there is John Nash's gloriously eccentric Royal Pavilion at Brighton, remodelled as an Indian palace for the Prince Regent in the early 1800s and fittingly converted into a hospital for wounded Indian soldiers during the First World War; Osborne House on the Isle of Wight with its Indian-style Durbar Room (1890–91), designed by Lockwood Kipling (Rudyard's father, and head of the Government School of Art in Lahore) and Bhai Ram Singh (an expert on Indian decoration); and Swansea City Hall (1930), designed by Sir Percy Thomas with its series of large British empire painted panels.[17] Nor need we confine ourselves to civic buildings. Of the three hundred or so metropolitan statues catalogued by A. Byron around two dozen (8%) have a direct link to the empire.[18] Erected on London's most prestigious sites, their sculptors were among the best known of the day – Harry Bates, Sir Thomas Brock, Sir William Hamo Thornycroft and John Tweed, to name but a few.[19] There were also many war memorials to imperial service. The South African War, in particular, left a permanent mark on Britain's urban landscapes: nine hundred or so structures were erected to the memory of its dead.[20]

A more prosaic way of bringing home the glories of the empire was through the naming of streets.[21] As recently observed, 'colonial appellations are a clearly visible category of street-names in all European countries which ruled overseas empires'.[22] In Britain this task usually fell to developers, many of whom contrived to present the populace with an imperial view of the

[182] nation's past. There were streets named after imperial heroes: Gordon, Havelock, Kitchener, Milner, Napier and Roberts. There were streets reminding people of the extent of the Crown's possessions: Kashmir, Pretoria, Cairo, Adelaide, Cawnpore, Dunedin and the Sudan. And there were streets celebrating colonial military campaigns: especially the relief of Kimberley, Ladysmith and Mafeking. Yet we must not get carried away here. Many exotic street names came from beyond the boundaries of the formal empire, while developers were more likely to mark the military victories of the Napoleonic and Crimean wars than those of the African empire.

There is, in fact, surprisingly little agreement regarding how far the built urban environment reflected the country's imperial role. Some argue that later-Victorian politicians responded to a 'popular awareness of Britain's role as the centre of a world-wide empire' by building 'their own imperial administrative palaces',[23] and that capital cities across Europe – including London – were shaped by 'the global history of imperialism'.[24] Others express surprise that Europe was not *more* affected by the increasing knowledge of distant parts of the world: 'in fact, European countries tended to export architectural taste to their imperial outposts, and examples of importation at this time were exceptional'.[25] London is felt to be a case in point: unlike Rome it was not 'paved with the spoils and trophies of Empire' and was 'only incidentally an imperial capital'. The 'new imperialism' was apparently too new to have planted its own monuments in Britain's capital city.[26]

These differences of opinion point to the difficulty of interpreting expressions of national identity in architecture. As one scholar shrewdly remarks, 'there is seldom a secure or enduring consensus as to which, or rather whose, legends and landscapes epitomise a nation'.[27] Here two questions will be posed. First, how far were colonial architectural styles transposed back to Britain? Second, how far did British architects develop an imperial idiom or concept of imperial space? The former is more easily handled. While there are instances of English homes emulating Eastern styles – Sezincote house in Gloucestershire, inspired by the Nawab Siraj-ud-Daulah's garden palace in Faizabad, is perhaps the best known[28] – such properties are rare. Unlike literature, fashion and food, Anglo-Indian taste never really caught on in architecture. In the Georgian and Regency periods a few buildings were erected in a mixture of Muslim and Hindu styles, but they were not widely copied. The majority of the wealthy nabobs returning to Britain were eager to be accepted as members of the landed gentry and so preferred conventional Palladian residences.[29] A more indirect influence may be traced back to West Indian plantation owners and East India Company officials: their fortunes enabled some of England's [183] best-known country houses (Harewood, Dodington, Orchardleigh and Brodsworth) to be built, rebuilt and furnished.[30] Yet, to repeat: there was nothing manifestly colonial in the designs of these properties, which followed fashions from Europe (in particular France and Italy) rather than the wider world.[31] The one major exception is the bungalow – a Bengali peasant dwelling adopted and adapted by the European community in India, and developed in England as a specialised dwelling for middle-class holidays and retirement. Although the bungalow did not fully come into its own until between the wars, it is very much a legacy of the Raj.[32]

A more problematic issue is what makes public architecture or urban planning 'imperial'. Is this simply a matter of a capital city boasting build ings worthy of a nation's imperial role? Or does it imply something more – not a vague expression of pride in the empire through conventional architectural forms, but architects and sculptors whose careers (and commissions) depended on the colonies and who were imperially inspired when designing and decorating buildings? Edwin Lutyens (1869–1944) and Herbert Baker (1862–1945) immediately spring to mind. Lutyens made his name as a domestic architect. His career began with the 'arts and crafts' houses of his native Surrey, and he was heavily influenced by Richard Norman Shaw (1831–1912) and the 'English vernacular' style.[33] Later he received several colonial commissions,[34] most famously the Viceroy's House in India. The then Viceroy, Lord Hardinge, wanted to placate Indian opinion by adopting an Eastern style of architecture.[35] Lutyens, however, saw little of substance in traditional Indian design.[36] He sought to revive the 'great artistic discipline' of English Classical style in India – the chosen mode of the East India Company until its dissolution[37] – and rejected a mere 'grafting of Eastern excrescences onto a Western building'.[38] From Mughal architecture he gained an understanding of colour and form in the Indian landscape and the use to which wide-projecting cornices (chajjas) and pierced stone lattices (jaalis) could be put in protecting buildings from the heat.[39] Meanwhile Buddhist architecture influenced his design of the dome.[40] In this way Indian features and motifs were introduced to the Viceroy's House but they were rigorously subordinated to the classical idiom, thus betraying Lutyens's superficial commitment to Indian forms.[41]

Baker is best known for his work in South Africa, in particular on the Union Buildings. He admired Rhodes (building several houses for him) and was closely connected to Milner's Kindergarten.[42] In 1909 he published a manifesto on the 'Architectural Needs of South Africa'. This expressed admiration for the dignity and beauty of Cape Dutch architecture, and

[184] reflected Rhodes and the Kindergarten's desire to evolve a wider South African patriotism (see pp. 137–9).[43] Yet Baker too was a believer in the enduring forms of classicism, both in South Africa, where he appreciated their appeal to the European-descended Boer, and in India where he saw that architecture had to 'fearlessly put the stamp of British sovereignty'.[44] In India, Baker and Lutyens worked together on the planning of imperial Delhi; Baker was responsible for the Secretariat Buildings. Back in Britain Baker pipped Lutyens to the post for the job of rebuilding the Bank of England. His plans for the Bank strove to retain some of the features of Sir John Soane's building and to convey the 'historical continuity' of the institution; yet it was the Bank's world rather than 'imperial' role that was emphasised.[45] Baker also took charge of the building of India House (1925), South Africa House (1930) and the Royal Empire Society (1936). Interestingly, many of the sculptures in these buildings were carved by Charles Wheeler (1892–1974), a protégé of Baker's who was known for his decorative work on monuments and buildings. Wheeler's sculptures expressed the 'dignity' and 'exalted status' of the Raj, the 'romance and history' of the Cape, and the combination of 'thought and action' that made the colonising spirit. In addition to the above buildings, his commissions included Rhodes House in Oxford, the memorial to the Indian dead at Neuve Chapelle and the empire reliefs in the assembly hall of Church House in Westminster.[46]

Lutyens and Baker drew upon European classical traditions and reinterpreted them to further their own common ideal: a monumental architecture expressive of Britain's imperial mission. Buildings were to be of sufficient scale and splendour for an empire at the height of its powers. Whether this was an empire that could conceive of no challenge to its prestige or power,[47] or one intent upon impressing its subjects with the futility of dissent, is a moot point.[48] Either way, Lutyens and Baker consciously sought to state in their buildings the right (and determination) of Britain to govern its overseas possessions come what may. What they did not do was to produce a distinctively British imperial style. Baker had once written to Lutyens to say that their architecture should be neither Indian, South African nor English, but 'Imperial'.[49] And yet their buildings assimilated local colonial traditions only to a limited degree.[50] Moreover, in Lutyens's case this was probably more a matter of aesthetic judgement than political or ideological conviction. First and foremost, Lutyens wanted to build beautiful buildings.[51] This may help to explain why so few of the features from his colonial commissions influenced domestic designs. Plans for the Catholic Cathedral of Christ the King in Liverpool included a vast circular space beneath the dome, developed from his Durbar Hall at Delhi, and capable [185] of holding 10,000 people.[52] But for Lutyens such architectural exchanges were rare.

It is also worth emphasising that not all architects were as imperially-minded as Lutyens and Baker. External influences came from France (with Beaux-Arts methods);[53] America (especially on modern offices and company headquarters);[54] the eastern Mediterranean (from the Islamic and Byzantine arts);[55] and Germany (the 'Modern Movement', emphasising spatial freedom).[56] Nor was all 'imperial architecture' manifestly successful. The Imperial Institute rapidly became 'an expensive liability' and 'mausoleum of imperial hopes' – too far from Parliament and Whitehall, it was handed unceremoniously from ministry to ministry with some of its space rented out to the University of London.[57] Meanwhile, the imperial symbolism of the Victoria Memorial (1911) situated in front of Buckingham Palace was very muted indeed, notwithstanding the fact that the colonies had contri-buted nearly a third of the cost. Plans for groups of colonial statuary in the Mall were shelved in favour of barely visible depictions of the colonies on the monument's gateposts. India was not even directly represented on the monument – Lord Curzon had decided to build a Victoria Memorial in Calcutta instead.[58]

Private and commercial buildings do not seem to have been as amenable to formal imperial planning as official buildings. Take the rebuilding of Regent Street in London in the early 1900s: Edwardian retailers and shop-keepers thwarted plans to transform this purpose-built shopping street into a place more redolent of Britain's imperial glory.[59] Similarly, in the mid-1920s, the public reacted negatively to Liberty's unveiling of its carved frieze representing the trading ties between East and West.[60] Not until 1937 does the incorporation of imperial symbolism into commercial architecture seem to have met with general approval.[61] In that year the Oxford Street façade of Selfridge's was redecorated for the Coronation under the grand motif 'The Empire's Homage to the Throne'.[62] At the instigation of the American Anglophile Gordon Selfridge, eighteen plaster panels, each 20 feet (6 metres) high, were erected to mark the royal event. They illustrated episodes of British history: Clive of India (1757), Wolfe capturing Quebec (1759) and Rhodes in South Africa (1881) were all part of the display. At the four corners of the building sculptural groups represented the domin-ions of Australia, Canada and South Africa, and British rule in India, while in the Orchard Street window there was a huge painting by Clara Fargo Thomas showing the empire's great ports. The cost was close on £50,000, all the more staggering given that the decorations were temporary – they

[186]   were later transported to India to be erected at a Maharajah's palace.[63] E. M. Foster thought them 'awful' and 'vulgar', but the immense crowds that gathered for the Coronation were apparently impressed.[64]

Like language, therefore, public architecture and the built urban environment offer some support for the idea that British identities drew meaning and strength from the empire. And yet there are definite limits to imperialism's influence on our towns and cities.

Visiting colonials

Imperial expansion, it is said, 'made Britishness a more racist consciousness'.[65] But the question of what the perception of racial difference contributed to a sense of British nationhood is much more complex than this comment allows. There were, after all, a range of 'others' from which a belief in national superiority could also be derived – the Irish, Jews, French, Italians and Portuguese were all at times disdained.[66] The real issue is whether the contribution of colonial Africans and Asians to forming British identity was of a different order to that of, say, the Celts or continental Europeans. Here three groups of indigenous peoples have been singled out for consideration: Aboriginal cricketers, African princes and Indian students. Each visited Britain. How were they received?

One way in which the racism of Victorian society supposedly manifested itself is through organised sport, in particular cricket. Most famously, there was the star batsman, Prince Ranjitsinhji (1872–1933), who despite being more skilful than many of his Cambridge team-mates was not awarded a 'blue' until his final year. Ranjitsinhji's colour also led to opposition to his selection for England during the 1896 Australian Test, not least from the then president of the MCC, Lord Harris, previously Governor of Bombay.[67] Such bigotry is said to have been endemic in the game at this time.[68]

The first Australian cricketers to come to Britain were Aborigines; not for a further ten years did a team consisting only of white players tour.[69] Arriving in May 1868, the Aboriginal players competed in forty-seven games over five months. By late July they had established themselves as a competitive side that proved more than a match for many of their English opponents.[70] English spectators received them enthusiastically and crowds of several thousand gathered at many games. Each Aboriginal player sported a different colour sash to aid identification, and each was given a soubriquet – Jungunjinanuke, for example, was known as 'Dick-a-Dick' and Arrahmunijarrimun as 'Peter'. While this may seem disrespectful, it is worth remembering that the Aboriginal side was completely unknown to Victorian spectators; given the complexity of the players' names to English ears (and the difficulty of rendering them into English) soubriquets were perhaps understandable – more recently Brazilian footballers have suffered the same fate.[71] Some newspaper comment was negative. The sporting press expected the Aborigines to be 'savage' and 'uncivilised', expressing surprise when it found otherwise; and it remarked frequently on the players' colour and facial features. That said, there were surprisingly few incidents of racial tension during the tour, and the agility and intelligence of the visitors' star player, Johnny Mullagh, was widely praised. In general the Aborigines were recognised by the press as serious cricketers to be respected rather than exhibits to be poked fun at. If constructing a colonial 'other' requires a conscious or concerted effort to devalue and demean another culture, the Aboriginal cricket tour of 1868 does not seem to fit the bill.

Yet perhaps the colonial 'other' did not become firmly entrenched in British culture until the end of the nineteenth century. Deputations and envoys from the dependent colonies were commonplace by then.[72] Here I have focused on the region of Southern Africa. In 1894 a prince and five leading headmen from Swaziland visited Britain, and in 1895 three chiefs from Bechuanaland. Both territories faced an encroaching European imperialism that threatened to engulf them.

The Swazis came to ask Queen Victoria for protection against the Transvaal. Sir Ellis Ashmead-Bartlett championed their cause. He was a popular and pugnacious figure in the late-Victorian Tory party who founded the Patriotic Association (1877), edited the paper *England* (1880–98) and spoke passionately on imperial issues.[73] Named *Silomo* ('a man spoiling for a fight') by the Swazis, Ashmead-Bartlett told Conservative audiences up and down the country that the fate of these 'fine', 'brave' African people was 'trembling in the balance' as a result of Kruger's territorial designs.[74] His greatest triumph was in carrying a motion at the 1894 Conservative National Union conference that condemned the Liberal government's handling of the situation. However, the odds were stacked against the delegation's success: parliament was in recess, *The Times* was hostile,[75] and the government forbade it to court publicity. The Colonial Office took the view that Swaziland was not a truly independent nation, having already bartered away many of its farming and mineral rights to European concession hunters.[76] A convention signed in December 1894 gave the Transvaal the right to take over Swaziland as a 'protectorate'. Rhodes, in return, was given a free hand in expanding to the north and west without fear of Boer intervention.

Figure 9   The Aboriginal cricket team, Sydney, 1867
Source: State Library of New South Wales

Figure 10   The Swazi deputation to Britain, 1894
Source: *Illustrated London News*, 1 December 1894. British Library Shelfmark LD47. By permission of the British Library

By way of contrast, the visit of the Tswana chiefs – Khama, Sebele and Bathoen – was at least partly successful. They came to Britain to protest against the transfer of their tribal lands to Cecil Rhodes's chartered company and considerable reserves were kept under British protection.[77] Sponsored by the London Missionary Society, they conducted a whistle-stop tour of forty-four towns and gave countless press interviews. The LMS helped the deputation to attract publicity and lobby government; it was rewarded by patronage for future mission work. The humanity of the Tswana chiefs was widely remarked upon by several newspapers, while church congregations embraced them as Christian gentlemen and expressed sympathy with their plight.[78] Indeed, one of the chiefs contrasted the more tolerant racial attitudes of the 'English in England' with the more aggressive attitudes of white English settlers in Africa. 'Out here [in Africa] men call themselves Christians but we cannot see their spoor [i.e. tracks]. In England we can see their spoor very clearly', remarked Sebele, ruler of the BaKwena.[79] A recent study of the Eastern Cape suggests that Sebele may well have been right. It compares a settler vision of the colonial frontier, which had to be dominated in the interests of migrants' physical safety and economic survival, with a missionary vision of a 'zone of contact' across which civilising values and religious sentiment were to be transmitted. It goes on to show how late-Victorian settlers were hard at work trying to shift opinion at home toward their view of the intrinsic racial superiority of the British, employing 'extensive, partially globalised circuits of communication' to that end.[80]

The first coloured students to come to Britain for formal education date back to the late eighteenth century and were from West African coastal tribes;[81] initially they tended to study theology, later medicine and law.[82] Indian students arrived from the mid-nineteenth century. Though their early experiences appear to have been positive,[83] by the early twentieth century racist attitudes towards them were more and more in evidence.[84] Thus when in May 1907 Indian students honoured the fiftieth anniversary of the Mutiny (or 'War of Independence') by wearing badges commemorating the 'martyrs', British 'jingoes' tried to tear them off and a fight ensued. 'The Indian student problem', as *The Times* termed it, was considered sufficiently serious by this stage for the British authorities to restrict entrants, appoint guardians and financial guarantors and require character certificates; it also saw Scotland Yard putting students under surveillance and intercepting their post.

Did Asian students help to forge a sense of 'imperial Britishness'? It seems unlikely. The sight of Indians in London may not have been uncommon at this time,[85] yet there were only 700 to 800 of them studying in Britain by

1907–8 and only 1,500 by 1922. The ethnic minorities recognised to have [191] faced the most widespread hostility prior to 1945 were not from the empire – they were the much more numerous Catholic immigrants from Ireland and Jews from Eastern Europe.[86] That is not to say that colonial subjects who came to Britain were not disillusioned or disenchanted by their experiences.[87] It is, however, hard to believe that their presence gave rise to that ubiquitous or unthinking racism commonly associated with a British imperial identity.[88] If such racial antipathies did exist, they are much more likely to have been imported from abroad. We will return to this possibility when examining the experiences of soldiers serving in Britain's overseas empire.

Institutions

A country's established institutions, and the habits of mind that surround them, can shed light on the national character. Two such institutions are Britain's monarchy and armed forces. In the eyes of many, the Royal family, although of German descent, constituted the core of Britishness – the 'strongest cement' for an identity that was constantly in danger of fracturing along social, geographical and gender lines.[89] As the formal political power of the monarchy declined during the first half of the nineteenth century, so its ceremonial functions grew.[90] Reginald Brett (Viscount Esher) was responsible for their overall planning. In his hands royal pageants became pre-eminently imperial – opportunities for the colonies to express loyalty to the Crown, and for ordinary working people in Britain to embrace what he felt to be the leading political ideal of the day – the 'federation of the English race'.[91]

This 'imperialising' of the British monarchy can be traced back to the Royal Titles Bill of 1876 which proclaimed Victoria 'Empress of India'. It was hoped that the bill would please the Queen (who was eager for the inclusion of an imperial element in her royal title), cultivate a feudal relationship between the British monarch and Indian princes, and draw public attention to Britain's Asiatic empire and the power and prestige it conferred.[92] The bill was criticised heavily in parliament and the political press; the word 'Empress' smacked of European-style despotism and Disraeli's handling of the legislation was inept. Nonetheless it was passed on its first reading and pointed to a developing interest on the part of the monarchy in imperial affairs and a new era in royal representations.[93] In particular, imperialists trumpeted Victoria's diamond (1887) and golden (1897) jubilees as evidence of the empire's glory and goodness. Even the reaction of the socialist

[192] press, fiercely critical of the 'new' imperialism, was reasonably restrained.[94] The colonial prime ministers attended the former and were the central guests at the latter. Contingents of colonial troops formed parts of both processions. There was also an effusion of Jubilee literature which took the onward march of empire to be a defining characteristic of Victoria's reign.[95]

The monarchy, moreover, retained this imperial identity well after Victoria's death and, indeed, well beyond the First World War. Royal tours of the colonies were one of the main ways in which successive generations of the Royal family identified with the empire.[96] The Duke of Cornwall and York – the future George V – embarked on one of the longest excursions in 1901. The tour lasted almost eight months and was extensively reported in the British and colonial press. It took in Australia, New Zealand, Canada, South Africa, Gibraltar, Malta, Aden, Ceylon and Singapore, and gave the future monarch 'an understanding and affection for the empire that went beyond that of his father's'. It also paved the way for his spectacularly successful Christmas radio broadcasts to the empire during the 1930s.[97] Meanwhile, the future Edward VIII made his name with a series of empire tours during the 1920s, and George VI's visits to Canada in 1939 and South Africa in 1947 were considered high points of his reign.[98]

As late as 1953, Elizabeth II's coronation was still being invested with imperial significance. The 'vast machinery of [royal] reverence' was 'cranked up' to display the power, wealth and unity of the Empire-Commonwealth and to bring it before the British public as a powerful reality rather than an abstract idea;[99] or, as Britain's envoy to India pithily put it, 'the confetti of empire was still very visible in 1953'.[100] Yet change was in the air. Only two years before, the Festival of Britain (1951) had offered a rather different perspective on what it meant to be British. It too was a national public celebration, but as we saw in Chapter 4 it contained very few representations of the Empire-Commonwealth.[101] The gap between the rhetoric of a freedom-loving empire and the reality of racial prejudice toward colonial peoples had been more sharply exposed during the Second World War.[102] This may help to explain why Herbert Morrison and the Festival of Britain's planning committee decided to 'edit out' the empire from its 'representational repertoire' – political prudence, as well as an actual shortage of materials and labour, favoured a national rather than imperial celebration in 1951.[103]

The army bore an imperial imprint, though it presents us with a somewhat more complex case than the monarchy.[104] The machinery for strategic planning was decidedly deficient before the 1880s when the requirements [193] of imperial defence suffered from want of serious or systematic attention. It was the South African War that highlighted the need to correlate colonial defence plans with those of the home government. The Committee of Imperial Defence (1902) and Haldane's scheme for an Imperial General Staff were two of the proposed remedies. Yet the CID lacked the capacity to transform imperial defence planning (so too did the colonial conference system);[105] while the idea of an IGS, put forward at the 1907 colonial conference, smacked of imperial centralisation.[106] National prejudice against a large standing army, electoral pressures for economy, a diplomatic situation in constant flux and the overwhelming strength of the Royal Navy – all these stood in the way of longer-term planning for the empire's security. Not until Lloyd George established the Imperial War Cabinet in 1917 was a closer working partnership between the British and Dominion governments (temporarily) achieved.

To be sure, the Stanhope memorandum (1888) did try to give a clearer statement of the army's rationale – to aid the civil authorities, to garrison India and the colonies, to provide for home defence and ('subject to the foregoing considerations and to financial considerations') to deploy for expeditionary purposes during a European war.[107] In practice, however, there was little agreement among military strategists regarding the army's role. 'Traditionalists' hankered after the days of long service and the experienced soldier, and lamented the way in which the Cardwell reforms had turned the home forces into a vast nursery for overseas colonial units; 'Continentalists' looked to Prussian military organisation for inspiration, and urged Britain to prepare for a European war on a grand scale; and an 'Imperial School' chiefly concerned itself with training for colonial warfare, and saw action on the European mainland as a remote contingency.[108] Thus in the case of the army there was no equivalent of the 'Blue Water' school or imperial-naval conception of defence.[109] Curzon railed at Arthur Balfour – the 'Blue Water Prime Minister' – for precisely this reason. He protested that India did not appear to fit into the government's military strategy and was consequently left to look after itself.[110]

The empire loomed larger in terms of the distribution of Britain's armed forces and a soldier's military experience. The proportion of a career spent overseas varied over time. Soldiering in the colonies was not popular during the 1850s and 1860s when rates of mortality and disease were much higher there than in Europe.[111] In order to overcome problems of recruitment, the Cardwell system introduced the idea of 'linked battalions' and the possibility of short-term military service.[112] The intention was to

[194]   withdraw garrisons from the self-governing dominions and to station a greater proportion of soldiers at home to be despatched to colonial trouble-spots as the need arose. This aim of an army-in-balance was not easy to achieve, however.[113] Home-based battalions were squeezed as international competition intensified, colonial crises multiplied and more and more soldiers had to be sent abroad. The disparity was particularly marked after the Zulu war of 1879 when there were 82 battalions abroad but only 59 at home. There was further pressure to provide overseas drafts in the early 1920s when Britain took on new territorial responsibilities in the Middle East, and nationalist activities increased in Egypt and India.[114]

The need to defend a worldwide empire (in particular, to provide drafts for the army in India) was of continuous concern to British defence planners.[115] Table 5 provides peacetime figures for the total strength of the British army and its respective components from 1848 to 1925. By 1938 the British army numbered 197,338 troops: 106,704 (54%) were based in Britain[116] and 90,628 (46%) were based overseas. Of the latter,

Table 6   Distribution of Cavalry Regiments and Infantry Battalions of the British Regular Army in 1899, 1906, 1914 and 1935 (figures rounded to nearest whole percentage)

	1899	1906	1914	1935
Home	19 Cavalry	18	19	14
	71 Infantry	81	83	70
	90 (49%)	99 (50%)	102 (54%)	84 (53%)
India	9 Cavalry	9	9	5
	52 Infantry	52	52	45
	61 (33%)	61 (31%)	61 (32%)	50 (32%)
Colonies	3 Cavalry	4	3	3
	30 Infantry	33	22	21
	33 (18%)	37 (19%)	25 (13%)	24 (15%)
Total Cavalry	31	31	31	22
Total Infantry	153	166	157	136
Combined Total	184	197	188	158

Source: Adapted from J. K. Dunlop, *The Development of the British Army, 1899–1914* (Routledge, 1938), Appendix C, p. 309.

Table 7   Average strength and geographical distribution of the British army in 1848, 1881, 1895, 1905 and 1925

	Total strength	Home	Colonial	India
1848	129,726	61,623	39,403	28,700
		(48%)	(30%)	(22%)
1881	188,958	91,162	25,999	69,647
		(48%)	(14%)	(37%)
1895	220,309	107,636	37,084	75,589
		(49%)	(17%)	(34%)
1905	272,133	129,930	63,165	78,061
		(48%)	(23%)	(29%)
1925[a]	208,633	107,712	15,501[b]	62,179
		(52%)	(7%)	(30%)

Sources: A. Porter, *Atlas of British Overseas Expansion* (1994), pp. 118–21; *General Annual Return of the British Army for the Year 1895, PP* (1896) Cd.8,225, p. 3; *General Annual Report on the British Army for the Year Ending September 1905, PP* (1906) Cd.2,696, pp. 48–9; *Distribution of Regimental Establishments, Army Estimates for Year Ending 31/3/1926, PP* (1926) Cd.16,203, pp. 26–7.
[a] The period covered is from the end of March 1925 to the end of March 1926, rather than a calendar year.
[b] The figure is artificially low because at this time there was also the further category of 'Other Forces' (Rhine; Egypt and Sudan; Iraq; Palestine): 23,178 (11%). If the British troops in the Rhine were deducted and the others added to the colonial category the amended figure would be 28,487 (14%).

55,498 (28%) were stationed in India; 21,187 (11%) in the Middle East and Mediterranean; 12,143 (6%) in the Far East; and 1,806 (1%) in the West Indies.[117]

Of course, more of the army's manpower was tied up in the colonies during times of conflict.[118] It is estimated that 10,000–12,000 British troops were required for the Maori wars in New Zealand from 1845 to the 1860s; 20,000 for the Burmese war of 1852; 16,000 for Lord Chelmsford's second invasion of Zululand in 1879; and 35,000 (from India as well as England) for the Egyptian war of 1882.[119] A staggering 448,435 imperial troops saw service in South Africa from 1899 to 1902, the vast majority of them British. After the First World War, imperial policing duties in Iraq and Palestine meant that thirty-two infantry battalions had to be stationed there, a military presence that approximated to some 12,000 British and 53,000 indigenous Indian troops.[120]

[196]   Hence while wealthier officers in fashionable regiments may have avoided overseas duty, the majority could expect to spend a proportion of their time in the colonies, as could the ordinary soldier.[121] Whether the location of the army's overseas battalions mattered much to the life or spirit of their regiments at home is difficult to say. Regimental culture betrayed signs of colonial involvement – mascots, mess paintings, stuffed dogs, uniforms and various forms of imperial booty – but the roots of a regiment arguably lay in its home recruiting area.[122] From an individual's perspective, however, the empire takes on greater significance. By the late nineteenth century, when the tropics were no longer a white man's grave, imperial service began to be sought after as an avenue to promotion. This was especially true of officers from modest middle-class backgrounds lured by the higher pay of the Indian army and the prospect of maintaining a good showing in a regiment in England.[123] Yet wealthier officers were not immune to the enhanced status likely to be gained from participation in Victoria's small colonial wars.[124] In fact, all levels from lance-corporal and sergeant upwards probably saw some benefits in colonial military service whether it be in terms of promotion, civil jobs on the railways or the acquisition of land.

To recover the experience of officers and soldiers who saw service in the colonies is a different matter. It probably gave officers a wider vision and political awareness, and encouraged them to improvise tactically because of the multiplicity of adversaries.[125] On the other hand it provided them with few insights into large-scale warfare or the need for mechanisation, and did little to assist the introduction of modern armaments.[126] As for the rank-and-file, they were exposed to endemic diseases, extremes of climate and difficulties of terrain the like of which they had not previously encountered at home.[127] How far such drawbacks were offset by the freedom of wide-open colonial spaces,[128] or by retinues of servants to take care of daily chores, is unclear.[129] There was certainly a measure of pride and prestige in colonial soldiering by the end of the nineteenth century – some of those who returned from the Boer War 'were feted like proper heroes' by their local communities.[130]

What type of racial attitudes did colonial military service foster? This is a complex subject and only a few reflections can be offered here.[131] The main point to emphasise is that soldiers' views of colonial peoples are likely to have varied considerably according to their rank, their duties and the colony in question. Let us take each in turn. Family background, education and material incentives are all said to have inclined (some) officers to embrace the empire in a way that their men did not.[132] The dimensions of British troops' interactions with indigenous peoples must have been [197] important too. Expeditionary forces sent to conquer territory or put down a tribal revolt would have formed impressions of 'natives' mainly from fighting with and against them. For example, the Ashanti campaign of 1873–4 was the occasion for some hostile remarks toward the 'native' bearers who assisted British troops against the Kumasi but were felt to be frightened of the enemy. Similarly, during the Zulu war (1879) 'native' transports were rounded upon for delays, and parts of the Natal Native Contingent were criticised for fleeing their posts during battle.[133] Yet there was also recognition of the bravery and fighting skills of the loyal Swazis who were part of the second campaign against the Pedi in 1879, and of the Egyptians and Sudanese troops that helped Britain to reconquer the Sudan in 1898.[134] Garrison troops, meanwhile, had much more time to learn about the local populations among whom they lived, and appear to have been much more integrated into the wider social and cultural life of both settler and indigenous society.[135]

Oral testimony sheds further light on soldiers' racial attitudes. Those who served in Africa were frequently appalled by the barbarity that they considered their enemies to have displayed,[136] while the newly-arrived in India were soon 'inoculated by the older soldiers in the way natives should be treated'.[137] During his visit in 1875–6, the Prince of Wales (and future King Edward VII) rounded upon the army for the 'rough and ready manner' in which it treated the Queen's Indian subjects, especially the habit of referring to them as 'niggers'.[138] On their return home these same soldiers may well have helped to shape British society's perceptions of the extra-European world. We know, for instance, that 'service-pension-wallahs' liked to gather to share stories of 'natives' they had punched, booted or killed, and to regale their colleagues at work with these tales.[139] Yet we also know that letters from Zululand in 1879 reveal a much wider range of emotions: a sense of helplessness, a struggle for survival, a desire for revenge, a revulsion at the number of enemy slain, and a 'growing respect' for their courage and intelligence.[140] Much more work remains to be done here.

The regions and nations of the United Kingdom

Built by the Scots, Welsh and Irish as well as the English, the empire's prestige and profits accrued to them all.[141] The armies that fought in colonial wars were emphatically 'British': Scottish and Irish soldiers were prominent

[198] in the conquest of India, the suppression of the Mutiny and the Boer War, and the 24th Regiment of Foot (the South Wales Borderers) had a strong and enduring South African connection as a result of the Zulu war.[142] In the spheres of education, engineering, exploration, medicine, commerce and shipping, the Scots in particular earned a reputation for empire-building. But the Irish middle-class – educated Catholic as well as Protestant – was well represented in the Indian Civil and Medical services, while the Irish working class played a critical role in the colonisation process. The Welsh were somewhat more reticent – part of the purpose of the 1911 investiture of the Prince of Wales was to encourage them to take their full place in the British imperial enterprise. That said, Welsh emigrants to the colonies were deeply involved in establishing the gold-fields of Australia (where the Eisteddfod became a well-known institution), they pioneered the peopling of Patagonia, and there is a sense in which the very character of the industrial economy of South Wales and its working population can be considered to have been 'imperial'.[143]

Unity in a shared imperial cause did not, however, mean uniformity. While a range of domestic forces – railways, education, migration and sport – were working to 'blend' different cultures within the United Kingdom,[144] regional distinctiveness was as likely to be underlined as undermined by the empire. John Mackenzie has already urged the empire's tendency to 'perpetuate and enhance' regional identities with reference to Scotland.[145] Here we will take a closer look at the colonial connections of England and Ireland. The case of England was self-evidently *sui generis*: its political and demographic primacy in the UK raised the problem of whether British nationalism could ever transcend a narrower English patriotism. The assumption of the English that they were the senior partner in Britain's imperial enterprise suggests not.[146] Indeed, Westminster-based politicians like Milner and Rosebery were at pains to praise the imperial instincts of England's neighbours precisely because they felt that they needed re-assuring that the cry of a shared allegiance to empire was not a cloak for English aggrandisement.[147]

And yet there were at least two ways in which overseas expansion may have suppressed an English identity. First, as the dominant part of the United Kingdom the English were confident about who they were and did not feel the need to debate their identity.[148] Some of this self-confidence must surely have come from the empire, which lifted them above 'mere nationalist self-glorification' and gave them 'a leading role as an agent of civilisation and progress'.[149] Second, overseas expansion helped to stimulate and sustain a range of sub-English identities. The strength of localism in domestic British

life has been more widely recognised in recent historical writing.[150] What
has been overlooked is the fact that many English emigrants to the colonies took a particular pride in their place of origin within the British Isles. A key mechanism for encouraging sub-English identities among settlers was the regional society or county association.[151] Cultural rather than political, these voluntary bodies provided a forum in which settlers from the same region could meet and mix. Many were formed on an occupational basis, reflecting the way in which labour skills were tied to particular areas of the United Kingdom. They were prominent on the diamond- and gold-fields of South Africa where they helped the newly-arrived to find work, dispensed charitable aid to those who had fallen on hard times, and organised recreational activities that were intended to reflect the culture of the region concerned. Yet they were also to be found across Australia and Canada too.

Ireland's imperial involvement is complex and there is simply no way of doing it justice in a book of this scope.[152] The empire served a different function for the Irish to the Scottish or the Welsh, and was frequently conceived more negatively. This was the result of Ireland being an internally fractured society – the subject of systematic English and Scottish colonisation. Moreover, in so far as Ireland did take on an imperial identity it differed from that of England. So much is shown by the frontier mentality of Ulster 'loyalists' and their sense of themselves as a settler people.[153] Like other embattled groups in Natal and Rhodesia, Irish Unionists constantly sought reassurance that their loyalty to Britain and the empire would not go unrecognised or unrewarded.[154] They were an ultra-British community determined to remain within the UK rather than be ruled from Dublin.[155] As such, they saw themselves not as 'Irish British'[156] but as 'imperial British',[157] and took considerable pride in Britain's achievements overseas. Yet they also sensed that their interests were increasingly diverging from those of the 'mother country', which was felt to be losing its way and becoming more decadent; this was particularly true of evangelical Protestants who linked the spread of empire to religious values and a true Christian commitment.[158] Meanwhile, for certain types of (elite) Unionist the incorporation of the imagery and ideology of empire into Unionism may have been more instrumental.[159] Irish Unionist intellectuals apparently showed scant concern for imperial issues when they did not intersect with Irish affairs, while the Irish Protestant gentry is said to have undertaken colonial service as much for financial reasons as from a sense of imperial mission.[160]

As early as the 1880s Ulster began to take on an imperial consciousness, possibly before.[161] During the Home Rule crisis Irish Protestants embraced

[200] the empire as a way of legitimising their opposition to an ascendant Catholic nationalism and 'Rome Rule', and it was at this time that the north of Ireland began to represent itself as a bastion of imperial loyalty.[162] The South African War was important, too. For Irish Catholics it provided another example of colonial oppression – some actually fought alongside the Boers. But for Unionists the struggle in South Africa was a source of inspiration: volunteer companies, memorials, press reporting and commercial advertising all helped to 'propagate a mass audience for the imperial message'.[163] Ulster Protestant migration to Canada is also worth a mention: it was much higher than that to Australia or New Zealand. Hence the Orange Lodge Order – the fraternity at the heart of Ulster Unionism – was well established in Canada where its branches not only provided 'an avenue of social and political association for Protestants of Irish extraction', but extended 'a colonial frame of mind' among many Irish Protestant settlers who were becoming increasingly aware of the growing republican and Catholic threat at home and abroad.[164]

There is a greater recognition nowadays of how 'regional' forms of identity not only survived the rise of Britishness but remained integral to what it meant.[165] True domestically, this insight can equally be applied to the empire. As we have seen, the process of fashioning an imperial British identity was as much about building on regional forms of association as it was about liquidating them. 'Imperial Britishness' was not something superimposed over an array of disparate cultures and identities that made up the United Kingdom. Rather, to varying degrees, the Scottish, the Welsh, the Irish and the English regions were to find in the empire a form of self-affirmation that helped them better contend with the political and cultural challenges they were facing.

Conclusion

We need to resist overstating the colonies' contribution to creating British nationhood for there was always a fundamental tension in the British peoples' self-perception.[166] On the one hand they were a 'worldwide people' who took pride in their ability to command the seas and dispense their justice on a global scale. Yet, on the other, they were apt to retreat into their island fortress and to eschew the potentially corrupting influences of Catholic Europe and the outside world. That the empire was not the only frame of reference for national imagining is clear from what

was said earlier about the vocabulary of the English language and the built
urban environment. To a degree, each reflects Britain's imperial involvement; however, many more foreign words were borrowed from Europe
and the USA, while the empire was only one among many influences –
domestic and international – on architectural styles. Meanwhile, a sense
of imperial Britishness seems to have struck deeper roots in the country's
established institutions. Here the empire was in no small part responsible
for defining the role and enhancing the reputation of Britain's monarchy
and armed forces.

In so far as we can meaningfully speak of a British imperial identity,
it was constructed along at least two axes. It was partly negative and
oppositional, and dependent on the feeling of 'otherness' that the colonies
helped to create. But it was also positive and self-referential, and derived
from a feeling of 'sameness' that bound metropolitan Britons to the self-
styled British communities of the settler empire. This notion of a 'Greater
Britain' or 'British world' has gained a much wider currency in recent
historical writing. Discussions of emigration (Chapter 2) and the domestic
politics of imperialism (Chapter 6) showed how it resonated privately with
families and publicly with politicians, and the final section of this chapter
on regionalism reinforced this point by examining the preservation of
a range of sub-British identities by settler societies, clubs and lodges; a
similar function may have been served by the churches and other religious
associations.

This does not mean that imperial Britishness was a consensual or stable
identity, however.[167] One problem when studying national identities is
to establish how far their 'dominant groups' or 'principal carriers' were
reflecting or responding to a popular will.[168] Other parts of this book
have argued that different people could embrace an imperial identity for
different – even diametrically opposed – reasons.[169] In this chapter we have
seen how urban retailers were not nearly as eager as public planners to
redevelop the capital's shopping streets as imperial spaces: they embraced
the empire as a market, yet feared the expense of such an undertaking and
the fact that it threatened to drive away middle-class consumers. Official
and non-official (or commercial) conceptions of empire can be seen to have
collided, therefore. Indeed, what George Orwell observed of patriotism may
well have been equally true of imperialism, namely, it tended to take different forms among different classes, though it ran like a connecting thread
through nearly all of them.[170]

Finally, we need to reconsider the relationship between the loss of
the colonies and the supposed demise of Britishness. It has recently been

[202]   argued that the empire was no longer central to national identity in Britain by the time of the Suez crisis in 1956.[171] However, to say that 'the loss of imperial glory naturally created a situation of hostility to the concept of the United Kingdom seems to involve the belief that the Empire must have [previously] been a *vital cement* of that unity'.[172] There are grounds for doubt. The United Kingdom was not primarily established to form a basis for overseas expansion, while the 'revolt of the regions' antedated imperial decline in Britain and has troubled many states that were not formerly colonial powers. More than that, many of the supports that formerly propped up a sense of British nationality – Protestantism, Parliament, the countryside, the BBC and the folk memory of the Second World War – seem to be much weaker now than they were in 1945.[173] Thus if we are currently confused and uncertain about our national identity, we should not jump to the conclusion that this is solely (or even mainly) the result of the loss of an empire and 'post-imperial drift'. But that is to anticipate the next chapter.

CHAPTER 9

AFTER-EFFECTS

There is no escaping the sudden collapse of the (formal) British empire after 1945. The Second World War may not have shattered public belief in colonial rule, yet it did have deeply 'corrosive effects at . . . every level of the imperial connection'.[1] Within a few decades of granting independence to India on 14 August 1947, sixty-four countries and approximately 500 million people had ceased to be ruled by the British. The Commonwealth was the only consolation.

Two contrasting views can be identified in the surprisingly sparse literature on the after-effects of empire. Many on the Left have tried to explain the lack of radical dissent in Britain in terms of the cultural and constitutional legacies of colonialism.[2] The historian Ashis Nandy believes that imperial attitudes and values were thoroughly internalised by the British.[3] While Indians were largely able to confine the impact of empire to their urban centres, the British were 'overwhelmed' by their experience of being colonial rulers. The former cabinet minister and leading thinker on Labour's Left, Tony Benn, agrees. He regards Britain as the empire's last colony and the British people as the last to await liberation.[4] Nandy's case rests on the damage colonialism supposedly inflicted on British society. It did this by encouraging 'magical feelings of omnipotence and permanence', by justifying a limited role for women, by sanctifying institutionalised forms of violence and by fostering a false sense of homogeneity. Benn is more interested in government and Britain's claim to be a 'global' and 'imperial' power. He sees this mistaken belief as having stifled the development of a truly democratic political culture by obstructing constitutional reform and by privileging the Anglo-American 'special relationship', the result of which has been subservience to the United States. Yet both men share the same sense that while the empire has become less and less important to formerly colonial populations, the metropolitan British have yet to escape it.

[204]   Another and in many respects diametrically opposed view is that after 1945 the empire rapidly became irrelevant to the lives of people in Britain, if indeed it was not irrelevant already. It was a dwindling dimension of their past, more apparent to foreigners than to the British themselves.[5] Admittedly, the loss of an institution that was thought to have brought wealth and stability to Britain was deeply disconcerting for a few (especially the landed and professional middle-class families who had served it), but it was of little concern to the majority. Rather, Britain put her imperial past behind her surprisingly quickly: people 'ceased to relate to empire' and eventually even to remember it.[6] A recent survey of post-war propaganda, Empire Day, advertising, the school curriculum and overseas military service goes as far as to suggest that, by the 1940s, 'popular imperialism' was already in terminal decline. Stripped of its romance, invincibility and moral validity, the empire no longer lay at the core of national identity – this explains why the Suez crisis of 1956 proved much less of a shock to ordinary Britons than it did to their political leaders.[7]

For all European powers, the colonial legacy has proved difficult to disentangle. In Britain's case it could be the subject of a separate and substantial book. Hence this chapter is not comprehensive and confines itself to the exploration of three themes. The first is Britain's self-image. How did the loss of empire 'strike back' at Britain's view of its international role, and how disruptive was the process of adjusting to the status of a second-rank, middle-weight power? These questions are particularly pertinent given Britain's rather ambivalent relationship with the EU and critiques of its close alignment with the USA. (There is, however, no attempt here to present a sustained analysis of the 'empire to EEC' debate, partly because other historians have done this, partly because the colonial component of anti-Europeanism has arguably been exaggerated anyway.) Second, how has the migration of people from the 'new' Commonwealth – which is, after all, the most enduring legacy of empire – changed views of Britain? Did their experiences differ from immigrants from other parts of the world? And to what extent does today's multi-cultural society continue to suffer from preconceptions and prejudices inherited from the colonial period? Third, how far is the empire a factor in debates about Britain's contemporary condition, and what changes has the passing of the empire brought about in public thinking? Here we will examine attitudes toward Britain's last remaining colonies; issues of public policy that Britain's imperial past has recently thrust into the public domain (child migration, the repatriation of human remains, war memorials); and recent representations of that past in the media.

Throughout the chapter close attention will be paid to generational perspectives both of the 'indigenous' and 'immigrant' parts of the population.
Any child of the 1930s or 1940s was brought up at a time when much of
the world was 'British'. Does this mean that those born before the Second
World War tend to have an imperial outlook while those born since do
not?[8] Similarly, much of the literature on Commonwealth immigration contrasts the attitudes of first-generation migrants with those of their British-
born descendants: whereas until recently many of the former maintained at
least 'the myth of return' (the idea that their stay was only temporary), the
lives of the latter have been much more centred on Britain. Is this why they
have become more conscious of, and bitter about, racial discrimination?[9]
Yet there may be a danger of whiggism here. Several post-war public opinion surveys (cited below) suggest that, counter-intuitively, younger (white)
people tended to be better informed about the colonies and more willing
to consider emigrating to them. Neither is it apparent that the memory of
empire is now receding in public culture. On the contrary, as this chapter
was written, Britain's imperial involvement was being debated more widely
and vigorously than at any time the author (born in 1968) can remember.
We will conclude by asking why this is so, and how far other post-imperial
societies have felt the same need to revisit aspects of their colonial pasts.

Britain's place in the world

Dean Acheson, President Truman's Secretary of State from 1949 to 1953,
once famously said that Britain had 'lost an empire' but had 'not yet found
a role'. His remark was made at a time when the country's political leaders
appeared to be acting under the misapprehension that the nation was stronger
than it actually was.[10] Hence their willingness to maintain high levels
of defence spending (notwithstanding its adverse economic effects), and to
uphold a role in the Middle East and East of Suez. Not until devaluation
in 1967 did Britain finally scale down its overseas commitments.[11]
    The Suez crisis is often treated as a litmus test for Britain's view of its
international role.[12] For some Suez represents the last gasp of empire, a
'symbolic watershed' that paved the way for a gradual realignment away from
the Commonwealth and towards greater involvement in Europe.[13] For others
it is symptomatic of a 'post-imperial great power syndrome' that resurfaced
during the Falkland crisis of 1982 and even as recently as the repatriation
of Hong Kong in 1997.[14] Alternatively, Britain's diminished world role
after Suez may have reflected new economic realities. By the later 1950s

[206]   British prosperity turned on the expansion of trade with Western Europe and North America and not on the protection of 'soft' colonial markets.[15] Likewise with finance: in 1957 the Colonial Policy Committee reported that the Sterling Area, though important to the British economy, need not be jeopardised by dollar-earning colonies gaining their independence.[16]

Thus not even Suez provides a clear-cut case of an 'imperial hangover'. In trying to re-occupy the canal zone, Eden was undeniably moved by patriotic conviction and by a desire to maintain Britain as a first-class power. But Eden did not possess Churchill's instinctive love of empire nor Attlee's belief in the Commonwealth. Neither had he previously seen eye to eye with the Suez group, for whom the base was not only vital for access to oil, but a lifeline of empire and the chief military guarantee of Commonwealth ties.[17] Rather, as Foreign Secretary, Eden had persistently advocated and eventually achieved withdrawal in 1954.[18] When he did decide to use force two years later he was probably prompted as much by his memories of appeasement and hatred of Nasser as by any clinging to an imperial past.[19] Similarly, Thatcher's decision to send the Royal Navy to re-occupy the Falkland Islands in 1982 is open to more than one interpretation.[20] It could be portrayed as the jingoistic fulfilment of an 'imperial mission'. But it could equally be that the Falklands was as much about standing up to dictators – and (again) motivated by the memory of appeasement – as it was about nostalgia for a colonial past.

In fact, the very analogy of Britain trying to 'punch above its weight' may be false. It tends to conceive of Britain's overseas influence merely as a matter of military and material strength. Yet there have clearly been many conflicts that the international community has not been able to resolve by armed intervention or economic sanctions – in recent years the Congo, Somalia, Yugoslavia, Afghanistan and Iraq could all be counted in this category. Is it not possible that the imperial phase in British history may have played a more positive role in terms of fostering a belief within a post-war generation of political and military leaders that government was about more than ensuring the nation's stability and prosperity? Could it not have equipped them with the judgement and expertise necessary to resolve certain types of dispute and to exercise leadership on an international stage? Harold Macmillan certainly felt this to be the case. As he explained in 1960:

> Our leadership of the Commonwealth, the progressive fulfilment of our colonial responsibilities . . . the legacy of our imperial past, the maturity of our political experience outside Europe, our national quality of rising to an emergency and our reliability in the defence of freedom and justice: all these can continue to

justify for the United Kingdom a leading position among the Powers and a   [207]
higher place in their counsels than our material assets alone would strictly
warrant.[21]

A cynic would dismiss these remarks as self-justifying.[22] They could be read
another way, however. Britain's governing elite may have remained attached
to the empire during the 1950s and 1960s not just because of the status
and prestige that it conferred, but because they had grown up with it.
It was, in short, a vital source of political experience – a point of reference
that they (and others) could not easily erase.

So much for the politicians: what about the wider public? The capacity
of the empire to evoke different responses was as true after 1945 as it was
before.[23] Previous chapters have emphasised the range of relationships the
British people had with the colonies. There are several reasons why this
was so. Far from being a single entity, the empire was vast and varied, and
each part developed its own particular traditions and links to Britain.
Britain, moreover, was an increasingly diverse and pluralistic society in
which perceptions of the importance of the imperial connection differed
according to family background, social class, gender and regional belonging. Imperialism's impact was also uneven: it was probably more pronounced
(and is certainly easier to trace) in terms of religion, politics and established
institutions than in terms of the economy, education or organised leisure.
Finally, the range of issues raised by overseas expansion – the maintenance
of national prestige; the protection of expatriate British communities;
the use of force to counter terrorism or contain dissent; and the cost of
imperial commitments to the British taxpayer – tended to touch the public
nerve at different times and in different ways. Taken together, these factors
help to explain why the empire continued to have many and complex
effects on the home society during and after the Second World War.

What is new about the war and post-war era is the availability of
quantitative evidence about public attitudes. While it would be unwise
to regard opinion polls as a more 'scientific' type of data – pollsters have
their own agenda, questions can be skewed and samples are not always
representative – it nonetheless provides a useful perspective on the British
public's engagement with the empire.

My focus here is on a series of Mass Observation (MO) surveys from
1942 to 1948, a BBC report of 1943 and various Gallup Polls from 1937.
The first MO survey was published in March 1942, and based on a panel
of 1,300 observers, who were asked six questions including one about 'their
present feelings about the British Empire'.[24] The BBC Listener Research

[208] Report (Dec. 1942 to Jan. 1943) employed a 'local correspondents' system – a group of interviewers questioned people with whom they were in daily contact about the empire (sample A), and offered their own replies to a similar set of questions (sample B).[25] Another MO survey – for Kemsley Newspapers – asked a series of questions about the empire, in addition to exploring the nature of people's interest and participation in sport.[26] The best-known survey – for the Colonial Office in May–June 1948 – aimed to 'discover public knowledge of and interest in the British colonies'.[27] Finally, *A Report on the British Commonwealth and Empire* (Nov. 1948) was conducted for the *Daily Graphic* newspaper.[28]

The only one of these surveys to attract scholarly attention – the 1948 CO inquiry – has been quoted very selectively. The main conclusion drawn at the time (and subsequently) was that the British public knew very little about their empire.[29] Only one person in four knew the difference between a 'dominion' and a 'colony', and only a half of those questioned could name a colony. Yet is it any surprise that the general public could not define the difference between a 'colony' and a 'dominion' when these words were used so imprecisely?[30] Of the 980 respondents to the CO survey who failed to name a colony, 250 had offered a 'dubious' answer rather than no answer at all – some were way off the mark but many had simply referred to a 'dominion' instead. Nor was this the only type of knowledge tested, and in other respects people were much better informed about the empire. Thus 44% could cite an event that had recently occurred there; 67% had heard of the groundnuts scheme in Tanganyika; 59% were aware that Britain assisted the colonies financially; and 21% realised that the colonies helped earn dollars for Britain.[31] These are not the response rates of an imperially illiterate population.

The groundnuts scheme had, of course, attracted a lot of publicity. Although intended to show what the colonial state was capable of in tropical Africa, it did nothing to ease Britain's vegetable oil and fat shortages and by the mid-1950s had cost the British taxpayer £36 million.[32] Not surprisingly, the Conservative party saw it as a handy stick with which to beat Attlee's government; so too did comedians in the music and variety halls and on the radio.[33] The fact that the issue was controversial is significant. As the BBC's survey was at pains to point out, what turned listeners off the empire were anodyne reports of it, in particular the way in which radio programmes had frequently been 'hamstrung by sensitivities of the imperial relationship'.[34] Served uninspiring material, who could blame the public for losing its appetite for colonial news? What they really wanted was for 'the colonial point of view' to be 'frankly presented', and for mistakes in past colonial policy not to be 'glossed over'. In other words, they wanted [209] real news about the empire not propaganda.

To treat opinion surveys as empire IQ-tests which the public failed is misleading, therefore. In fact, these surveys tackled an array of subjects that ranged far beyond the merely factual. Those confused about the terminology of empire, or uncertain about its geography, were much more forthcoming when asked for their views on Britain's colonial record. Tax policy offers a good point of comparison here. The majority of people in post-war Britain would not have properly understood the impact of different taxes on their standard of living; nor would they necessarily have known the higher (or marginal) rate of tax for any given amount of extra income they earned. Yet they would have been aware of current controversies surrounding the tax system (e.g. compulsory savings and post-war tax credits), and they would have held firm opinions about its fairness. Likewise, the empire: people did not need to know a lot about it in order to have an opinion on it. Take the 1942 MO survey. It recorded a 'very considerable body of guilt' about how the dependent colonies had been acquired and administered, and went on to suggest that this 'guilt factor' was important in forming opinion about their future. There was a widespread feeling that these parts of the empire would have to be granted more freedom after the war. This was attributed partly to the loss of Singapore (which had dealt a severe psychological blow to the British),[35] partly to the way the colonies had rallied to Britain's side in 1939, and partly to the more general state of wartime anxiety that was easily transferred to the colonial stage.[36]

Guilty or proud, many people in Britain do seem to have thought about the empire. But how far did their views change during the 1950s and 1960s when the cost of defending Britain's colonial commitments became ever more difficult for the Exchequer to sustain, and when protecting the position (and privileges) of European settlers in Africa regularly required the use of force? It has been argued that it was only after the 'third implosion of empire' between 1959 and 1964 that 'both popular and intellectual culture . . . became fully aware of the underlying realities of power, of the extent to which empire was over in economic, political, military and conceptual terms'.[37] Is this correct?

Here Britain's post-war empire will be separated into three strands: strategic-military priorities in Suez, Aden and Singapore; responsibilities toward 'expatriate' British in tropical Africa; and leadership of the Commonwealth and its implications for Britain's relations with Europe. Together these issues go some way to capture the key concerns that the continuing exercise of colonial power thrust into the public arena during these decades.

[210]   Moreover, in each case we have direct insight into the 'public mind' in the form of the Gallup opinion polls. Founded in 1935, much of Gallup's early work was market research on the movie-going habits of the American public. It subsequently became known for tracking the public's attitudes on a wide range of political, social and economic issues. Already by 1937 the organisation was operating in several other countries including Britain. By weighing the evidence of the Gallup polls against other forms of historical research it should be possible to test the 'third implosion of empire' thesis.

The best place to start is Suez. Many of the soldiers who were sent to repossess the canal seem to have struggled to understand why they were there. Sir James Spicer recently spoke of the way in which company commanders had their doubts about the operation.[38] 'We were the last gasp of empire', he recalled. What oral testimony we have from the troops shows a similar lack of commitment – a desire to get the job done mixed with a feeling of the absurdity of it all.[39] Whether Suez points to a wider rejection of the 'imperial mission' that had previously motivated the armed forces is unclear; further study of the experiences of the national servicemen who served in Aden, Cyprus, Egypt, Kenya and Malaya would help here. Meanwhile in the country opinion was deeply divided.[40] Gallup asked a series of questions in September 1956. Almost 70% of people disapproved of Nasser's action in nationalising the Suez Canal Company, but when asked whether Britain and France should have opted for immediate military action a similar number said not.[41] Even in response to the *Daily Express*'s heavily-weighted question about whether Eden was right to send 'British forces' to protect 'British interests' and to guarantee the freedom of transit of 'British ships', 39% of respondents expressed their opposition.[42] Looking back on the crisis a year later, 48% defended the decision to send in the troops (though government propagandists had shrewdly played the Cold War card in the intervening months).[43] Yet 32% still criticised Britain's use of armed force and Eden's handling of the situation. Moreover, a sizeable body of opinion, supported by the liberal press, favoured a peaceful end to the dispute by referring the issue to the UN Security Council, notwithstanding the danger of appearing disloyal to the troops.[44]

Suez called into question Britain's aspirations to be an independent player on the world stage.[45] It may also have helped to prepare people for the withdrawal from East of Suez the following decade. In the mid-1960s Britain still retained much of the global network of bases that had long been the lynchpin of imperial defence. Sizeable forces were stationed in the Far East (Singapore, Hong Kong), the Middle East (Aden and the Gulf) and Southern Africa (Simonstown).[46] Harold Wilson's government entered office

in 1964 committed to maintaining a British presence in these regions.[47]
The public, however, did not seem so sure. When asked that year about the
defence of Aden and Singapore, 42% favoured Britain shouldering the
responsibility alone but 28% were willing to ask the United States for help.
By July 1966, 28% could contemplate withdrawing completely from East
of Suez, while in May 1967, when the government finally announced its
intention to leave Aden, 52% approved – violence against British troops
had long been escalating, and only weeks after this poll twenty-two servicemen were killed and a further thirty-one wounded by a terrorist attack.[48]
For some people, at least, the prospect of maintaining a large military presence overseas was not very attractive.[49] Overall, however, public opinion
was probably mixed, and, unlike immigration, the question of Britain's East
of Suez role was not to be settled by it. It was more a matter of politicians,
who had grown up with the assumption that Britain was a world military
power, gradually recognising that external pressures and economic necessity were driving them toward withdrawal from the Middle East and South-
East Asia.[50] They did not need to ask the electorate for its approval: there
was no legislation to pass, and by the time of devaluation in 1967 Britain's
financial position left them with little alternative. Two years later, Philip
Larkin derided the cost cutting of the final stages of colonial withdrawal
in one of his few politically explicit poems, 'Homage to a Government':

> Next year we are to bring the soldiers home
> For lack of money, and it is all right.
> Places they guarded, or kept orderly,
> Must guard themselves, and keep themselves orderly.
> We want the money for ourselves at home
> Instead of working. And this is all right.
>
> It's hard to say who wanted it to happen,
> But now it's been decided nobody minds.
> The places are a long way off, not here,
> Which is all right, and from what we hear
> The soldiers there only made trouble happen.
> Next year we shall be easier in our minds.
>
> Next year we shall be in a country
> That brought its soldiers home for lack of money.
> The statues will be standing in the same
> Tree-muffled squares, and look nearly the same.
> Our children will not know it's a different country.
> All we can hope to leave them now is money.[51]

[212]   Larkin may well have expressed a mood of resignation tinged by shame that greeted Britain's foreign policy at this time; his poem oversimplified events, however. There had actually been many obstacles to rapid withdrawal. According to Denis Healey, then Defence Secretary, who played a pivotal role in Britain's retreat from East of Suez, these included the need to make sure that newly-independent colonies did not further destabilise their regions; the hope of establishing another Far Eastern military base in Australia, or failing that an airfield on the island of Aldabra off Mozambique; the pressure from the United States to stay on, and the fear of financial aid being jeopardised if Britain did not; and the fact that British troops were still fighting alongside Commonwealth troops in Borneo during the Confrontation between Malaya and Indonesia.[52] Thus it was not until the 1966 Defence White Paper was published that a majority of Healey's cabinet colleagues fully accepted the logic of scaling down British bases in Aden and Singapore, and, moreover, could see their way to achieving this. By this date only Harold Wilson seemed to have the stomach for continuing an East of Suez role.

Increasingly felt to be an encumbrance during the 1950s and 1960s, the empire was becoming something of an embarrassment too. The year 1959 was a turning point. Two separate events in Africa questioned the continuation of colonial rule. The first was the revelation of brutality at the Hola Camp for Mau Mau rehabilitants in Kenya,[53] where during a riot eleven detainees were beaten to death by guards under the jurisdiction of a British prison official. The second was the Devlin report on the imposition of emergency rule in Nyasaland (part of the white-run Central African Federation under British colonial administration) that referred to a territory run like a 'police state'. Parliament and the press scrutinised the Macmillan government's handling of these incidents, and there was a high level of public awareness of them: 90% of those polled by Gallup had heard about the troubles in Kenya, and 80% about what was happening in Nyasaland. In the case of the Mau Mau a majority of people supported the authorities' actions: 41% in favour to 23% against. (Whereas the press had turned a blind eye to counter-terrorist measures in Malaya, it was much more uneasy over this campaign.[54]) Opinion was more finely balanced toward Nyasaland: 25% were prepared to back the British government, 23% were not; more people's sympathies also lay with the Africans (30%) than with the European settlers (18%).

After the outcry over the Hola camp massacres and the Nyasaland emergency, gradualism in the transfer of power looked less realistic. Politically, supporters of more rapid constitutional advance in Africa were able to unite in a number of non-partisan organisations including the Africa 1960 Committee and the Committee on Northern Rhodesia. Among Tories they were initially a minority and centred on the Bow Group, although with every new intake of MPs the party's attachment to empire weakened – here generational differences did matter.[55] In fact, by the end of the 1950s the whole concept of empire no longer seemed such an electoral asset.[56] On the doorsteps few Conservative candidates were willing to risk embarrassing voters with evocations of imperial greatness which only ten years before had been a standard part of their repertoire.[57] What had changed? It seems likely that sympathy for the highly privileged European settlers in Africa was beginning to dwindle. Macmillan disliked their decadence;[58] they were more frequently the butt of contemporary satire, not least in Vicky's cartoons in the *Evening Standard;*[59] 'kith and kin' sentiment had much more limited appeal for an emerging group of professional middle-class Tory MPs;[60] and the Gallup polls point to a growing body of support for political rights and social equality for Rhodesia's 'coloured population', and for withholding independence from a government consisting only of Europeans.[61]

The final strand of our analysis of Britain's self-image concerns the Commonwealth, views of which differ markedly among both academics and politicians. For some it has been an important instrument for collective action, and provided crucial economic, political and strategic support for Britain's claim to remain a world power.[62] For others it has been no more than 'the residue of a far-flung empire', a mere 'myth' or 'historical souvenir'[63] that concealed the extent and eased the pain of national decline.[64] Yet these are retrospective judgements: what did it mean to British people during the 1950s and 1960s? There is no doubt that Suez exposed the Commonwealth's limitations. A senior Canadian official later recalled that it was 'like discovering that your spouse had had an affair: divorce was not possible, but neither was trust'.[65] Britain had not consulted the Canadians for fear that they would not endorse their action. Meanwhile, Canada's Secretary of State for External Affairs, Lester Pearson, set about negotiating an Anglo-French withdrawal and the despatch of a force by the UN – he hoped to stop non-aligned countries being driven into the hands of the Soviet Union, and to prevent a rift opening up between Britain and the United States. (For his efforts in conflict moderation he was rewarded with a Nobel Prize.) Nehru went further and forthrightly condemned the British and French attempt to coerce Egypt as a 'reversion to past colonial methods'. He also saw it as an added justification for India's non-aligned foreign policy.[66]

[214]   Equally, it should be remembered that politicians in Britain remained committed to the Commonwealth ideal. So much is evident from their reaction to the 1948 election in South Africa, which brought D. F. Malan's Nationalist party to power. This was widely seen as a major setback for the Commonwealth and the principles on which it was founded.[67] Apartheid not only 'damaged the moral authority of whites to rule anywhere in Africa', it 'challenged the British conception of a multi-racial partnership'.[68] In 1960, many British politicians accepted the inevitability of South Africa's transition to a Republic precisely because they feared the impact of the apartheid policies and ideology of Hendrik Verwoerd's government on the idea of the Commonwealth as a progressive association. (When Verwoerd was assassinated in Cape Town in September 1966 little sympathy was expressed in Britain – *Private Eye*'s cover famously showed four Zulu warriors jumping for joy above the caption 'A Nation Mourns'.)

The commitment of much of Britain's political class to the Commonwealth is further evident from debates about the European Economic Community. Britain's obligations to the dominions (Australia and New Zealand, especially) were repeatedly and successfully invoked as a reason for not joining. 'The (white) bonds of history and culture', it is said, 'gripped hard on the public mind.'[69] For example, during the 1961 debate the Tories lauded the Commonwealth connection and insisted that it had to be preserved. They 'yearned for the vanished, English-speaking world' and the power and prestige that Britain's leadership of that world had conferred.[70] This strongly suggests that the 'old' dominions enjoyed at least a measure of public affection or esteem at this time.[71] From the Labour backbenches concern was expressed about the impact of EEC entry on the growth of the 'new' multi-racial Commonwealth. Might Britain not be sacrificing long-standing interests in Africa and Asia for a new venture in Western Europe?

It is, of course, Macmillan who is credited with initiating the major reversal in British thinking about the virtues of European integration and the need for a corresponding re-evaluation of Britain's colonial commitments.[72] Was this new 'Europeanist phase' in British politics an 'elite' or 'popular' phenomenon? Historians think the former, explaining the failure of the first application for EEC entry (1961–3) in terms of the rather downbeat campaign that Macmillan had to conduct at home in deference to the Commonwealth, and the resulting difficulty in persuading de Gaulle and the French that Britain was psychologically ready for the change.[73] Pro-Europeanists in particular lament the way in which European integration was portrayed (negatively) as a necessary response to decline – 'the only place left to go'.[74] How far, then, can this reluctance to proclaim Europe's [215] virtues be blamed on the Commonwealth? There were certainly other obstacles to joining the fledgling EEC, not least the feared loss of national sovereignty and scepticism regarding Europe's economic benefits. The Commonwealth's influence was less obtrusive. Many people clearly felt that Britain stood apart from continental Europe. Much of this insularity stemmed from Britain's geographical position on its periphery, reinforced by the sense of 'relative impregnability' that came from victory in two world wars. (These must have been hugely significant in shaping popular perceptions of Britain's place in the world if only because millions were personally involved.[75]) Yet Britain's insularity was probably also a product of its imperial experience in so far as this gave rise to the feeling that the British were different from (and superior to) other Europeans.[76]

The appeal of an 'imperial political economy' was more significant still.[77] Not only did Commonwealth trade bulk large in the Treasury's calculations regarding the EEC, it seems to have influenced public opinion too.[78] As late as 1969 two-thirds of those asked by Gallup thought it would be 'serious' or 'very serious' for Britain if the Commonwealth were to break up. While only a half of these people saw the Commonwealth as 'important' or 'very important' to Britain's military role and standing in world politics, 80% were convinced that the Commonwealth was vital to British overseas trade. Why did so many people think this was so? Part of the explanation may lie in the shifting contours of Britain's post-war economy. Commonwealth exports supplied scarce dollars to the Sterling Area from 1945 to 1952,[79] by which time a combination of higher exports and lower imports had brought the UK's dollar problem under control.[80] The years from the mid-1940s to the early 1950s also saw a significant re-direction of exports toward empire markets;[81] only from the late 1960s did this massive post-war preference of the Commonwealth for the products of British industry give way to expanding intra-European trade. Hence when Britain applied for a second time to join the EEC in 1967 the Commonwealth may diplomatically and militarily have looked like a 'broken reed',[82] but from an economic viewpoint it probably looked a much better bet. Here it is worth recalling how, for several years, the Labour party had been busy criticising the Tories for jeopardising Commonwealth trading links. Britain's commitment to the Commonwealth was felt to be perfectly compatible with Labour's attempts to modernise the economy.[83]

A few closing remarks about Britain's self-image are required. The Gallup polls gave people the option to answer 'don't know', and the tendency to do so became more marked over time. Most people expressed a view on the control of the Suez canal: only 10–20% had no opinion. Suez, however, was very firmly etched on the public consciousness. Two years later, almost a third of those asked about the Mau Mau, and a half of those about Nyasaland, could not say whether they approved or disapproved of the way Britain was handling these situations. Similarly, depending on the question, a quarter to a third of people asked about the rights of coloured people in Rhodesia, or about the desirability of Britain maintaining a presence in Aden and Singapore, did not feel able to respond. Of course, some sections of society would have felt more keenly the winding down of the empire – especially those who had spent substantial periods of time in the colonies. Anglo-Indian memsahibs struggled with their abrupt departure from India and the gender constraint reimposed on them by their return;[84] colonial civil servants experienced difficulty in finding new jobs 'compatible with their real if fragile self-esteem';[85] and children from colonial families who returned to lives of 'genteel poverty' in suburban semis were conscious that they were different from others at school.[86] That said, there does seem to have been something like a 'third implosion of empire' between 1959 and 1964. During these years an increasing number of people became disengaged from the empire in the sense that they were less likely to support or hold an opinion about it.

New Commonwealth immigration

The exception here is immigration; after the war this was to become a live issue politically and a source of wide public concern. The British Nationality Act of 1948 reaffirmed the right of people from the colonies to settle permanently in the United Kingdom.[87] An 'open door' policy (which survived until 1962) was felt to have the virtues of remedying shortages of labour, of presenting a liberal, progressive image of Britain to the rest of the world (especially America) and of helping to stabilise the Commonwealth system. During the 1950s and 1960s most immigrants came from the West Indies and South Asia. In 1953, a mere two thousand Caribbean people entered the country; by the mid-1960s there were a quarter of a million West Indians in Britain.[88] The growth of Britain's South Asian population occurred just as the movement from the Caribbean peaked. One hundred thousand people from the Indian subcontinent had come to Britain by 1961; almost half a million by 1971.[89] They included Punjabi Sikhs from Jullundur and Hoshiarpur, Hindus from central and southern Gujarat,

and Pakistani Muslims from the regions of Mirpur and Sylhet – after independence in 1971 the latter became part of Bangladesh.[90] There was also a
smaller movement of people from Hong Kong, Singapore and Malaysia
who together formed Britain's Chinese community, which numbered around
96,000 by the early 1970s.

Tables 8 and 9 provide a breakdown of immigration by source.
Approximately one and a half million 'new' Commonwealth migrants were
resident in Britain by the mid-1970s. Other migrant groups included the
100,000 or so former members of the Polish armed forces who did not
want to return to the newly-Communist Poland;[91] 'displaced persons' from
the Ukraine, Yugoslavia, Estonia, Latvia and Lithuania; people from the
English-speaking world (the dominions and the USA); and the Irish. The
latter increased markedly after a slump in Ireland's economy in 1951. There
were at least three-quarters of a million Irish-born immigrants in the 1960s
– the largest single immigrant group.[92] At this time people from the new
Commonwealth formed no more than a third of the immigrant population,

Table 8   Estimated net immigration from the New Commonwealth, 1953–62

	West Indies	India	Pakistan	Others	Total
1953	2,000				2,000
1954	11,000				11,000
1955	27,500	5,800	1,850	7,500	42,650
1956	29,800	5,600	2,050	9,350	46,800
1957	23,000	6,600	5,200	7,600	42,400
1958	15,000	6,200	4,700	3,950	29,850
1959	16,400	2,950	850	1,400	21,600
1960	49,650	5,900	2,500	−350	57,700
1961	66,300	23,750	25,100	21,250	136,000
1962	31,800	19,050	25,080	18,970	94,900
Total	272,450	75,850	67,330	69,670	484,900

Source: Z. Layton-Henry, The Politics of Immigration: Race and Race Relations in Postwar Britain (Blackwell
Publishers, 1992), p. 13.
Note: 1962 figures only include first six months up to introduction of immigration controls.

Table 9   Population by birthplace and ethnic origin: Britain, 1971

Birthplace		New Commonwealth Ethnic Origin
Total	53,826,375	
UK	50,514,820 (94%)	
Irish Republic	720,985 (1%)	
Old Commonwealth	145,250 (0.3%)	
New Commonwealth	1,157,170 (2%)	1,486,000
India	322,670	384,000
Pakistan	139,445	169,000
West Indies	302,970	548,000
Cyprus	72,665	155,000
Africa	176,060	157,000
Other	143,355	73,000
Foreign (not stated)	1,076,935	

Source: Adapted from C. Peach, 'Patterns of Afro-Caribbean Migration and Settlement in Great Britain, 1945–1981', in C. Brock (ed.), *The Caribbean in Europe: Aspects of the West Indian Experience in Britain, France and The Netherlands* (Frank Cass, 1986), p. 64.

and only 3% of the total population. However, as the majority lived in the major conurbations of Greater London, the West Midlands, Manchester, Merseyside and Yorkshire, they were much more visible to the rest of society.

Coloured immigration provoked heated debate.[93] One index of this is the rising number of motions at Tory party conferences calling for tighter controls, another the willingness of Conservative candidates to exploit hostility to immigrants in local and parliamentary elections – Smethwick in the West Midlands in 1964 is notorious when a Labour MP was defeated against the national swing.[94] But the most explosive intervention came in 1968 from Enoch Powell. His 'rivers of blood' speech played on white people's fears of immigrants overrunning their neighbourhoods, schools, hospitals and jobs. It also spoke of the possibility of US-style race riots. The speech struck such a strong chord that for a while Powell was among the country's most popular politicians, although Heath considered his remarks sufficiently inflammatory to merit dismissal from the shadow cabinet.[95] Nor was 1968 the last time Powell prophesied the dangers of immigration. His hard-line rhetoric was to be heard again at the party conference in 1972, this time in response to the expulsion of Ugandan Asians. Again he received overwhelming support from Conservative associations.

What is the significance of the racism and xenophobia that surrounds the immigration debate? It is worth remembering that if some of the extreme fringe groups who were the most hostile to coloured immigrants (League of Empire Loyalists, the National Front) were nostalgic for the empire, Powell by then was an 'ex-imperialist' prepared to go to great lengths to deny that it had ever been a factor in England's past.[96] Hence immigration is hardly a reliable barometer of attitudes to decolonisation. What it does show is just how little the empire had done to prepare the British for a more cosmopolitan future, and just how rigidly construed national identity was at this time. Identified primarily by their skin colour, and by the fact that they had not descended from people born in this country, West Indian and Asian migrants were not generally regarded as 'British'.[97] Policymakers, moreover, opted for restrictive legislation rather than embark on a programme of public education to challenge such perceptions.[98]

The focus of our enquiry, however, will not be on the 'high' politics of immigration or on the sequence of legislative controls. Both of these subjects have already received plenty of attention.[99] Indeed, writing in this field is so heavily weighted toward official, party and media perspectives that the voices of Commonwealth immigrants are all too rarely heard.[100] These immigrants first arrived as cheap labour at a time of labour scarcity, and later as a late manifestation of continuing imperial responsibilities.[101] How did they view themselves? Speaking in parliament in 1961, Hugh Gaitskell insisted that West Indians felt 'British'.[102] Oral testimony backs up his claim.[103] Interviews with West Indian students show how they saw Britain as the 'mother country';[104] while a Caribbean man (whose parents had worked on a sugar plantation) recalled: 'we West Indians were given the title "British" and encouraged to come to Britain'.[105] There was also an expectation among West Indian migrants that their knowledge of Britain would be matched by British knowledge of the West Indies. Barrington Young – who came to Manchester from Jamaica via New York – expressed surprise that, considering the West Indies were ruled by Britain, its people 'knew nothing about us': 'I had to keep telling people where Jamaica was, and why we were here.'[106] Equally upsetting was the tendency 'to lump all immigrants together into one generic group'.[107] The typical British person seemed barely

[220] aware of the differences between West Indians and Asians let alone the differences between settlers from within the Caribbean. For many migrants this was hard to comprehend. As a person from Trinidad later reflected:

> The whole experience of living in England, though at first traumatic, is of extreme value for the West Indian . . . he has the colonial myth of his almost British personality completely destroyed. In the end realisation of this makes it impossible to be bitter about his stay in England. The English have at last rendered him a service.[108]

Whereas West Indians had grown up in Anglicised British colonies, Indian and Pakistani migrants were not nearly so familiar with English society and values.[109] In the words of one scholar:

> To Pakistanis it [Britain] was a foreign land whose language, customs, religion, and way of life were totally alien to them. Their loyalties were to their own new nation, to their region, to their village, and above all to their kin. They came to England asking nothing of their hosts except to settle for a while, work, and earn for their families at home, to whom they meant to return.[110]

Less clear is what happened to first-generation Asian migrants after they arrived. Language barriers, low employment rates, residential separation and the continued centrality of kinship groups all tended to reinforce their loyalty to the society they had left behind and to impede their assimilation.[111] Here it is important to remember that the majority of people from South Asia expected their stay in Britain to be temporary and maintained the so-called 'myth of return'. A continuing history of mobility, bolstered by strong and enduring trans-national ties, was a marked feature of Asian migration,[112] and so it was not uncommon for people to go home to retire in their old age, or for their bodies to be repatriated for burial.[113] For some Asian men the arrival of wives and families during the 1970s prompted a new commitment to make a permanent life in Britain; for others it may merely have been a strategy to ensure that a migrant fulfilled his obligations to relatives back home and did not succumb to the 'temptations' and 'corrupting influences' of the West.[114] Another possible turning point for first-generation Asian migrants was the realisation that their children and grandchildren intended to remain in Britain: to return to the Indian subcontinent meant leaving them behind.[115] Recent research suggests that many now see Britain as their 'home' and expect to stay here for the rest of their lives; their links with family and friends in the Indian subcontinent have gradually eroded over time.[116]

How far is the issue of racial discrimination toward Britain's ethnic minorities linked to an ongoing imperial legacy? Several scholars seem to think so.[117] According to one study, 'most whites literally prejudged West Indian men and saw no reason to revise attitudes unaltered in their essentials since colonial days'.[118] We are also told that it was impossible for the British to accept West Indian immigrants as equals because the empire had erected 'caste-like barriers' between black and white.[119] More generally, it is argued that those growing up in a country that ruled vast areas of the world were naturally inclined to think that it was good to be 'British' and unfortunate to be 'black' – thus making it all the more difficult to respond positively to immigration.[120]

Yet the idea of a structural relationship between Britain's colonial past and today's domestic racism merits closer consideration. Britain is not the only European country with difficult race relations; in Germany the minority facing the strongest hostility, the Turks, were not former colonial subjects,[121] while white newcomers to Britain – Jews from Eastern Europe, the Irish, Italians and Germans – have faced plenty of intolerance too.[122] Moreover, the variety of experiences of new Commonwealth immigrants, and the very different levels of economic success they have achieved, caution us against explaining exclusion and hardship simply in terms of racial prejudice. Thus, in the view of Birmingham's Centre for Contemporary Cultural Studies, the racial segmentation of the 1960s and 1970s may have been historically connected to the 'high' colonial period but it was significantly different from it.[123] Coloured colonial immigrants came to Britain at the very same time that it was in 'decline', or at least felt that it was so; they were linked to the loss of its material wealth and global power, and regarded as an unwanted burden on its dwindling resources.[124]

How far did migrants themselves feel that racial prejudice was 'imperial' in origin? Memories of slavery, incidents of brutal repression, failure to reward acts of loyalty – all these are supposed to have provided ready-made explanations for discrimination.[125] For example, Salman Rushdie, the Indian-born novelist who emigrated to Britain in 1965, once explained how it is impossible to grasp the essence of British racism without accepting its historical and colonial roots:

> Four hundred years of conquest and looting, four centuries of being told that you are superior to the Fuzzy-Wuzzies and the wogs, leave their stain. This stain has seeped into every part of the culture, the language and daily life; and nothing much has been done to wash it out.[126]

[222] In similar vein, a study of mid-1960s Slough claimed that members of the town's Asian community were conscious of the historical background of British rule, and apt to link their history to present-day difficulties in race relations.[127]

Nevertheless, it can just as well be argued that hostile reactions to Commonwealth immigration have been 'local' and 'economic'. Certainly, competition for scarce local resources – education, social services and, above all, housing – can be seen to have inspired much anti-immigrant sentiment in post-war Britain: 'where local autonomy has retained a significant fiscal and administrative role . . . the rights of "strangers" have been insecure'.[128] In addition to local welfare, experiences of the labour market were probably a factor too. The majority of migrants had to take jobs in the relatively stagnant sectors of the British economy where the pay was low, the hours long, and shift work plentiful,[129] and where friction and resentment between coloured and white factory workers was not uncommon.[130] Other explanations of racism that are not framed around colonialism include forms of prejudice deriving from the real or imagined links between immigration and crime,[131] and from concerns about the impact of immigration on public health. There was also a more general fear of loss of national characteristics arising out of the 'ethnic distance' of the migrant population in question.[132] (It is perhaps also worth mentioning that the racism of the extreme Right, which emerged during the late 1960s out of renegade empire loyalist and anti-immigrant groups, has of late become increasingly localist in terms of its strategy and isolationist-nationalist in terms of its tone.)[133]

After almost half a century, Caribbean and South Asian people have begun to be accepted as 'British'.[134] A younger generation of 'white' people, however, are decidedly more liberal on issues of immigration, while to varying degrees the rest of the population continues to find it hard to live with racial difference at home. In this sense there does seem to remain a 'critical gap' between notions of 'metropolitan superiority' and 'colonial inferiority' upon which British power was for so long predicated.[135] Part of the challenge has been for Western states to accept that African and Asian migrants belong to more than one society – home is partly where they 'hang their hat', partly 'where their heart remains'.[136] Of course, the difficulty of responding to this challenge cannot solely be attributed to an ongoing imperial legacy; all states with major immigrant populations have legitimate concerns about 'citizenship' and common values regardless of how and why migrants arrived and from whence they came. But perhaps it may *partly* be attributed to it. A comparison with the only other European power to have experienced major intra-imperial immigration – France – is instructive here. Whereas Britain's approach to immigrants is often said to have differed from that of France – the former reluctant to interfere with the cultural life of ethnic minorities, the latter eager to make them full *citoyens* and an integral part of metropolitan society[137] – debates about immigration in both countries have in practice evinced a strong assimilationist streak. Today much media discussion centres on religious differences and the question of how far liberal societies can accommodate Islamic beliefs and practices. But first-generation migrants have long encountered difficulty in preserving their cultural heritage and maintaining their religion: only lately has their impact on British culture come to be seen as a matter for celebration (see pp. 234–5 below). The empire may have provided part of the impulse to immigration; it has hardly helped the transition to a multi-racial society, however.

After empire

The purpose of this book has been to show that Britain should not be studied separately from the empire. If true of the past, is this equally true of today? Having let go of (or abandoned) their colonies have the British become more parochial? Or have the many years of imperial adventure given rise to an international and cosmopolitan perspective that has survived decolonisation? Did the end of empire effectively put pay to the notions of service, loyalty and deference that had previously helped to convince the British people of their 'right' and 'duty' to rule?[138] Or are Nandy and Benn right to argue for a residual colonialist mentality that has stifled the development of a more open and democratic society?[139]

Several of the problems presently facing the British state – hostility towards immigrants, the unravelling of a British identity, anti-Europeanism and sectarianism in Northern Ireland – are perceived to be a legacy of empire. We have already cautioned against overstating the imperial dimension of the first two of these issues. The same point needs to be emphasised in respect of anti-Europeanism and the conflict in Northern Ireland. It is possible to portray the Tory party's anti-Maastricht rebels as 'the true heirs of the Suez Group'.[140] Yet there are many other ways of accounting for Euroscepticism, including xenophobia (especially toward Germany); the defence of parliamentary sovereignty (especially the fear of becoming enmeshed in a big super-state); socialism (the perception of the Common Market as a capitalists' club); neo-liberalism (the perception of the Common Market as too corporatist); and internationalism (the desire to forge links with the wider world, and not just the EU).[141] Meanwhile, Irish Nationalists have

[224] blamed the 'troubles' in the North on British colonialism and insisted on British withdrawal as the only solution. Yet recent historical writing resolutely rejects this perspective. The weakness of the Nationalist case, it is argued, is that 'an accurate depiction of the past is used to validate a misleading portrait of the present'.[142] Most of Ireland's colonial characteristics had already been shed by Partition; the current conflict in the North is better understood, therefore, in terms of recent European ethnic conflagrations.[143] Even Unionist ideology and propaganda, which cannot be properly understood without reference to its colonial-settler origins (see pp. 199–200), seems to have adapted to the demise of empire and now betrays many other influences.[144]

If the evidence of the latest crop of opinion polls is anything to go by, half of the population of Britain is largely or totally ignorant of its imperial history,[145] teenagers do not take any pride in their country's past (colonial or otherwise),[146] few of those considered to be 'Great Britons' (at a push, six of the top hundred) were empire-builders,[147] and Spain and France now rank as highly as Australia and Canada among would-be migrants' preferred destinations – they would be even higher if speaking another language were not a problem.[148] It is, moreover, difficult to deny that certain aspects of the British empire are fast fading from the public memory. During the continuing controversy over the empty plinth in Trafalgar Square, the London Mayor, Ken Livingstone, remarked that he had no idea why the two Victorian generals – Charles Napier and Henry Havelock (famous for their service in India) – were there. In fact, there are some one hundred and twenty-nine Havelock roads, streets and avenues in today's Britain, but the Indian Mutiny of 1857–8 appears to be long forgotten.[149]

British India is remembered in other ways, however.[150] During the 1980s a series of imperial 'heritage' films – *The Jewel in the Crown*, *The Far Pavilions* and *A Passage to India* – invested the Raj with considerable glamour.[151] Critics complained that this 'Raj revival' portrayed India primarily through European eyes, and that in the films Indians had only walk-on parts. But the whirligig of time seems to have turned full circle here. For hard on the heels of the 'Raj revival' came the spread of Bollywood's appeal to Western audiences in the early twenty-first century.[152] Bollywood's cross-over potential was uncertain until the 2002 release of *Lagaan: Once Upon A Time In India*, a period drama written and directed by Ashutosh Gowariker and set in 1893 in a small village in central India. The film's wildly implausible plot focuses on the hardships of the village as it is forced to pay a double *lagaan* – a land tax collected as a portion of every farmer's crops – after years of drought. An appeal to the local British administrator results in a challenge: the tax will be waived if the villagers can beat the British team at cricket – a game they have never seen – but tripled if they lose. The climax is a life-or-death match in which the downtrodden Indians predictably triumph over their arrogant imperial masters. Featuring the Indian screen superstar Aamir Khan, and two British actors, Rachel Shelley and Paul Blackthorne, the film cost $6 million to make, the most expensive Bollywood production ever. Though intended primarily for an Indian audience,[153] it made a major breakthrough in terms of its appeal to non-Asian audiences in Britain and across Europe where it was screened at twenty-seven cinemas and film festivals.[154]

So much for the Raj: what about the 'colonial remnants', the bits of the map that remain stubbornly pink?[155] A mixture of sought-after tourist destinations,[156] low-tax regions,[157] military bases[158] and isolated, sparsely populated areas,[159] there are a surprisingly large number of territories over which the Union Flag still flies.[160] A few have proved diplomatic nuisances, though not necessarily through any fault of their own: the inhabitants of Diego Garcia were removed to make way for an American military base and have been fighting for restitution ever since. Others are seen as an unwelcome drain on UK resources; here the Channel Islands are the main exception for they are arguably more affluent and successful than the UK. Drug-trafficking, financial scandals and contraventions of human rights have also posed problems to Britain. Yet the vast majority of these places have not sought to end their connection with the Crown, even if Britain has been prepared to let them go.[161] This is partly because many are practically self-governing, partly because they tend to be too small to protect themselves (particularly in the face of a close and powerful neighbour), partly because they can look to Britain (and the EU) as a source of aid and welfare, partly because they usually have the right of abode in the UK, and partly because many of their inhabitants consider themselves to be thoroughly 'British' (albeit protective of their own separate identity).[162] This last factor has been especially true of the peoples of Gibraltar and the Falkland Islands who have tenaciously defended their right to manage their own affairs albeit under British protection, and who were eventually exempted from the discriminating provisions of the 1981 Nationality Act, the former the result of their particular status in the European Union, the latter as a result of the Falklands War.[163]

The conflict over the Falklands is instructive. Before 1982 few people in Britain were aware that this remote and neglected colony existed, fewer still of where it was. Nonetheless, when Argentina invaded the islands the government and media happily portrayed the Royal Navy's expedition to

[226] rescue them as a national crusade in defence of British people and values. The Falklands, after all, could boast an old-fashioned fire station and red pillar boxes; their inhabitants still smoked Woodbine cigarettes; and the Governor, Rex Hunt, drove around in a London taxi – each of which was singled out by the press for special mention. Indeed, the Falkland islanders were regarded as 'quintessentially British in a way that Britain had not been for a very long time, or perhaps never had been'.[164] For the then Prime Minister, Margaret Thatcher, the success of the operation signified the reversal of the long years of decline stretching back to Suez. Addressing the party faithful at Cheltenham in July, she declared, 'We have to see that the spirit of the South Atlantic – the real spirit of Britain – is kindled not only by war but can now be fired by peace . . . the spirit has stirred and the nation has begun to assert itself.' Is this, then, an example of 'an atavistic imperialism'? Not surprisingly some on the Left were inclined to think so.[165] Yet it is worth remembering that, immediately after the Argentine invasion in April, one in four of those polled by Gallup expressed disapproval of the British government's military response, and that even after the islands had been recaptured in June one in five still felt that more effort should have been put into negotiating a peaceful solution. Moreover, when reminded of the cost of securing the Falklands and keeping them 'British' – hundreds of millions of pounds – over 50% said it was too high a price to pay.[166] Massive support for the war there may have been, yet it was not an unrestrained and unthinking jingoism.[167] A Garland cartoon in the *Spectator* (rather than the headlines of the *Sun*) perhaps came closest to capturing what many people in Britain felt toward the Falklands.[168] To be sure, there was a lingering nostalgia for the empire which, alongside the anger provoked by the naked aggression of the Argentine military dictatorship, and the need to restore Britain's international credibility, helps to explain the public's reluctance to abandon the islands. However, it was tempered by the recognition that they were an anachronism,[169] a hangover from a colonial past that Britain had more of a duty than a desire to defend. To some extent this is borne out by the polls. At the beginning of the crisis they revealed reservations about the worth of the islands and whether they justified the cost of recapture. At its end they showed majority support for UN trusteeship as doubts resurfaced about the viability of Britain's long-term economic and strategic commitment to the region.[170]

The return of Hong Kong to China in 1997 sheds further light on public attitudes toward the end of empire. After the handover there were still sixteen British-ruled territories with a combined population of approximately

Figure 11   'Victory in the South Atlantic', *The Spectator*, 19 June 1982
Source: By permission of *The Spectator*

[228]   160,000. Yet Hong Kong was Britain's last significant colony by virtue of the size of its population (some six million) and its wealth (some of which was remitted to the UK). Hence the *Guardian* spoke of 'Britain's final imperial retreat'[171] and of Britain 'shutting down the empire that once encompassed a quarter of the globe'.[172] *The Times* referred to 'the close of an extraordinary era in British history'[173] and the *Independent* (ironically) to 'the curtain finally falling on the greatest empire the world has ever known'.[174] Yet one newspaper columnist also observed that Hong Kong's return to China had hardly stirred any public emotion: 'despite the fact that we sometimes seem to the outside world to be perpetually looking backwards, there is very little sense of loss in Britain'. This may reflect the 'curious' insulation of Hong Kong from British domestic politics during previous decades: 'there was little sign . . . that British domestic opinion displayed either embarrassment with the ideological burden of domestic rule over a remote colony or resentment at a redundant imperial obligation'.[175] In all probability, those who did care to think about Hong Kong had been resigned to separation for some time. Not only had the transfer been widely heralded,[176] it was clear that if China chose to invade Britain was in no position to defend the territory. Simply cutting off the water supply from the Pearl River could have brought Hong Kong to its knees.[177] This is not to deny that Hong Kong was reported as a 'domestic' rather than 'international' news story, or that some people were moved by the handover ceremony. But the ceremony had been deliberately staged by the British government and portrayed by the British media as a ritualised act of colonial withdrawal: it would have been highly surprising if it had not resonated.[178] Scratch beneath the surface and pockets of opinion in Britain evinced rather mixed feelings toward the colony. Some on the Right rue-fully reflected that it was nothing more than a 'gravy train for those [white] expatriates whose life-style mattered far more than their job', and that there were no more than a 'small handful of Hong Kong people' who wished to preserve the British legacy.[179] Meanwhile, some on the Left expressed frustration with the lack of progress toward democracy, the lack of protection of workers' rights and the lack of interest on the part of any major political organisation or trade union in the UK in such issues.[180] Whatever pride in the empire a *Daily Telegraph* poll revealed a month or so later,[181] the subdued reaction to the repatriation of Hong Kong to China adds weight to the contention that Britain no longer valued her last remaining colonies.[182] Once 'dependent territories', now 'British overseas territories', Britain has not even seemed sure what to call them let alone what to do with them.

If Britain's vestigial colonies are no longer considered important, the empire [229] has nonetheless struck back in other ways. The anti-apartheid movement of the 1970s and 1980s merits a mention here. Britain's long-standing cultural and historical connection to South Africa informed its opposition to the injustices of apartheid and placed it at the forefront of the international campaign for majority rule.[183] The ANC's largest overseas office was in London, and South African exiles came to Britain from as early as the 1940s; they did not need a visa and a common language facilitated communication. It was they, moreover, who provided the initial strength of the anti-apartheid movement. Whether conceived as a fight for democracy and humanity in Africa, or against racism and the capitalist system in Britain, anti-apartheid activism was central to left-wing politics and also to student activism for much of this period. Disinvestment, economic and sporting boycotts, public marches and anti-apartheid music and film all ensured the issue a high political profile.

Our focus, however, is on three more recent attempts to make amends for the errors of Britain's colonial past – the repatriation of cultural artefacts and human remains, the honouring of the colonial war dead, and compensation offered to post-war child migrants. On 26 January 1988 the author, actor and activist Burnum Burnum (1936–97) planted the Aboriginal flag on Brighton beach. In taking symbolic possession of England on behalf of Australia's Aboriginal people he assured the assembled journalists that he did not intend to poison their waterholes, to sterilise their young women, to separate children from their families, or to pickle British skulls for public display. Burnum Burnum was one of the 'stolen generation' – Aboriginal children forcibly removed from their parents during the first half of the twentieth century.[184] In the 1960s he joined the battle for Aboriginal rights and led a movement at the University of Tasmania to reclaim the remains of Truganini from the Tasmanian Museum. The purpose of his journey to the UK was to publicise the problem of human remains held by museums in England and Scotland and to argue for their return. Collected by British explorers, officials, traders and scientists during the colonial period, at the time of writing these remains continue to be held by the Duckworth Laboratory in Cambridge University, the National History Museum in London and the Marischal Museum in Aberdeen.

In July 2000, after Edinburgh University had handed back over three hundred Aboriginal skeletons to Australia, the House of Commons Select Committee on Culture, Media and Sport urged that guidelines on restitution give greater weight to requests for return.[185] Its recommendations were based on the recognition of the primary rights of indigenous peoples over

[230] the remains of their ancestors (already conceded by the United States and Australia). A Working Group on Human Remains was then established in May 2001. In November 2003 it reported the results of a survey of 132 museums in England. Of these institutions, 39 held remains of Australian Aborigines and New Zealand Maori – 569 items in total, though actual holdings may be significantly higher. The Working Group accepted that these remains had often been acquired by colonial collectors in unethical circumstances, that indigenous peoples were unable to prevent their removal ('because of the dynamics of power in colonial situations'), and that retention and research on them continued to cause great distress. It reiterated the need for museums to be able to make discretionary decisions about specimens in their care, urged the establishment of a panel to oversee repatriation and acknowledged the right of leaders and elders of affected communities (not just direct descendants) to lodge repatriation requests.[186] Though this was welcomed by Australia's Aborigines, they continue to call for a wider inquiry into how human remains – ranging from locks of hair to full skeletons – came into the possession of UK institutions.[187]

Another heart-wrenching story concerns the few thousand child migrants shipped out from Britain (and Malta) after the Second World War.[188] Some were sent to Canada, Southern Rhodesia and New Zealand, but the majority ended up in Australia. The policy ended in 1967 when charities in Britain effectively ran out of children to send. The appalling fate suffered by child migrants is now very much in the public domain thanks to the International Association of Former Child Migrants, the Child Migrants Trust (founded in 1987 by Margaret Humphreys, a Nottingham social worker and key figure in the campaign) and the poignant testimony of the migrants themselves. These children were mostly aged between 7 and 10 and came from orphanages run by charities. It was not unusual for them to be removed without parental knowledge or consent. They were sent without passports or even the most basic documentation. Brothers and sisters were separated on arrival. In order to prevent them from tracing their parents, names were altered, different birth dates given and letters withheld. Most depressingly, they were frequently subjected to years of harsh institutional care. At best their lives were highly regimented and starved of affection; at worst they were full of abuse. Almost all of the one hundred and fifty interviewees for Charles Wheeler's series of radio programmes, *The Child Migrants*, testified to the cruelty of their 'carers'.[189] Having been promised fairy-tale conditions on their departure, the children came to feel abandoned, neglected, confused and betrayed. For many of them their 'stolen childhoods' led on to profoundly damaged adult lives. For the most severely

Figure 12 Burnum Burnum on Brighton beach, 26 January 1988
Source: Copyright Carmen Ky. Reproduced with permission

[232] traumatised it proved impossible to trust or love again. A few committed suicide.

Restitution for these people, belated and inadequate as it may be, has taken various forms. Some charities have apologised for their actions and set aside money for former child migrants to trace their families. The British government has also admitted failing in its responsibility. In July 1988 a House of Commons Select Committee recognised the policy of relocation to have been misguided, and that many migrants had suffered emotional and psychological problems as a result.[190] Practically, it offered to set up a Support Fund and committed £1 million for three years. It did not explain why the Home Office and Commonwealth Relations Office had not acted on the findings of the Ross Committee some forty years earlier, which had condemned the policy and highlighted the deficiencies of particular institutions.[191] Most of the support for the migrants has come from the Child Migrants Trust – a voluntary organisation helping them to re-establish their identities and to find their families.[192] Yet this has proved a protracted process that, sadly, many child migrants commenced after their parents had died. For others family reunions were not all that they had hoped for. Actions for legal damages in courts have been difficult too. Many of those who abused child migrants were deceased or considered too old and infirm to stand trial. Perhaps the best that can be said is that the historical record is now being set straight and that the stories of the migrants are being told. Once the pawns of an imperial state – part of the rationale for the policy had been to populate the empire with 'good white British stock' – the individuals involved are at long last the centre of concern.

On a more positive note, the millions of largely forgotten Indian, African and Caribbean soldiers who fought alongside Britain in the last century's two world wars have fittingly been recognised by the erection of commemorative memorial gates on the top of Constitution Hill near Hyde Park Corner.[193] The driving force behind this project was Baroness Flather, the first Asian woman peer. Her father had served as a medical orderly in Mesopotamia during the First World War, and later ran a cutlery factory in India that made bayonets during the Second World War.[194] From 1997 she devoted herself to the campaign and raised some £2.8 million. In addition to a £1 million lottery grant from the Millennium Commission, other major benefactors included the former RAF pilot and Grand Bahama businessman, Sir 'Union' Jack Hayward, and the Hong Kong businessman, Eric Hotung. There were also many individual donors (often with a wartime connection) who gave smaller sums of money. Designed by the architect Liam O'Connor, the Memorial Gates consist of a square defined by four stone piers and paved with granite sets in the form of a radiating fan. Between the piers to the north there is an Indian-style chattri (domed pavilion) inscribed inside with the names of those who were awarded the Victoria Cross and George Cross and the major campaigns in which those commemorated fought. The Queen unveiled the memorial on 6 November 2002.

It is worth emphasising that selective lapses of memory regarding the two world wars were not confined to 'new' Commonwealth soldiers. British soldiers in the Far East similarly saw themselves as having been forgotten – for understandable reasons the global aspects of these conflicts receded from public memory in a way that their European aspects did not. Indeed, it could be argued that colonial soldiers were remembered by the War Graves Commission in just the same way as British soldiers, namely where they fell and in their home countries. Yet one consequence of this was that their contribution was never adequately acknowledged within Britain; Baroness Flather was painfully aware of the bitterness of veterans living in the UK who recalled how quickly they had slipped from the memory of the British government after 1945.[195] To her credit, however, the memorial was always intended to look as much to the future as the past. It is, she says, a message for race relations, celebrating not only the courage of Asian, African and West Indian soldiers from the empire but the contribution that their descendants continue to make to the rich diversity of Britain today:

> It is our fervent hope that the volunteers from the Indian subcontinent, Africa and the Caribbean, whom this memorial commemorates, will find a permanent place in the hearts of the British people . . . We believe the memorial should become a symbol for today's multi-racial Britain. By remembering our shared sacrifice in the darkest days of two world wars, we are certain that we can build together a truly cohesive society based on mutual respect and understanding.

Each of the above examples raises the bigger question of how we relate to our history, and how far we feel a part of it. To the extent that we do, the door is opened for the sins and successes of the past to be visited upon us.[196] Not that the British are alone in trying to apportion or accept responsibility for events that may not have happened during their lifetime. German politicians have recently broken decades of silence to argue that the Allies must take their share of the guilt for the suffering of the *Vertriebenen* – the Germans expelled from Poland and other countries after the Second World War. The Poles meanwhile have asked awkward questions about how far the Communist 'old guard' were implicated in the persecution of the Jews. The British differ not in the act of revisiting and reappraising

[234] their past but in the prominence of empire in this process. Among continental Europeans not even those with a significant colonial inheritance have been willing to confront it. The Belgians, in particular, have tried to bury the injustices of the Congo: 'a striking example of the politics of forgetting'.[197] The French have also shown amnesia toward their empire.[198] The painful legacy of the Algerian war (1954–62), and the injury inflicted by decolonisation on a more state-centred empire, may help to explain why.[199] Conversely, during the last decade or so there has been a collective surge of interest in 'imperial Britain'. Unfashionable during the 1970s and for much of the 1980s, Britain's imperial past is now firmly in the public domain; media dons, radio presenters and press pundits all want to have their say about it. In bringing this book to a close, I want to ask what purpose is served by society continuing to consider the empire and its legacies into the twenty-first century.

My window on the imperial present is the exhibition of empire in museums.[200] How many people have recently been reached in this way? Fifteen thousand visitors went to the National Portrait Gallery's exhibition on 'The Raj' in October 1990,[201] and 60,000 to the 'Transatlantic Slavery' gallery at the Merseyside Maritime Museum within the space of three months in 1994.[202] In 1999–2000, the National Maritime Museum's 'Trade and Empire' gallery helped to attract 850,000 people; subsequently as many as half a million may have walked through its displays.[203] In 2002–3, there were approximately 80,000 visitors to the Bristol Empire and Commonwealth Museum; from May to September 2002, 107,534 to the British Library's exhibition 'Trading Places: The East India Company and Asia, 1600–1834';[204] and 56,366 to the 'Indian Encounter' exhibition at the National Gallery from November 2002 to January 2003.[205] Clearly, these are striking figures; estimating conservatively, well over half a million people must have gone to a museum to see an empire-related exhibition in the last fifteen years.

The curators of these museums seem convinced that people really do want (and need) to know more about Britain's imperial past.[206] In terms of the empire's domestic impact, the meaning of multiculturalism and the management of race relations have understandably been key concerns. Museums have sought to reclaim the histories of oppressed minorities and their struggles against imperialism,[207] to show how ethnic and racial identities have been inherited from the empire and, above all, to catalogue the contribution of immigrants to British society.[208] This contribution has clearly been considerable, spanning a range of cultural forms from fashion and food to music, comedy and film.[209] Moreover, the very act of celebrating multiculturalism in Britain has probably helped to empower ethnic minorities and to develop a stronger sense of their identity; it also highlights how a younger generation of 'white' people have become increasingly open and receptive to extra-European cultures more generally and not just post-colonial ones. Many of the displays of Bristol's Empire and Commonwealth museum focus on the cross-cultural exchanges made possible by the empire. Other examples of the way museums have celebrated the rich diversity of our culture include the NMM's exhibits on multicultural crewing and Black and Asian seamen in the British mercantile marine, the National Gallery's depiction of Indian influences upon Queen Victoria's royal household,[210] and the British Library's study of 'Asia in Britain' and the changes wrought by Anglo-Indian trade.[211] Not all minority groups within Britain have perhaps been given their due consideration. Britain's Chinese community remains fairly marginalised, though their campaign against the British Library's 'Trading Places' exhibition for failing to reflect the darker side of the East India Company's activities may herald a more prominent profile in immigrant debates.[212]

Museums have explored two aspects of the empire's impact beyond the British Isles. First, how far the rest of the world's perceptions of Britain are still swayed by its imperial past; second, the consequences of colonialism for international stability and global welfare today. Both have provoked considerable controversy. For example, several of those who put pen to paper to complain about the NMM's 'Trade and Empire' gallery were evidently frustrated that, by highlighting Britain's role in the slave trade, the gallery was simply providing foreign visitors and parties of ethnic minority schoolchildren 'with another stick with which to beat us'.[213] Presumably the British Library's 'Trading Places' exhibition only confirmed their fears: it led several left-leaning newspaper commentators to castigate the East India Company as the world's first 'global narcotics cartel'.[214] The rise of the so-called 'new American empire' in Afghanistan and Iraq has been the occasion for a similar polarisation of views. To be sure, the Left has long maintained that decolonisation did not result in any major change to the international system, and that after the Second World War colonial relationships were simply reconfigured in the form of the neo-imperialism of the United States. But only lately has the Right tried to rehabilitate the British empire as a model for US foreign policy. Niall Ferguson's *Empire: How Britain Made the World* (serialised on Channel 4, and watched by nearly 2.5 million people) argued that British imperialism is pregnant with lessons for contemporary America.[215] *Inter alia*, he urged Americans to face up to their global responsibilities and stop being in denial about their (informal)

[236] empire; to follow Britain's example and practice as well as preach free trade; and to develop a capacity for liberal self-criticism.[216] Ferguson reiterated some of these points at a round table debate at Bristol's Empire and Commonwealth museum. Here he suggested that the imperial baton had passed to the USA during the Second World War, but that America was suffering from an 'attention deficit' in terms of its approach to international affairs. Unsurprisingly, his remarks found little favour with the former International Development Secretary, Clare Short, who berated American foreign policy for its 'dismissal of the basic quality of humanity', and who availed herself of an alternative imperial analogy to shed light on the actions of the Bush administration in the Middle East – that of a 'fading Rome'.[217]

What is striking is how little the public debate about Britain's imperial record appears to have moved on over the last forty or fifty years. Museum curators and directors may understandably have felt the time was ripe for a more considered assessment. This has not proved so, however.[218] Rather, to judge by public and media reaction to their galleries and displays, the empire is still wrapped up in feelings of pride, shame, anger and guilt. There has been a persistent tendency to think in terms of a 'moral balance sheet'; imperial costs and benefits are weighed and the empire is declared to have been a good or a bad thing.[219] On balance, nowadays, the verdict is more likely to be negative than positive. There are several reasons why this may be so. Most obviously, the empire has increasingly been shorn of its more positive meanings. Before the Second World War it could be embraced as a modernising and progressive force; subsequently it was held responsible for economic 'decline' and the unravelling of a 'British' identity.[220] The latter seems to have been particularly significant. Part of the current interest in empire stems from uncertainty about what it now means to be 'British' and, moreover, who will be left calling themselves 'British' in twenty or thirty years time. It is, of course, far too early to say. But perhaps it will be only the Ulster Unionists, still in their own mind 'colonists' or 'frontier' people, and the ethnic minorities, another product of empire. What is not in doubt is that in certain quarters of society the fashion for scapegoating the empire for much of what we dislike about ourselves endures. Racism, cultural chauvinism, xenophobia and misogyny – all these have been (partly) attributed to an ongoing imperial legacy. This chapter has questioned how far such attitudes can be said to derive from the possession of an empire which may be the largest the world has ever known, but will shortly be half a century or so in our past. But even if they could, there would still be a danger here. By becoming too steeped in their imperial history, the British may avoid squaring up to the problems of the present. This is especially true of the integration of immigrants and the management of race relations. To be sure, there is a sense in which the acceptance of Caribbean and South Asian migrants has been made more difficult by persistent notions of inferiority and superiority inherited from the colonial period. However, current concerns about community cohesion need to be understood primarily in terms of lower levels of ethnic achievement in employment and education, and residential segregation – social inclusion is key.

There is also a sense in which Commonwealth-Imperial history has become more politicised in recent years. Admittedly, there is nothing novel about politicians turning to the past to prove a point. But they do seem increasingly inclined to invoke, interpret and try to control the historical record.[221] Take the current controversy over the honours system. The Asian pop musician, John Pandit, and the Rastafarian poet, Benjamin Zephaniah, both publicly turned down awards because of their colonial connotations.[222] Their very title – containing, as it does, the word 'empire' – provoked a hostile response. It reminded them of years of brutality, exploitation and slavery. Even in the wider public debate about the honours system there has been general agreement that such references to the empire are unhelpful and need to be removed.[223] Why should awards be given in the name of a contentious and outdated aspect of Britain's past? Why should the nomenclature of the honours system be framed around an institution that no longer plays a living part in the sense of our national identity? These are fair questions, and the British people are beginning to see themselves rather differently as their imperial past recedes. Yet the modernisation of the honours system is arguably about a lot more than titles. There is a lack of clarity about its purpose, political patronage looms too large in the selection process and there are too few women and ethnic minorities among recipients. Hence the word 'empire' has merely highlighted a need for wider restructuring.[224]

As much as any other cultural institution, museums have in recent years taken upon themselves the task of constructing an 'honest' relationship with our imperial past. Given their centrality to contemporary culture and learning, this makes sense.[225] But what have they actually achieved? Their major success may have been to usher in a new openness to our explorations of imperial history, partly by presenting to a wider public audience British rule as it was seen at the time and from all sides,[226] and partly by raising awkward questions about the spirit in which it is reappraised. To be sure, some people continue to suspect the 'moral integrity' of any such exercise: 'what holds us back from confronting truths about the Empire is not censorship or self-censorship, but an entire historical legacy which dwells on

[238]   the good that the Empire spread, and which is still sustained by traditionalists'.[227] Others, meanwhile, decry the way in which history now seems to
be full of 'self-deprecation and envy', and largely devoid of respect for past
achievements in which British people could justifiably take some pride.[228]
Why not bat for the home team, and indulge 'our own view of the Raj'?[229]
Why deny the idealism of many colonial officials? Why disparage all that
we were and most of what we did? These were some of the questions asked
by critics of the NPG and NMM exhibitions. And yet by bringing such
complex and contradictory feelings about the empire to the surface of
public life museums have underscored the fact that imperial history means
different things to different people, and that no settled historical assessment of the subject is about to be achieved.[230] They have also exposed the
fallacy of the so-called 'new' imperial history and its Olympian detachment;
all historians are inclined to detect the sympathies of others and to write as
if they are free of their own, but in the case of Commonwealth-Imperial
history this has recently been a pronounced trait. Above all, they have challenged people to think more carefully and critically about the criteria they
employ when assessing Britain's colonial record.

Nietzsche once said that 'only something that has no history can be
defined'.[231] In today's Britain, a variety of imperial pasts are being remembered. In view of its multiplicity of meanings it has simply not been possible (or desirable) to tell a single story about the empire.[232] How people
view it depends not only on their background knowledge but upon who
they are: family, ethnicity and collective memory are all significant. This
perhaps is the main reason for continuing to consider the contested legacies of colonialism into the twenty-first century: by doing so, we become
more self-aware. Indeed, consciously or otherwise, in forming opinions
about the nature and extent of imperial influences upon Britain we will be
reflecting on what type of society we once were, now are, and (arguably)
wish to be.

AFTERWORD

This book has sought to re-situate the empire in a reading of modern
Britain's political culture, social development and economic performance. It has reviewed a range of activities – public and private – in order to
establish how far Britain was influenced and modified by its long imperial
involvement. To what extent were people in Britain aware of the empire?
In what ways (if any) did it change their lives? How far was it fundamental
to Britain's identity? How long-lived have its legacies been? In responding
to these questions, some scholars have played up the domestic impact of
imperialism, others have played it down. Their conflicting views stem partly,
of course, from different readings of the evidence. Yet they also reflect more
deep-seated disagreements about British state formation, the grand narratives of which ('difference', 'decline' and 'disintegration') continue to look
to Britain's imperial past to legitimate themselves. In arguing about the
empire's effects on Britain, therefore, we are not simply disputing the
archival record: there is a wider ideological context in which conclusions
about this subject must be set.

Previous chapters have shown how the British people developed a remarkably rich relationship with their empire that markedly extended the
boundaries of their domestic society. They reject the idea that Britain was
an 'empire-free zone' – a relatively self-contained country in which there
was relatively little involvement in the imperial project. They also reject the
idea that the British people were imperially illiterate – it was not only
middle-class families with a tradition of imperial service who knew about
the empire; nor did one have to be a walking encyclopaedia of colonial
knowledge in order to have an opinion about colonial rule. Equally, these
chapters suggest that the existing literature glosses over some serious
methodological problems with the influential 'popular imperialism' thesis.

To begin with, 'enthusiasm' for empire may be too global and abstract a
category. There were various strands of discourse – trans-national family

[240] ties; international labour solidarity; the adventure, excitement and spectacle of faraway and exotic places – that resonated with ordinary working people, and other strands – the empire as an economic or political concept – that had a more limited purchase. Nor were these discourses exclusive to the empire, though they may have been more deeply embedded in the colonial than non-colonial parts of the extra-European world. Moreover, what the empire meant to the masses is unlikely to be decided by studies of their leisure and recreation habits alone. The evidence is too ambiguous, and the conceptual frameworks are too flimsy – especially the idea of 'social control'. Even in the case of exhibitions and the cinema, which actively propagated an imperial message to large audiences, it is difficult to know how people responded. In other cultural spheres, it is not always clear who the audience actually was. We need therefore to pay more attention to the home and the workplace. These were the most formative influences on working people, and it is from these perspectives that we can restore to working people a sense of agency in the way they reacted to the empire. Contrary to what is often supposed, labour movements and trade unions did not have imperial beliefs foisted on them from above; rather, they had their own reasons for paying attention to what was happening in the empire, in particular for forging bonds with British workers overseas. The propagandist impulse was certainly stronger in the case of popular literature and the celebration of Empire Day. But even here reader surveys, oral histories, and working-class memoirs show how propaganda did not always have its desired effect. Meanwhile, several key aspects of popular imperial belief remain under-explored, in particular the experiences of emigrants, as reflected by their correspondence and remittance patterns, and of immigrants, as reflected by their oral testimony. Both experiences, though not well served by the secondary literature, are integral to what 'imperial Britain' actually meant.[1]

It is not only the 'popular imperialism' thesis that is open to methodological criticism, however. When trying to measure imperialism's impact at home there may be just as big a danger of setting the bar artificially high. Should we demand the type of evidence for 'popular' support for the empire that even historians of Chartism, temperance or women's suffrage would find it hard to produce? And what do we mean by the word 'popular' – an activity that was predominantly working-class or one that appealed across classes? Further comparison of Britain's imperial experience with that of, say, France, Belgium, Germany or Russia, might help to show how far there was a popular consciousness of empire, and whether it really matters if there was. But the very search for explicit and emphatic expressions of

empire in British culture may be mistaken. Britain is perhaps better understood as an assimilative society that tended to absorb, incorporate and
internalise external influences, and not to let such influences eradicate all
that had gone before. Thus, the empire's 'impact', far from being forceful
and aggressive, was often subtle and unobtrusive – this is well illustrated
by the repercussions of Victorian expansion for patterns of working-class
consumption, and consumer consciousness of the origins of staple items of
food and drink.

The empire, then, was a significant factor in the lives of the British people.
It was not, however, all-pervasive. Indeed, it is necessary to break down
Britain's imperial experience in order to appreciate how different parts of
society became caught up in the process of overseas expansion in different
ways. In that sense, the 'big theory' behind this book is that there is no 'big
theory': no uniform imperial impact, no joined-up or monolithic ideology
of imperialism, no single source of enthusiasm or propaganda for the empire, no cohesive imperial movement. Notwithstanding the relatively high
levels of awareness of empire in Britain, its appeal and meaning varied considerably. Family background, social class, region and gender all shaped
people's perceptions of empire; so did the sphere of their life in which they
encountered it, and the type of colony with which they were concerned.
The latter is particularly significant. Each colony had its own traditions
and links with the UK, and these in turn manifested themselves at different
times and in different spheres of British public life. For example, during the
nineteenth century, there was a sea change in public attitudes to the settler
colonies, which became ever more central to the economic and political
dimensions of imperial ideology; India was far more prominent in the literary and linguistic than the political culture of empire, but of continuous
regional importance to certain branches of manufacturing, and, more broadly,
to the armed forces; South Africa had a high profile in the British labour
movement after the discovery of gold but only until the First World War;
the West Indies 'struck back' toward the beginning of our period (with
the Governor Eyre controversy) and again toward the end (with new
Commonwealth immigration), but made a relatively modest impression in
between; the Scots had particularly strong links to India (as administrators
and engineers) and the Irish (as soldiers), the Irish and Scots to Canada (as
migrants), and the Cornish to South Africa (as miners). One could go on.

In drawing attention to the diverse ways in which imperialism influenced the 'domestic' history of modern Britain, this study may be swim-
ming against a historiographical tide. Commonwealth-Imperial history has
tended to attract more 'lumpers' than 'splitters'[2] over the years – more scholars

[242] seeking to sketch the general patterns than to perceive differences and draw distinctions. Recent postcolonial theory has perhaps reinforced this tendency by failing to deconstruct the European 'centre' in the way it has so successfully deconstructed the extra-European 'periphery'. And yet this book has shown how the British developed a variety of connections to their empire, and how their imperial involvement must be approached from many different angles. For this reason, we must be wary of generalisations: the domestic culture of empire was much more fragmented than some of the existing literature is apt to allow.

So much for activities: what of the question of *power*? How successfully did the British people adjust to and accommodate their empire? Did the exercise of colonial rule come at an unacceptable cost to the British in terms of their moral standing, or their social, economic and political progress, or their fitness to govern the 'multi-racial society' that came with decolonisation? As we have seen, there was always more than one type of imperialism at work on Britain. The empire faithfully reflected the increasing pluralism and growing complexity of British society, and provided an arena in which competing social values and visions could be contested. This is not to deny that imperialism could act as a reactionary force that worked to preserve the status quo. Yet it could equally be dynamic and progressive, providing a catalyst for change (in particular, for the professions), or a competitive spur (for entrepreneurs), or reassurance for risk-takers (such as investors or migrants), or an expanded public sphere (for a variety of women's movements). Moreover, even if we accepted that the exercise of international power sometimes damaged British society, we would need to exercise caution before attributing this solely to its imperialist dimensions. The empire was an integral facet of Britain's broader international relations, and as such was more likely to reflect and reinforce a deepening involvement in the wider world than to stand apart from it. This is especially true of the economy, but migration and women's missionary activity fit comfortably in this framework of analysis too.

The preceding pages have emphasised how Britain's liberal state and society displayed a considerable capacity for self-criticism of particular aspects of imperialism. By their very nature, empires involve the exercise of force and the assumption of superiority. The real question, therefore, is how far the British were complacent or callous about the consequences of their rule with respect both to the welfare of the people who came under its sway, and its negative repercussions at home. We know that elements of British society underestimated Britain's capacity to stir up colonial societies. We also know that they were capable of displaying a marked lack of sensitivity to extra-European cultures and religions. Equally, however, they were sufficiently confident in their own institutions, and sufficiently mindful of their own standards of government, not to allow what they cherished and valued (or aspired to) at home to be completely compromised by their colonial commitments. In fact, tub-thumping imperialists were always regarded with suspicion in Britain because they were alien to the dominant political culture. The sanctioning of martial law, the suspension of judicial process, restrictions on the press and the use of armed force – all these galvanised liberal, humanitarian and anti-imperial sentiment. Furthermore, the dependent empire was not the only source of influence on the British political process. To be set against acts of settler oppression and rapacity, and the brutality of colonial rule, were the new perspectives on constitutional and social reform to be gained from the neo-Britains. Indeed, from the 1890s, the empire of settlement became an increasingly important influence on the thinking of politicians of all persuasions (including many British socialists and labour leaders).

Yet the liberal state has proved somewhat weaker when trying to deal with the diversity of culture and religion in Britain's post-colonial society. It has not been assertive enough in facing the challenges of new Commonwealth immigration; and it is conceivable that a more vigorous programme of public education in the immediate post-war period could have restrained racial prejudice, and furthered the integration of West Indian and Asian migrants – though that must remain a matter of speculation. 'Integration', of course, is now firmly back on the public policy agenda. Many of our 'ethnic minority' communities stretch back three generations. In what ways do they feel themselves to be British; what are the shared values they espouse? As Trevor Phillips at the Commission for Racial Equality has pointed out, multi-culturalism (or the toleration of difference) is all very well; yet, in itself, it is unlikely to prove a sufficiently strong buffer against fragmentation and division in society, or to provide the social 'glue' that helps society to cohere. We need to discover what we have in common. Is there really a core of Britishness that is not the preserve of 'white' people? If so, of what does it consist?[3] Continuing to consider the legacies of colonialism may be of help here. The stories of Britain's empire now being told by the media are much more inclusive. Museums, especially, have played a leading role in showing how African and Asian peoples contributed to British history well before the large-scale Commonwealth immigration after the Second World War, not least by reminding us that so many colonial soldiers fought in the conflicts that helped to forge modern Britain. What is particularly interesting about the role of these soldiers is why many

[244] of them thought they were fighting – namely, from a sense of duty to the King-Emperor, or for the future of the empire; the assumption that they invariably resented British rule is far from the truth.[4] Thus, as a result of the widespread discussion of empire in today's media a much wider range of colonial voices is now being heard, as official and heroic narratives of empire are increasingly displaced by other forms of public memory that range from personal reflection, to lobby and pressure group activism, to debate in the media and public exhibitions.[5] In this way, the empire has become an ever more 'present' past in recent years. This may be no bad thing.

APPENDIX

Table A   Money order transactions between the United Kingdom and the principal colonies and foreign countries, 1873

	Issued in Colonies (£)	Issued in UK (£)
Australia	143,014	29,921
Canada	163,138	33,899
Cape Colony	11,231	2,800
India	57,725	2,673
New Zealand	48,760	6,656
South & West Africa	23,308	1,207
West Indies	91,126	2,909
	£538,302	£80,065

	Issued Overseas (£)	Issued in UK (£)
Belgium	15,652	10,738
Denmark	2,005	2,176
France	1,857	8,638
Germany	30,246	39,321
Italy	4,997	7,097
Netherlands	4,000	3,197
Switzerland	5,403	11,516
United States	275,453	48,370
	£339,613	£131,053

Table B   Money orders received in Britain from the colonies, selected years, 1856–1910

	Number	Amount (£)
1856	3,965	12,961
1860	13,605	40,256
1871	123,472	520,550
1880–1	187,837	690,465
1888–9	350,902	1,252,606
1900–1	539,598	1,625,012
1909–10	1,012,062	2,929,397
1913–14	2,003,000	5,450,000

Table C   Money orders received in Britain from foreign countries, selected years, 1871–1910

	Number	Amount (£)
1871	28,662	107,911
1880–1	241,351	626,032
1888–9	593,090	1,495,951
1900–1	780,744	1,764,336
1909–10	1,550,215	4,013,117
1913–14	1,796,000	4,672,000

Table D   Money orders to the United Kingdom from Britain's colonies, 1909–10

	Amount (£)	Percentage
Australia	298,713	10
Canada	1,161,741	40
India	389,044	13
New Zealand	204,997	7
South Africa	592,292	20
West Indies	78,684	2
Other colonies & postal agencies	203,926	7

Table E   Money orders issued in the United Kingdom and sent to the colonies and to foreign countries, 1900–10

	To the Colonies (£)	To Foreign Countries (£)
1900–1	449,483	1,080,975
1901–2	456,901	1,175,142
1902–3	559,941	1,329,582
1903–4	584,954	1,445,655
1904–5	611,864	1,375,197
1905–6	646,821	1,409,749
1906–7	699,268	1,420,532
1907–8	865,913	1,480,061
1908–9	862,163	1,513,333
1909–10	884,534	1,556,939
	£6,621,842	£13,787,165

Source for all tables: Postmaster General's Annual Reports, Post Office Archives.

NOTES

Introduction

1. For the value of counter-factual history, see N. Ferguson (ed.), *Virtual History: Alternatives and Counterfactuals* (1997); A. Roberts (ed.), *What Might Have Been? Leading Historians on Twelve 'What Ifs' of History* (2004).

2. For the antithetical view, see J. G. A. Pocock, 'British History: A Plea for a New Subject', *JMH* (1975), pp. 603–4. As late as 1982, Pocock could still claim that 'We have little or no "British history" . . . most of what passes by that name is English history and makes little pretense of being anything else': 'The Limits and Divisions of British History: In Search of the Unknown Subject', *AHR* (1982), p. 311. For the dominance of 'English' history in the degree syllabuses of British universities in the first half of the twentieth century, see J. Kenyon, *The History Men: The Historical Profession in England since the Renaissance* (1983), p. 270.

3. See the essays by R. Gott ('Little Englanders') and E. Green and M. Taylor ('Further Thoughts on Little Englandism'), as well as the Preface and Introduction to R. Samuel (ed.), *Patriotism: The Making and Unmaking of British National Identity. Volume I: History and Politics* (1989), pp. x–lxvii, 91–109. Ironically, this volume of essays was subsequently criticised for that very same 'Little England parochialism' which its editor had identified as a weakness of the Left. See D. Cannadine, 'Patriotism' in *History In Our Time* (Penguin edn, 2000), pp. 91–2.

4. The *locus classicus* remains Enoch Powell's 'England: St George's Day Lecture' in *Reflections of a Statesman: The Writings and Speeches of Enoch Powell. Selected by Rex Collings* (1991).

5. For the revival of 'Little Englander' history by Lady Thatcher, and her successor John Major, see D. Cannadine, 'British History as a "New Subject": Politics, Perspectives and Prospects' in A. Grant and K. J. Stringer (eds), *Uniting the Kingdom: The Making of British History* (1995), pp. 12–13, 27–8.

6. For a commentary on the Left, see S. Howe, 'Labour Patriotism, 1939–83' in Samuel (ed.), *Patriotism. Vol. 1*, p. 132. For an example from the Right, see J. Enoch Powell, *Freedom and Reality* (Surrey, 1969), ch. 14.

7. For the link between nationalist historiography and contemporary politics see J. G. A. Pocock, 'The New British History in Atlantic Perspective: An Antipodean Commentary', *AHR* (1999), pp. 492–3 and 'History and Sovereignty: The Historiographical Response to Europeanization in two British Cultures', *JBS* (1992), pp. 363–4, 377–8.

8. For English history set in the larger context of the British Isles, see L. Colley, *Britons: Forging the Nation, 1707–1837* (1992); Grant and Stringer (eds), *Uniting the Kingdom?*; H. Kearney, *The British Isles: A History of Four Nations* (Cambridge, 1989); K. Robbins, *Nineteenth Century Britain: Integration and Diversity* (Oxford, 1988).

9. N. Davies, *The Isles: A History* (1999); S. Schama, *A History of Britain. Vol. 1: At the Edge of the World? 3000BC–AD1603* (2000), *Vol. 2: The British Wars 1603–1776* (2001), and *Vol. 3: The Fate of Empire, 1776–2000* (2002). See also the 'Britain and Europe' series, edited by Keith Robbins, which challenges the traditional separation of 'British' and 'European' history.

10. See, especially, the Manchester University Press series, *Studies in Imperialism*, edited by John Mackenzie.

11. For the subversive possibilities of 'comparative religion', from William Jones onwards, see C. Allen, *The Buddha and the Sahibs: The Men who Discovered India's Lost Religion* (2002).

12. J. F. Codell and D. S. Macleod (eds), *Orientalism Transposed: The Impact of the Colonies on British Culture* (Aldershot, 1998), ch. 1; J. P. Waghorne, *The Raja's Magic Clothes: Re Visioning Kingship and Divinity in England's India* (Pennsylvania, 1994).

13. For the burgeoning post-colonial literature on Indian fiction, see E. Boehmer, *Empire Writing: An Anthology of Colonial Literature, 1870–1918* (Oxford, 1998), pp. xliv–liii. Of particular interest is H. Trivedi's *Colonial Transactions: English Literature and India* (Calcutta, 1993), esp. pp. 15–22.

14. J. Majeed, *Ungoverned Imaginings: James Mill's 'The History of British India' and Orientalism* (Oxford, 1992); U. S. Mehta, *Liberalism and Empire: A Study in Nineteenth Century British Liberal Thought* (Chicago, 1999); P. van der Veer, *Imperial Encounters: Religion and Modernity in India and Britain* (Princeton, 2001).

15. A. Burton, *Burdens of History: British Feminists, Indian Women, and Imperial Culture, 1865–1915* (Chapel Hill, 1994); K. Jayawardena, *The White Woman's Other Burden: Western Women and South Asia During British Rule* (1995); B. Ramusack, 'Cultural Missionaries, Maternal Imperialists, Feminist Allies: British Women Activists in India, 1865–1945' in N. Chaudhuri and M. Strobel (eds), *Western Women and Imperialism: Complicity and Resistance* (Bloomington, 1992) and 'Catalysts or Helpers? British Feminists, Indian Women's Rights, and Indian Independence' in G. Minault (ed.), *The Extended Family. Women and Political Participation in India and Pakistan* (Delhi, 1981).

16. P. Buckner, 'Whatever Happened to the British Empire?', *Journal of the Canadian Historical Association* (1994), pp. 17ff; S. Constantine, *Emigrants and Empire:*

[250]   *British Settlement in the Dominions between the Wars* (Manchester, 1990); K. Fedorowich, *Unfit for Heroes: Reconstruction and Soldier Settlement in the Empire between the Wars* (Manchester, 1995); M. Harper, 'British Migration and the Peopling of the Empire', Vol. 3 *OHBE*, ch. 4.

17. S. Dubow, 'Colonial Nationalism, the Milner Kindergarten and the Rise of White South Africanism, 1902–10', *HWJ* (1997), pp. 53–85; E. H. H. Green, *The Crisis of Conservatism: The Politics, Economics and Ideology of the British Conservative Party, 1880–1914* (1995); A. S. Thompson, *Imperial Britain: The Empire in British Politics, c. 1880–1932* (Longman, 2000); P. Williamson, *Stanley Baldwin: Conservative Leadership and National Values* (Cambridge, 1999), ch. 8.

18. Much of the scholarship is focused on South Africa and the Boer War. See J. Bush, *Edwardian Ladies and Imperial Power* (Leicester, 2000); H. Callaway, 'Journalism as Active Politics: Flora Shaw, *The Times*, and South Africa' in D. Lowry (ed.), *The South African War Reappraised* (Manchester, 2000); E. van Heyningen, 'The Voices of Women in the South African War', *SAHJ* (1999), pp. 22–43; E. Reidi, 'Imperialist Women in Edwardian Britain: The Victoria League, 1899–1914', University of St Andrews Ph.D. (1998); A. S. Thompson, 'Publicity, Philanthropy and Commemoration: British Society during the War' in D. E. Omissi and A. S. Thompson (eds), *The Impact of the South African War* (Basingstoke, 2002).

19. J. Hyslop, 'The Imperial Working Class Makes Itself "White": White Labourism in Britain, Australia and South Africa before the First World War', *Journal of Historical Sociology* (1999), pp. 398–421 and 'A Ragged Trousered Philanthropist and the Empire: Robert Tressell in South Africa', *HWJ* (2001), pp. 65–86.

20. For examples, see n. 3 above on the 'Little Englander' school.

21. See, for example, J. Harris, *Private Lives, Public Spirit: A Social History of Britain, 1870–1914* (Oxford, 1993), p. 4: 'The very fact of British economic and political power in the wider world was in itself a major determinant of the character of domestic society throughout the period [1870–1914], perhaps more markedly so in the 1900s than in the mid-Victorian era'; and A. Burton, *At the Heart of Empire: Indians and the Colonial Encounter in Late-Victorian Britain* (Berkeley, 1998), pp. 7–8, which refers to empire as a 'fundamental and constitutive part of English culture and national identity at home'.

22. P. J. Marshall, 'No Fatal Impact? The Elusive History of Imperial Britain', *TLS*, 12/3/1993, p. 10; 'Imperial Britain', *JICH* (1995), pp. 392–3; and 'Imperial Britain' in Marshall (ed.), *The Cambridge Illustrated History of the British Empire* (Cambridge, 1996), pp. 336–7.

23. J. A. Schumpeter, 'The Sociology of Imperialisms' in *Imperialism and Social Classes*, trans. H. Norden, ed. P. M. Sweezy (Oxford, 1951), pp. 29, 84–5, 123–5, 130.

24. D. Cannadine, *Ornamentalism: How the British Saw Their Empire* (New York, 2001) and *Class in Britain* (New Haven, 1998), p. 19.

25. Harris, *Private Lives, Public Spirit*, pp. 254–5.

26. E. Stokes, *The English Utilitarians and India* (Oxford, 1959); van der Veer, *Imperial Encounters*.

27. P. Mandler, 'The Consciousness of Modernity? Liberalism and the English "National Character", 1870–1940' in M. Daunton and B. Rieger (eds), *Meanings of Modernity: Britain from the Late-Victorian Era to World War II* (Oxford, 2001), p. 129.

28. N. Owen, 'Critics of Empire in Britain' in Vol. 4 *OHBE*, p. 193.

29. B. Conekin, F. Mort and C. Waters (eds), *Moments of Modernity: Reconstructing Britain 1945–64* (1999), pp. 1–21; Daunton and Rieger (eds), *Meanings of Modernity*, pp. 12–13.

30. A similar framework of analysis is to be found in Miles Taylor's engaging essay, 'The 1848 Revolutions and the British Empire', *P&P* (2000).

31. In what was arguably becoming a more secular society, the evangelical missionary movement was potentially a powerful source of revival and renewal within the British churches. See, especially, S. Thorne, *Congregational Missions and the Making of an Imperial Culture in Nineteenth Century England* (Stanford, 1999). There are, of course, conflicting views on the extent to which Britain was becoming a more secular society in this period. For the view that it was, see R. Currie, A. Gilbert and L. Horsley, *Churches and Churchgoers: Patterns of Church Growth in the British Isles since 1700* (Oxford, 1977).

32. At a time when the aristocracy's grip on power gradually began to weaken, the empire is said to have breathed new life into hierarchical conceptions of society, and to have prolonged the belief of traditional ruling groups in their inborn right to govern. See, especially, A. Adonis, *Making Aristocracy Work: The Peerage and the Political System in Britain, 1884–1914* (Oxford, 1993), pp. 210–39, 276–9; D. Cannadine, *The Decline and Fall of the British Aristocracy* (New Haven, 1990), pp. 391–3, 420–9, 594–605. Chapter 1, however, offers a different perspective.

33. Imperialism may in several ways have impeded the progress of female emancipation, but some women's philanthropic and political energies seem to have found an outlet in various forms of imperial activism. For the crux of the debate, see R. O'Hanlon, 'Gender in the British Empire' in Vol. 4 *OHBE*, pp. 395–6. For further discussion, see Chapters 5 and 6.

34. The empire has been held responsible for Britain's 'extravagant' defence spending and for feather-bedding British industry, but it has also been identified as the driving force behind the dynamic and enterprising service sector. See P. J. Cain, 'Economics and Empire: The Metropolitan context', Vol. 3 *OHBE*; D. K. Fieldhouse, 'The Metropolitan Economics of Empire', Vol. 4 *OHBE*. These issues are investigated further in Chapter 7.

35. J. Darwin, 'Civility and Empire' in P. Burke, B. Harrison and P. Slack (eds), *Civil Histories: Essays Presented to Sir Keith Thomas* (Oxford, 2001), p. 333.

[252] 36. For the fluidity of these terms, see Jack Gallagher's Ford Lectures, *The Decline, Revival and Fall of the British Empire*, ed. Anil Seal (Cambridge, 1982).

37. P. J. Cain, 'Hobson, Wilshire and the Capitalist Theory of Imperialism', *History of Political Economy* (1985); 'Financial Capitalism and Imperialism in Late Victorian and Edwardian England', *JICH* (1985); and 'British Radicalism, the South African Crisis and the Origins of the Theory of Financial Capitalism' in Omissi and Thompson (eds), *The Impact of the South African War*. See also M. Taylor, 'Imperium et Libertas? Rethinking the Radical Critique of Imperialism during the Nineteenth Century', *JICH* (1991). Anti-Semitism was far from uncommon amongst early 20th-century liberals: some striking examples can be found in M. Bonham Carter and M. Pottle (eds), *Lantern Slides: The Diaries of Violet Bonham Carter, 1904–14* (1996).

38. G. L. Bernstein, *Liberalism and Liberal Politics in Edwardian Britain* (Winchester, Mass., 1986); P. Clarke, *Liberals and Social Democrats* (1988); M. Freeden (ed.), *Minutes of the Rainbow Circle, 1894–1924* (1989).

39. M. Weiner, *English Culture and the Decline of the Industrial Spirit, 1850–1980* (Harmondsworth, 1985).

40. P. Cain and A. G. Hopkins, *British Imperialism, 1688–2000* (Harlow, 2002); W. Hutton, *The State We're In* (1995).

41. For a parallel case, see Raphael Samuel's observations on the concept and study of 'patriotism': *Patriotism. Vol. I*, p. xvii.

42. V. S. Berridge, *Popular Journalism and Working Class Attitudes, 1854–86: A Study of Reynolds' Newspaper, Lloyd's Weekly Newspaper and the Weekly Times*, University of London Ph.D. (1976), pp. 301–2.

43. J. C. D. Clark, 'English History's Forgotten Context: Scotland, Ireland and Wales', *HJ* (1989), pp. 211–28.

44. For a useful commentary on the literature, see J. Tomlinson, *The Politics of Decline: Understanding Post-War Britain* (Harlow, 2000).

45. For an early and forceful statement of this view, see T. Nairn, *The Break-Up of Britain: Crisis and Neo-Nationalism* (2nd edn, 1981), pp. 13, 19–24.

46. For the argument that historical periods do not possess inherent characteristics, but have such characteristics imposed upon them by historians, see D. Eastwood, 'The Age of Uncertainty: Britain in the Early-Nineteenth Century', *TRHS* (1998), pp. 91–2.

47. A. Jones and B. Jones, 'The Welsh World and the British Empire, c. 1851–1939: An Exploration', *JICH* (2003), pp. 58, 75.

48. J. Mackenzie, 'The Second City of the Empire: Glasgow – Imperial Municipality' in F. Driver and D. Gilbert (eds), *Imperial Cities: Landscape, Display and Identity* (Manchester, 1999), p. 219.

49. Pocock, 'The Limits and Divisions of British History', p. 314.

50. R. Evans, 'Our Job is to Explain; it is for Others to Judge', *THES*, 13/6/ 2002, p. 20.   [253]

51. D. Kennedy, 'The Boundaries of Oxford's Empire', *IHR* (2001), pp. 606–7.

52. For press commentary on the opening of the museum, see *Daily Telegraph*, 28/9/02, p. 15. For a return to a more upbeat view of empire (albeit with qualifications), see Niall Ferguson's *Empire: How Britain Made the Modern World* (2003), and the accompanying Channel 4 TV series screened in January 2003.

53. See, especially, Corelli Barnett's trilogy: *The Audit of War: The Illusion and Reality of Britain as a Great Nation* (Basingstoke, 1986); *The Lost Victory: British Dreams, British Realities, 1945–50* (1996); *The Verdict of Peace* (Basingstoke, 2001).

54. See, for example, Stephen Howe on how the postcolonialists regard Commonwealth-Imperial history as a field of 'moral instruction in the evils of racism, sexism and colonialism': 'The Slow Death and Strange Rebirths of Imperial History', p. 139.

55. A. G. Hopkins, 'Accounting for the British Empire', *JICH* (1988), p. 245.

Chapter 1 Elites

1. L. Colley, 'Britishness and Otherness' and *Britons: Forging the Nation, 1707–1837* (1992); J. MacKenzie, 'Essay and Reflection: On Scotland and the Empire', *IHR* (1993) and 'Empire and National Identities: The Case of Scotland', *TRHS* (1998); A. Jones and B. Jones, 'The Welsh and the British World, 1851–1939' in C. Bridge and K. Fedorowich (eds), *The British World: Diaspora, Culture and Identity* (2003); K. Jeffery, *An Irish Empire? Aspects of Ireland and the British Empire* (Manchester, 1996).

2. For contemporary views of emigration and for its effects, see Darwin, 'Civility and Empire', p. 328; Harris, *Public Spirit, Private Lives*, p. 5.

3. Cannadine, *Class in Britain*, pp. 65, 104–5, 137–42, 157–60 and *Ornamentalism*, pp. xviii–xx, 4–10, 56–7, 85, 121–2, 128–31.

4. Cain and Hopkins, *British Imperialism, 1688–2000*, pp. 47–50; H. J. Field, *Toward a Programme of Imperial Life: The British Empire at the Turn of the Century* (Oxford, 1982); M. Hechter, *Internal Colonialism: The Celtic Fringe in British National Development, 1536–1966* (1975), p. 261; Mackenzie, *Propaganda and Empire*, pp. 254–8; B. Semmel, *Imperialism and Social Reform: English Social Imperial Thought, 1895–1914* (1960), pp. 13, 19, 22–4.

5. A. Burton, *At the Heart of Empire: Indians and the Colonial Encounter in Late-Victorian Britain* (Berkeley, 1998), pp. 7–8, 191–2; C. Hall, *Civilising Subjects: Metropole and Colony in the English Imagination, 1830–67* (Oxford, 2002); A. McClintock; *Imperial Leather: Race, Gender, and Sexuality in the*

Colonial Contest (New York, 1995). For a sceptic, see B. Porter, 'Edward Elgar and Empire', *JICH* (2001), p. 7: 'Some ludicrous errors have been made by cultural scholars who, glimpsing a flash of the dolphin's fin in the water, have assumed it belonged to an imperial shark.'

6. P. Smith, 'Refuge for the Aristocracy', *LRB*, 21/6/2001, p. 31.

7. T. Metcalf, *Ideologies of the Raj: The New Cambridge History of India* (Cambridge, 1994); D. Washbrook, 'India, 1818–60: The Two Faces of Colonialism' in Vol. 3 *OHBE*.

8. M. Girouard, *The Return to Camelot: Chivalry and the English Gentleman* (Yale, 1981), p. 226.

9. B. R. Tomlinson, 'The British Economy and the Empire, 1900–39' in C. Wrigley (ed.), *A Companion to Early Twentieth Century Britain* (Oxford, 2003), p. 208.

10. J. V. Beckett, *The Aristocracy in England, 1660–1914* (Oxford, 1986), p. 464.

11. A. Adonis, 'Aristocracy, Agriculture and Liberalism: The Politics, Finances and Estates of the 3rd Lord Carrington', *HJ* (1988), pp. 887–9; F. Bedarida, *A Social History of England, 1851–1975* (1976), pp. 44–5, 127; E. J. Evans, 'Landownership and the Exercise of Power in an Industrialising Society: Lancashire and Cheshire in the Nineteenth Century' in R. Gibson and M. Blinkhorn (eds), *Landownership and Power in Modern Europe* (1991), pp. 152–3; D. Spring, 'The Role of the Aristocracy in the Late Nineteenth Century', *VS* (1960), p. 63 and *The English Landed Estate in the Nineteenth Century* (Baltimore, 1963).

12. Beckett, *The Aristocracy in England*, ch. 14; F. M. L. Thompson, *English Landed Society in the Nineteenth Century* (1963); W. L. Gutsman, *The British Political Elite* (1963).

13. L. Namier, *Skyscrapers and Other Essays* (1931), p. 48.

14. R. Perren, 'The Marketing of Agricultural Products: Farm Gate to Retail Store' in E. J. T. Collins (ed.), *The Agrarian History of England and Wales* (Cambridge, 2000), p. 959.

15. Adonis, 'Aristocracy, Agriculture and Liberalism', pp. 885–7; Thompson, *English Landed Society*, pp. 327–9.

16. Beckett, *The Aristocracy in England*, pp. 460–1.

17. D. Eastwood, *Governing Rural England: Tradition and Transformation in Local Government, 1780–1840* (Oxford, 1994), pp. 261–5; Spring, 'The Role of the Aristocracy', p. 60.

18. Another possibility, not explored here, is that the empire was useful to the aristocracy in terms of finding a role for the less able and hiding away its defects overseas. While not denying that this was true for some, I am sceptical whether enough members of the landed elite found refuge in the colonies for the fortunes of aristocracy *as a whole* to have been affected in this way.

19. Cannadine, *The Decline and Fall of the British Aristocracy*, p. 598.

20. C. A. Hughes and J. F. Nicholson, 'A Provenance of Proconsuls: British Colonial Governors, 1900–60', *JICH* (1975), pp. 77–105; and Table 5.2 in A. Kirk-Greene, *On Crown Service: A History of HM Colonial and Overseas Civil Services, 1837–1997* (1999), p. 102.

21. A. Adonis, 'The Survival of the Great Estates: Henry, 4th Earl of Carnarvon and his Dispositions in the Eighteen-Eighties', *BIHR* (1991), pp. 54–62.

22. S. Checkland, *The Elgins, 1766–1917: A Tale of Aristocrats, Proconsuls and their Wives* (Aberdeen, 1988), pp. 107–17, 136–40, 188, 260–1.

23. A. Lyall, *The Life of the Marquis of Dufferin and Ava* (1905), pp. 203–4.

24. T. Anbinder, 'From Famine to Five Points', *AHR* (2002), pp. 356–7; C. G. Carroll, *The Lansdowne Irish Estates and Sir William Petty* (Dublin, 1881); G. L. Lyne, *The Lansdowne Estate in Kerry under the Agency of William Steuart Trench, 1849–72* (Dublin, 2001).

25. Lord Newton, *Lord Lansdowne: A Biography* (1929), pp. 24–5, 45–6, 129.

26. M. Harper, *Emigration from North-East of Scotland. Vol. 2: Beyond the Broad Atlantic* (Aberdeen, 1988), ch. 3.

27. P. Dunae, *Gentleman Emigrants: From the British Public Schools to the Canadian Frontier* (Vancouver, 1981), pp. 1–12, 215–35.

28. Quotation from B. Berman and J. Lonsdale, *Unhappy Valley: Conflict in Kenya and Africa* (Ohio, 1992), p. 1.

29. D. A. Low and A. Smith, *History of East Africa* (Oxford, 1976), pp. 450–3.

30. Adonis, *Making Aristocracy Work*, p. 211.

31. For others, however, a colonial posting signified failure in domestic politics: Cannadine, *The Decline and Fall of the British Aristocracy*, pp. 603–4.

32. Adonis, *Making Aristocracy Work*, p. 239.

33. J. L. Morison, *The Eighth Earl of Elgin: A Chapter in Nineteenth-Century Imperial History* (1928), p. 43.

34. T. Walrond (ed.), *Letters and Journals of James, Eighth Earl of Elgin* (1872), pp. 395–6.

35. Checkland, *The Elgins*, pp. 196–7.

36. Lyall, *Life of the Marquis of Dufferin*, pp. 265–75.

37. Newton, *Lord Lansdowne*, p. 123.

38. J. Marsh, *Back to the Land: The Pastoral Impulse in England from 1880 to 1914* (1982); M. Weiner, *English Culture and the Decline of the Industrial Spirit, 1850–1950* (Cambridge, 1981).

39. J. A. Froude, *Oceana or England and her Colonies* (1886), p. 338.

40. P. Mandler, 'Against "Englishness": English Culture and the Limits to Rural Nostalgia, 1850–1940', *TRHS* (1997), p. 170.

[256] 41. Cain and Hopkins, *British Imperialism*, ch. 1.

42. G. Crossick, 'From Gentlemen to the Residuum: Languages of Social Description in Victorian Britain' in P. J. Corfield (ed.), *Language, History and Class* (Oxford, 1991), pp. 164–5; E. J. Hobsbawm, 'The Example of the English Middle Class' in J. Kocka and A. Mitchell (eds), *Bourgeois Society in Nineteenth Century Europe* (Oxford, 1993), pp. 134–5.

43. See, especially, the claims made by R. Drayton, *Nature's Government: Science, Imperial Britain, and the 'Improvement' of the World* (New Haven, 2000), p. 170.

44. D. Duman, 'The Creation and Diffusion of a Professional Ideology in Nineteenth Century England', *Sociological Review* (1979), pp. 113–38.

45. P. J. Corfield, *Power and the Professions in Britain 1700–1850* (1995).

46. Bedarida, *A Social History of England*, pp. 50–1; T. R. Gourvish, 'The Rise of the Professions' in Gourvish and A. O'Day (eds), *Later-Victorian Britain, 1867–1900* (Basingstoke, 1988), pp. 13–35; K. T. Hoppen, *The Mid-Victorian Generation, 1846–86* (Oxford, 1998), pp. 40–9; H. Perkin, *The Rise of Professional Society: England since 1880* (1990, paperback edn).

47. N. Gardiner, *Sentinels of Empire: The British Colonial Administrative Service, 1919–54*, University of Yale Ph.D. (1998), ch. 3; L. H. Gunn and P. Duigan, *The Rulers of British Africa, 1870–1914* (1978), p. 198; Kirk-Greene, *On Crown Service*, p. 95.

48. C. Jeffries, *The Colonial Empire and its Civil Service* (Cambridge, 1938), pp. 10, 18. See, for example, the sizes of the Ceylon and Malay civil services, tabulated in J. de Vere Allen, 'Malayan Civil Service, 1874–1941: Colonial Bureaucracy/Malayan Elite', *Comparative Studies in Society and History* (1970), p. 160.

49. Kirk-Greene, *On Crown Service*, pp. 16, 37, 52–3.

50. Technical recruitment comprised medical and veterinary; education; agriculture; and forestry.

51. Approximately a fifth of recruits to the technical services came from the former and just over a quarter from the latter.

52. On the size and composition of the ICS, see T. H. Beaglehole, 'From Rulers to Servants: The ICS and the British Demission of Power in India', *MAS* (1977), pp. 245–6; H. A. Ewing, *The Indian Civil Service, 1919–42: Some Aspects of Control in India*, Cambridge University Ph.D. (1980), pp. 177–80, 238–40; and D. C. Potter, *India's Political Administrators, 1919–83* (Oxford, 1986), pp. 21–2, 33–4, 56–80, 84–5, 90, 97.

53. *Report of a Committee on the Appointment in the Colonial Office and the Colonial Services.* April 1930. Cmd 3554. *Parliamentary Papers* (1929–30), pp. 32–5, 50–3. Also compare R. Furse, *Aucuparius: Recollections of a Recruiting Officer* (1962) with R. Heussler, *Yesterday's Rulers: The Making of the British Colonial Service* (Syracuse, 1963), pp. 6, 15, 23–4, 34–5; H. Kuklick, *The Imperial*

Bureaucrat: The Colonial Administrative Service in the Gold Coast, 1920–39   [257]
(Stanford, 1979), pp. 20–39; and Vere Allen, 'Malayan Civil Service', p. 164.

54. Ewing, 'The Indian Civil Service', pp. 164–9, 238–44; Potter, *India's Political Administrators*, pp. 86–9; R. Symonds, *Oxford and Empire: The Last Lost Cause* (1986), p. 192.

55. See, for example, J. M. Peterson, *The Medical Profession in Mid-Victorian London* (Berkeley, 1978), pp. 124–5, which shows how serving as a doctor in the army or navy in India could make it possible to accumulate the funds to buy a practice at home. I am grateful to Brian Harrison for this reference.

56. J. M. Orpen, *Reminiscences of Life in South Africa from 1846 to the Present Day,* Vol. 1 (Cape Town, 1964), p. 3.

57. For two professions that took on an imperial identity, see the example of engineering below, and the description of the Institute of Chartered Accountants' offices in London in Chapter 8, p. 181.

58. For a detailed discussion of the introduction of open competition see J. M. Compton, 'Open Competition and the Indian Civil Service, 1854–76', *EHR* (1968), pp. 265–84.

59. C. Dewey, 'The Education of a Ruling Caste: The Indian Civil Service in the Era of Competitive Examination', *EHR* (1973), pp. 283–5.

60. On patronage and its gradual decline, see G. Kitson Clark, ' "Statesmen in disguise": Reflections on the History of the Neutrality of the Civil Service' in P. Stansky (ed.), *The Victorian Revolution: Government and Society in Victoria's Britain* (New York, 1973), pp. 64–5; W. J. Reader, *Professional Men: The Rise of the Professional Classes in Nineteenth-Century England* (1966), chs 5–6; A. M. Saunders and P. A. Wilson, *The Professions* (Oxford, 1933), pp. 239–40.

61. Searle, *Entrepreneurial Politics*, p. 124.

62. Under this system, patrons who had the right to nominate candidates still exercised that right, but they nominated more people than there were vacancies for. The Civil Service Commissioners then ran competitions to determine who should be appointed. It was a diluted form of patronage where competitions were open only to patrons' nominees.

63. J. Roach, *Public Examinations in England, 1850–1900* (Cambridge, 1971), pp. 203–9; Reader, *Professional Men*, pp. 93–6.

64. For the comparison see Corfield, *Power and the Professions*, pp. 226–35; A. J. Guy, ' "People who will stick at nothing to make money"? Officers' Income, Expenditure and Expectations in the Service of John Company, 1750–1840' in Guy and P. B. Boyden (eds), *Soldiers of the Raj: The Indian Army 1600–1947* (Coventry, 1997), p. 50; G. Harries-Jenkins, *The Army in Victorian Society* (1977), p. 13; T. A. Heathcote, *The Indian Army: The Garrison of British Imperial India, 1822–1922* (1974), pp. 122–30; D. E. Omissi, *The Sepoy and the Raj: The Indian Army, 1860–1940* (Basingstoke, 1994), pp. 103–5; G. B. Otley, 'The Social Origins of British Army Officers', *Sociological*

Review (1970), pp. 213–39; P. E. Razzell, 'Social Origins of Officers in the Indian and British Home Army: 1758–1962', *British Journal of Sociology* (1963), pp. 248–60.

65. Lieut.-Col. E. T. Paul, *The Imperial Army of India* (Calcutta, 1902), p. 52.

66. R. A. Buchanan, 'The Diaspora of British Engineering', *Technology and Culture* (1986), pp. 501–24.

67. R. A. Buchanan, *The Life and Times of Isambard Kingdom Brunel* (2002), ch. 6.

68. A. Martin Wainwright, 'Representing the Technology of the Raj in Britain's Victorian Periodical Press' in D. Finkelstein and D. M. Peers (eds), *Negotiating India in the Nineteenth Century Media* (Basingstoke, 2000), ch. 9.

69. D. R. Headrick, *The Tentacles of Progress: Technology Transfer in the Age of Imperialism, 1850–1940* (Oxford, 1988), p. 196.

70. Earl of Cromer, *Modern Egypt* (1911), p. 821. See also R. Tignor, *Modernisation and British Colonial Rule in Egypt, 1882–1914* (Princeton, 1966), p. 114.

71. M. A. Hollings (ed.), *The Life of Sir Colin C. Scott-Moncrieff* (1917), pp. 162, 172–3, 177, 180.

72. Cromer, *Modern Egypt*, p. 820.

73. A. L. al Sayyid Marsot, *Egypt and Cromer: A Study in Anglo-Egyptian Relations* (New York, 1969), pp. 85–6; Tignor, *Modernisation and British Colonial Rule*, p. 115.

74. R. Appleyard, *The History of the Institution of Electrical Engineers, 1871–1931* (1939), pp. 153–4.

75. R. A. Stafford, 'Scientific Exploration and Empire' in Vol. 3 *OHBE*; T. Richards, *The Imperial Archive: Knowledge and the Fantasy of Empire* (1993), pp. 1–3.

76. A. Godleska and N. Smith (eds), *Geography and Empire* (Oxford, 1994), pp. 4–5; B. Hudson, 'The New Geography and the New Imperialism, 1870–1918', *Antipode*, Vol. 9 (1977), pp. 12–19; D. R. Stoddart, *On Geography: And its History* (Oxford, 1996), pp. 128–9. The RGS's efforts to cash in on the publicity surrounding African exploration were also the cause of anxiety within the institution: see F. Driver, *Geography Militant: Cultures of Exploration and Empire* (Oxford, 2001), ch. 2.

77. For the French case, see D. Lejeune, *Les Sociétés de géographie en France et l'expansion coloniale au XIX siècle* (Paris, 1993) and A. M. C. Godlewska, *Geography Unbound: French Geographic Science from Cassini to Humboldt* (Chicago, 1999).

78. A. S. Goudie, 'George Nathaniel Curzon – Superior Geographer', *Geographical Journal* (1980), pp. 203–9.

79. Hudson, 'The New Geography', p. 14.

80. R. Oliver, *Sir Harry Johnston and the Scramble for Africa* (1964).

81. W. H. Parker, *Mackinder: Geography as an Aid to Statecraft* (Oxford, 1982).   [259]

82. MacKenzie, 'Empire and Metropolitan Cultures' in Vol. 3 *OHBE*, pp. 287–8.

83. H. M. Stanley, 'Central Africa and the Congo Basin; or, the Importance of the Scientific Study of Geography', *Journal of the Manchester Geographical Society* (1885), pp. 7–25.

84. Stafford, 'Scientific Exploration and Empire', pp. 298–9.

85. J. A. Second, 'King of Siluria: Roderick Murchison and the Imperial Theme in Nineteenth Century British Geology', *VS* (1982), pp. 413–42.

86. Although university geology departments trained the career geologists who manned geological surveys and managed mining enterprises throughout the empire. See R. Porter, 'The Natural Sciences Tripos and the "Cambridge School of Geology", 1850–1914', *History of Universities* (1982), pp. 193–200.

87. Drayton, *Nature's Government*, chs 6–7.

88. C. Pinney, 'Colonial Anthropology in the "Laboratory of Mankind"' in C. Bayly (ed.), *The Raj: India and the British 1600 1947* (1990), pp. 252–63.

89. G. W. Stocking, *Victorian Anthropology* (New York, 1987), chs 3, 6.

90. J. Falconer, *India: Pioneering Photographers, 1850–1900* (2001), pp. 8–33.

91. Thompson, *Imperial Britain*, ch. 3.

92. I am indebted to Professor Rubinstein who supplied me with copies of the notebooks of newspaper editors, and to Professor Perkin for guiding me to this source. See also J. D. Startt, *Journalists for Empire: The Imperial Debate in the Edwardian Stately Press* (Westport, CT, 1991), ch. 2.

93. S. J. Potter, *News and the British World: The Emergence of an Imperial Press System* (Oxford, 2003). ch. 5.

94. B. Griffen-Foley, 'Before the "Dirty-Digger": The Australian Journalist on Fleet Street, *c.* 1900–1939', unpublished paper given to the British World Conference, University of Cape Town, Jan. 2002.

95. Potter, *Nationalism, Imperialism and the Press*, p. 50.

96. T. Johnson, 'The State and the Professions: Peculiarities of the British' in A. Giddens and I. Neustadt (eds), *Social Class and the Division of Labour* (Cambridge, 1982), pp. 186–208.

97. The place to begin is the informative if congratulatory account compiled by Sarah Tooley, *The History of Nursing in the British Empire* (1906), esp. pp. 174–86, 341–68.

98. E. A. Friend, *Professional Women and the British Empire, 1880–1939*, University of Lancaster Ph.D. (1998), p. 238.

99. H. P. Dickson, *The Badge of Britannia: The History and Reminiscences of the Queen Elizabeth Overseas Nursing Service, 1886–1966* (Haddington, E. Lothian, 1990), pp. vii–ix, 3–7, 16.

[260]   100.   On the nursing profession and empire see D. Birkett, 'The "White Woman's Burden" in the "White Man's Grave": The Introduction of British Nurses in Colonial West Africa' in Chauhuri and Strobel (eds), *Western Women and Imperialism*, pp. 177–88; A. Summers, *Angels and Citizens: British Women as Military Nurses, 1854–1914* (1988), ch. 7. On the impact of the South African War (1899–1902) specifically see: *Report by the Central British Red Cross Committee on Voluntary Organisations in the Aid of the Sick and Wounded during the South African War* (1902), pp. 3, 8; B. Oliver, *The British Red Cross in Action* (1966), p. 182; S. Marks, 'British Nursing and the South African War' in G. Cuthbertson, A. Grundlingh and M.-L. Suttie (eds), *Writing a Wider War* (Ohio, 2002).

101.   J. Moore, *A Zeal for Responsibility: The Struggle for Professional Nursing in Victorian England, 1868–1883* (Athens, GA, 1988), pp. ix–x, 180–6.

102.   Friend, *Professional Women and the British Empire*, pp. 240–5.

103.   Thompson, 'Publicity, Philanthropy and Commemoration', pp. 99–123.

104.   Perkin, *The Rise of Professional Society*, p. xii.

105.   S. J. D. Green, 'In Search of Bourgeois Civilisation: Institutions and Ideals in Nineteenth-Century Britain', *Northern History* (1995) [quote from p. 257].

106.   Furse, *Aucuparius*, pp. 221, 228–32.

107.   Before 1945, the 'industrial north' provided 18% of recruits to the technical and professional services, rising to 26% thereafter. Gardiner, *Sentinels of Empire*, p. 156. A study of the CAS in the Gold Coast suggests that recruits with a business background may have been more numerous still. See Kuklick, *The Imperial Bureaucrat*, pp. 29, 38.

108.   On the importance of empire markets to British industry, see A. S. Thompson and G. Magee, 'A Soft Touch? British Industry, Empire Markets and the Self-Governing Dominions, 1870–1914', *EcHR* (2003), pp. 689–717.

109.   L. E. Davis and R. A. Huttenback, *Mammon and the Pursuit of Empire: The Economics of British Imperialism* (Cambridge, 1988), ch. 7.

110.   A. Howe, *The Cotton Masters, 1830–60* (Oxford, 1984), pp. 38–43.

111.   W. J. MacPherson, 'Investment in Indian Railways, 1845–75', *EcHR* (1955–6), pp. 177–86. Quite a few English novelists were drawn to Indian railway stock: see N. Henry, *George Eliot and the British Empire* (Cambridge, 2002), pp. 77, 95.

112.   B. Lenman and K. Donaldson, 'Partners' Incomes, Investment and Diversification in the Scottish Linen Area, 1850–1921', *Business History* (1971), pp. 1–18.

113.   C. Bright, *Submarine Telegraphs: Their History, Construction and Working* (1898), pp. 31–2, 166; H. Barty-King, 'Pender, Sir John (1816–96)', *Dictionary of Business Biography*, Vol. 4, pp. 609–13; B. J. Hunt, 'Doing Science in a Global Empire: Cable Telegraphy and Electrical Physics in Victorian Britain' in B. Lightman (ed.), *Victorian Science in Context* (Chicago, 1997), p. 321.

114. For Manchester's apathy to John Bright's campaigns for changes to the [261] structure of Indian government, see J. L. Sturgis, *John Bright and the Empire* (1969), pp. 25–31, 53–76.

115. On the pragmatism of provincial manufacturers, see Searle, *Entrepreneurial Politics*, pp. 127–8, 316–17.

116. G. Timmins, *Made in Lancashire: A History of Regional Industrialisation* (Manchester, 1998), pp. 230–1.

117. A. W. Silver, *Manchester Men and Indian Cotton, 1847–1872* (Manchester, 1966), p. 59.

118. Howe, *The Cotton Masters*, pp. 199–202.

119. Palmerston to Milner Gibson [President of the Board of Trade], 7/6/1861, quoted in Silver, *Manchester Men*, p. 144.

120. Worboys, *Science and British Colonial Imperialism*, pp. 58–65.

121. Thompson, *Imperial Britain*, pp. 101–2.

122. A. Porter, *Victorian Shipping, Business and Imperial Policy: Donald Currie, the Castle Line and Southern Africa* (Suffolk, 1986).

123. P. N. Davies, *Sir Alfred Jones: Shipping Entrepreneur Par Excellence* (1978).

124. F. Harcourt, 'The P&O Company: Flagships of Imperialism' in S. Palmer and G. Williams (eds), *Charted and Uncharted Waters: Proceedings of a Conference on the Study of British Maritime History* (1981), pp. 6–28; N. A. Pelcovits, *Old China Hands and the Foreign Office* (New York, 1948), pp. 160–89, 296–9; Report on the Hong Kong and Shanghai Bank 3rd Annual Dinner, 6/12/1909 (extract of speech given by Sir Thomas Sutherland), HSBC archives, London.

125. H. Robinson, *The British Post Office: A History* (Princeton, 1948), pp. 391–3.

126. Porter, *Victorian Shipping*, p. 266.

127. Quotes from Davies, *Sir Alfred Jones*, pp. 104, 121.

128. On Rowntree's politics, imperial attitudes and response to the Boer War, see M. Higham, 'Rowntree, Joseph (1836–1925)', *Dictionary of Business Biography*, Vol. 4, pp. 965–72; R. Fitzgerald, *Rowntree and the Marketing Revolution, 1862–99* (Cambridge, 1995), pp. 99, 553, 557; D. Rubinstein, *Faithful to Ourselves and the Outside World: York Quakers in the Twentieth Century* (York, 2001), p. 60; A. Vernon, *A Quaker Business Man: The Life of Joseph Rowntree, 1836–1925* (1958), pp. 9–10, 14, 104, 139, 153–5, 161–3, 173–7, 196–7.

129. On Cadbury's politics, imperial attitudes and response to the Boer War, see C. Dellheim, 'The Creation of a Company Culture: *Cadburys, 1861–1931*', *AHR*, 92 (1987), pp. 13–44; A. G. Gardiner, *Life of George Cadbury* (1923), pp. 78–9, 139, 211–19, 242–51, 308–9; H. H. Hewison, *Hedge of Wild Almonds: South Africa, the Pro-Boers and the Quaker Conscience, 1890–1910* (Portsmouth, NH, 1989), pp. 109, 112, 116, 180–1, 221; I. Williams, *The Firm*

of Cadbury, 1831–1931 (1931), ch. 8. [Quote from Gardiner, *Life of George Cadbury*, p. 79.]

130. Africa did not displace Latin America as the main source of cocoa beans until the 1920s. See J. Othick, 'The Cocoa and Chocolate Industry in the Nineteenth Century' in D. Oddy and D. Miller (eds), *The Making of the Modern Diet* (1976), p. 90.

131. Williams, *The Firm of Cadbury*, pp. 214–15.

132. For the claim that it was the latter, see R. Robinson and J. Gallagher, *Africa and the Victorians* (Basingstoke, 1981, 2nd edn), pp. 2–4.

Chapter 2 The Lower Middle Class and the Working Class at Home

1. Hoppen, *The Mid-Victorian Generation*, p. 56; R. McKibbin, *Classes and Cultures: England, 1918–51* (Oxford, 1998), p. 106.

2. White-collar workers rose from 2.3 to 5.7% of the occupied population from 1851 to 1891, and from 6.7 to 10.7% from 1921 to 1951: *British Labour Statistics: Historical Abstract, 1886–1968* (1971), pp. 102–3; Hoppen, *The Mid-Victorian Generation*, p. 46; McKibbin, *Classes and Cultures*, p. 46.

3. For the counter-case, see P. Bailey, 'White Collars, Gray Lives? The Lower Middle Class Revisited', *JBS* (1999), p. 273; T. Jeffery, 'A Place in the Nation: The Lower Middle Class in England' in R. Koshar (ed.), *Splintered Classes: Politics and the Lower Middle Classes in Interwar Europe* (New York, 1990), p. 72; Perkin, *The Rise of Professional Society*, p. 99.

4. Bedarida, *A Social History of England*, p. 208.

5. C. Hughes, 'Imperialism, Illustration and the *Daily Mail*, 1896–1904' in M. Harris and A. Lee (eds), *The Press in English Society from the Seventeenth to the Nineteenth Centuries* (Cranbury, NJ, 1986), p. 187.

6. R. Price, 'Society, Status and Jingoism: The Social Roots of Lower Middle Class Patriotism, 1870–1900' in G. Crossick (ed.), *The Lower Middle Class in Britain* (1977), pp. 89–112.

7. See, in particular, the books published under the imprint of John Mackenzie's 'Studies In Imperialism' Series, especially *Propaganda and Empire* and *Imperialism and Popular Culture* and Mackenzie's impressive contributions to the *OHBE*: Vols 3 and 4.

8. Mackenzie, *Propaganda and Empire*, pp. 2–3, 7–9 and *Imperialism and Popular Culture*, pp. 3–4, 9.

9. P. Corrigan and D. Sayer, *The Great Arch: English State Formation as Cultural Revolution* (Oxford, 1991), pp. 122–3, 193–5.

10. V. Kiernan, 'Working Class and Nation in Nineteenth-Century Britain' in M. Cornforth (ed.), *Rebels and Their Causes* (1978), p. 126.

11. J. Foster, *Class Struggle and the Industrial Revolution: Early Industrial Capitalism in Three English Towns* (1974), pp. 6–7, 203–7, 250; Kiernan, 'Working Class and Nation', p. 130.   [263]

12. G. Elton, *The English* (Oxford, 1992), p. 234.

13. Paper given by Bernard Porter, 'Metropolitan Culture and Imperial Decline' symposium, 5/12/2001, Institute of Commonwealth Studies, London. See also *The Lion's Share*, pp. 349–50.

14. A. S. Thompson, 'Is Humpty-Dumpty Together Again? Imperial History and the *OHBE*', *TCBH* (2001), p. 523; Omissi and Thompson, 'Investigating the Impact of the War', pp. 10–11.

15. A conclusion reached by H. J. Booth and N. Rigby (eds), *Modernism and Empire* (Manchester, 2000), p. 3.

16. B. Semmel, *The Governor Eyre Controversy* (1962), pp. 134–5.

17. F. Cooper and A. L. Stoler (eds), *Tensions of Empire: Colonial Cultures in a Bourgeois World* (Berkeley, 1997), pp. 9–10; S. Marks, 'History, the Nation and Empire: Sniping from the Periphery', *HWJ* (1990), p. 115.

18. Crossick, 'From Gentleman to the Residuum', pp. 161–3.

19. This distinction is largely absent from the literature, but is rightly emphasised in Kumar's *The Making of English National Identity*, p. 195.

20. A. James Hammerton, 'Pooterism or Partnership? Marriage and Masculine Identity in the Lower Middle Class, 1870–1920', *JBS* (2001), p. 320.

21. Compton, 'Open Competition and the Indian Civil Service', pp. 281–2.

22. They formed 15% of the total intake.

23. Gardiner, *Sentinels of Empire*, pp. 256–8.

24. Ibid., pp. 112–13.

25. Ibid., pp. 114–15.

26. Ibid., chs 4–5.

27. Berridge, *Popular Journalism and Working Class Attitudes*, pp. 2–3, 95–7, 299–303.

28. K. Jones, *Fleet Street and Downing Street* (1919), pp. 147–9.

29. *Daily Express*: 16/5/1900, 8/6/1900, 16/6/1900, 23/6/1900, 13/9/1900, 19/9/1900, 20/9/1900; *Daily Mail*: 14/8/1899, 4/9/1899, 13/9/1899.

30. *Daily Express*: 22/8/1900, 24/8/1900, 20/6/1901; *Daily Mail*: 4/9/1899, 18/9/1899, 25/9/1899.

31. *Daily Express*: 3/5/1900, 10/5/1900, 21/5/1900, 20/12/1900; *Daily Mail*: 4/12/1899, 21/12/1899.

32. *Daily Mail*: 4/9/1899, 13/9/1899.

33. *Daily Express*: 14/2/1901, 25/6/1901, 10/8/1901.

[264]   34. 'Whatever your Harmsworths and Pearsons don't know, they do know the public': Moberley Bell to Leo Amery, 13/5/1900, quoted in S. Koss, *The Rise and Fall of the Political Press in Britain. Vol. 1: The Nineteenth Century* (1981), p. 419. See also R. Allen, *Voice of Britain: The Inside Story of the Daily Express* (Cambridge, 1983), p. 17 and S. J. Taylor, *The Great Outsiders: Northcliffe, Rothermere and the Daily Mail* (1996), pp. 36–7.

35. R. Bourne, *Lords of Fleet Street* (1990), p. 31.

36. J. M. Golby and A. W. Purdue, *The Civilisation of the Crowd: Popular Culture in England 1750–1900* (1984), pp. 179–80; L. A. Loeb, *Consuming Angels: Advertising and Victorian Women* (Oxford, 1994), pp. 8–13, 83–4, 125, 173; Thompson, 'Publicity, Philanthropy and Commemoration', p. 101.

37. R. Price, *An Imperial War and the British Working Class: Working Class Attitudes and Reactions to the Boer War, 1899–1902* (1972), pp. 132–77. Price's conclusions are endorsed by J. H. Grainger's *Patriotisms: Britain 1900–1939* (1986), p. 150.

38. Perkin, *The Rise of Professional Society*, p. 99.

39. S. Pennybacker, *A Vision for London, 1889–1914: Labour, Everyday Life and the LCC Experiment* (1995), pp. 33–95; C. Waters, *British Socialists and the Politics of Popular Culture, 1884–1914* (1990), pp. 161–5; S. Pierson, *British Socialists: The Journey from Fantasy to Politics* (1979), p. 18; K. Hardie, *My Confession of Faith in the Labour Alliance* (1910), p. 7.

40. W. Fest, 'Jingoism and Xenophobia in the Electioneering Strategies of British Ruling Elites before 1914' in P. Kennedy and A. Nicholls (eds), *Nationalist and Racialist Movements in Britain and Germany before 1914* (Oxford, 1981), pp. 174–5; L. P. Gartner, *The Jewish Immigrant in England, 1870–1914* (3rd edn, 2001), p. 28.

41. *Daily Express*, 26/5/1900.

42. P. Krebs, *Gender, Race and the Writing of Empire: Public Discourse and the Boer War* (Cambridge, 1999), pp. 1–2, 7, 14, 22.

43. Ibid., pp. 3, 21–2, 145; T. Packenham, 'Mafficking' in I. Smith (ed.), *The Siege of Mafeking. Vol. 2* (Johannesburg, 2001), pp. 399–435.

44. *Labour Leader*, 6/1/1900.

45. *Labour Leader*, 17/3/1900.

46. J. B. Glasier, Unpublished Diary, 8/3/1900 and 14/3/1900, Sydney Jones Library, University of Liverpool, GP/2/1/7.

47. Glasier Diary, 10/3/1900 and 13/3/1900.

48. P. Snowden, *An Autobiography* (1934), p. 94.

49. McKibbin, *Ideologies of Class*, p. 297; E. P. Thompson, *The Making of the English Working Class* (1963), pp. 9–12.

50. See, in particular, Joanna Bourke's reflections on working-class reactions to the Boer War: *Working-Class Cultures in Britain, 1890–1960: Gender, Class and*

Ethnicity (1994), p. 172; and Stanley Meacham's discussion of the efforts of 'educational bureaucrats' to instil middle-class patriotism into workers: *A Life Apart: The English Working Class, 1890–1914* (Cambridge, Mass., 1977), pp. 196–8.   [265]

51. For a critique of the concept of 'social control', which lays bare its limitations, see F. M. L. Thompson, 'Social Control in Victorian Britain', *EcHR* (1981), pp. 189–208.

52. M. Anderson, *Family Structure in Nineteenth Century Lancashire* (Cambridge, 1971), pp. 111–61, 171; T. Griffiths, *The Lancashire Working Classes, c. 1880–1930* (Oxford, 2001), pp. 222, 265.

53. J. Humphries, 'Class Struggle and the Persistence of the Working-Class Family', *Cambridge Journal of Economics* (1977), pp. 241–58.

54. L. Davidoff, 'The Family in Britain' in F. M. L. Thompson (ed.), *The Cambridge Social History of Britain, 1750–1950. Vol. 2: People and their Environment* (Cambridge, 1990), p. 129; M. Dupree, *Family Structure in the Staffordshire Potteries, 1840–1880* (Oxford, 1995), pp. 344–5; McKibbin, *Classes and Cultures*, pp. 172–3.

55. McKibbin, *Classes and Cultures*, pp. 166–8.

56. R. Floud, *The People and the British Economy, 1830–1914* (Oxford, 1997), p. 97.

57. H. Cunningham, *The Challenge of Democracy: Britain 1832–1918* (Harlow, 2002), p. 188.

58. R. Opie, *Rule Britannia: Trading on the British Image* (Harmondsworth, 1985), p. 18. For the growth of advertising more generally, see T. R. Nevett, *Advertising in Britain: A History* (1982), pp. 67, 72–4, 145.

59. Marks, 'Sniping at the Periphery', p. 116.

60. McClintock, *Imperial Leather*, ch. 5 [quotes from p. 209].

61. E. J. Hobsbawm, *Worlds of Labour: Further Studies in the History of Labour* (1984), pp. 186–7.

62. G. Magee and A. S. Thompson, 'A Soft Touch? British Industry, Empire Markets and the Self-Governing Dominions, 1870–1914', *EcHR* (2003), pp. 697–700.

63. P. Hadley, *The History of Bovril Advertising* (1972), pp. 3, 13–18; Thompson, 'Publicity, Philanthropy and Commemoration', pp. 101–3.

64. Amery, *My Political Life*, Vol. II, p. 352; D. Meredith, 'Imperial Images: The Empire Marketing Board, 1926–32', *History Today* (1987), pp. 30–5; S. Constantine, 'Bringing the Empire Alive: The Empire Marketing Board and Imperial Propaganda, 1926–33' in MacKenzie (ed.), *Imperialism and Popular Culture*, pp. 192–231.

65. D. S. Ryan, *The Daily Mail Ideal Home Exhibition and Suburban Modernity, 1908–51*, University of East London Ph.D. (1995), pp. 186–93.

[266]   66. Such, at least, was the opinion of the British Poster Advertising Association.

67. J. C. Drummond and A. Wilbraham, *The Englishman's Food* (revised edn, 1958), pp. 327–31; P. Mathias, *Retailing Revolution* (1973), pp. 26–9; K. F. Kiple and K. C. Ornelas (eds), *The Cambridge History of Food*, Vol. 2 (Cambridge, 2000), pp. 1223–4; D. J. Oddy, 'Food and Drink' in Thompson (ed.), *The Cambridge Social History*, Vol. 2, pp. 253, 262.

68. Berridge, *Popular Journalism and Working Class Attitudes*, pp. 244–8, 281.

69. Oddy, 'Food, Drink and Nutrition', pp. 261–2 and 'A Nutritional Analysis of Historical Evidence: The Working-Class Diet, 1880–1914' in D. Oddy and D. Miller (eds), *The Making of the Modern Diet* (1976), pp. 215–21.

70. R. Scola, *Feeding the Victorian City: The Food Supply of Manchester, 1770–1870* (Manchester, 1992), pp. 49–50.

71. For example, when the Glasgow merchant and banker, James Morton, expanded into the Australian trade in the 1870s, he strove to create a market in Scotland for Australian tinned meat. See D. S. Macmillan, 'Scottish Enterprise in Australia, 1798–1879' in P. L. Payne (ed.), *Studies in Scottish Business History* (1967), p. 340.

72. J. Burnett, *Plenty and Want: A Social History of Food in England from 1815 to the Present Day* (1966), p. 116; S. Shephard, *Pickled, Potted and Canned: The Story of Food Preserving* (2000), pp. 246–7.

73. Quoted in S. Thorne, *The History of Food Preservation* (Cumbria, 1986), p. 130.

74. Shephard, *Pickled, Potted and Canned*, p. 292.

75. B. McNamee, 'Trends in Meat Consumption' in T. C. Barker, J. C. McKenzie and J. Yudkin (eds), *Our Changing Fare: Two Hundred Years of British Food Habits* (1966), p. 83.

76. M. Winstanley, *The Shopkeeper's World, 1830–1914* (Manchester, 1983), p. 141.

77. It is difficult to generalise about the extent of meat consumption among other workers, not least because of the considerable regional and rural/urban differences. For a contemporary estimate for the mid-nineteenth century, see F. Engels, *The Condition of the Working-Class in England in 1844* (1892 edn), p. 72. For further discussion see McNamee, 'Trends in Meat Consumption', pp. 78–80, 90.

78. Burnett, *Plenty and Want*, pp. 134–5.

79. See ibid., Table 2.2, p. 288.

80. J. Burnett, *Liquid Pleasures: A Social History of Drinks in Modern Britain* (1999), p. 185.

81. W. G. Clarence-Smith, *Cocoa and Chocolate, 1765–1914* (2000), p. 24.

82. Ibid., p. 27.

83. C. Booth quoted in P. Keating (ed.), *Into Unknown England, 1866–1913: Selections from the Social Explorers* (Manchester, 1976), pp. 128–31. See also D. J. Richardson, 'J. Lyons & Co Ltd. Caterers and Food Manufacturers, 1894–1939' in Oddy and Miller (eds), *The Making of the Modern Diet*, pp. 162–4.

84. The quote is from Floud, *The People and the British Economy*, pp. 99–100. For the growth of cocoa consumption, see J. Othick, 'The Cocoa and Chocolate Industry in the Nineteenth Century' in Oddy and Miller (eds), *The Making of the Modern Diet*, pp. 77–8.

85. J. R. Ward, 'The Industrial Revolution and British Imperialism, 1750–1850', *EcHR* (1994), p. 53; Berridge, *Popular Journalism and Working Class Attitudes*, p. 250.

86. P. Mathias, 'The British Tea Trade in the Nineteenth Century' in Oddy and Miller (eds), *The Making of the Modern Diet*, pp. 91–8.

87. Oddy, 'Food, Drink and Nutrition', p. 266.

88. Mathias, *Retailing Revolution*, pp. 101–2, 329–30. See also Lyons' acquisition of the Lujeri tea estates in Nyasaland in the mid-1920s, in P. Bird, *The First Food Empire: A History of J. Lyons & Co* (Chicester, 2000), ch. 14.

89. D. Northrup, *Indentured Labour in the Age of Imperialism, 1834–1922* (Cambridge, 1995), pp. 24, 31–3, 37–8, 68.

90. Cunningham, *The Challenge of Democracy*, p. 188.

91. S. Mintz, *Sweetness and Power: The Place of Sugar in Modern History* (New York, 1985), pp. 133–4, 161.

92. See here A. Torode, 'Trends in Fruit Consumption' in Barker, McKenzie and Yudkin (eds), *Our Changing Fare*, pp. 122–4.

93. Mintz, *Sweetness and Power*, pp. 147–9.

94. V. G. Kiernan makes a similar claim when he states that empire-grown 'creature comforts' like sugar, tobacco and tea kept factory hands 'quiet and contented' and better able 'to meet the brutal pace of work'. See 'Working Class and Nation', p. 123.

95. F. W. Pavy, *A Treatise on Food and Dietetics: Physiologically and Therapeutically Considered* (1874), pp. 325–6. Further evidence to support Pavy's claims can be found in Henry Mayhew's *The Morning Chronicle Survey of Labour and the Poor: The Metropolitan Districts*, conducted in 1850: see pp. 144, 158, 161 (reprinted by Caliban Books, Horsham, 1982). See also J. Burnett's remarks on the significance of tea, 'Trends in Bread Consumption' in Barker, McKenzie and Yudkin (eds), *Our Changing Fare*, pp. 62–3.

96. Mintz, *Sweetness and Power*, pp. 180, 186.

97. Ibid., p. 186.

98. R. C. Terry, *Victorian Popular Fiction, 1860–80* (1983), p. 1.

[268]   99. R. Altick, *Victorian People and Ideas* (1974), pp. 59–60 and *The English Common Reader: A Social History of the Mass Reading Public 1800–1900* (Chicago, 1957), pp. 306–7; W. Donaldson, *Popular Literature in Victorian Scotland: Language, Fiction and the Press* (Aberdeen, 1986), p. 18; J. A. R. Pimlott, *Recreations* (1968), pp. 44–6; Stevenson, *British Society, 1914–45*, pp. 398–9.

100. A. Esquiros, *The English at Home* (1861, trans. and ed. L. Wraxall), Vol. 1, p. 347.

101. Between two-thirds and three-quarters of the working class are said to have achieved a basic level of literacy: see R. K. Webb, *The British Working-Class Reader* (1955), p. 13.

102. Altick, *Victorian People and Ideas*, pp. 61–2; J. Feather, *A History of British Publishing* (1988), pp. 156–7; L. James, *Fiction for the Working Man, 1830–50: A Study of the Literature Produced for the Working Classes in Early Victorian Urban England* (Harmondsworth, 1974), chs 2–4.

103. Berridge, *Popular Journalism and the Working Class*, pp. 285–91.

104. A. Beever, 'From a Place of "Honourable Destitution" to a Paradise of the Working Class: The Transformation of British Working Class Attitudes to Australia, 1841–1851', *Labour History* (1981), pp. 13–14.

105. J. S. Bratton, *The Victorian Popular Ballad* (1975); E. King, 'Popular Culture in Glasgow' in R. A. Cage (ed.), *The Working-Class in Glasgow, 1750–1914* (1987), pp. 148–51.

106. J. Holloway and J. Black (eds), *Later English Broadside Ballads*. Vol. 2 (1979), pp. 1–7; V. E. Neuburg, *Popular Literature: A History and Guide* (1977), pp. 123–41.

107. Neuburg, *Popular Literature*, p. 141.

108. Golby and Purdue, *The Civilisation of the Crowd*, pp. 128–9. See also the remarks of Alphonse Esquiros on the popularity of ballads in London in the early 1860s, *The English at Home*, Vol. 1, pp. 287–89.

109. M. Kilgarriff (ed.), *Sing Us One of the Old Songs: A Guide to Popular Song, 1860–1920* (Oxford, 1998).

110. J. Richards, *Imperialism and Music: Britain 1876–1953* (Manchester, 2001), p. 324.

111. Bratton, *The Victorian Popular Ballad*, p. 61.

112. Digitised copies are displayed electronically and indexed by title, first line and subject on *http://www.bodley.ox.ac.uk/ballads*. My analysis of Victorian ballads is based on a reading of some two hundred examples from the Bodleian Library's Catalogue of 30,000-plus ballads.

113. Bratton, *The Victorian Popular Ballad*, pp. 62–73.

114. See, for example, 'The Late Indian War' from the Harding collection B 15 (169a), Bodleian Library, University of Oxford. Another good example of a Mutiny ballad, from the working-class poet Gerald Massey (1828–1907),

is 'Havelock's March' (1860) reprinted in C. Brooks and P. Faulkner (eds), [269]
The White Man's Burden: An Anthology of British Poetry of the Empire (Exeter,
1996), pp. 193–9.

115. J. Ashton, *Modern Street Ballads* (1968), pp. 358–63.

116. Bratton, *The Victorian Popular Ballad*, pp. 74–6; P. J. Keating, *The Working
Classes in Victorian Fiction* (1971), ch. 6; R. H. MacDonald, *The Language of
Empire: Myths and Metaphors of Popular Imperialism, 1880–1918* (Manchester,
1994), ch. 5; Richards, *Imperialism and Music*, p. 354.

117. Examples taken from the South African War Box of the John Johnson
Collection of Ephemera, Bodleian Library, University of Oxford. See also
R. Durbach, *Kipling's South Africa* (Plumstead, South Africa, 1988), pp. 41–
2.

118. J. G. Leigh, 'What Do the Masses Read?', *Economic Review*, 14 (1904),
pp. 166–77. On the CSU and its journal (published 1891–1914) see
P. d'A. Jones, *The Christian Socialist Revival, 1877–1914* (Princeton, 1968),
ch. 6. For corroboration of Leigh's findings, with a particular emphasis on
the popularity of 'gambling', 'sporting' and 'Sunday' papers, see J. Haslam,
*The Press and the People: An Estimate of Reading in Working-Class Districts,
Reprinted from the 'Manchester City News'* (Manchester, 1906), pp. 3–19.
Haslam's study was based on conversations with slum newsagents in Salford,
Ancoats and Harpurhey.

119. A story of negro life in the slave states of America which created a consider
able furore in Britain because of the comparison it drew between American
slaves and British workers.

120. For the striking if long-forgotten popularity of Mrs Henry Wood (1814–
87), see the chapter by Adekleine Sergeant in Mrs Oliphant *et al.*, *Women
Novelists of Queen Victoria's Reign* (1897), pp. 174–92 and George Elliott's
reader survey, 'Our Readers and What They Read', *Library*, 7 (1895),
pp. 276–81. Wood's novels included clever plots about murders, thefts and
forgeries; they were a forerunner of the modern detective story.

121. Alongside Haggard, Henty is the 'imperial' author most frequently mentioned
in studies of popular reading habits. See C. E. Russell (Hon. Secretary of the
Heyrod Street Lads' Club in Ancoats, Manchester), *Manchester Boys: Sketches
of Manchester Lads at Work and Play* (Manchester, 1905), pp. 104–5. Russell
claimed that, up to the age of 16, Henty was 'the god of a lad's literary
idolatry'. See also F. Gordon Roe, *The Victorian Child* (1959), pp. 95, 98.

122. For the growth and popularity of the sporting press, see T. Mason, 'Sporting News, 1860–1914' in Harris and Lee (eds), *The Press in English Society*,
pp. 168–85.

123. The newspaper was a staple of working-class reading in other regions,
too. See, for example, Donaldson on serialisations and popular fiction in
Scotland: *Popular Literature*, pp. 99, 149–50.

[270]   124. By the end of the nineteenth century, many working-class readers could probably have afforded the luxury of an evening, local or daily paper: see P. Keating, *The Haunted Study: A Social History of the English Novel, 1875–1914* (1989), pp. 409–10.

125. J. Rose, *The Intellectual Life of the British Working Classes* (New Haven, 2002).

126. Ibid., pp. 338, 342, 349.

127. Ibid., pp. 350–62.

128. Ibid., p. 322.

129. See, for example, J. Hyslop, 'A Scottish Socialist Reads Carlyle in Johannesburg: J. T. Bain and The Fort, 1900: Reflections on the Literary Culture of the Imperial Working Class', unpublished paper, University of Witwatersrand, 2002.

130. J. McAleer, *Popular Reading and Publishing in Britain, 1914–50* (Oxford, 1992), p. 89.

131. Significantly, 9 of the 14 authors who figured in an advertisement for a small suburban circulating library in 1929 are also mentioned in this list: see Q. D. Leavis, *Fiction and the Reading Public* (1932), pp. 7–8.

132. M. N. Cohen, *Rider Haggard: His Life and Work* (1968), pp. 230–2.

133. Leavis, *Fiction and the Reading Public*, pp. 5, 7. See also Stevenson, *British Society, 1914–45*, p. 399.

134. Keating, *The Haunted Study*, p. 418.

135. For the claim that it did, see McKibbin, *Classes and Cultures*, p. 492. McKibbin's observation is made specifically about Mills & Boon novels. However, at least two of the authors he mentions – J. Sutherland and L. Gerrard – were fond of imperial romances: the former favoured the colonial frontier (in particular NW India), the latter West Africa. For a corrective view, see R. Anderson, *The Purple Heart Throbs: The Sub-Literature of Love* (1974), pp. 96–7, 144–8, 200.

136. N. Beauman, *A Very Great Profession: The Woman's Novel, 1914–39* (1983), p. 195.

137. D. Kirkwood, 'Settler Wives in Southern Rhodesia: A Case Study' in H. Callan and S. Ardener (eds), *The Incorporated Wife* (1984), pp. 150, 163.

138. See *Tropical Tales and Others* (1909); *Hands Across the Sea!* (1914); *Exile: An Outpost of Empire* (1916).

139. R. Hoggart, *The Uses of Literacy: Aspects of Working-Class Life, with Special Reference to Publications and Entertainments* (1957), pp. 172–84; Leavis, *Fiction and the Reading Public*, p. 7; McAleer, *Popular Reading and Publishing*, pp. 94–5, 99; McKibbin, *Classes and Cultures*, p. 503; Stevenson, *British Society, 1914–45*, pp. 398–9.

140. See, for example, D. Bowker, 'Libraries, Leisure and Reading in Inter-War Ashton-Under-Lyne', *Journal of Regional and Local Studies*, 8 (1988), pp. 9, 15–16.

141. E. Said, *Culture and Imperialism* (1993), pp. xv–xviii, 95–115.

142. Quoted in P. Miles, 'The Painter's Bible and the British Workman: Robert Tressell's Literary Activism' in J. Hawthorn (ed.), *The British Working-Class Novel in the Twentieth Century* (1984), p. 4.

143. J. Hyslop, 'A Ragged Trousered Philanthropist and the Empire: Robert Tressell in South Africa', *HWJ* (2001), pp. 65–86 [quote from p. 82].

144. For Tressell in South Africa, see D. Harker, *Tressell: The Real Story of the Ragged Trousered Philanthropists* (2003), pp. 3–10.

145. D. Feldman, 'Migration' in M. Daunton (ed.), *The Cambridge Urban History of Britain. Vol. III: 1840–1950* (Cambridge, 2000), pp. 185–6; D. M. MacRaild and D. E. Martin, *Labour in British Society, 1830–1914* (Basingstoke, 2000), pp. 62–5, 84–5.

146. J. Benson, *The Working Class in Britain, 1850–1939* (1989), pp. 120–1, 127.

147. C. Bridge and K. Fedorowich, 'Mapping the British World' in Bridge and Fedorowich (eds), *The British World: Diaspora, Culture and Identity* (2003).

148. G. M. Trevelyan, *English Social History: A Survey of Six Centuries: Chaucer to Queen Victoria* (1944), pp. 582–3.

149. Ibid., p. 583.

150. For this possibility, see McKibbin, *The Ideologies of Class*, p. 23; Kiernan, 'Working Class and Nation', p. 131.

151. For migration scholarship, see M. Harper, 'British Migration and the Peopling of the Empire' and S. Constantine, 'Migrants and Settlers' in Vols 3 and 4 of the *OHBE* respectively. For its impact on the wider literature, see Jeremy Black, who refers to the empire as 'a tap-root of self-identity', an expansive sense of Britishness being 'underpinned by families with relatives in Australia, New Zealand, Canada and South Africa': *Modern British History Since 1900* (Basingstoke, 2000), p. 285.

152. Quote from Darwin, 'Empire and Civility', p. 328.

153. See, for example, the correspondence of the Petworth project emigrants (1832–7): W. Cameron and M. M. Maude, *Assisting Emigration to Upper Canada: The Petworth Project 1832–1837* (Montreal, 2000), part 1.

154. M. Vicinus, *The Industrial Muse: A Study of Nineteenth Century British Working-Class Culture* (1974), pp. 37–8.

155. An 1893 Guide and Catalogue is preserved in the John Johnson Collection, Bodleian Library, Oxford, 'Empire & Colonies', Box 1.

156. Beever, 'From a Place of "Horrible Destitution"', pp. 1–15.

157. R. A. Buchanan, 'The Diaspora of British Engineering', *Technology and Culture* (1986), p. 509; Berridge, *Popular Journalism and Working Class Attitudes*, ch. 5; C. L. Mowat, *The Charity Organisation Society 1869–1913: Its Ideas and Work* (1961), pp. 89–90.

[272]   158.   See M. Harper and M. E. Vance (eds), *Myth, Migration and the Making of Memory: Scotia and Nova Scotia, c. 1700–1990* (Edinburgh, 1999), p. 16.

159.   Mackay twice visited Canada (1858, 1865), strongly supported confederation, and lobbied the CO for the better treatment of Canadian officials visiting London: see C. Mackay, *Forty Years' Recollections of Life, Literature and Politics: From 1830 to 1870*, Vol. 2 (1877), pp. 227–9 and *Through the Long Day: Memorials of a Literary Life during Half a Century*, Vol. 2 (1887), pp. 286–9.

160.   These songs were first issued as part of a series of musical supplements to the *ILN*, then published under the title of *Songs by Charles Mackay* and reissued in popular form in 1856 as *Songs for Music*.

161.   M. Harper, *Emigration from North-East Scotland. Vol. 1: Willing Exiles* (Aberdeen, 1988), pp. 156, 167–8.

162.   M. Fairburn, *The Ideal Society and its Enemies: The Foundations of Modern New Zealand Society, 1850–1900* (Auckland, 1989), p. 21; P. Hudson, 'English Emigration to New Zealand, 1839–50: Information Diffusion and Marketing a New World', *EcHR* (2001), pp. 692–3.

163.   Fairburn, *The Ideal Society*, pp. 20–2; R. G. Moyles and D. Owram, *Imperial Dreams and Colonial Realities: British Views of Canada, 1880–1914* (Toronto, 1988), ch. 5.

164.   R. F. Haines, *Emigration and the Labouring Poor: Australian Recruitment in Britain and Ireland, 1831–60* (Houndmills, Basingstoke, 1997), ch. 3.

165.   On emigration agents, see M. Harper, *Emigration from North-East Scotland. Vol. 2: Beyond the Broad Atlantic* (Aberdeen, 1988), pp. 21–3 and *Emigration from Scotland between the Wars* (Manchester, 1988), pp. 53–66; Hudson, 'English Emigration to New Zealand'.

166.   M. Rose, *Australia, Britain and Migration, 1915–1940: A Study of Desperate Hopes* (Cambridge, 1995), pp. 192–3.

167.   Harper, *Emigration from North-East Scotland, Vol. 2*, pp. 16–18 and *Emigration from Scotland Between the Wars*, pp. 65–6. It would, for example, be hard to explain the remarkable interest in Canada in the quarter century before the First World War without reference to the dominion's extensive network of emigration agents in Britain.

168.   Fairburn, *The Ideal Society*, pp. 201–2; K. S. Inglis, *The Australian Colonists: An Exploration of Social History, 1788–1870* (Melbourne, 1974), pp. 33–5.

169.   D. Fitzpatrick, *Oceans of Consolation: Personal Accounts of Irish Migration to Australia* (Ithaca, 1994), p. 20.

170.   A. Lester, *Imperial Networks: Creating Identities in Nineteenth-Century South Africa and Britain* (2001), pp. 73–4.

171.   D. Baines, *Migration in a Mature Economy: Emigration and Internal Migration in England and Wales, 1861–1900* (Cambridge, 1985), p. 282.

172. Before 1855, the cost of colonial letters had been a shilling or more, but it [273] was then reduced to an average of about 6d. Unlike the domestic rate within the UK, it was not uniform, and the rates to several foreign countries were considerably lower: H. Robinson, *The British Post Office: A History* (Princeton, 1948), p. 394.

173. See, for example, A. K. Hamilton Jenkin, *The Cornish Miner: An Account of his Life Above and Underground from Early Times* (first published in 1927; 4th edn, Newton Abbot, Devon, 1972), pp. 326–7.

174. During this decade, the volume of correspondence between Britain and Australia grew by 8% in a single year from 2,693,000 to 2,915,000 letters.

175. *11th Report of the Postmaster General on the Post Office* (1865), p. 7; *20th Report of the Postmaster General on the Post Office* (1874), p. 15: Post Office Archives, Farringdon Road, London, Ref Post 92.

176. R. M. Pike, 'National Interest and Imperial Yearnings: Empire Communications and Canada's Role in Establishing the Imperial Penny Post', *JICH* (1998), pp. 22–48.

177. *34th Report of the Postmaster General on the Post Office* (1888), p. 14.

178. Robinson, *The British Post Office*, pp. 398–400.

179. For the suggestion that, after 1945, the British were still corresponding far more regularly with people beyond than within Europe, see Eden's remarks to his private secretary, Evelyn Shuckburgh, quoted in H. Young, *This Blessed Plot: Britain and Europe from Churchill to Blair* (1998), p. 73. I am grateful to Brian Harrison for this reference.

180. For a fuller study of money, postal and telegraph orders (the main mechanisms for transferring money to and from the colonies), based on the Post Office Archives, the reader is directed to Chapter 7.

181. *19th Report of the Postmaster General on the Post Office* (1873), p. 12.

182. Harper, *Emigration from North-East Scotland, Vol. 1*, pp. 146, 207–9, 308.

183. For a sharp analysis of the social impact of remittances, see A. Ross McCormack, 'Networks Among British Immigrants and Accommodation to Canadian Society, 1900–1914' in H. Tinker (ed.), *The Diaspora of the British: Collected Seminar Papers of the Institute of Commonwealth Studies*, 31 (1982), pp. 58–9.

184. See also A. Bielenberg (ed.), *The Irish Diaspora* (Harlow, 2000), pp. 55, 59.

185. Information provided by Paddy Fitzgerald, Ulster American Folk Park, Omagh.

186. G. M. Burke, *The Cornish Miner and the Cornish Mining Industry, 1870–1921*, University of London Ph.D. (1981), pp. 413–15. I am grateful to the staff of the Cornish Studies Library in Redruth for guiding me to many of the texts that I have used on the history of Cornish miner-migrants and their families.

[274] 187. R. Dawe, *Cornish Pioneers in South Africa: 'Gold and Diamonds, Copper and Blood'* (St Austell, 1998), pp. xv, 123.

188. S. Schwartz and R. Parker, *Tin Mines and Miners of Lanner: The Heart of Cornish Tin* (2001), pp. 157–8.

189. C. Lewis Hind, *Days in Cornwall* (2nd edn, 1907), p. 352 quoted in P. Payton, *The Cornish Overseas* (Fowey, 1999) p. 347.

190. Payton, *The Cornish Overseas*, p. 245.

191. G. B. Dickason, *Cornish Immigrants to South Africa: The Cousin Jack's Contribution to the Development of Mining and Commerce, 1820–1920* (Cape Town, 1978), p. 71.

192. Payton, *The Cornish Overseas*, p. 367; Dawe, *Cornish Pioneers*, pp. 118, 129, 272.

193. Burke, *The Cornish Miner*, pp. 440–51.

194. Payton, *The Cornish Overseas*, p. 346.

195. Ibid., pp. 352, 362, 366.

196. See, especially, the papers presented at the conference organised by Marjory Harper and the AHRB Centre for Irish and Scottish Studies, University of Aberdeen: 'Emigrant Homecomings: The Return Movement of Emigrants, *c.* 1700–*c.* 2000'. For the European context, see E. Morawska, 'Return Migrations: Theoretical and Research Agenda' in R. J. Vecoli and S. M. Sinke (eds), *A Century of European Migrations 1830–1930* (Urbana, 1991), pp. 277–92.

197. The 1860s and 1870s appear to have been the key decades: before then, the cost of the journey was too high for many migrants to contemplate returning.

198. In several years there was an inward balance of migration from South Africa (1883–5, 1899, 1904 and 1906–8): see E. Bradlow, *Immigration into the Union 1910–1948: Policies and Attitudes*, University of Cape Town Ph.D. (1978), p. 409.

199. Figures for the period 1895–1914 from Harper, *Emigration from Scotland Between the Wars*, p. 3.

200. The most detailed study of return migration is that by Dudley Baines: see *Migration in a Mature Economy*, ch. 5.

201. Interview with Gwennie Edmondson, b. 9/6/1912, recorded Sept. 1995, North West Sound Archive, Record No. 646, Identification 1995.0217.

202. For the flow of Australians and New Zealanders to Britain see K. S. Inglis, 'Going Home: Australians in England, 1870–1900' in D. Fitzpatrick (ed.), *Home or Away? Immigrants in Colonial Australia. Visible Immigrants* (Canberra, 1992), pp. 105–30 and A. Woollacott, '"All that is the empire, I told myself": Australian Women's Voyages "Home" and the Articulation of Colonial Whiteness', *AHR* (1997), pp. 1003–29.

Chapter 3 The Working Class at Work [275]

1. Benson, *The Working Class in Britain, 1850–1939*, p. 9; Thompson, 'Social Control in Victorian Britain', p. 204.

2. P. Joyce (ed.), *The Historical Meanings of Work* (Cambridge, 1987), p. 24.

3. D. J. Newton, *British Labour, European Socialism and the Struggle for Peace, 1889–1914* (Oxford, 1985), pp. 57–8, 68–73; H. Pelling, *A History of British Trade Unionism* (5th edn, 1992), pp. 319–22; C. Wrigley, 'Labour and the Trade Unions' in K. D. Brown (ed.), *The First Labour Party* (1985), pp. 129–57.

4. Hechter, *Internal Colonialism*, pp. 236–7.

5. A. Kilpatrick and T. Lawson, 'On the Nature of Industrial Decline in the UK', *Cambridge Journal of Economics* (1980), pp. 88–9.

6. S. Howe, 'The Slow Death and Strange Rebirths of Imperial History', *JICH* (2001), p. 136.

7. E. Royle, *Modern Britain: A Social History, 1750–1985* (1987), pp. 137–8.

8. E. J. Hobsbawm, *Worlds of Labour: Further Studies in the History of Labour* (1984), p. 55; R. A. Huttenback, *Racism and Empire: White Settlers and Coloured Immigrants in the British Self-Governing Colonies, 1830–1910* (Ithaca, 1976).

9. M. Jackson, 'Pride and Prejudice: West Indian Men in Mid-Twentieth Century Britain', *JBS* (2002), pp. 400–2; B. Jackson, *Working Class Community: Some General Notions Raised by a Series of Studies in Northern England* (1968), pp. 85–6.

10. C. Bolt, *Victorian Attitudes to Race* (1971), pp. 207, 214–15; K. Malik, *The Meaning of Race: Race, History and Culture in Western Society* (Basingstoke, 1996), pp. 116–19; Price, *British Society, 1680–1880*, p. 341.

11. C. Hall, *Civilising Subjects: Metropole and Colony in the English Imagination, 1830–1867* (Oxford, 2002), p. 8. See also Kiernan: 'an inbred contempt for the Irish among English workers must have predisposed them to take an arrogant view of other colonial races': 'Working Class and Nation', pp. 127–30.

12. J. Schneer, *London 1900: The Imperial Metropolis* (New Haven, 1999), pp. 50–63. The quotes that follow are from this book.

13. See Thompson, 'Publicity, Philanthropy and Commemoration', pp. 106–13.

14. This includes the National Amalgamated Sailors' and Fireman's Union of Great Britain as well as the National Union of Seamen.

15. L. Tabili, *'We ask for British justice': Workers and Racial Difference in Late Imperial Britain* (Ithaca, 1994), pp. 1–14, 39, 42, 55, 82–8, 95–112, 182–4.

16. H. Llewellyn Smith and V. Nash, *The Story of the Dockers' Strike: Told by Two East Londoners* (first published 1889; 1970 reprint, Portway, Bath), pp. 119–25. But see also E. Hopkins, *A Social History of the English Working Classes*

1815–1945 (1979), p. 161 and *Industrialisation and Society: A Social History, 1830–1951* (2000), pp. 103–4; J. Lovell, *Stevedores and Dockers: A Study of Trade Unionism in the Port of London, 1870–1914* (Basingstoke, 1969), pp. 109–11 and 'The Significance of the Great Dock Strike of 1889 in British Labour History' in W. J. Mommsen and H.-S. Husung (eds), *The Development of Trade Unionism in Great Britain and Germany, 1880–1914* (1985), pp. 100–13; H. Pelling, *A History of British Trade Unionism* (1963), pp. 93–7.

17. T. A. Coghlan, *Labour and Industry in Australia, from the First Settlement in 1788 to the Establishment of the Commonwealth in 1901* (1918), Vol. 4, pp. 1840, 1896–7. Coghlan was a government statistician in Australia from 1886 until 1905, when he became the Australian Agent-General in London.

18. R. Glover, 'Australian Unions and the 1889 London Dock Strike', *Bowyang* (1982), p. 10.

19. For a breakdown and analysis of the figures, see P. F. Donovan, 'Australia and the Great London Dock Strike: 1889', *Labour History* (1972), pp. 17–26.

20. For Mann's time in New Zealand and Australia see B. Holton, *British Syndicalism, 1900–1914: Myths and Realities* (1976), pp. 53–5; C. Tsuzuki, *Tom Mann, 1856–1941: The Challenges of Labour* (Oxford, 1991), ch. 8; J. White, *Tom Mann* (Manchester, 1991), ch. 5.

21. On the history of syndicalism in Britain, see Holton, *British Syndicalism*, pp. 17–69 and 'Revolutionary Syndicalism and the British Labour Movement' in Mommsen and Husung (eds), *The Development of Trade Unionism in Great Britain and Germany*, pp. 266–82; Hopkins, *Working-Class Self-Help*, pp. 169–77; R. Hyman, 'Mass Organisation and Militancy in Britain: Contrasts and Continuities' in Mommsen and Husung (eds), *The Development of Trade Unionism in Great Britain and Germany*, pp. 250–65.

22. Holton, 'Revolutionary Syndicalism', pp. 270–3.

23. The same claim has been made for Ben Tillett, for example: W. Hamish Fraser, *A History of British Trade Unionism, 1700–1998* (Basingstoke, 1999), pp. 116, 125.

24. For further biographical information, see E. Gitsham and J. F. Trembath, *A First Account of Labour Organisation in South Africa* (Durban, 1926), pp. 159–79: twenty-nine of the forty major labour leaders featured in this book are in fact British-born, the majority having acquired trade union experience in the UK before moving to South Africa.

25. There was not the same degree of connectedness with American workers – unionisation rates were significantly lower in the USA.

26. J. Burnett, *Idle Hands: The Experience of Unemployment, 1790–1990* (1994), pp. 117–18; Fairburn, *The Ideal Society*, p. 22; E. H. Hunt, *British Labour History 1815–1914* (1981), pp. 204–5; A. E. Musson, *The Typographical Association: Origins and History up to 1949* (1954), pp. 34–5, 106–7, 178–9,

306, 312–13, 322–5; J. Neville Barlett, *Carpeting the Millions: The Growth of* [277] *Britain's Carpet Industry* (Edinburgh, 1978), pp. 31–3.

27. Minutes of the proceedings of the Emigration Aid Committee (1853–7), London Typographical Society, MSS 28/CO/1/2/1/1, Modern Records Centre, University of Warwick.

28. J. B. Jefferys, *The Story of the Engineers, 1800–1945* (1945), pp. 128–9.

29. The union did not make similar progress in the United States – by 1914, for example, 8.4% of members were from the colonies, but only 1.8% from the United States. This suggests that the empire had its own particular organisational dynamic.

30. *Annual* and *Monthly* Reports of the Amalgamated Society of Boilermakers, 1880–1914, MSS 192/BM/4/1, Modern Records Centre, University of Warwick.

31. For the opposing view that race hatred rather than fear of economic competition was the vital driving force behind settler attitudes, see R. A. Huttenback, *Racism and Empire: White Settlers and Coloured Immigrants in the British Self-Governing Colonies, 1830–1910* (Ithaca, 1976).

32. Nearly 64,000 Chinese workers were imported over four years, on three-year contracts ending in compulsory repatriation.

33. ASE *Monthly Journal* (Feb. 1904), p. 4.

34. Letter dated August 1903, published in ASE *Monthly Journal* (Oct. 1903), pp. 8–9.

35. ASE *Monthly Journal* (Dec. 1903), pp. 2–3.

36. Thompson, 'Imperial Propaganda during the South African War', pp. 318–20; Pelling, *Popular Politics and Society*, pp. 97–8.

37. ASE *Monthly Journal* (Mar. 1904), p. 21.

38. Ibid.

39. ASE *Monthly Journal* (Apr. 1904), pp. 2–5.

40. ASE *Monthly Journal* (Dec. 1903), p. 3.

41. ASE *Monthly Journal* (Apr. 1904), p. 3. Campaigns were also staged on the Rand opposing the introduction of Italian workers in the mines. See E. N. Katz, *A Trade Union Aristocracy: A History of White Workers in the Transvaal and the General Strike of 1913* (Johannesburg, 1976), pp. 65–70.

42. ASE *Monthly Journal* (Jan. 1905), p. 4.

43. There seems to be little point in listing the trade councils concerned, but they cover the length and breadth of the country, and their responses can be studied in the *Trade Councils Annual Reports* (1904), arranged alphabetically in Board of Trade Library, Modern Records Centre, University of Warwick.

44. TUC *Annual Report* (1904), p. 48.

[278]   45. TUC *Parliamentary Committee Reports*, 18/3/1904; *The Times*, 28/3/1904, p. 7.

46. P. Richardson accepts the TUC figure: see *Chinese Labour in the Transvaal* (1982), p. 6.

47. *The Times*, 28/3/1904, p. 7.

48. Ibid.

49. Ibid.

50. J. Hyslop, 'The Imperial Working Class Makes Itself White: White Labourism in Britain, Australia and South Africa before the First World War', *Journal of Historical Sociology* (1999), pp. 398–421.

51. L. Barrow, 'White Solidarity in 1914' in Samuel (ed.), *Patriotism*, Vol. 1, p. 275.

52. Burke, *The Cornish Miner*, p. 438.

53. Dickason, *Cornish Immigrants*, p. 69.

54. B. Hirson and G. A. Williams, *The Delegate for Africa: David Ivon Jones, 1883–1924* (1995), pp. 134–5.

55. ASE *Monthly Journal* (Feb. 1914), p. 13.

56. Ibid., pp. 59–60.

57. ASB *Monthly Report* (Mar. and Apr. 1914).

58. ASB *Monthly Report* (June 1914).

59. The amendment was defeated by a vote of 214 to 50: T. F. Tsiang, *Labour and Empire* (New York, 1923), p. 87.

60. Interestingly, Mann refused to be drawn on the question of the 'colour bar'. Moreover, through the offices of the liberal temperance activist, Theo Schreiner, he met with and formed a favourable impression of at least one black labour spokesman.

61. 'Visit to South Africa' (1914), MSS 334/7/2/, Tom Mann papers, Modern Records Centre, University of Warwick.

62. It was denounced as a Bolshevist uprising by the Conservative press in Britain: see N. Herd, *1922: The Revolt on the Rand* (Johannesburg, 1966), pp. 163–4.

63. A. Christie, *The Man in the Brown Suit* (first published 1924; 1993 Harper Collins edn), pp. 47–8. Christie herself had been caught up on the fringes of the Rebellion during her 'empire tour': see J. Morgan, *Agatha Christie: A Biography* (1984), pp. 86–93.

64. J. E. Mortimer, *History of the Boilermakers' Society. Volume 2, 1906–39* (1982), p. 52.

65. Hyman, *The Workers Union*, pp. 112, 153.

66. See the editorials in the ASE's *Monthly Reports* (Jan.–June 1922).

67. M. Nicholson, *The TUC Overseas: The Roots of Policy* (1986), pp. 48–50.   [279]

68. Detail taken from D. A. Farnie, *The English Cotton Industry and the World Market, 1815–1896* (Oxford, 1979), pp. 98–105.

69. D. A. Farnie, 'The Metropolis of Cotton Spinning, Machine Making and Mill Building' in D. Gurr and J. Hunt (eds), *The Cotton Mills of Oldham* (Oldham, 1989), pp. 7–11.

70. S. J. Chapman, *The Lancashire Cotton Industry: A Study in Economic Development* (Manchester, 1904), p. 156.

71. G. Timmins, *Made in Lancashire: A History of Regional Industrialisation* (Manchester, 1998), p. 240.

72. J. K. Walton, *Lancashire: A Social History, 1558–1939* (Manchester, 1987), pp. 329–30.

73. *Blackburn Power-Loom Weavers' Protection Society* (1895), p. 1, Board of Trade Library, Modern Records Centre, University of Warwick.

74. *Annual Report of the Blackburn & District Power-Loom Weavers' Association* (1894), pp. 5–6 and (1895), pp. 1–2, Board of Trade Library, Modern Records Centre, University of Warwick.

75. P. Harnetty, 'The Indian Cotton Duties Controversy, 1894–1896', *EHR* (1962), pp. 694–5.

76. One of Blackburn's leading cotton spinners and manufacturers, William Coddington MP, had played a significant role in securing these concessions.

77. Sir Griffiths Evans, *Legislative Council Proceedings* (1896), quoted ibid., p. 701.

78. *The Bolton Operative Cotton Spinners' Provincial Association* (1896), p. 22 and (1897), p. 12, Board of Trade Library, Modern Records Centre, University of Warwick.

79. I am grateful to Dr Alan Fowler for supplying me with a copy of Tom Shaw's *Report of Investigations into the Conditions of Indian Textile Workers* (May 1927). See also A. Fowler, *Lancashire Cotton Operatives and Work, 1900–1950: A Social History of Cotton Operatives in the Twentieth Century* (Aldershot, 2002), pp. 102–5.

80. The IFTWA's report was received positively by the United Textile Factory Workers' Association, and Shaw and his colleagues were thanked for their work: see *UTFWA's Report on Proceedings at the Annual Conference of 1927*, printed at the office of the *Cotton Factory Times* (1927).

81. See, for example, B. Bowker, *Lancashire Under the Hammer* (1928), which documented in painful detail Lancashire's loss of exports in linear yards, the closure of Lancashire mills, and export of their (redundant) machinery to Indian and Japanese producers: pp. 48–50, 79, 105–15.

82. My analysis here is partly based on 'A Visit From Gandhi', Granada TV programme. Copy of video of programme kindly lent to the author by Dr Alan Fowler.

[280]   83. For a contemporary assessment of the impact of the boycott (which held it partly responsible for the deterioration of the cotton trade), see A. R. Burnett-Hurst, 'Lancashire and the Indian Market', *Journal of the Royal Statistical Society*, Part III (1932), pp. 407–8, 425.

84. R. Vizram, *Asians in Britain: 400 Years of History* (2002), pp. 265–6.

85. We are fortunate to have some oral testimony of Gandhi's visit. In addition to the several interviewees for the Granada TV programme, see A. Foley, *A Bolton Childhood* (Manchester, 1973), p. 90, and the North West Sound Archive, W. R. Hill, Record No. 43 (b. 1897, Blackburn) and J. Hudson, Record No. 30 (b. 3/3/1913, Burnley).

86. Harnetty, 'The Indian Cotton Duties Controversy', p. 693.

87. Tsiang, *Labour and Empire*, p. 72.

88. B. Chatterji, *Trade, Tariffs, and Empire: Lancashire and British Policy in India, 1919–39* (Delhi, 1992), p. 352.

89. Recollection of Raymond Street from Granada TV programme, based on what appears to have been a rather fraught meeting between Gandhi and representatives of cotton manufacturers at Greenthorn country house in Edgeworth near Bolton.

90. See, for example, *The Cotton Factory Times*, 2/10/1931; *Darwen News*, 26/9/1931 and 3/10/1931; and *The Manchester Guardian*, 28/9/1931. Apparently, when the Hindu social reformer, Rammohun Roy (1772–1833) visited a Manchester factory in 1831, crowds had rushed to see him too: see Visram, *Asians in Britain*, p. 34.

91. A deputation of operatives from the Clitheroe Weaver's Association, led by Mr Brame, responded to Gandhi in very similar terms, *Clitheroe Advertiser and Times*, 2/10/1931, as did the editor of the *Darwen News*, 10/10/1931.

92. H. Trivedi, 'Gandhi, Language and the Subaltern Historians', seminar paper given to the School of English, University of Leeds, 12/5/2003.

93. M. Dupree (ed.), *Lancashire and Whitehall: The Diary of Sir Raymond Street, 1931–39* (Manchester, 1987), Vol. 1, entry for Saturday 26 September 1931, p. 97.

94. See also Gandhi's recollections in *The Collected Works of Mahatma Gandhi* (Delhi, 1971), XLVIII, entry for 27 September 1931, pp. 76–7: 'I have certainly been very happy here and have experienced nothing but the greatest affection and kindness.'

95. G. Stewart, *Jute and Empire: The Calcutta Jute Wallahs and the Landscapes of Empire* (Manchester, 1998), p. 4.

96. E. Gordon, *Women and the Labour Movement in Scotland, 1850–1914* (Oxford, 1991), p. 139.

97. The Calcutta industry was not the only menace to Dundee; the emergence of jute mills in Europe, especially in Germany, and the protection of European markets by tariffs, was a further blow.

98. W. M. Walker, *Juteopolis: Dundee and its Textile Workers, 1885–1923* (Edinburgh, 1979), pp. 529–30.

99. Stewart, *Jute and Empire*, p. 11.

100. This was not the first time such a visit had been made. In the winter of 1895–6, Dundee's Liberal MP, Sir John Leng, had travelled to Calcutta.

101. Sime was not known for his moderation. He had spent his early days as a labour organiser trying to crush the (rival) Dundee Mill and Factory Workers' Union, and berated Dundee employers for investing in Indian jute companies while complaining of foreign competition.

102. *Parliamentary Debates*, Fifth Series, Vol. 326, 22/7/1937, 2533.

103. For the 1938 debate, see *Parliamentary Debates*, Fifth Series, Vol. 331, 2/2/1938, 248–306.

104. Many people from Dundee made their fortunes in Calcutta industry, and then bought country houses or substantial villas back in the West of Scotland with their newly acquired wealth. See, for example, the comment of Eugenie Fraser, a married man who made his way up from mill assistant to mill manager: 'India offered the opportunity to reap a rich harvest. The mansions in West Ferry testify to the truth of my statement', quoted in Stewart, *Jute and Empire*, pp. 149–50.

105. Sandeman was a Lancashire MP but had spent the larger part of his life among the jute mills of Dundee.

106. Stewart, *Jute and Empire*, pp. 137–9.

107. B. James, 'Labour Banners: What Can They Tell Us?' in J. E. Martin and K. Taylor (eds), *Culture and the Labour Movement: Essays in New Zealand Labour History* (Palmerston North, 1991), pp. 234, 236.

Chapter 4 The Working Class at Play

1. See, in particular, the Manchester University Press *Studies in Imperialism* series, discussed in the introduction to this book (pp. 2–3).

2. D. A. Reid, 'Playing and Praying' in M. Daunton (ed.), *The Cambridge Urban History of Britain. Vol. III* (2000), pp. 746–51; Pimlott, *Recreations*, p. 42; F. M. L. Thompson, *The Rise of Respectable Society: A Social History of Victorian Britain, 1830–1900* (1988), pp. 276, 302–3.

3. J. Belchem, *Industrialisation and the Working Class: The English Experience, 1750–1900* (Aldershot, 1990), p. 225; Hopkins, *A Social History of the English Working Classes*, p. 117; B. C. Hollingsworth, 'Working Class Recreation in the Nineteenth Century as Reflected in Lancashire Dialect Poetry', *Journal of Local Studies*, 2 (1982), pp. 35, 40.

4. For the seminal study of working-class hobbies, see McKibbin, 'Work and Hobbies in Britain, 1880–1950' in *Ideologies of Class*, pp. 139–66. For

[282]   an earlier recognition of their significance, see Hoggart, *The Uses of Literacy*, pp. 266–8.

5. For an amusing example, see A. Grundlingh, 'Gone to the Dogs: British Greyhound Racing and Afrikaner Working Class Culture on the Witwatersrand', unpublished paper given at the British Worlds conference, University of Cape Town, Jan. 2002.

6. J. Auerbach, *The Great Exhibition of 1851: A Nation on Display* (Yale, 1999), p. 102.

7. P. H. Hoffenberg, *An Empire on Display: English, Indian and Australian Exhibitions from the Crystal Palace to the Great War* (Berkeley, 2001), p. 8; Mackenzie, *Propaganda and Empire*, pp. 96–9. For explicitly imperial events, see the Colonial and India exhibition (1886); the 'Stanley and Africa' exhibition (1890); the 'Greater Britain' exhibition (1899); and the 'South African Products' exhibition (1907).

8. P. Greenhalgh, *Ephemeral Vistas: The Expositions Universelles, Great Exhibitions and World's Fairs, 1851–1939* (Manchester, 1988), ch. 3; A. Maxwell, *Colonial Photography and Exhibitions: Representations of the 'Native' and the Making of European Identities* (1999), pp. 1–14; Mackenzie, *Propaganda and Empire*, pp. 101–18; N. Macmaster, *Racism in Europe, 1870–2000* (Basingstoke, 2001), pp. 73–8. The last interpretation was raised by Professor Keith Jeffery at the Exhibiting Empire conference, National Maritime Musuem, Greenwich, 15–16 Oct. 1999.

9. R. Dixon and S. Muthesius, *Victorian Architecture* (1978), pp. 94–103.

10. A. Briggs, *Victorian People: A Reassessment of Persons and Themes, 1851–67* (Chicago, 1972), pp. 16, 38, 43; Mackenzie, *Propaganda and Empire*, p. 97; C. H. Gibbs-Smith, *The Great Exhibition of 1851* (1981), p. 7. See also W. Gaspey, *Tallis's Illustrated London: In Commemoration of the Great Exhibition of 1851* (1851), pp. 1–2 and *The Crystal Palace Exhibition Illustrated Catalogue: London (1851)* (1970 Dover reprint, New York), xi–xiii. It was not purely self-congratulatory, however: genuine concern was expressed regarding the quality of British design and its implications for Britain's position in world markets. On this point, see T. A. Sparling, *The Great Exhibition: A Question of Taste* (Yale, 1982), pp. ix, 1, 6.

11. S. Johansen, 'The Great Exhibition of 1851: A Precipice in Time?', *Victorian Review* (1996), p. 61.

12. There is a caveat: some of the European nations used the exhibition to display the commercial success of their colonial relationships. See L. Purbrick (ed.), *The Great Exhibition of 1851: New Interdisciplinary Essays* (Manchester, 2001), p. 18. Yet it would be difficult to argue that this was a major theme of 1851.

13. C. Babbage, *The Exposition of 1851* (1851), p. 42 (my italics). See also *Tallis's History and Description of the Crystal Palace, and the Exhibition of the World's Industry in 1851*, 6 vols (1851), Vol. 1, pp. iii, 14–17.

14. Mackenzie, *Propaganda and Empire*, p. 98. Exhibits for the UK took up 156 [283] pages, for the Colonies, 27 pages and for Foreign countries, 135 pages. Indian exhibits occupied 6 pages, the same as Spain and Russia; the USA's display accounted for 9 pages, Germany's 32 pages and France's 34 pages. See *Official Catalogue of the Great Exhibition of the Workers of Industry of All Nations, 1851* (1851). America had secured the second largest area of the foreign exhibitors, but was unable to fill it: Sparling, *The Great Exhibition*, p. 31.

15. See here *Tallis's History and Description*, Vol. 1, p. 17: 'To give the rest of the world its chance, the British colonies had their assigned space'.

16. Auerbach, *The Great Exhibition of 1851*, p. 100.

17. L. Kriegel, 'Narrating the Subcontinent in 1851: India at the Crystal Palace' in Purbrick (ed.), *The Great Exhibition of 1851*, pp. 150–2.

18. For a description see *Hunt's Hand-Book to the Official Catalogues. An Explanatory Guide to the Natural Productions and Manufactures of the Great Exhibition of the Industry of All Nations*, 2 vols (1851), pp. 753–7.

19. *Tallis's History and Description*, Vol. 1, pp. 54–5. Not all the Australian colonies had the time or the money to participate in the exhibition, and there was a delay in the arrival of some of the Australian exhibits. Anxious to attract settlers, Canada put on a more impressive display, including a grand timber-trophy, a collection of sleighs, a twenty-man birchbark canoe and a fire-engine from Montreal. See Hoffenberg, *An Empire on Display*, pp. 9, 107, 129, 132, 142.

20. *Tallis's History and Description*, Vol. 1, p. 31.

21. Ibid., p. 31; S. Phillips, *A Guide to the Palace and Park* (1856), pp. 124–5. The latter is a description of the Crystal Palace after its move to Sydenham.

22. Tallis's *History and Description*, Vol. 1, p. 17; Phillips, *A Guide to the Palace*, pp. 118–28.

23. Comment on the Indian exhibition was particularly ambivalent. Its decorative arts were praised for their high standard of production and their aesthetic qualities, but criticised for their extravagance: *Tallis's History and Description*, Vol. 1, pp. 33–8; Sparling, *The Great Exhibition*, p. 35.

24. For these two possibilities see Maxwell, *Colonial Photography and Exhibitions*, pp. 3, 10, 14 *versus* Greenhalgh, *Ephemeral Vistas*, p. 225 and MacMaster, *Racism in Europe*, p. 77.

25. S. Barton, 'Why Should Working Men Visit the Exhibition?: Workers and the Great Exhibition and the Ethos of Industrialism' in I. Inkster (ed.), *The Golden Age. Essays in British Social and Economic History, 1850–1870* (Aldershot, 2000), pp. 146–63; J. R. Davis, *The Great Exhibition* (Sutton, 1999), pp. 98, 188–92; P. Gurney, 'An Appropriated Space: The Great Exhibition, the Crystal Palace and the Working Class' in Purbrick (ed.), *The Great Exhibition of 1851*, pp. 114–45.

[284]   26. P. H. Hoffenberg, 'Equipoise and its Discontents: Voices of Dissent during the International Exhibitions' in M. Hewitt (ed.), *An Age of Equipoise? Reassessing Mid-Victorian Britain* (Aldershot, 2000), pp. 53, 60.

27. D. Judd, *The British Imperial Experience from 1765 to the Present* (1996), ch. 21; K. Walthew, 'The British Empire Exhibition of 1924', *History Today* (1981), Vol. 31, pp. 34–9.

28. *Reader's Digest: Yesterday's Britain* (1998), p. 61.

29. Lord Stevenson, quoted in Richards, *Imperialism and Music*, p. 177.

30. Quoted in Mackenzie, 'The Popular Culture of Empire in Britain', p. 214.

31. Here I draw on the excellent papers by Stephen Constantine and Edel Mahony at the National Maritime Museum's conference, 'Exhibiting Empire', 1999.

32. Mackenzie, 'The Popular Culture of Empire in Britain', p. 215; Richards, *Imperialism and Music*, pp. 196–207.

33. Rose, *The Intellectual Life of the British Working Classes*, p. 349.

34. Richards, *Imperialism and Music*, pp. 207–8.

35. Walthew, 'The British Empire Exhibition', p. 39; C. Tait, 'Brushes, Budgets and Butter: Canadian Culture and Identity at the British Empire Exhibition, 1924–5', 3rd British World Conference, University of Calgary, Canada, July 2003. Tait's paper also makes it clear that Canadian participation at Wembley provided the opportunity not merely for an expression of imperial solidarity, but for 'small and subtle hints of national identity and cultural differentiation . . . as well'.

36. For the view that the Festival was a key event dividing the immediate postwar world from the 1950s, see B. Donoughue and G. W. Jones, *Herbert Morrison: Portrait of a Politician* (1973), p. 493; K. O. Morgan, *Labour in Power, 1945–51* (Oxford, 1984), p. 314; H. Pelling, *Modern Britain, 1885–1955* (1960), pp. 187–8.

37. *The Times*, 30/1/1951.

38. *The Story of the Festival of Britain, 1951* (1952), pp. 15–16. See also R. Morrison, 'What did the Festival of Britain organisers get so right that the perpetrators of the Dome got so wrong?', *The Times*, 26/4/2001, p. 7.

39. R. Weight, *Patriots: National Identity in Britain, 1940–2000* (Basingstoke, 2002), pp. 197–8.

40. Lord Ismay in the Royal Society of Arts, *The Story of the Festival of Britain, 1951* (1951), p. 3.

41. Mainly with regard to agriculture, mineral resources and modern communications.

42. See, for example, the *Festival of Britain 1951* – a leaflet given to visitors.

43. Quoted in M. Banham and B. Hillier (eds), *A Tonic to the Nation: The Festival of Britain, 1951* (1976), p. 8. See also B. E. Conekin, 'The autobiography of

a nation': The 1951 Festival of Britain (Manchester, 2003), ch. 7 [quote from
p. 198].

44. See, for example, the various recollections of the Festival, ibid., pp. 37, 54, 59, 161, 178. A lot of emphasis was placed on recent developments in polar exploration, weather forecasting, astronomy and nuclear research.

45. See the account of the Dome of Discovery in I. Cox, *The South Bank Exhibition* (1951), pp. 41–66.

46. A. J. P. Taylor, *English History, 1914–45* (Oxford, 1965), p. 313.

47. P. Corrigan, 'Film Entertainment as Ideology and Pleasure: A Preliminary Approach to a History of Audiences' in J. Curran and V. Porter (eds), *British Cinema History* (1983), pp. 24–35; A. Davies, *Leisure, Gender and Poverty. Working-Class Culture in Salford and Manchester, 1900–1939* (Buckingham, 1992), pp. 73–6; P. Stead, 'The People and the Pictures: The British Working Class and Film in the 1930s' in N. Pronay and D. W. Spring (eds), *Propaganda, Politics and Film, 1918–45* (Basingstoke, 1982), pp. 77–95.

48. Stevenson, *British Society, 1914–39*, pp. 395–6.

49. Davies, *Leisure, Gender and Poverty*, pp. 95–6.

50. S. G. Jones, *The British Labour Movement and Film, 1918–1939* (1987), p. 26.

51. Rose, *The Intellectual Life of the British Working Classes*, p. 385.

52. Ward (ed.), *British Culture and the End of Empire*, p. 15.

53. Mackenzie, 'The Popular Culture of Empire in Britain', p. 225.

54. Mackenzie, *Propaganda and Empire*, p. 72.

55. J. Barnes, *The Beginnings of the Cinema in England, 1894–1901* (Exeter, 1997), p. xxxi.

56. See J. Barnes, *Filming the Boer War* (1992), pp. 19–22.

57. S. Popple, ' "But the khaki-covered camera is the latest thing": The Boer War Cinema and Visual Culture in Britain' in A. Higson (ed.), *Young and Innocent? The Cinema in Britain, 1896–1930* (Exeter, 2002), p. 25.

58. Barnes, *Filming the Boer War*, p. 7.

59. Popple, ' "But the Khaki-covered camera" ', pp. 19–21.

60. A. Roberts, 'Non-Fiction Film of Africa before 1940', *Historical Journal of Film, Radio and TV* (1988), p. 203.

61. F. Robinson, 'The Raj and the Nationalist Movements, 1911–1947' in C. Bayly (ed.), *The Raj: India and the British, 1600–1947* (1990), p. 350.

62. S. Bottomore, ' "Have you seen the Gaekwar Bob?": Filming the 1911 Delhi Durbar', *Historical Journal of Film, Radio and Television* (1997), p. 309.

63. On Urban, see L. McKernan, 'Putting the World Before You: The Charles Urban Story' in Higson (ed.), *Young and Innocent?*, pp. 65–77.

64. Information kindly provided by Michael Harvey, Curator of Cinematography, National Musueum of Photography, Film & Television, Pictureville, Bradford.

[286] 65. Bottomore, '"Have you seen the Gaekwar Bob?"', pp. 327–8.

66. Curzon had long thought him duplicitous, gushing loyalty on his visits to England but refusing to have anything to do with the Government of India when in Baroda: see S. Lahiri, 'British Policy Towards Indian Princes in Late Nineteenth and Early Twentieth Century Britain', *Immigrants and Minorities* (1996), p. 220.

67. Ibid., pp. 332–5.

68. D. L. Le Mahieu, *A Culture for Democracy: Mass Communication and the Cultivated Mind in Britain between the Wars* (Oxford, 1988), p. 168.

69. Mackenzie, *Propaganda and Empire*, p. 86 and 'The Popular Culture of Empire in Britain', p. 227.

70. R. Low, *Documentary and Educational Films of the 1930s* (1979), p. 66.

71. P. Swann, *The British Documentary Film Movement, 1926–1946* (Cambridge, 1989), pp. 34–5, 45.

72. Information kindly provided by James Taylor, Cataloguer, National Film and Television Archive, 21 Stephen Street, London, W1P 2LN.

73. J. Sedgwick, 'Cinema-Going Preferences in Britain in the 1930s' in J. Richards (ed.), *The Unknown 1930s: An Alternative History of the British Cinema, 1929–39* (1998), pp. 24–34.

74. For example: *The Hurricane* (1937), *Old Bones of the River* (1938) and *Song of Freedom* (1936). See Jones, *The British Labour Movement and Film*, p. 25.

75. My observations about these films draw heavily on Jeffrey Richards, '"Patriotism with profit": British Imperial Cinema in the 1930s', *British Cinema History* (1983), pp. 245–56; 'The Admirable Briton', *Movie* (1982/3), pp. 324–6; and *Films and British National Identity: From Dickens to Dad's Army* (Manchester, 1997), ch. 2. I am equally indebted to my father-in-law, Mr Norman Lenton, who supplied me with extracts of reviews and analysis of all the films mentioned below from his own extensive film library: J. Walker (ed.), *Halliwell's Film Guide* (1991, 8th edn); D. Shipman, *The Story of the Cinema: An Illustrated History. Vol. 1: From the Beginnings to Gone With The Wind* (1982); J. D. Eames, *The Paramount Story* (1985); R. Pickard, *The Hollywood Studios* (1978); J. Kobal, *People Will Talk* (1986); S. Morley, *Tales from the Hollywood Raj: The British Film Colony on Screen and Off* (1983), and *British Sound Films: The Studio Years, 1928–59* (1984); D. Pirie, *Anatomy of the Movies* (1981); P. Robertson, *The Guinness Book of Movie Facts and Feats* (Enfield, 1993); G. Perry, *Forever Ealing: A Celebration of the Great British Film Studio* (1981); R. B. Jewell and V. Harbin, *The RKO Story* (1982); C. Hirschorn, *The Universal Story* (1983).

76. For the latest study, see C. Drazin, *Alexander Korda: Britain's Only Movie Mogul* (Basingstoke, 2002).

77. K. Kulik, *Alexander Korda: The Man Who Could Work Miracles* (1975), p. 135.

78. On Korda's philosophy, see B. Baillieu and J. Goodchild, *The British Film Business* (Chichester, 2002), pp. 37–8.

79. The other major trilogy of imperial films produced in Britain was that by   [287]
    Michael Bacon for Gaumont-British. Unlike Korda's films, their focus was
    mainly on the (economic) benefits of the empire as opposed to the sacrifices
    that it demanded. See, for example, *Rhodes of Africa* (1936), *The Great Barrier*
    (1936) and *King Solomon's Mines* (1937). For Zoltan's rather different approach
    to imperial subjects, and his fascination with indigenous populations, see Kulik,
    Alexander Korda, pp. 136–7, 211.

80. J. Richards, *The Age of the Dream Palace: Cinema and Society in Britain, 1930–*
    1939 (1984), p. 151.

81. See, for example, M. F. Thorp, *America at the Movies* (1946), p. 171.

82. Kobal, *People Will Talk*, p. 619.

83. Radio-Keith-Orpheum: formed in 1928; among its prestigious films in the
    1930s and 1940s were Astaire-Rogers musicals; comedies starring Katherine
    Hepburn and Cary Grant; and individual productions such as Hitchcock's
    Suspicion and Welles's *Citizen Kane*.

84. Morley, *Tales from the Hollywood Raj*, p. 134.

85. H. M. Glancy, *When Hollywood Loved Britain: The Hollywood 'British' Film, 1939–*
    45 (Manchester, 1999), pp. 189–93.

86. The other film was a Scottish comedy, *The Ghost Goes West* (1935): see
    P. Tabori, *Alexander Korda* (1959), p. 178.

87. The film is thought to have been influential in shaping perceptions of the
    Colonial services in the 1930s: see Gardiner, *Sentinels of Empire*, pp. 100–1.

88. Tabori, *Alexander Korda*, p. 197.

89. Thorp, *America at the Movies*, p. 172.

90. J. L. Finer, *The Movie Directors Story* (1985), p. 150.

91. Jewell and Harbin, *The RKO Story*, p. 126.

92. G. Macdonald Fraser, *The Hollywood History of the World* (Harmondsworth,
    1988), p. 155.

93. Walker (ed.), *Halliwell's Film Guide*, p. 1052.

94. It certainly did not escape my father-in-law, who thought her character was
    'ludicrous'.

95. Tentatively rather than conclusively because the evidence is hard to read.
    Korda's imperial epics, for example, were in many ways Edwardian, and based
    on literary texts written by Rudyard Kipling, Edgar Wallace and A. E. W.
    Mason before the First World War. Yet the empire he described was in the
    process of transformation. For this reason, it is not entirely clear whether they
    reflected or disguised how the British people felt about their empire at this
    time. For this point, see M. Paris, 'Africa in Post-1945 British Cinema', *SAHJ*
    (2003), pp. 61–2.

96. This seems to be an inconsistency in Bernard Porter's approach. See, for
    example, his review of J. Richards's *Imperialism and Music: Britain 1876–1953*

in *JICH* (2002), pp. 138–42, and the speculations then made at the end of his own essay, 'Edward Elgar and Empire', *JICH* (2001), p. 26.

Chapter 5 Women and Children

1. The 'high walls' referred to in the quote are those on either side of a narrow road from Tower Bridge which led to the dock warehouses and St Katherine's Way.

2. R. O'Hanlon, 'Gender in the British Empire' in Louis and Brown (eds), Vol. 4 *OHBE*, p. 379. For two recent examples, see Midgley (ed.), *Gender and Imperialism*, esp. pp. 1–15; Hall, *Civilising Subjects*, pp. 16–18.

3. Such scholars also question the notion of a 'global sisterhood': G. Spivak's 'Three Women's Texts and a Critique of Imperialism', *Critical Inquiry* (1985), pp. 243–61; V. Amos and P. Parmar, 'Challenging Imperial Feminism', *Feminist Review* (1984), pp. 3–8; B. Melman, 'Changing the Subject: Women's History and Historiography, 1900–2000' in I. Zweiniger-Bargielowska (ed.), *Women In Twentieth-Century Britain* (Harlow, 2001), p. 25; and B. Gartrell, 'Colonial Wives: Villains or Victims?' in H. Callan and S. Ardener (eds), *The Incorporated Wife* (1984), pp. 182–3. It is argued that the racist views of Western women have been glossed over in the search for female role models: D. Birkett and J. Wheelwright, '"How could she?" Unpalatable Facts and Feminist Heroines', *Gender and History*, 2 (1990), pp. 49–55; I. Ghose, *Women Travellers in Colonial India: The Power of the Female Gaze* (Calcutta, 1998), pp. 3, 9; S. Mills, *Discourses of Difference: An Analysis of Women's Travel Writing and Colonialism* (1991), pp. 4, 196.

4. Contrast, for example, the position of privileged public school boys aspiring to a career in colonial service, for whom the empire apparently held an almost magnetic attraction, with the plight of young children in institutional care, whom a new generation of imperially-minded philanthropists were only too willing to ship off to one of Britain's colonies without taking the time or trouble to find out what would await them on their arrival. G. Sherrington, 'British Youth and Empire Settlement: The Dreadnought Boys in New South Wales', *Journal of the Royal Australian Historical Society* (1996), pp. 1–22 and '"A better class of boy": The Big Brother Movement, Youth Migration and Citizenship of Empire', *Australian Historical Studies* (2002), p. 283. See also the post-war schemes of child migration discussed in Chapter 9, pp. 230–2.

5. For general studies of women and children in this period, which show the empire was only one of a range of social, economic and political factors that shaped their lives, see S. Bruley, *Women in Britain since 1900* (Basingstoke, 1999), pp. 178–81; H. Cunningham, *Children and Childhood in Western Society since 1500* (Harlow, 1995), pp. 186–90; K. Gleadle, *British Women in*

the Nineteenth Century (Basingstoke, 2001), pp. 187–90; E. Hopkins, *Child-hood Transformed: Working-Class Children in Nineteenth-Century England* (Manchester, 1994), pp. 314–22; L. Rose, *The Erosion of Childhood: Child Oppression in Britain, 1860–1918* (1991), p. 244; J. Walvin, *A Child's World: A Social History of English Childhood, 1800–1914* (Harmondsworth, 1982), pp. 193–99.

6. J. De Groot, '"Sex" and "Race": The Construction of Language and Image in the Nineteenth Century' in S. Mendus and J. Rendall (eds), *Sexuality and Subordination: Interdisciplinary Studies of Gender in the Nineteenth Century* (1989), p. 122. See also the new interdisciplinary studies of masculinity: J. Tosh and M. Roper (eds), *Manful Assertions: Masculinities in Britain since 1800* (1991), pp. 1–24 and J. Tosh, *A Man's Place: Masculinity and the Middle-Class Home in Victorian England* (New Haven, 1999), ch. 8. Of further interest is J. Mangan and J. A. Walvin (eds), *Manliness and Morality: Middle-Class Masculinity in Britain and America, 1800–1940* (Manchester, 1987).

7. Tosh, *A Man's Place*, p. 175.

8. J. Tosh, 'Imperial Masculinity and the Flight from Domesticity in Britain, 1880–1914' in *Gender and Colonialism*, pp. 72–85 and *A Man's Place*, ch. 8.

9. Hyam, *Empire and Sexuality*, pp. 71–3; S. K. Kent, *Gender and Power in Britain, 1640–1990* (1999), ch. 9.

10. See, especially, the negative assessment offered by A. Davin, 'Imperialism and Motherhood', *HWJ* (1978), pp. 9–65. Davin's arguments are broadly endorsed by Jose Harris for the late-Victorian and Edwardian period: see *Private Lives, Public Spirit*, pp. 80–4; by Wendy Webster for the inter-war years, see '"Race", Ethnicity and National Identity', p. 294; and by Jane Mackay and Pat Thane for both: see 'The Englishwoman' in Colls and Dodd (eds), *Englishness*, pp. 192, 202–3, 223. In a similar vein, historians have drawn attention to the plight of Anglo-Indian children and their long periods of estrangement from their parents in India: see E. Buettner, 'Parent–Child separations and colonial careers: The Talbot Family Corres-pondence in the 1880s and 1890s' in A. Fletcher and S. Hussey (eds), *Childhood in Question: Children, Parents and the State* (Manchester, 1999), pp. 115–32 and *Families, Children and Memories: Britons in India, 1857–1947*, University of Michigan Ph.D. (1998); P. Barr, *The Dust in the Balance: British Women in India, 1905–45* (1989), pp. 17–18.

11. M. A. Procida, *Married to the Empire: Gender, Politics and Imperialism in India, 1883–1947* (Manchester, 2002); M. Macmillan, *Women of the Raj* (New York, 1998), pp. 234–6.

12. A. Davin, *Growing Up Poor: Home, School and Street in London, 1870–1914* (1996), pp. 208, 214–17.

13. Hopkins, *Childhood Transformed*, pp. 315–16, 322.

14. David, *Rule Britannia*, pp. 7–8, 207, 212–13; F. Azim, *The Colonial Rise of the Novel* (New York, 1993), pp. 7–9, 145–6, 173.

15. See, for example, Anna Jameson's comparison of the position of 'native' Indian women in Canada and middle-class European women, which questions whether the 'drudgery' of the lives of the former is really any worse than the 'idleness' of the latter: *Winter Studies and Summer Rambles in Canada*, 3 vols (1838), discussed in Norma Clarke's 'Anna Jameson: "The idol of thousands of young ladies"' in Hilton and Hirsch (eds), *Practical Visionaries*, pp. 79–81.

16. S. L. Meyer, *Imperialism at Home: Race and Victorian Women's Fiction* (Ithaca, 1996), pp. 7–11, 28, 200–1.

17. L. Peach, 'No Longer a View: Virginia Woolf in the 1930s' in M. Joannou (ed.), *Women Writers of the 1930s: Gender, Politics and History* (Edinburgh, 1999), pp. 192–204.

18. The more modest claims made by Susanne Howe, *Novels of Empire* (New York, 1949), pp. 4, 163–5, seem to me to be closer to the mark.

19. N. Henry, *George Eliot and the British Empire* (Cambridge, 2002), p. 3: 'there was no imperialist agenda behind either her actions or her writing'.

20. Ibid., pp. 107–8 and ch. 4.

21. Brooks and Faulkner, *The White Man's Burden*, p. 184.

22. Mitchell, *The New Girl*, p. 142; S. Kemp *et al.* (eds), *Edwardian Fiction: An Oxford Companion* (Oxford, 1997), p. 252. She wrote under a pseudonym; her real name was Ada Ellen Bayly.

23. I am using this term loosely to group together novels, collections of short stories, contributions to magazines and periodicals, and (published) memoirs and autobiographies written by women who were either born into Anglo-Indian society, or who stayed in India for an extended period, and thus felt themselves to be a part of the *Raj*.

24. Mills, *Discourses of Difference*, pp. 1–2; R. Ray, 'The Memsahib's Brush: Anglo-Indian Women and the Art of the Picturesque, 1830–80' in J. F. Codell and D. S. Macleod (eds), *Orientalism Transposed: The Impact of the Colonies on British Culture* (Aldershot, 1998), p. 89; Dominic Omissi, *The Mills and Boon Memsahibs: Women's Romantic Indian Fiction, 1877–1947*, University of Lancaster Ph.D. (1995), pp. 18–20.

25. Between 1880 and 1900, 48 new titles appeared in the women's magazine and periodical market. Of those that reported most regularly on India, the *Englishwomen's Domestic Magazine* (first published in 1852) claimed to have around 50,000 subscribers: N. Chaudhuri, 'Issues of Race, Gender and Nation in *Englishwomen's Domestic Magazine* and *Queen*, 1850–1900' in Finkelstein and Peers (eds), *Negotiating India*, p. 53. Alice Perrin's *The Anglo-Indians* (1912) went through at least eight editions: see Procida, *Married to the Empire*, p. 24. Maud Diver's *Lonely Furrow* (1923) went through six reprints in the same number of months; 10,280 copies of the 'Cheaper Edition' and 25,250 copies of the 'Cheap Edition' were printed in 1925 and 1926 respectively: see

Omissi, *The Mills and Boon Memsahibs*, pp. 19–20. Omissi's study of eleven Anglo-Indian women, writing between 1877 and 1947, numbers 171 novels, short story collections and volumes of poetry to their names.   [291]

26. A point well made by the only study to focus on the lighter or lowbrow end of this market: see Omissi, *The Mills and Boon Memsahibs*, p. 190.

27. Ray, 'The Memsahib's Brush', pp. 92–9, 107–8; Omissi, *The Mills and Boon Memsahibs*, p. 327; Ghose, *Women Travellers in Colonial India*, esp. p. 161. Memsahibs, for example, circulated Indian recipes and spread the latest fashions in Indian goods through newspaper and magazine articles, letters to editors, cookery and exchange columns, and household manuals: see N. Chaudhuri, 'Shawls, Jewelry, Curry, and Rice in Victorian Britain' in Chaudhuri and Strobel (eds), *Western Women and Imperialism*, pp. 231–46, 'Memsahibs and their Servants in Nineteenth Century India', *WHR* (1994), pp. 549–62 and 'Issues of Race, Gender and Nation', pp. 51–62. A note of caution is, however, sounded by Jane Robinson in her analysis of the books and journals of the 'Mutiny memsahibs' that appeared in Britain from 1858 and were still being published as late as 1911: *Angels of Albion: Women of the Indian Mutiny* (1996), pp. 251 5.

28. S. Suleri, *The Rhetoric of English India* (Chicago, 1992), pp. 75–6.

29. Ghose, *Women Travellers in Colonial India*, pp. 142, 162. See also C. S. Bremner, *A Month in a Dandi: A Woman's Wanderings in Northern India* (1891).

30. T. E. Tausky, *Sara Jeanette Duncan: Novelist of Empire* (1980), pp. 183, 191, 193, 260.

31. Mills, *Discourses of Difference*, pp. 3–6.

32. Chaudhuri, 'Memsahibs and their Servants', pp. 554, 558.

33. Omissi, *The Mills and Boon Memsahibs*, p. 67.

34. Tausky, *Sara Jeanette Duncan*, pp. 187, 201, 217, 260–2.

35. F. Parks, *Wanderings of a Pilgrim in Search of the Picturesque during Four-and-Twenty Years in the East: With Revelations of Life in the Zenana*, 2 vols (1850).

36. A. Sattin (ed.), *An Englishwoman in India: The Memoirs of Harriet Tytler, 1828–1858* (Oxford, 1986).

37. Suleri, *The Rhetoric of English India*, pp. 80–1, 92, 94, 98.

38. Omissi, *The Mills and Boon Memsahibs*, ch. 4.

39. I. Ghose, *Memsahibs Abroad: Writings by Women Travellers in Nineteenth Century India* (Delhi, 1998), pp. 1–2.

40. Strictly-speaking, Carpenter was not an orthodox evangelical but an 'evangelical Unitarian': for the difference see R. Watts, 'Mary Carpenter: Educator of the Children of the "Perishing and Dangerous Classes"' in M. Hilton and P. Hirsch (eds), *Practical Visionaries and Social Progress, 1790–1930* (2000), p. 40.

41. Burton, 'Institutionalising Imperial Reform', pp. 26–9.

[292]   42. Tausky, *Sara Jeanette Duncan*, pp. 235ff.

43. Ghose, *Women Travellers in Colonial India*, p. 103.

44. P. Horn, *The Victorian Town Child* (Stroud, 1997), pp. 163–8.

45. B. Alderson, 'Tracts, Rewards and Fairies: The Victorian Contribution to Children's Literature' in A. Briggs (ed.), *Essays in the History of Publishing* (Longman, 1974), pp. 247–57, 272–7; F. J. Harvey Darton, *Children's Books in England* (Cambridge, 1958), pp. 266–71, 321.

46. For an introduction to the juvenile market for periodical publishers, see D. Dixon, 'Children and the Press, 1866–1914' in Harris and Lee (eds), *The Press in English Society*, pp. 133–45.

47. McKibbin, *Classes and Cultures*, p. 497.

48. Rose, *The Intellectual Life of the British Working Classes*, pp. 321–35.

49. For an endorsement of Rose's views on children's literature see S. Collini, 'The Cookson Story', *LRB*, 13/12/2001, pp. 33–5.

50. Recollections are not, of course, unproblematic, especially when they are from people on the Left who are reading back into their childhood the anti-imperialism they came to feel as adults. But for a strident statement that reading mattered, see the IRA member (and one of Michael Collins's assassins) Todd Andrews, *Dublin Made Me: An Autobiography* (Dublin, 1979), p. 45: 'From the comics we read, *Chips*, *Comic Cuts* and later the *Magnet* and the *Gem* and the *Union Jack*, we absorbed the correct British imperial attitudes to the "Fuzzy Wuzzies", the "Niggers" and the Indian Nabobs.'

51. G. Arnold, *Held Fast for England: G. A. Henty, Imperialist Boys' Writer* (1980), pp. 75–80; K. Castle, *Britannia's Children: Reading Colonialism through Children's Books and Magazines* (Manchester, 1996), pp. 167–74; Mackenzie, 'Empire and Metropolitan Cultures', Vol. 3 *OHBE*, p. 289 and 'The Popular Culture of Empire in Britain', Vol. 4 *OHBE*, p. 223; J. Richards (ed.), *Imperialism and Juvenile Literature* (Manchester, 1989), pp. 1–10. See also Walvin's *A Child's World*, p. 178: 'it is reasonable to suggest that children's books, at school and at home, played a remarkable role in encouraging a sense of superiority among the young which lasted into adult life'.

52. E. James and H. R. Smith, *Penny Dreadfuls and Boys' Adventures: The Barry Ono Collection of Victorian Popular Literature in the British Library* (The British Library, 1998).

53. It then became *Boys of the Empire, An Up-To-Date Boys' Journal* (1901–6).

54. *Penny Dreadfuls and Comics: English Periodicals for Children from Victorian Times to the Present Day* (1983), p. 21.

55. These were published under various titles, including *Boys of England, Jack Harkaway's Journal for Boys* and *Jack Harkaway and his Son's Adventures*. The character was created by Bracebridge Hemyng (1829–1904). For Hemyng and Harkaway, see P. Haining, *The Penny Dreadful* (1975), ch. 23.

56. James and Smith, *Penny Dreadfuls*, pp. 43–5; L. James, 'Tom Brown's Imperialist Sons', *VS* (1973), pp. 94–6.

57. K. Boyd, 'Knowing Your Place: The Tensions of Manliness in Boys' Story Papers, 1918–39' in Roper and Tosh (eds), *Manful Assertions*, pp. 145, 158.

58. For the significance of this theme more generally, see E. S. Turner, *Boys Will Be Boys: The Story of Sweeney Todd, Deadwood Dick, Sexton Blake, Billy Bunter, Dick Barton et al.* (Harmondsworth, 1976), pp. 192ff.

59. P. Keating, *The Haunted Study: A Social History of the English Novel, 1875–1914* (1989), p. 354.

60. A weekly publication costing a penny, the paper could also be purchased as a monthly edition, featuring a large colour plate illustrating one of the articles of the month, and bound in a more durable cover. An annual edition was available for the Christmas market, at the cost of eight shillings, featuring all the weekly issues and colour plates, plus a title page and index, bound in a stiff cover. The paper was effectively under the control of George Andrew Hutchison (its sub-editor) from 1879 to 1912. Hutchison was editor of the *Sunday School World* from 1865, and part of the editorial panel of *The Baptist*.

61. For a contemporary assessment of their popularity, see E. Salmon, *Juvenile Literature As It is* (1888) based on Charles Welsh's 1884 survey of 2,000 schoolchildren aged 11–19: the *BOP* received 404 out of 1,000 votes and *GOP* received 315 out of 1,000 votes.

62. McAleer, *Popular Reading and Publishing*, p. 242.

63. P. A. Dunae, 'New Grub Street for Boys' in Richards (ed.), *Imperialism and Juvenile Literature*, pp. 22–3.

64. Ibid., p. 28.

65. D. Gorham, 'The Ideology of Femininity for Girls' in F. Hunt (ed.), *Lessons for Life: The Schooling of Girls and Women, 1850–1950* (Oxford, 1987), p. 48.

66. K. Reynolds, *Girls Only? Gender and Popular Children's Fiction in Britain, 1880–1910* (1990), p. 142.

67. McAleer, *Popular Reading and Publishing*, p. 216.

68. Dunae, 'Boys' Literature and the Idea of Empire', pp. 106–16.

69. Hopkins, *Childhood Transformed*, p. 305; R. Noakes, 'The Boy's Own Paper, Science, and Late-Victorian Juvenile Magazines' in G. N. Cantor *et al.* (eds), *Science in the Nineteenth-Century Periodical: Reading the Magazine of Nature* (Cambridge, 2003), p. 6; J. Springhall, 'Building Character in the British Boy: The Attempt to Extend Christian Manliness to Working-Class Adolescents, 1880–1914' in Mangan and Walvin (eds), *Manliness and Morality*, pp. 67–8.

70. I. Dancyger, *A World of Women: An Illustrated History of Women's Magazines* (1978), p. 84; Reynolds, *Girls Only?*, p. 142; W. Forrester, *Great Grandma's Weekly: A Celebration of the Girls' Own Paper, 1880–1901* (Guildford, 1980), p. 25; Gorham, 'The Ideology of Femininity', p. 49.

[294]   71. J. Mackay and P. Thorne, 'The Englishwoman' in Colls and Dodd (eds), *Englishness*, p. 194.

72. *Penny Dreadfuls and Comics*, pp. 45–6.

73. Ibid.

74. D. Reed, *The Popular Magazine in Britain and the United States, 1880–1960* (1997), p. 86; McAleer, *Popular Reading and Publishing*, p. 219.

75. Jack Cox, himself an editor of the *BOP* in later years, estimates a circulation of around 250,000 copies: *Take a Cold Tub, Sir! The Story of the Boys' Own Paper* (Guildford, 1982), p. 76.

76. The RTS' general committee (packed with Baptist pro-Boers) dared not run the risk of damaging sales by actually speaking out against the conflict: see Dunae, 'Boys' Literature and the Idea of Empire', p. 115.

77. Before writing for the *BOP*, Kingston had published the *Magazine for Boys* (1859), which was discontinued. He was honorary secretary of the Colonisation Society, and worked for the SPCK as a dockside missionary distributing tracts and bibles to intending colonial settlers.

78. A one-time apprentice of the Hudson Bay Company, Ballantyne produced some of the most popular children's fiction of the period: *Black Ivory* was written in support of the anti-slavery movement, while *Dusty Diamonds* promoted emigration for London orphans.

79. G. Avery, *Nineteenth Century Children: Heroes and Heroines in Children's Stories, 1780–1900* (1965), p. 145; S. Hannabus, 'Ballantyne's Message of Empire' in Richards (ed.), *Imperialism and Juvenile Literature*, pp. 58–9, 62, 68–9; R. H. Macdonald, 'Reproducing the Middle-Class Boy: From Purity to Patriotism in the Boys' Magazines, 1892–1914', *JCH* (1989), pp. 527–8.

80. Dunae, 'Boys' Literature and the Idea of Empire', p. 111. Stables had served for nine years as a surgeon in the Royal Navy, but was forced to leave the service after contracting 'jungle fever'.

81. For the debate on how far Henty's popularity survived the First World War, see Mackenzie, 'The Popular Culture of Empire in Britain', p. 222, and Stevenson, *British Society, 1914–45*, p. 399, who argue that it did; and McAleer, *Popular Reading and Publishing*, p. 142, who argues that, by the 1920s, Henty's popularity was very much in decline.

82. M. Beetham and K. Boardman, *Victorian Women's Magazines: An Anthology* (Manchester, 2002), p. 4.

83. J. Grace, *Advice to Young Ladies: From the Nineteenth Century Correspondence Pages of The Girl's Own Paper* (1997); Mackay and Thorne, 'The Englishwoman', pp. 191–2, 196–7, 212–13; Reynolds, *Girls Only?*, p. 139.

84. J. Rowbotham, *Good Girls Make Good Wives: Guidance for Girls in Victorian Fiction* (Oxford, 1989), ch. 5.

85. S. Mitchell, *The New Girl. Girls' Culture in England, 1880–1915* (New York, [295] 1995), pp. 116–17.

86. J. S. Bratton, 'British Imperialism and the Reproduction of Femininity in Girls' Fiction' in Richards (ed.), *Imperialism and Juvenile Literature*, pp. 201–6.

87. B. Melman, *Women and the Popular Imagination in the Twenties: Flappers and Nymphs* (Basingstoke, 1988), ch. 9.

88. Mackay and Thorne, 'The Englishwoman', pp. 212–13.

89. For a 'real life' example, see the interview of the Lancashire textile worker, Gwennie Edmondson (b. 1912) in the North-West Sound Archive, Iden. 1995.0217, Record No. 646 – as an adolescent girl she recalls 'going mad' on the books of Edgar Wallace, borrowed from the local library by her father. A contemporary commentator, Edward Salmon, felt that boys' fiction offered the 'stirring and lively plots' largely absent from that written specifically for girls: see 'What Girls Read', *The Nineteenth Century*, 20 (1886), pp. 515–29.

90. My own inclination is toward the variety, autonomy and unpredictability of readers' responses, as argued for by Jonathan Rose. For supporting evidence, see Robert Snape's discussion of the National Home Reading Union in the *Journal of Victorian Culture* (2002), pp. 86–110; and Kate Flint's study *The Woman Reader, 1837–1914* (Oxford, 1993), pp. vii–viii, 14–15, 42, 187, 325–6, 330. The debate remains wide open, however.

91. R. Lloyd, *The Church of England, 1900–1965* (1966), p. 46.

92. See, in particular, S. S. Maughan, *Regions Beyond and the National Church: Domestic Support for the Foreign Missions of the Church of England in the High Imperial Age, 1870–1914*, University of Harvard Ph.D. (1995), ch. 3.

93. A. F. Walls, 'British Missions' in T. Christensen and W. R. Hutchison (eds), *Missionary Ideologies in the Imperialist Era, 1880–1920* (Aros, Denmark, 1982), p. 161.

94. A. Porter, 'Religion, Missionary Enthusiasm, and Empire', Vol. 3 *OHBE*, p. 229.

95. J. Haggis, 'White Women and Colonialism: Towards a Recuperative History' in Midgley (ed.), *Gender and Imperialism*, p. 51.

96. Ibid., p. 52.

97. J. Murray, 'The Role of Women in the Church Missionary Society, 1799–1917' in K. Ward and B. Stanley (eds), *The Church Mission Society and World Christianity 1799–1999* (Richmond, Surrey, 2000), p. 75.

98. Trollope, *Britannia's Daughters*, pp. 30–1, 186–92.

99. Haggis, '"A heart that has felt the love of God"', p. 179; M. Hill, 'Women in the Irish Protestant Foreign Missions, c. 1873–1914: Representations and Motivations' in P. N. Holtrop and H. McLeod (eds), *Missions and Missionaries* (2000), pp. 178, 181.

[296] 100. C. Clear, *Nuns in Nineteenth Century Ireland* (Dublin, 1988); J. Scott, *Weapons of the Weak: Everyday Forms of Peasant Resistance* (New Haven, 1985); B. G. Smith, *Ladies of the Leisure Class: The Bourgeoises of Northern France in the Nineteenth Century* (Princeton, 1981).

101. Heeney, *The Women's Movement*, pp. 22–6, 46–53, 68–74; A. Summers, 'A Home from Home – Women's Philanthropic Work in the Nineteenth Century' in S. Burman (ed.), *Fit Work for Women* (1979), pp. 33–63.

102. F. Knight, *The Nineteenth-Century Church and English Society* (Cambridge, 1995), p. 200. Here the comment applies to the Anglican church, but it could easily be extended to the field of Nonconformity.

103. S. Swain, 'In These Days of Female Evangelists and Hallelujah Lasses: Women Preachers and the Redefinition of Gender Roles in the Churches in Late Nineteenth-Century Australia', *Journal of Religious History* (2002), pp. 65–77; J. Walker, 'Baeyertz, Emilia Louise (nee Aronson)' in B. Dickey (ed.), *Australian Dictionary of Evangelical Biography* (Sydney, 1994), pp. 18–19.

104. J. Holmes, *Religious Revivals in Britain and Ireland, 1859–1905* (2000); O. Anderson, 'Women Preachers in Mid-Victorian Britain: Some Reflections on Feminism, Popular Religion and Social Change', *HJ* (1969), pp. 467–84.

105. Salvationist women preached and assumed positions of leadership at a time when few Protestant denominations allowed women to perform such work: P. J. Walker, 'A Chaste and Fervid Eloquence: Catherine Booth and the Ministry of Women in the Salvation Army' in B. M. Kienzle and P. J. Walker (eds), *Women Preachers and Prophets through Two Millennia of Christianity* (Berkeley, 1998), pp. 288–302.

106. For an account of the holiness movement, see D. W. Bebbington, *Evangelicalism in Modern Britain: A History from the 1730s to the 1980s* (1989), ch. 5.

107. I am grateful to Dr Rhonda Semple for sharing her thoughts on the CIM, and women missionaries more generally. See, in particular, '"The conversion and highest welfare of each pupil": The Work of the CIM at Chefoo', *JICH* (2003), and her two papers: 'Representation and Experience: The Role of Women in British Missions and British Society, 1860–1910' and 'Women, Gender and Changing Roles in the Missionary Project: The LMS and the CIM, 1885–1910'.

108. For the suggestion that it did, see Murray, 'The Role of Women in the CMS', p. 81.

109. For an example and explanation, see C. F. Pascoe, *Two Hundred Years of the SPG: An Historical Account of the Society for the Propagation of the Gospel in Foreign Parts, 1701–1900* (1901), pp. 846, 846a; and R. Seton, '"Open doors for female labourers": Women Candidates for the LMS, 1875–1914' in R. A. Bickers and R. Seton (eds), *Missionary Encounters: Sources and Issues* (Surrey, 1996), pp. 55–6, 68.

110. A. Porter, 'Church History, History of Christianity, Religious History: Some [297] Reflections on British Missionary Enterprise Since the Late Eighteenth Century', *Church History* (2002), p. 576.

111. The word is derived from the Persian, 'zan' (woman). It referred to those parts of households from which all males outside the immediate family were excluded, and was also used to describe the women of the family themselves. Though zenanas were only prescribed for Muslim women, the influence of the Mughal rulers of India led to upper-caste Hindus emulating this practice.

112. I am aware that if the notion of imperialism is expanded to include 'informal' as well as 'formal' regions of expansion, then China can be taken from the international and placed in the imperial sphere. However, China's status as a region of informal empire seems to rest heavily on the (internationally-administered) treaty-ports, and the effective loss of Manchu sovereignty therein. It is far harder to incorporate inland China in a British informal empire – and this is where much missionary activity occurred.

113. Rev. J. S. Dennis, *Christian Missions and Social Progress: A Sociological Study of Foreign Missions* (1899), pp. xiv–xvii.

114. J. C. Pollock, *Shadows Fall Apart: The Story of the Zenana Bible and Medical Mission* (1958), pp. 22, 32–3. By 1871, Bengal had more zenana pupils than the other six Indian Provinces together: see G. A. Oddie, *Social Protest in India: British Protestant Missionaries and Social Reforms, 1850–1900* (New Delhi, 1979), p. 77, n. 8.

115. M. G. Taylor, *The Story of the China Inland Mission* (2nd edn, 1893–4), Vol. 2, pp. 293–5.

116. K. L. Lodwick, *Crusaders Against Opium: Protestant Missionaries in China, 1874–1917* (Lexington, 1996), pp. 36–8.

117. See, for example, the comparisons drawn by the Rev. E. S. Carr in the CEZMS' magazine, *India's Women and China's Daughters* (June 1896), p. 140.

118. M. C. Gollock, 'Women in the Church on the Mission Fields' in C. C. B. Bardsley (ed.), *Women and Church Work* (1917), pp. 78–80; G. Piercy, *Love for China: Exemplified in the Memorials of Mary Gunson, the First Female Teacher in Connection with the Wesleyan Methodist Mission at Canton*. See also P. Barr, *To China With Love: The Lives and Times of Protestant Missionaries in China, 1860–1900* (1972), pp. 127, 131 and Semple, 'Women, Gender and Changing Roles', p. 24.

119. I. Barnes, *Behind the Great Wall: The Story of CEZMS' Work and Workers in China* (1896) and *Behind the Pardah: The Story of CEZMS' Work in India* (1897); A. N. Duncan, *The City of Springs or Mission Work in Chinchew* (1902), p. 91; S. C. Potter, *The Social Origins and Recruitment of English Protestant Missionaries in the Nineteenth Century*, University of London Ph.D. (1974), pp. 260–1.

[298]   120.   *India's Women and China's Daughters* (Jan. 1897), p. 5; Piercy, *Love for China*, p. 3; A. H. Small, *Light and Shade in Zenana Missionary Life* (Paisley, 1890), pp. 92–5. See also J. Hunter, *The Gospel of Gentility: American Women Missionaries in Turn-of-the-Century China* (New Haven, 1984), p. 11; Williams, 'The Recruitment of Women Missionaries', p. 51.

121.   Semple, 'Women, Gender and Changing Roles', p. 8.

122.   Williams, 'The Recruitment of Women Missionaries', p. 45.

123.   Ibid., p. 23.

124.   The CIM did set up a school at Chefoo, but the decision was mainly motivated by financial considerations, and by the desire of families to get together more often, rather than by any sympathy for the Chinese. See Semple, ' "The conversion and highest welfare of each pupil" ', pp. 2, 5, 10, 22–3.

125.   Ibid., p. 9.

126.   Murray, 'The Role of Women in CMS', p. 88.

127.   J. S. Dennis, *Centennial Survey of Foreign Mission* (New York, 1902), p. 23.

128.   For the (contrary) suggestion that 'the origins of the missionary movement's feminisation lay as much in colonial relations of power as in gender relations at home', see S. Thorne, *Congregational Missions and the Making of an Imperial Culture in C19th England* (Stanford, 1999), pp. 94–8.

129.   For examples, see: Anon., *Dr David Livingstone: The Great Missionary Traveller* (1875); B. K. Gregory, *The Story of David Livingstone: Weaver Boy, Missionary and Explorer* (1896), published by the Sunday School Union; W. M. Harris, *David Livingstone: A Hero of Peace; a Study for Young People* (1913), published by the Congregational Union and the LMS. For secondary studies see B. W. Lloyd, J. Lashbrook and T. A. Simons, *A Bibliography of Published Works by and about David Livingstone, 1843–1975* (Cape Town, 1978), pp. 12–39; J. M. MacKenzie, 'David Livingstone: The construction of the myth' in G. Walker and T. Gallagher (eds), *Sermons and Battle Hymns: Protestant Popular Culture in Modern Scotland* (Edinburgh, 1990), p. 38; J. Wolffe, *Great Deaths. Grieving, Religion, and Nationhood in Victorian and Edwardian Britain* (Oxford, 2001), p. 142.

130.   F. R. Prochaska, *Women and Philanthropy in Nineteenth-Century England* (Oxford, 1980), p. 91.

131.   K. D. M. Snell, 'The Sunday-School Movement in England and Wales: Child Labour, Denominational Control and Working-Class Culture', *P&P* (1999), p. 126.

132.   A. Briggs, *Victorian Cities* (1963), p. 255.

133.   Green, *Religion in the Age of Decline*, p. 231.

134.   Thorne, *Congregational Missions*, pp. 115–16.

135.   Green, *Religion in the Age of Decline*, p. 232.

136. Ibid., p. 255.   [299]

137. H. McLeod, *Religion and Society in England, 1850–1914* (Basingstoke, 1996),
     p. 148.

138. For a review of the debate, see W. B. Stephens, *Education in Britain, 1750–*
     1914 (Basingstoke, 1998), pp. 77–81.

139. Rose, *The Erosion of Childhood*, p. 6.

140. R. D. Anderson, *Education and the Scottish People* (1995), pp. 68–9; A. Green,
     Education and State Formation: The Rise of Education Systems in England, France
     and the USA (1990), pp. 300–1; B. Simon, *Studies in the History of Education,*
     1780–1870 (1960), pp. 354–7.

141. Hopkins, *Childhood Transformed*, p. 230; Stephens, *Education in Britain*, p. 180.

142. A. Digby and P. Searby, *Children, School and Society in Nineteenth-Century Eng-*
     land (1981), pp. 20–8; S. Humphries, *Hooligans or Rebels? An Oral History of*
     Working-Class Childhood and Youth, 1889–1939 (Oxford, 1981), pp. 174–5;
     K. P. Stannard, 'Ideology, Education and Social Structure: Elementary Schools
     in Mid-Victorian England', *History of Education*, 19 (1990), p. 121.

143. S. Heathorn, *For Home, Country and Race: Constructing Gender, Class and Eng-*
     lishness in the Elementary School, 1880–1914 (Toronto, 2000), pp. 1–7; Horn,
     The Victorian Town Child, p. 96; MacKenzie, *Propaganda and Empire*, pp. 174–
     97; D. Rubinstein, 'Socialization and the London School Board, 1870–1904:
     Aims, Methods and Public Opinion' in P. McCann (ed.), *Popular Education*
     and Socialization in the Nineteenth Century (1977), p. 233.

144. A. Davin, *Growing Up Poor*, pp. 170, 208–14; Horn, *The Victorian Town*
     Child, pp. 12–13; J. Stewart, 'Children, Parents and The State: The Chil-
     dren Act, 1908', *Children and Society* (1995), pp. 90–9; A. Sumner Holmes,
     '"Fallen Mothers": Maternal Adultery and Child Custody in England, 1886–
     1925' in C. Nelson and A. Sumner Holmes (eds), *Maternal Instincts: Visions of*
     Motherhood and Sexuality in Britain, 1875–1925 (Basingstoke, 1997), p. 50.

145. For an overview of child migration, see Thompson, *Imperial Britain*, pp. 146–
     51.

146. For the work of Rye and MacPherson, see I. Pinchbeck, *Children in English*
     Society. Vol. II: From the Eighteenth Century to the Children Act of 1948 (1973),
     pp. 562–75.

147. L. Rose, *Rogues and Vagabonds: Vagrant Underworld in Britain, 1815–1985*
     (1988), p. 131.

148. T. A. Spalding, *The Work of the London School Board* (1900), p. 142.

149. Harper, *Emigration from North-East Scotland*, Vol. 2, p. 206.

150. C. Birchenough, *History of Education in England and Wales: From 1800 to the*
     Present Day (1938), p. 120.

151. Initially, by-laws empowering Local School Boards to enforce attendance
     were permissive: only 450 of the 2,000 or so Boards made use of them.

[300]   See J. Lawson and H. Silver, *A Social History of Education in England* (1973), p. 321.

152. J. Morgan, *The Work of the Leeds School Board, 1870–1903*, University of Leeds MA (1986), p. 47.

153. R. Smith, *Schools, Politics and Society: Elementary Education in Wales, 1870–1902* (Cardiff, 1999).

154. N. Middleton, 'The Education Act of 1870 as the Start of the Modern Concept of the Child', *British Journal of Education Studies*, 18 (1970), pp. 174–5.

155. W. E. Marsden, *Educating the Respectable: A Study of Fleet Road Board School, Hampstead, 1879–1903* (1991), p. 41.

156. Children at school beyond the age of 12 accounted for only 14% of the total on school registers: see Morgan, *The Work of the Leeds School Board*, p. 139.

157. J. G. Greenlee, *Education and Imperial Unity, 1901–26* (New York, 1987).

158. J. G. Greenlee, 'Imperial Studies and the Unity of the Empire', *JICH* (1979), pp. 323–4.

159. R. Aldrich, 'Imperialism in the Study and Teaching of History' in J. A. Mangan (ed.), *'Benefits bestowed'? Education and British Imperialism* (Manchester, 1988), pp. 27–8. For the RCI's earlier efforts to promote imperial studies in schools, see MacKenzie, *Propaganda and Empire*, p. 175.

160. B. J. Elliott, *The Development of History Teaching in England for Pupils Aged 11–18 Years, 1918–39*, University of Sheffield Ph.D. (1975), pp. 41ff.

161. Greenlee, 'Imperial Studies and the Unity of Empire', pp. 329–31.

162. P. Gordon and D. Lawton, *Curriculum Change in the Nineteenth and Twentieth Centuries* (1978), pp. 12–32.

163. P. Horn, 'English Elementary Education and the Growth of the Imperial Ideal: 1880–1914', in Mangan (ed.), *'Benefits bestowed?'*, pp. 40–1. For the handbooks see *Board of Education, Suggestions for the Consideration of Teachers and Others Concerned in the Work of Public Elementary Schools*, HMSO (1905), p. 61; (1914), p. 82; (1923), p. 92; (1927), pp. 122–4; (1937), p. 413.

164. Lawson and Silver, *A Social History of Education*, pp. 329–30.

165. J. S. Hurt, *Elementary Schooling and the Working Classes, 1860–1918* (1979), pp. 30–1.

166. Greenlee, *Education and Imperial Unity*, p. 197.

167. J. S. Hurt, 'Drill, Discipline and the Elementary School Ethos' in P. McCann (ed.), *Popular Education and Socialisation in the Nineteenth Century* (1977), pp. 171, 176, 187.

168. Ibid., pp. 182–3.

169. Davin, *Growing Up Poor*, p. 201.

170. The Board paid for several courses of lectures on imperial subjects, and credit could be gained toward teacher training certificates by attending them: see Spalding, *The Work of the London School Board*, pp. 204–5.

171. Marsden, *Educating the Respectable*, p. 151.

172. Greenlee, *Education and Imperial Unity*, pp. 41ff, 77, 181–7; M. Barber, 'Two Homes Now: The Return Migration of the Fellowship of the Maple Leaf', unpublished paper, Emigrant Homecomings Conference, Aberdeen, July 2002; J. Sturgis and M. Bird, *Canada's Imperial Past: The Life of F. J. Ney 1884–1973* (Edinburgh, 2000).

173. C. Steedman, *Childhood, Culture and Class in Britain: Margaret McMillan, 1860–1931* (1990), pp. 67, 94, 98–9.

174. D. Copelman, *London's Women Teachers: Gender, Class and Feminism, 1870–1930* (1996), pp. 119–20, 220–6; A. Oram, *Women Teachers and Feminist Politics, 1900–39* (Manchester, 1996), pp. 19–20.

175. Feather, *A History of British Publishing*, pp. 144, 165–6.

176. F. Glendenning, *The Evolution of History Teaching in British and French Schools in the Nineteenth and Twentieth Centuries with Special Reference to Attitudes to Race and Colonial History in History Schoolbooks*, University of Keele Ph.D. (1971).

177. Quoted in I. J. Steele, *A Study of the Formative Years of the Development of the History Curriculum in English Schools, 1833–1901*, University of Sheffield Ph.D. (1974), p. 69.

178. Ibid., pp. 253–85.

179. V. Chancellor, *History for their Masters: Opinion in the English History Textbook, 1800–1914* (Bath, 1970), pp. 114, 122, 128, 137.

180. It was not unknown for teachers and inspectors to object to racial prejudice in school texts: see Steele, *A Study of the Formative Years*, pp. 71–2.

181. Elliott, *The Development of History Teaching*, pp. 83ff, 102.

182. Horn, 'English Elementary Education', pp. 43–4; F. M. Mannsaker, 'The Dog that Didn't Bark: The Subject Races in Imperial Fiction at the Turn of the Century' in D. Dabydeen (ed.), *The Black Presence in English Literature* (Manchester, 1985), p. 113.

183. A. Davin, '"Mind that you do as you are told": Reading Books for Board School Girls, 1870–1902', *Feminist Review* (1979), pp. 90, 98; D. G. Paz, 'Working-Class Education as Social Control in England, 1860–1918', *History of Education Quarterly* (1981), p. 498; Walvin, *A Child's World*, p. 196.

184. J. M. Goldstrom, *The Social Content of Education, 1808–1870: A Study of the Working Class School Reader in England and Ireland* (Shannon, 1972).

185. Heathorn, *For Home, Country and Race*, pp. 9–11, 17.

186. Ibid., p. 211.

[302]   187.   For example, some scepticism was expressed regarding their influence by the school inspectors, who argued that little historical insight was gained through their use: see Steele, *A Study of the Formative Years*, pp. 225–6.

188.   S. Humphries, *Hooligans or Rebels? An Oral History of Working-Class Childhood and Youth, 1889–1939* (Oxford, 1981).

189.   Ibid., pp. 25–6, 43–4, 135.

190.   Ibid., p. 43.

191.   For studies of Lord Meath and Empire Day, see D. H. Hume, 'Empire Day in Ireland, 1896–1962' in Jeffery (ed.), *'An Irish Empire?'*, pp. 149–68; Richards, *Imperialism and Popular Music*, pp. 164–76; J. Springhall, 'Lord Meath, Youth and Empire', *JCH* (1970). I have also drawn on the work of one of my postgraduate students: see S. Pymer, *An Imperial Philanthropist? The Earl of Meath and the Empire Day Movement, c. 1900–29*, University of Leeds, MA by Research (2001).

192.   See his letter to *The Times*, 28/12/1896. However, the real inspiration behind the event appears to have come from Clementina Fessenden, a woman from Hamilton, Ontario, who in 1890 had proposed that a patriotic 'flag' day be held in all Canadian schools. See R. Fessenden, *The Founding of Empire Day* (Bermuda, c. 1930), p. 5, and also Meath in *The Times*, 24/5/1921, p. 11.

193.   Half and full day school holidays had previously been granted in the spring of 1900 to mark the relief of Mafeking and Ladysmith, while the anniversaries of great historical events (e.g. Trafalgar Day) figured in the calendars of many public schools. See Betsy Barton, 24/7/1983, Record No. 499, NW Sound Archive; S. Schwartz and R. Parker, *Tin Mines and Miners of Lanner: The Heart of Cornish Tin* (Cornwall, 2001), p. 158.

194.   H. Hendrick, *Images of Youth: Age, Class, and the Male Youth Problem, 1880–1920* (Oxford, 1990), ch. 6.

195.   These figures were published in the annual reports, and it is likely that the EDM simply added up the number of schools in approving LEAs. This, however, would have been an inflated figure because even after Empire Day received official recognition in 1916, it was left to LEAs to decide if they would celebrate it. Moreover, even with an LEA's encouragement, it is doubtful whether all schools would have complied.

196.   P. Bright, *Imperialism and Popular Culture in Lancashire, 1875–1920*, MA Thesis, University of Lancaster (1985), p. 5.

197.   Greenlee, *Education and Imperial Unity*, p. 61.

198.   Pymer, *An Imperial Philanthropist?*, pp. 76–8.

199.   N. Mansfield, 'Farmworkers and Local Conservatism in South-West Shropshire, 1916–23' in S. Ball and I. Holliday (eds), *Mass Conservatism: The Conservative and the Public since the 1880s* (2002), p. 48.

200. MSH 78A Female, Record 16, NW Sound Archive.

201. Fenella Fearson (b. 1908), 00063, MA200064/064, Mantle Collection, East Midlands Oral History Archive (EMOHA), Centre for Urban History, University of Leicester; Observer at the Coston Junior Mixed School, Topic Collection (Children & Education), TC 59 (1937–52), Mass-Observation Archive; P. Gordon (ed.), *Politics and Society: The Journals of Lady Knightley of Fawsley, 1885–1913* (Northampton, 1999), p. 24.

202. *A Memento of Empire Day at Batley, Saturday August 24th, 1907* (Farsley, nr. Leeds, 1907).

203. Ian White (b. 1941), 15/2/2000, Record 1301, NW Sound Archive.

204. Doris Joll (b. 1914), 2/10/1997, Record 4, NW Sound Archive.

205. Richards, *Imperialism and Music*, p. 166.

206. Grange Junior School, Topic Collection, TC 59/1//E, Mass-Observation Archive.

207. Glendenning, *The Evolution of History Teaching*, p. 430.

208. Bramford Senior Area School, Suffolk, Topic Collection, TC 59/1/E, Mass-Observation Archive.

209. Extract from Ian Hislop's TV series, 'School Rules. 2: Class Struggles', Channel 4. I am grateful to Richard Grayson for lending me the recording.

210. Grange Junior School, Topic Collection, TC 59/1/E, Mass-Observation Archive.

211. R. Blythe, *Akenfield: Portrait of an English Village* (1969), p. 146.

212. Selena Gee (1910), Acc. 96, Collection MA200/105/105, 7/8/1991 and Fenella Fearson (1908), Acc. 00063MA200/064/064, EMOHA.

213. *Pall Mall and Globe*, 24/5/23, Meath Archives, L/1/34, p. 70, quoted in Pymer, *An Imperial Philanthropist?*, p. 83.

214. I am, of course, aware here that with the passage of time, and the advent of old age, people's recollections can become dim and distorted. But the striking thing about oral history records that mention Empire Day is how clear the recollections were of what had happened, but how uncertain they were as to the significance of it all.

215. Lena Gee, Acc. 00096, Collection MA200/105/105, EMOHA.

216. Isabella Curle (1908), London, C707/404/1–3, 8/08/1972, 'Family Life and Work Experience Summaries before 1918', University of Essex.

217. See, for example, P. B. Ballard (ed.), *The Practical Infant Teacher* (1929), p. 222, which recognised that it was unrealistic to think that young children would appreciate much of Meath's purpose.

218. Elvy Morton, Acc. 01042, Collection EM/038/A, Mantle Oral History Project, EMOHA.

[304] 219. Hence this chapter needs to be cross-referenced with the discussions of nursing in Ch. 1; consumption, migration and family economy, and women's reading habits, in Ch. 2; Dundee jute workers (many of whom were female) in Ch. 3; and women's political activism in Ch. 6.

Chapter 6 Domestic Politics

1. J. Gallagher, *The Decline, Revival and Fall of the British Empire: The Ford Lectures and Other Essays* (Cambridge, 1982), pp. 75–81.

2. H. S. Jones, *Victorian Political Thought* (Basingstoke, 2000), pp. 55–9; A. S. Mehta, *Liberalism and Empire: A Study in Nineteenth-Century British Liberal Thought* (Chicago, 1999), pp. 4–9. For J. S. Mill see p. 151.

3. C. Hall, 'Rethinking Imperial Histories: The Reform Act of 1867', *New Left Review* (1994), pp. 9, 14–15, 29 and *Civilising Subjects*, pp. 12, 21, 424–5; M. Taylor, 'The 1848 Revolutions and the British Empire', *P&P* (2000), pp. 178–9.

4. M. Pugh, *The Tories and the People, 1880–1935* (Oxford, 1985).

5. P. J. Cain, 'The Economic Philosophy of Constructive Imperialism' in C. Navari (ed.), *British Politics and the Spirit of the Age* (Keele, 1996); E. H. H. Green, *The Crisis of Conservatism: The Politics, Economics and Ideology of the British Conservative Party, 1880–1914* (1995); A. Sykes, 'Radical Conservatism and the Working Classes in Edwardian England: The Case of the Workers Defence Union', *EHR* (1998); A. S. Thompson, 'Tariff Reform: An Imperial Strategy, 1903–13', *HJ* (1997) and *Imperial Britain*, ch. 4.

6. S. Howe, *Anti-Colonialism in British Politics: The Left and the End of Empire, 1918–64* (Oxford, 1993).

7. See Thompson, *Imperial Britain*, pp. 178–83, for a summary of the literature.

8. B. H. Harrison, *The Transformation of British Politics 1860–1995* (Oxford, 1996), p. 56. The rest of this paragraph is based on this study.

9. R. Hyam, 'Bureaucracy and Trusteeship in the Colonial Empire', Vol. 4 *OHBE*, p. 255.

10. William Baillie Hamilton quoted in R. C. Snelling and T. J. Barron, 'The Colonial Office and its Permanent Officials, 1801–1914' in G. Sutherland (ed.), *Studies in the Growth of Nineteenth-Century Government* (1972), p. 153.

11. R. B. Pugh, 'The Colonial Office, 1801–1925' in E. A. Benians (ed.) *CHBE*, Vol. III (1959), p. 747.

12. B. L. Blakeley, *The Colonial Office, 1868–1892* (Durham, NC, 1972), pp. xiii–xiv.

13. R. V. Kubicek, *The Administration of Imperialism: Joseph Chamberlain at the Colonial Office* (Durham, NC, 1969), pp. 14–16, 23, 26–9, 42, 174–6.

14. Though he did fix the issue of development on the CO's agenda: see [305] M. Havinden and D. Meredith, *Colonialism and Development: Britain and its Tropical Colonies, 1850–1960* (1993), p. 90.

15. For example, suggestions for a scheme of staff exchange between the CO and the colonies – which promised to provide bureaucrats with much-needed local knowledge – were 'ignored or parried'. See Pugh, 'The Colonial Office', p. 767; Sir C. Parkinson, *The Colonial Office from Within, 1909–45* (1947), pp. 46–7. See also *Downing Street and The Colonies: Report Submitted to the Fabian Colonial Bureau* (Woking, 1942), pp. 26–7, which argues that the limited exchange of senior officials compromised the CO's understanding of the aspirations of colonial peoples.

16. This was partly in the hope that colonial development would aid post-war British economic recovery: Parkinson, *The Colonial Office from Within*, pp. 63–5.

17. Havinden and Meredith, *Colonialism and Development*, pp. 138–40, 167–8, 191, 198–9; H. L. Hall, *The Colonial Office: A History* (1937), pp. 269–70.

18. See also the lament of the 'Member for India', Henry Fawcett, during the Royal Titles Bill debate (1876): 'the Indian people would be a great deal more grateful for a little attention from Parliament than they will be for having the Queen called "Empress of India"': Fawcett to Harcourt, 20/2/1876, quoted in L. Goldman (ed.), *The Blind Victorian: Henry Fawcett and British Liberalism* (Cambridge, 1989), p. 32.

19. J. G. Darwin, 'The Fear of Falling: British Politics and Imperial Decline since 1990', *TRHS* (1986), pp. 39–41.

20. A. Lester, *Imperial Networks and the Cape Eastern Frontier* (2001). See also John Darwin's perceptive review in *JSAS* (2003), pp. 316–17. For a study of such interactions and exchanges see A. S. Thompson, 'Imperial Propaganda during the South African War' in G. Cuthbertson, A. Grundlingh and M.-L. Suttie (eds), *Writing a Wider War: Rethinking Gender, Race and Identity in the South African War, 1899–1902* (Ohio, 2002), pp. 303–28.

21. Taylor, 'The 1848 Revolutions', p. 179.

22. Hall, *Civilising Subjects*, p. 424.

23. *Birmingham Daily Post*, 19/1/1865, quoted in Hall, 'Rethinking Imperial Histories', p. 15.

24. R. Knight, *Illiberal Liberal* (Melbourne, 1966), p. 213.

25. R. Lowe, *Speeches and Letters on Reform* (1867), p. 88.

26. E. Van Heyningen, 'The Voices of Women in the South African War', *SAHJ* (1999), p. 29.

27. L. N. Mayhall, 'The South African War and the Origins of Suffrage Militancy in Britain, 1899–1902' in Fletcher *et al.* (eds), *Women's Suffrage in the British Empire*, pp. 3–17.

[306]   28.   Thompson, 'Imperial Propaganda during the South African War', pp. 303–28.

29.   Mayall, 'The South African War', p. 9.

30.   J. Bush, *Edwardian Ladies and Imperial Power* (Leicester, 2000), p. 185.

31.   B. Caine, 'Vida Goldstein and the English Militant Campaign', *WHR* (1993), pp. 365–6.

32.   *Votes For Women*, 29/12/1911.

33.   A. Woollacott, 'Australian Women's Metropolitan Activism: From Suffrage, to Imperial Vanguard, to Commonwealth Feminism' in Fletcher *et al.* (eds), *Women's Suffrage in the British Empire*, pp. 207–23.

34.   J. Kendle, *Federal Britain: A History* (1997), pp. ix–xiii.

35.   N. Mansergh, *The Commonwealth Experience* (1969), p. 24; H. C. G. Matthew, *Gladstone, 1875–98* (Oxford, 1995), pp. 216, 225, 227.

36.   Ibid., p. 250.

37.   D. M. Schreuder, 'The Role of Morley and Knaplund' in B. L. Kinzer (ed.), *The Gladstonian Turn of Mind: Essays Presented to J. B. Conacher* (Toronto, 1985), p. 229.

38.   J. Morley, *The Life of William Ewart Gladstone* (1903), Vol. III, p. 317.

39.   Mr Gladstone to Queen Victoria, 13/2/1882 in P. Guedalla, *The Queen and Mr Gladstone, 1880–1898* (1933), pp. 176–8.

40.   Kendle, *Federal Britain*, pp. 170–6.

41.   J. A. Hobson, *Imperialism: A Study* (1938 edn), p. 151.

42.   M. Bryant (ed.), *The Complete Colonel Blimp* (1991).

43.   Harris, *Private Lives, Public Spirit*, p. 6.

44.   G. Hueman, 'The British West Indies', Vol. 3 *OHBE*, pp. 486–7; D. Judd, *Empire: The British Imperial Experience, from 1765 to the Present* (1996), pp. 82–3.

45.   For public reaction to the event, see C. Bolt, *Victorian Attitudes to Race* (1971), pp. 82–108; B. Semmel, *The Governor Eyre Controversy* (1962), chs 1, 3, 4, 6; G. B. Workman, *The Reactions of Nineteenth-Century English Literary Men to the Governor Eyre Controversy*, University of Leeds Ph.D. (1973).

46.   Bolt, *Victorian Attitudes*, pp. 102–6; Hall, *Civilising Subjects*, pp. 25, 424; D. A. Lorimer, *Colour, Class and the Victorians: English Attitudes to the Negro in the Mid-Nineteenth Century* (Leicester, 1978), pp. 12, 200.

47.   G. Dutton, *The Hero as Murderer* (1967), p. 390.

48.   N. Ferguson, *Empire: How Britain Made the Modern World* (2003), p. 195.

49.   M. Taylor, 'Imperium et Libertas? Rethinking the Radical Critique of Imperialism during the Nineteenth Century', *JICH* (1991), pp. 1–18.

50. C. Kaul, 'England and India: The Ilbert Bill, 1883: A Case Study of the Metropolitan Press', *Indian Economic and Social History Review* (1993), pp. 413–36.

51. S. Gopal, *The Viceroyalty of Lord Ripon, 1880–1884* (Oxford, 1953), pp. 151–2.

52. Although the distinction between Indian and English district magistrates and session judges was abolished, the difficulty of empanelling such a jury, and the costs and delays of transferring cases to the high courts, made it very difficult to secure a conviction.

53. A. Denholm, *Lord Ripon, 1827–1909: A Political Biography* (1982), p. 156; J. L. Sturgis, *John Bright and the Empire* (1969), pp. 74–5.

54. There was a single NUCCA pamphlet issued on the Ilbert Bill (*Lord Ripon's Policy in India*, 1883), while the party's campaign guide described the bill as a 'misguided' but nevertheless 'innocuous' measure: NUCCA *Campaign Guide* (1885), p. 18.

55. L. Wolf, *Life of the First Marquess of Ripon*, Vol. II (1921), pp. 128, 141. Atkins also asked the Secretary of the TUC for support, but was again rebuffed: Gopal, *The Viceroyalty of Lord Ripon*, p. 155.

56. Gopal, *The Viceroyalty of Lord Ripon*, pp. 136–7, 150–1, 153–4; Kaul, 'England and India', p. 418.

57. C. Hobhouse, 'Plain Facts in India Policy', *Macmillan's Magazine* (Oct. 1883), pp. 465–73. See also W. Summer, 'Mr Ilbert's Bill', *British Quarterly Review* (Oct. 1883), pp. 432–41.

58. 'India and Our Colonial Empire', *Westminster Review* (Apr. 1883), pp. 610–14.

59. J. Goldsmid, 'Questions of the Day in India', *Nineteenth Century* (May 1883), pp. 740–58.

60. For Dyer's supporters, see D. Sayer, 'British Reaction to the Amritsar Massacre, 1919–20', *P&P* (1991), pp. 149–50, 157–63.

61. K. Morgan, *Consensus and Disunity: The Lloyd George Coalition Government, 1918–22* (Oxford, 1979), ch. 10; Thompson, *Imperial Britain*, pp. 163–5.

62. G. Studdart-Kennedy, 'The Christian Imperialism of the Diehard Defenders of the Raj, 1926–35', *JICH* (1990), pp. 342–35.

63. Sir W. Sutherland to D. Lloyd George, 9/7/1920 in M. Gilbert (ed.), *Winston S. Churchill*, Vol. IV [Companion, Part 2, Documents] (1977), pp. 1140–1.

64. 'Unionist Revolt', *Manchester Guardian*, 9/7/1920, pp. 6–7.

65. H. Fein, *Imperial Crime and Punishment: The Massacre at Jallianwala Bagh and British Judgement, 1919–1920* (Honolulu, 1977), pp. 138–44. Most of Fleet Street remained critical of Dyer: see, especially, C. Kaul, *Reporting the Raj: The British Press and India, c. 1880–1932* (Manchester, 2003), pp. 212–13, 220–1.

[308]   66. J. Lawrence, 'Forging a Peaceable Kingdom: War, Violence and the Fear of Brutalisation in Post First World War Britain', *JMH* (forthcoming).

67. J. W. Cell, 'Colonial Rule', Vol. 4 *OHBE*, pp. 233–4.

68. Morley to Minto, 8/1/1908 and 3/9/1908, quoted in Thompson, *Thesis*, p. 168.

69. W. Nimocks, *Milner's Young Men: The Kindergarten in Edwardian Imperial Affairs* (1970), p. ix.

70. Several of these apostles of appeasement started out their careers as protégés of Milner – Brand, Curtis, Dawson, and Kerr. See N. Rose, *The Cliveden Set: Portrait of an Exclusive Fraternity* (2000).

71. Nimocks, *Milner's Young Men*, pp. viii–ix.

72. See, especially, S. Dubow, 'Imagining the New South Africa in the Era of Reconstruction' in Omissi and Thompson (eds), *The Impact of the South African War*, pp. 76–98 and 'Colonial Nationalism, the Milner Kindergarten and the Rise of "South Africanism", 1902–10', *HWJ* (1997).

73. A. S. Thompson, 'The Languages of Loyalism in Southern Africa, c. 1870–1939', *EHR* (2003), pp. 679–80.

74. C. Dewey, *Anglo-Indian Attitudes: The Mind of the Indian Civil Service* (1993), pp. 10–14, 262.

75. See, for example, Jose Harris's description of the district judge, Henry Beveridge, in her biography, *William Beveridge* (Oxford, 1977), pp. 7–11.

76. For the BCINC, see M. Morrow, *The Origins and Early Years of the BCINC, 1885–1907*, University of London Ph.D. (1977); Thompson, *Thesis*, chs 2, 5.

77. For the IPC and this episode, see Thompson, *Thesis*, pp. 162–7.

78. See, especially, J. Vernon, *Politics and the People: A Study in English Political Culture, c. 1815–67* (Cambridge, 1993), pp. 6–7, 103–4, 182; T. A. Jenkins, *Parliament, Party and Politics in Victorian Britain* (Manchester, 1996), pp. 11–26; and P. J. Waller, *Democracy and Sectarianism: A Political and Social History of Liverpool, 1868–1939* (Liverpool, 1981), pp. 48–52.

79. Thompson, *Imperial Britain*, ch. 2.

80. A. Chisholm and M. Davie, *Beaverbrook: A Life* (1993, Pimlico edn), pp. 275–81, 293–5.

81. For German women's active participation in imperialism, see L. Wildenthal, *German Women for Empire, 1884–1945* (Durham, 2001).

82. Bush, *Edwardian Ladies*; G. E. Maguire, *Conservative Women: A History of Women and the Conservative Party, 1874–1997* (Oxford, 1998), pp. 49–57; E. Reidi, *Imperialist Women in Edwardian Britain: The Victoria League, 1899–1914*, University of St Andrews Ph.D. (1998) and 'Women, Gender, and the Promotion of Empire: The Victoria League, 1901–14', *HJ* (2002), pp. 569–99; Thompson, *Imperial Britain*, pp. 55–8, 142–6.

83. P. Gordon, *Politics and Society: The Journals of Lady Knightley of Fawsley, 1885–1913* (Northampton, 1999), pp. 11–43.

84. See, for example, the attraction of eugenics to feminist women: Lucy Bland, *Banishing the Beast: English Feminism and Sexual Morality, 1885–1914* (1995), pp. 229–47.

85. A. Burton, *Burdens of History: British Feminists, Indian Women and Imperial Culture, 1865–1914* (Chapel Hill, 1994); V. Ware, *Beyond the Pale: White Women, Racism and History* (1992), pp. 119–66.

86. B. Ramusack, 'Catalysts or Helpers? British Feminists, Indian Women's Rights, and Indian Independence' in G. Minault (ed.), *The Extended Family: Women and Political Participation in India and Pakistan* (Delhi, 1981), pp. 109–50.

87. S. Koss (ed.), *The Anatomy of an Anti-War Movement: The Pro-Boers* (Chicago, 1973), pp. xxxvi, 207.

88. *The Manchester Guardian*, 9/5/1901 and 10/5/1901.

89. K. Grant, 'Christian Critics of Empire: Missionaries, Lantern Lectures, and the Congo Reform Campaign in Britain', *JICH* (2001), pp. 27–58.

90. B. Bush, '"Britain's conscience on Africa": White Women, Race and Imperial Politics in Inter-War Britain' in C. Midgley (ed.), *Gender and Imperialism* (Manchester, 1998), pp. 200–23.

91. E. Morton, *Women Behind Mahatma Gandhi* (1954). See also J. Liddington on Mrs Despard, *The Life and Times of a Respectable Rebel: Selina Cooper, 1864–1946* (1984), pp. 151–2.

92. J. Hannam and K. Hunt, *Socialist Women: Britain 1880s to 1920s* (2002), pp. 179–80, 190–4.

93. Bush, '"Britain's conscience on Africa"', pp. 218–20.

94. Hobson, *Imperialism*, p. 141.

95. See, for example, the discussion of the origins of the 1870 Education Act in Ch. 5, p. 112.

96. The increasing interest has been explained in terms of the evolution of British attitudes toward the state; the softening of Australian views on social policy; and the advent of Australian Federation: see, C. D. W. Goodwin, *The Image of Australia: British Perception of the Australian Economy from the Eighteenth to the Twentieth Century* (Durham, NC, 1974), pp. 209–14.

97. Quoted in K. Sinclair, *William Pember Reeves* (Oxford, 1966), p. 212.

98. D. Hamer, 'Centralisation and Nationalism (1891–1912)' in K. Sinclair (ed.), *The Oxford Illustrated History of New Zealand* (2nd edn, 1996).

99. D. Denoon and P. Mein-Smith, with M. Wyndham, *A History of Australia, New Zealand and the Pacific* (Oxford, 2000), p. 235.

100. D. Bythell, 'The Working Man's Paradise? Myth and Reality in Australian History, 1850–1914', *Durham University Journal* 81 (1988–9), pp. 4–11.

[310]   101.   J. Rickard, 'The Anti-Sweating Movement in Britain and Victoria: The Politics of Empire and Social Reform', *Historical Studies* (1978–9), pp. 582–97 [quote from p. 594].

102.   See pp. 66–74 above. See also J. D. B. Miller, *Britain and the Old Dominions* (1966), p. 43.

103.   This was equally true of the Canadian labour movement: see A. Ross McCormack, 'British Working-Class Immigrants and Canadian Radicalism: The Case of Arthur Puttee', *Canadian Ethnic Studies* (1978), pp. 22–37.

104.   Donovan, 'Australia and the Great London Dock Strike', p. 24; Glover, 'Australian Unions', p. 14; R. B. Walker, 'Media and Money: The London Dock Strike of 1889 and the Australian Maritime Strike of 1890', *Labour History* (1981), p. 45.

105.   Harrison, *The Transformation of British Politics*, p. 69.

106.   A. G. Austin (ed.), *The Webbs' Australian Diary, 1898* (Melbourne, 1965), pp. 113–15.

107.   Ibid., pp. 15–16; D. A. Hamer, *The Webbs in New Zealand, 1898: Beatrice Webb's Diary with Entries by Sidney Webb* (Wellington, 1974 edn), p. 10.

108.   R. J. Harrison, *The Life and Times of Sidney and Beatrice Webb, 1858–1905: The Formative Years* (Basingstoke, 1999), pp. 315–17, 333.

109.   Harrison, *The Transformation of British Politics*, pp. 69–82.

110.   B. Tillett, *Memories and Reflections* (1931), p. 210.

111.   Bythell, 'The Working Man's Paradise?', pp. 9, 12.

112.   G. Parker to C. Shorter, 27/7/1898 and 19/11/1901, Gilbert Parker papers, Special Collections, Brotherton Library, University of Leeds. See also his obituary in *The Times*, 7/9/1932, p. 14. For the novels, see *Donovan Pasha* (1902), *The Weavers* (1907), *Northern Lights* (1909) and *The Judgement House* (1913). Parker claimed that each of these made him £20,000.

113.   Chisholm and Davie, *Beaverbrook*, pp. 16, 70–1, 279.

114.   R. J. Q. Adams, *Bonar Law* (1999), p. 26.

115.   J. Stapleton, 'Political Thought and National Identity in Britain, 1850–1950' in S. Collini *et al.* (eds), *History, Religion and Culture: British Intellectual History, 1750–1950* (Cambridge, 2000), p. 249.

116.   S. Howe, *Anti-Colonialism in British Politics: The Left and the End of Empire, 1918–64* (Oxford, 1993), p. 48.

117.   D. Steele, *Lord Salisbury: A Political Biography* (1999), pp. 15–18.

118.   M. Campbell, 'John Redmond and the Irish National League in Australia and New Zealand', *History* (2001), pp. 348–62.

119.   Thompson, *Thesis*, pp. 148–9.

120.   Muir was the first holder of Manchester University's newly-created chair of Modern History (1914–21) and became an important figure in the

inter-war Liberal party. See R. Grayson, *Liberal, International Relations and Appeasement: The Liberal Party, 1919–39* (2001), pp. 42–3. [311]

121. B. Pimlott, *Harold Wilson* (1992), pp. 18–20.

122. I am grateful to Patrick Higgins for sharing his thoughts on Rab's involvement with the empire.

123. P. Williamson, *Stanley Baldwin: Conservative Leadership and National Values* (Cambridge, 1999), pp. 260, 265, 272.

124. F. M. Leventhal, *The Last Dissenter: H. N. Brailsford and His World* (Oxford, 1985), pp. 217–21.

125. R. L. Ashcroft, *Haileybury, 1908–61* (1961), pp. 181–3, 200–1.

126. T. Burridge, *Clement Attlee: A Political Biography* (1985), p. 14.

127. C. Attlee, *Empire into Commonwealth* (1961), pp. 5–6.

128. J. G. Darwin, 'A World University' in B. Harrison (ed.), *The History of the University of Oxford*, Vol. VIII (Oxford, 1994), pp. 609–10, 621.

129. It included Amery, Dawson, Malcolm, Brand and Curtis. Only Amery entered parliament. See A. L. Rowse, *All Souls in My Time* (1993), pp. 78, 83–7; W. R. Louis, *In the Name of God, Go! Leo Amery and the British Empire in the Age of Churchill* (New York, 1992), pp. 38, 40.

130. A. Gambles, *Protection and Politics: Conservative Economic Discourse, 1815–52* (Woodbridge, Suffolk, 1999), pp. 148–50, 174–5, 197–9; R. Price, *British Society, 1680–1880: Dynamism, Containment and Change* (Cambridge, 1999), pp. 62–4.

131. L. J. Butler, 'Reconstruction, Development and the Entrepreneurial State: The British Colonial Model, 1939–51', *CBH* (1999), p. 30; J. Callaghan, 'In Search of Eldorado: Labour's Colonial Economic Policy' in J. Fyrth (ed.), *Labour's High Noon: The Government and the Economy 1945–51* (1993), pp. 115–34.

132. K. Morgan, 'The Rise and Fall of Public Ownership in Britain' in Bean (ed.), *The Political Culture of Modern Britain*, pp. 294–5.

133. For the variety of forms of collectivism that emerged during the period 1880–1930, and their different connections to imperialism, see M. Langan and B. Schwarz (eds), *Crises in the British State, 1880–1930* (1985), pp. 7–8, 21–5.

134. D. Marquand, 'How United is the Modern United Kingdom?' in A. Grant and K. J. Stringer (eds), *Uniting the Kingdom? The Making of British History* (1995), pp. 286–8.

135. Quoted in Jones, *Victorian Political Thought*, p. 58.

136. Quoted in Thompson, *Imperial Britain*, p. 18.

137. My discussion of Stapleton draws on Professor David Howell's excellent entry on Stapleton for the *New Dictionary of National Biography* (Oxford, 2004).

138. Mehta, *Liberalism and Empire*, pp. 30–2, 99, 105–6, 111–12, 198–9.

139. E. P. Sullivan, 'Liberalism and Imperialism: J. S. Mill's Defence of the British Empire', *Journal of the History of Ideas* (1983), pp. 615–16.

140. L. Zastoupil, *John Stuart Mill and India* (Stanford, 1994), pp. 183–91.

141. A. Vincent and R. Plant, *Philosophy, Politics and Citizenship: The Life and Thought of the British Idealists* (Oxford, 1984), p. 90.

142. A view shared by Liberals of varying philosophical outlooks: see D. Boucher and A. Vincent, *A Radical Hegelian: The Political and Social Philosophy of Henry Jones* (Cardiff, 1993), pp. 148, 152–3.

143. Green, *The Crisis of Conservatism*, p. 182; Thompson, 'The Languages of Imperialism', pp. 156–8.

144. O. Mosley, *My Life* (1968), p. 91.

145. Ibid., pp. 168, 186, 248, 254; R. Skidelsky, *Oswald Mosley* (1975), p. 229.

146. There was a group of 19 MPs who voted for imperial preference in June 1925, though some of these were not fully-fledged protectionists and would not have endorsed all of Mosley's views. See Howe, *Anti-Colonialism in British Politics*, p. 50.

147. M. Daunton, *Trusting Leviathan: The Politics of Taxation in Britain, 1799–1914* (Cambridge, 2001), pp. 30, 124, 135, 239, 311, 314, 332.

148. Cain, 'The Economic Philosophy of Constructive Imperialism', pp. 47–8, 54–5; Green, *The Crisis of Conservatism*, pp. 165–6, 171.

149. Leo Amery quoted in Thompson, *Imperial Britain*, p. 87.

150. Thompson, *Imperial Britain*, p. 25; E. H. H. Green, 'The Political Economy of Empire, 1880–1914', Vol. 3 *OHBE*, pp. 349–50.

151. Green, *The Crisis of Conservatism*, p. 180.

152. For some acute reflections on the relationship between imperial politics and public opinion see J. G. Darwin, *The End of the British Empire: The Historical Debate* (Oxford, 1991), pp. 18–24.

Chapter 7 Metropolitan Economics

1. B. R. Tomlinson, 'The British Economy and the Empire' in C. Wrigley (ed.), *A Companion to Early Twentieth-Century Britain* (Oxford, 2003), pp. 200–1.

2. S. Constantine, 'Migrants and Settlers', Vol. 4 *OHBE*, p. 181.

3. A. Offer, *The First World War: An Agrarian Interpretation* (Oxford, 1989), pp. 130–4, 'The British Empire, 1870–1914: A Waste of Money?', *EcHR* (1993), pp. 233–4 and 'Costs and Benefits, Prosperity, and Security, 1870–1914', Vol. 3 *OHBE*, pp. 696–7.

4. M. Harper, 'British Migration and the Peopling of the Empire', Vol. 3 *OHBE*, [313] p. 86.

5. Bridge and Fedorowich, 'Mapping the British World', p. 3; Constantine, 'British Emigration to the Empire-Commonwealth', pp. 17, 19–20, 23. This, however, is not an uncontested view. For the argument that migrants to Canada were more concerned about raising their standard of living than living under the Union Jack, see A. G. Green, M. Mackinnon and C. Minns, 'Dominion or Republic? Migrants to North America from the United Kingdom, 1870–1910', *EcHR* (2002), pp. 666–96.

6. Constantine, 'Migrants and Settlers', pp. 172, 175.

7. Ibid., pp. 166–7.

8. Bridge and Fedorowich, 'Mapping the British World', p. 4.

9. Constantine, 'Migrants and Settlers', p. 167: Table 7.4.

10. Haines, *Emigration and the Labouring Poor*, p. 22.

11. K. Cardell, C. Cumming, P. Griffiths and B. Jones, 'Welsh Identity on the Victorian Goldfields in the Nineteenth Century' in K. Cardell and C. Cumming (eds), *A World Turned Upside Down: Cultural Change on Victoria's Goldfields, 1851–2001* (Canberra, 2001), pp. 25–60.

12. Constantine, 'Migrants and Settlers', pp. 171–2.

13. Offer, *The First World War*, p. 134.

14. J. McAloon, *No Idle Rich: The Wealthy in Canterbury and Otago, 1840–1914* (Dunedin, 2002), pp. 172–4.

15. Offer, *The First World War*, p. 315. For a powerful evocation of the egalitarian mood of Australia in the early twentieth century, see D. H. Lawrence, *Kangaroo* (first published 1923; 1966 reprint), esp. pp. 16–18: 'nobody felt *better* than anybody else, or higher; only *better off*'; 'it was a granted condition of Australia, that Demos was his own master'; 'in Australia authority was a dead letter. There was no giving of orders here; or, if orders were given, they would not be received as such.'

16. Bridge and Fedorowich, 'Mapping the British World', pp. 5–6.

17. Other studies place greater emphasis on the sense of uncertainty and social dislocation suffered especially by first-generation migrants, and on the fact that there was not always an obvious gain in the standard of living: see, in particular, Fairburn, *An Ideal Society and its Enemies*, pp. 192–3 and chs 7–9 and Belich, *Making Peoples*, pp. 339–40, 379–81, 388–91. These different interpretations may be taken to reinforce my broader point about the indeterminate economic impact of empire migration.

18. Charles Feinstein's brave effort to quantify remittances to the UK probably underestimates the sums involved: *National Income, Expenditure and Output of the United Kingdom, 1855–1965* (Cambridge, 1972), pp. 113, 124–7 and Table 37.

[314]   19. My survey is based on research in the Post Office Archives. For a fuller treatment of the subject, see G. Magee and A. S. Thompson, '"Lines of credit, debts of obligation": Migrant Remittances to Britain, c. 1875–1914' (forthcoming).

20. H. Robinson, *The British Post Office: A History* (Princeton, 1948), pp. 149–50; M. J. Daunton, *Royal Mail: The Post Office since 1840* (1985), p. 84; C. R. Perry, *The Victorian Post Office: The Growth of a Bureaucracy* (Woodbridge, 1992), p. 16.

21. The Army Post Office sent money home from the soldiers, and it later agreed to issue orders to civilians at inland rates. After the war, the system was extended to Malta and Gibraltar, though orders could only be sent homeward.

22. Robinson, *The British Post Office*, p. 405.

23. *Annual Reports of the Money Orders Office* (1899–1903 and 1904–8), Post Office Archives, Post 27 (80–1).

24. *PMG 19th Annual Report* (1873), p. 11. British Central Africa and Southern Rhodesia joined the money order system in 1901.

25. L. Stephen, *Life of Henry Fawcett* (1885), pp. 427–9.

26. British postal orders were issued for every complete sixpence from 6d. up to 20s. and also for 21s. The sender could increase the value by an amount not exceeding 5d. by affixing postal stamps not exceeding three in number to the face of the order. The colonies could use their own stamps to do this.

27. Robinson, *The British Post Office*, p. 405.

28. 'Imperial Postal Order Service: Heads of Arrangement, 11/7/1904' and 'Report on the Imperial Postal Order Scheme Two Years After Its Commencement', Post Office Archives, Post 27 (131).

29. *PMG 18th Annual Report* (1872), p. 15.

30. This sum was equivalent to a fifth of total customs revenue collected during this period.

31. *PMG Annual Report* (1913–14), p. 8.

32. There is also the issue of Egypt's classification as a 'foreign country'. Egypt was 'temporarily occupied' by Britain in 1882. However, many Commonwealth-Imperial historians write about Egypt as though it was effectively part of the British empire at this time. Egypt remitted £1,039,869 to the UK from 1900 to 10.

33. For the distribution of British investment across the empire, and how it varied over time, see L. E. Davis and R. E. Gallman, *Evolving Financial Markets and International Capital Flows: Britain, the Americas, and Australia, 1865–1914* (Cambridge, 2001), p. 59.

34. Though Michael Edelstein claims that as much as 40% of the 1850–75 surge in overseas investment went to the British empire, with Australia and

India as major recipients: *Overseas Investment in the Age of High Imperialism: The*
United Kingdom, 1850–1914 (1982), p. 291.

35. Hoppen, *The Mid-Victorian Generation*, pp. 298–304. For the lack of domestic demand (especially from the 1890s), see Edelstein, *Overseas Investment in the Age of High Imperialism*, pp. 299–302, 304, 306–9. I am, of course, aware that the debate on this issue is still raging, but for works that support my position, see F. Capie and M. Collins, *Have the Banks Failed British Industry? A Historical Survey of Bank/Industry Relations in Britain, 1870–1990* (1992) and P. L. Cottrell, *Industrial Finance, 1830–1914: The Finance and Organisation of English Manufacturing Industry* (1980), ch. 7.

36. M. Dintenfass, *The Decline of Industrial Britain, 1870–1980* (1992), pp. 43–5.

37. I am grateful to Professor Mike Collins for his advice on this subject, and for providing me with a copy of M. Collins and M. Baker, 'The Durability of Transaction Banking Practices in the Provision of Finance to the Business Sector by British Banks', *Entreprises et Histoire* (1999), pp. 78–92.

38. For the factors that prompted direct investment, see G. Jones (ed.), *British Multinationals: Origins, Management and Performance* (Aldershot, 1986), Table 1.1, p. 8.

39. The shift from foreign to imperial lending during the inter-war years focused on government rather than private company issues: see J. M. Aitken, *British Overseas Investment, 1918–31* (New York, 1977), p. 161.

40. Ibid., pp. ii–iii, 109, 266–7, 272, 278.

41. B. Waites, *Europe and the Third World: From Colonisation to Decolonisation, c. 1500–1998* (Basingstoke, 1999), p. 240.

42. Proprietorships, partnerships, private companies and mercantile groups are all excluded from Davis and Huttenback's sample.

43. According to Edelstein, domestic stocks were at least as good if not a better bet from 1870 to 1876 and from 1887 to 1896.

44. Cain and Hopkins, *British Imperialism*, p. 168.

45. Investment in Asia surged in the 1860s (accounting for almost a quarter of total overseas investment) and the majority of this finance was directed to Indian railways. Only one country – the USA – had more listed railway securities than India. See also the Colonial Stock Act (1900) under which the colonies were able to issue loan stock with trustee status – tantamount to an imperial guarantee: Havinden and Meredith, *Colonialism and Development*, p. 88.

46. It is estimated that, as a result of the railway guarantee system, Rs 568 million was paid out of Indian tax revenues to British investors in subsidies from 1849–1900: see J. M. Hurd, 'Railways' in D. Kumar (ed.), *The Cambridge Economic History of India, Vol. 2: c. 1757–1970* (Cambridge, 1983), p. 743.

[316]   47. Macpherson, 'Investment in Indian Railways, 1845–75', *EHR* (1955), p. 181. See also D. Thorner, *Investment in Empire: British Railway and Steam Shipping Enterprise in India, 1825–49* (Philadelphia, 1950), chs 6–7.

48. I am grateful to Simon Potter for drawing this to my attention. Davis and Gallman emphasise the willingness of investors in the 'frontier' economies of Australia, Canada, Argentina and the USA to tolerate higher levels of risk or uncertainty, arising partly from the greater variations in return on investments in these regions: see *Evolving Financial Markets*, esp. pp. 232–3.

49. For speculative investment see J. F. Gilpin, *The Poor Relation has Come into Her Fortune: The British Investment Boom in Canada, 1905–15*, Canada House Lecture Series, No. 53 (Leeds, 1992); R. C. Michie, 'Options, Concessions, Syndicates, and the Provision of Venture Capital, 1880–1913', *Business History* (1981), pp. 156–7. It should, however, be acknowledged that the geographical distribution of investment trusts, many of which, in their initial phase, were speculative, and some of which were downright fraudulent, was more heavily weighted to the USA and Latin America than it was to the British empire: see Y. Cassis, 'The Emergence of a New Financial Institution: Investment Trusts in Britain, 1870–1939' in J. J. Van Helten and Y. Cassis (eds), *Capitalism in a Mature Economy. Financial Institutions, Capital Exports and British Industry, 1870–1939* (Aldershot, 1990), pp. 145–7. Moreover, as regards Canada, British investors tended to minimise risk by buying existing mineral claims and developed properties rather than engaging in exploration – this was more frequently undertaken by Canadian and American companies: see D. G. Paterson, *British Direct Investment in Canada, 1890–1914* (Toronto, 1976), pp. 96–9.

50. R. Michie, 'The Social Web of Investment in the Nineteenth Century', *Revue Internationale d'histoire de la banque* (1979), pp. 158–75. I am grateful to Professor Michie for supplying me with a copy of this essay.

51. For the South African mining boom, see D. Kynaston, *The City of London. Vol. II: Golden Years, 1890–1914* (1995), pp. 109–25. For the 'Kaffir Circus' beyond London, see W. A. Thomas, *The Provincial Stock Exchanges* (1973), pp. 189–90, 311.

52. For the sharp business practices that were involved, see I. Phimister, 'Corners and Company-Mongering: Nigerian Tin and the City of London, 1909–12', *JICH* (2000), pp. 23–4, 38–9.

53. I. Phimister, 'Mining, Engineers and Risk Management: British Overseas Investment, 1894–1914', (forthcoming).

54. Paterson, *British Investment in Canada*, p. 102.

55. R. Kubicek, 'Economic Power at the Periphery: Canada, Australia and South Africa, 1850–1914' in R. E. Dumett (ed.), *Gentlemanly Capitalism and British Imperialism: The New Debate on Empire* (Harlow, 1999), p. 119.

56. My information on Cornwell came from: 'Interview with Miss Alice Cornwell', *Women's Penny Paper*, 19/10/1899, No. 52, Vol. I, pp. 1–2;

P. Mansfield, 'Midas and the Pope' and 'Downtrodden, yes – downhearted,   [317]
no' in the *Ballarat Courier*, 12/3/1987 and 19/9/1997; correspondence from the Premier's Department, Tasmanian Archives, PD1/43/286;
F. W. Niven and Co., *Guide to Ballarat* (Ballarat, 1890), p. 12. I am grateful
to Mrs H. M. Lay for supplying the essays from the Australian press, to
Dr Glyn Roberts for sharing the material from the Tasmanian Archives,
and to Dr William Jones for supplying the reference to the Midas mine.

57. A. K. Cairncross, 'Investment in Canada, 1900–13' in A. R. Hall (ed.), *The Export of Capital from Britain, 1870–1914* (1968), pp. 159–60, 167. Indus-trial ventures in Canada were risky too: all five of the Canadian companies created by British funds between 1901 and 1905 were in liquidation by 1910, though in general Canadian industrial stocks found less favour on the London market.

58. Quoted in A. Offer, 'Empire and Social Reform: British Overseas Invest-ment and Domestic Politics, 1908–14', *IIJ* (1983), pp. 123–4.

59. Potter, *Nationalism, Imperialism and the Press in Britain and the Dominions*, p. 43.

60. Cain and Hopkins, *British Imperialism*, p. 172.

61. For Barclays, see J. Crossley and J. Blandford, *The DCO Story: A History of Banking in Many Countries, 1925–71* (1975); M. Ackrill and L. Hannah, *Barclays: The Business of Banking, 1690–1996* (Cambridge, 2000); and the entry on F. C. Goodenough by P. E. Smart in the *Dictionary of Business Biography*, Vol. 2, pp. 603–6. For Standard Life, see M. Moss, *Standard Life, 1825–2000: The Building of Europe's Largest Mutual Life Company* (Edinburgh, 2000) and J. H. Treble, 'The Pattern of Investment of the Standard Life Assurance Company, 1875–1914', *Business History* (1980), pp. 170–87.

62. A. Baster, *The Imperial Banks* (1929), p. 235.

63. The new company was dissolved in 1866, its activities having been taken over by Standard Life.

64. Atkin, *British Overseas Investment*, p. 120; A. R. Hall, *The London Capital Market and Australia* (1963), pp. 53–4; Treble, 'The Pattern of Investment of the Standard Life Assurance Company', Tables I and II. For a comparison, see B. Supple, *The Royal Exchange Assurance: A History of British Insurance, 1720–1970* (Cambridge, 1970), p. 346: by 1907, 34% of the Company's port-folio of Stock Exchange securities were held in the UK, 25% in the USA, 20% in the Empire, 9% in Europe and 5% in Argentina.

65. After the First World War, Canada continued to be Standard Life's most im-portant overseas market, accounting for some 30% of all new sums assured.

66. A. N. Porter, 'London and the British Empire, *c.* 1815–1914' in H. Diederiks and D. Reeder (eds), *Cities of Finance* (Amsterdam, 1996), pp. 53–68. I am grateful to Professor Porter for supplying me with a copy of his excellent essay.

67. P. T. Marsh, *Bargaining on Europe: Britain and the First Common Market, 1860–1892* (New Haven, 1999), pp. 5–7, 209.

[318]   68.   F. Crouzet, 'Trade and Empire: The British Experience from the Establishment of Free Trade until the First World War' in B. M. Ratcliffe (ed.), *Great Britain and Her World, 1750–1914* (Manchester, 1975), pp. 209–35 [quote from p. 223].

69.   D. K. Fieldhouse, 'The Metropolitan Economics of Empire', in Vol. 4 *OHBE*, pp. 90–1; T. Rooth, *British Protectionism and the International Economy: Overseas Commercial Policy in the 1930s* (Cambridge, 1993), p. 83.

70.   K. Tsokhas, *Markets, Money and Empire: The Political Economy of the Australian Wool Industry* (Carlton, Victoria, 1990), pp. 89–104.

71.   Rooth, *British Protectionism*, pp. 84, 95–9, 317–19; Tomlinson, 'The British Economy', pp. 203–4.

72.   Cain and Hopkins, *British Imperialism*, pp. 174–8.

73.   For the complexities, and some tentative conclusions, see S. Pollard, 'Capital Exports, 1870–1914: Harmful or Beneficial?', *EcHR* (1985), pp. 512–14 and *Britain's Prime and Britain's Decline: The British Economy, 1870–1914* (1989), ch. 2.

74.   For a fuller treatment, see A. S. Thompson and G. Magee, 'A Soft Touch? British Industry, Empire Markets and the Self-Governing Dominions, 1870–1914', *EcHR* (2003), pp. 689–717. For the inter-war years, see the debate on foreign direct investment and the performance of British multinationals between G. Jones (ed.), *British Multinationals: Origins, Management and Performance* (1986) and S. Nicholas, 'Locational Choice, Performance and the Growth of British Multinational Firms', *Business History* (1989), pp. 122–41. For different versions of the 'soft market' thesis, see the bibliography provided by 'A Soft Touch?' For its attractiveness to a more general readership, see G. Owen, *From Empire to Europe: The Decline and Revival of British Industry Since the Second World War* (1999), esp. pp. 458–60.

75.   W. T. Goodge, *Hits! Skits! And Jingles!* (Singapore, 1972), p. 34.

76.   Thompson and Magee, 'A Soft Touch?', pp. 703–11.

77.   Ibid., pp. 693–700.

78.   For the argument that it did, see M. W. Kirby, *The Decline of British Economic Power Since 1870* (1981), p. 7; P. Mathias, *The First Industrial Nation: An Economic History of Britain, 1700–1914* (1969), pp. 413–15.

79.   Crouzet, 'Trade and Empire', p. 224.

80.   B. Chatterji, *Trade, Tariffs and Empire: Lancashire and British Policy in India, 1919–39* (Delhi, 1992), pp. 60, 112.

81.   S. B. Saul, *Studies in British Overseas Trade, 1870–1914* (1960), p. 198.

82.   German manufacturers entered the market, but only for rush orders when British suppliers were quoting long delivery dates: S. B. Saul, 'The Engineering Industry' in D. H. Aldcroft (ed.), *The Development of British Industry and Foreign Competition, 1875–1814* (1968), p. 199.

83. B. R. Tomlinson, 'British Business in India, 1860–1970' in R. P. T.   [319]
Davenport-Hines and G. Jones (eds), *British Business in Asia since 1860*
(Cambridge, 1989), pp. 107, 111–13; B. R. Tomlinson, *The New Cambridge
History of India, III.3, The Economy of Modern India, 1860–1970* (Cambridge,
1993), pp. 99–100; B. R. Tomlinson, 'Imperial Power and Foreign Trade:
Britain and India, 1900–70' in P. Mathias and J. A. Davis (eds), *The Nature
of Industrialisation. Vol. 5: International Trade and British Economic Growth from
the Eighteenth Century to the Present Day* (Oxford, 1996), pp. 160–2. I am grateful
to Professor Tomlinson for supplying me with a copy of the latter.

84. On the setting of tariffs, see Chatterji, *Trade, Tariffs and Empire*, pp. 206–7,
348–9.

85. Tomlinson, *The New Cambridge History*, pp. 133–4.

86. See, for example, John Brunton, chief resident engineer on the Scinde
railway, who constructed a line from Karachi to Kotri from 1858 to 1862:
John Brunton's Book: Being the Memories of John Brunton (Cambridge, 1939),
pp. 82–3. For the broader point, see J. N. Sahni, *Indian Railways: One
Hundred Years, 1853–1953* (New Delhi, 1953), pp. 90–1.

87. Even in 1931, when the general tariff rate was increased to 25%, railway
plant and rolling stock were exempted and entered on a lower duty of 10%:
B. R. Tomlinson, *The Political Economy of the Raj, 1914–47: The Economics of
Decolonisation* (1979), p. 62.

88. Hurd, 'Railways', p. 749; F. Lehmann, 'Great Britain and the Supply of
Railway Locomotives of India: A Case Study of "economic imperialism"',
Indian Economic and Social History Review (1965), pp. 301–2; J. N. Westwood,
Railways of India (1974), p. 173.

89. A. G. Clow, *The State and Industry: A Narrative of Indian Government Policy and
Action in Relation to Industry under the Reformed Constitution* (Calcutta, 1928),
pp. 84–8.

90. Tomlinson, *The New Cambridge Economic History*, pp. 134–5.

91. Clow, *The State and Industry*, pp. 90–1.

92. L. G. Sanberg, *Lancashire in Decline: A Study in Entrepreneurship, Technology and
International Trade* (1974), pp. 165–7; R. E. Tyson, 'The Cotton Industry'
in Aldcroft (ed.), *The Development of British Industry and Foreign Competition*,
p. 111.

93. A. Slaven, 'A Glasgow Firm in the Indian Market: John Lean and Sons, Muslin
Weavers', *Business History* (1969), pp. 496–522.

94. Saul, *Studies in British Overseas Trade*, pp. 198–203.

95. This was the conclusion reached by British officials who looked into the
question of Indian trade: see, especially, the views of Sir Charles Elliott and
Sir Roper Lethbridge examined in Thompson, *Imperial Britain*, pp. 99–100.

96. Tomlinson, 'Imperial Power and Foreign Trade', pp. 155–6.

[320]   97.   D. K. Fieldhouse, *Unilever Overseas: The Anatomy of a Multinational, 1895–1965* (1978), pp. 151–2, 164–5.

98.   L. Carter, *Chronicles of British Business in Asia, 1850–1960* (New Delhi, 2002), pp. 106–8, 169–70, 184–5, 196–7; W. J. Reader, *Metal Box: A History* (1976), pp. 100–4.

99.   Tomlinson, *The New Cambridge History*, pp. 142–3.

100.   R. Kirk and C. Simmons, 'Lancashire and the Equipping of the Indian Cotton Mills: A Study of Textile Machinery Supply, 1854–1939', *Salford Papers in Economics*, 81–6 (1981).

101.   In the case of Platt Brothers of Oldham, India accounted for 15% of foreign sales and 9% of total sales over the period 1873–1913, 23% of total sales 1919–23, and 33% of total sales 1931–9: see Kirk and Simmons, 'Lancashire and the Equipping of the Indian Cotton Mills', pp. 23–4. For Platt Brothers more generally, see D. A. Farnie, 'The Textile Machine-Making Industry and the World Market, 1870–1960', *Business History* (1990), pp. 150–3, 157–61.

102.   It faced only a small duty of 2.5%, rising to 10% in 1931.

103.   Kirk and Simmons, 'Lancashire and the Equipping of the Indian Cotton Mills', p. 22.

104.   Farnie, 'The Textile Machine-Making Industry', pp. 152–3.

105.   C. Barnett, *The Lost Victory: British Dreams, British Realities, 1945–50* (1996), pp. 8–12, 51, 84.

106.   Davis and Huttenback, *Mammon and the Pursuit*, ch. 5.

107.   Pollard, *Britain's Prime and Britain's Decline*, p. 107.

108.   O'Brien, 'The Costs and Benefits', p. 188.

109.   A. G. Hopkins, 'Accounting for the British Empire', *JICH* (1988), p. 239; Offer, 'The British Empire', pp. 222–31. [Quote from Offer, p. 226.]

110.   P. Kennedy, 'The Costs and Benefits of British Imperialism, 1846–1914', *P&P* (1989), pp. 189–91. [Quote from p. 191.]

111.   P. P. O'Brien, 'The Titan Refreshed: Imperial Overstretch and the British Navy Before the First World War', *P&P* (2001), pp. 152–3.

112.   Offer, 'The British Empire', p. 231 and *The First World War*, pp. 217–32.

113.   A. J. Marder, *From the Dreadnought to Scapa Flow: The Royal Navy in the Fisher Era, 1904–19. Vol. 1: The Road to War, 1904–14* (1961), chs 3–4; Thompson, *Imperial Britain*, pp. 112–19; O'Brien, 'The Titan Refreshed', pp. 153–6.

114.   Thompson, *Imperial Britain*, pp. 119–22; O'Brien, 'The Titan Refreshed', pp. 165–7.

115.   Offer, 'The British Empire', p. 229.

116.   Edelstein, 'Imperialism: Cost and Benefit', pp. 215–16.

117.   Offer, 'The British Empire', p. 235.

118. See, for example, Tomlinson, 'Imperial Power and Foreign Trade', p. 162. [321] But for the view that the quantity and quality of information flowing between Britain and its colonies may have been better than that flowing between Britain and foreign countries, and that this conferred certain commercial and financial advantages, see G. Magee and A. Thompson, 'Imperial Globalisation? A Cultural Economy of the British Empire, 1860–1914' (forthcoming). That said, the argument advanced in this paper rejects the idea that the empire was fundamental to Britain's development (for better or worse); indeed it draws many parallels between Britain's economic interaction with its colonies and with the United States.

119. Fieldhouse, 'The Metropolitan Economics of Empire', pp. 89, 111.

120. C. Feinstein, 'The End of Empire and the Golden Age' in P. Clarke and C. Trebilcock (eds), *Understanding Decline: Perceptions and Realities of British Economic Performance* (Cambridge, 1997), p. 232.

121. Apart from the above problems, there is the question of 'informal empire' – where imperial power ends and mere influence begins. If only for sanity's sake, most of the scholars who have written on this subject have confined their analysis to the formal empire, and so have I. Argentina, Brazil and China are thus all treated alongside the USA as independent states.

122. The phrase is taken from Offer, 'Costs and Benefits', p. 708.

Chapter 8 The Forging of British Identities

1. It cannot, of course, be dated precisely, but was given a major impetus by R. Samuel, *Patriotism: The Making and Unmaking of a British National Identity* (1989); H. Kearney, *The British Isles: A History of Four Nations* (Cambridge, 1989); L. Colley, *Britons: Forging the Nation* (1992).

2. T. Nairn, *The Break-Up of Britain* (1977); P. Hitchens, *The Abolition of Britain* (1999); A. Marr, *The Day Britain Died* (2000); and R. Weight, *Patriots: National Identity in Britain, 1940–2000* (Basingstoke, 2002).

3. K. Tidrick, *Empire and the English Character* (1992, 2nd edn).

4. L. Colley, 'Britishness and Otherness: An Argument', *JBS* (1992), pp. 309–29; J. K. Walton, 'Britishness' in C. Wrigley (ed.), *A Companion to Early Twentieth Century Britain* (Oxford, 2003), pp. 518, 522; Weight, *Patriots*, p. 725.

5. J. Ayto, *Twentieth Century Words* (Oxford, 1999), p. iv.

6. M. S. Serjeantson, *A History of Foreign Words in English* (2nd impression, 1961), p. 1; A. W. Ward and A. R. Waller, *The Cambridge History of English Literature* (Cambridge, 1916), p. 459.

7. A 'malingerer'.

8. R. Rankin, *A Subaltern's Letters to His Wife* (1901), p. 108.

[322]

9. A. D. King, *The Bungalow: The Production of a Global Culture* (1984), p. 67.

10. H. Yule and A. C. Burnell, *Hobson-Jobson: The Anglo-Indian Dictionary* (Ware, 1996, Wordsworth edn). For an entertaining commentary, see S. Rushdie, 'Hobson-Jobson' in *Imaginary Homelands: Essays and Criticism, 1981–1991* (1991), pp. 81–3.

11. 'Indian English', *The Times*, 26/7/03, 31/7/03, 2/08/03/, 7/08/03.

12. Nigel Hankin states that the *Concise OED* shows that there are 500 words in English usage connected with the Indian subcontinent, and that the real number may be much greater: see *Hanklyn-Janklin or A Stranger's Rumble-Tumble Guide to Some Words, Customs and Quiddities Indian and Indo-British* (New Delhi, 1992), p. iii. For the borrowing of foreign words from French, Latin, Scandinavian, Greek and Italian, see Serjeantson, *A History*, pp. 223–5; Ward and Waller, *The Cambridge History*, p. 457.

13. I am grateful to Sarah Crellin for sharing her thoughts on Lutyens, Baker and Wheeler, and for the references she supplied. See also her paper, 'Architecture, Artisans and Applied Sculpture' in *Sculpture in Twentieth Century Britain. Vol. 1: Infrastructures, 1925–50*, pp. 88–100.

14. J. Ruskin, *The Seven Lamps of Architecture* (1925 edn), p. 361: 'every form of noble architecture is in some sort the embodiment of the Polity, Life, History and Religious Faith of nations'; N. Pevsner, *A History of Building Types* (1976), pp. 9–10, 289–93.

15. L. Handley-Read, 'Legacy of a Vanished Empire: The Design of the India Office', *Country Life*, 9/7/1970, pp. 110–12.

16. Mackenzie, *Propaganda and Empire*, pp. 122–5; P. Ward-Jackson, *Public Sculpture of the City of London* (Liverpool, 2003), pp. 152–7.

17. M. H. Port, *Imperial London: Civil Government Building in London, 1850–1915* (New Haven, 1995), pp. 21–2; I. Black, 'Rebuilding "The Heart of the Empire": Bank Headquarters in the City of London, 1919–39', *Art History* (1999), pp. 593–618; M. Girouard, *The Victorian Country House* (New Haven, 1990, 4th edn), p. 152; A. Whittick, *European Architecture in the Twentieth Century*, Vol. II (1953), p. 60.

18. A. Byron, *London Statues* (1981), pp. 14–56. They include Major-General Charles Napier (1855), General Henry Havelock (1861), Sir Henry Bartle Frere (1887–8), General Gordon (1888), Alfred Beit (1910), Lord Robert Clive (1917), Field Marshal Earl Roberts (1924), Lord Kitchener (1926), Lord Curzon (1931), Viscount Milner (1931) and the Earl of Meath (1934). It could, of course, be argued that some of these figures were primarily military, and only secondarily imperial.

19. B. Read, *Victorian Sculpture* (New Haven, 1982), pp. 294, 345–7, 352, 365–9.

20. Thompson, 'Publicity, Philanthropy and Commemoration', pp. 113–20. But monuments to Nelson and Wellington proliferated in the early 19th

century: see A. Yarrington, *The Commemoration of the Hero, 1800–64: Monuments to British Victors of the Napoleonic Wars* (1988), pp. 333–6. In the 20th century, there was the Cenotaph, which rapidly became a national shrine to the Commonwealth servicemen who died in its two world wars. How far the absence of Christian symbolism on the monument reflected a desire not to offend India, or Edwin Lutyens's pantheist and theosophist sympathies, is not entirely clear. See A. Gregory, *The Silence of Memory: Armistice Day, 1919–46* (Oxford, 1994), p. 15; E. Homberger, 'The Story of the Cenotaph', *TLS*, 12/11/1976, pp. 1429–30; C. Hussey, *The Life of Sir Edwin Lutyens* (1950), p. 394; D. Lloyd, *Tourism, Pilgrimage and the Commemoration of the Great War in Britain, Australia and Canada, 1919–39*, University of Cambridge Ph.D. (1994), pp. 61ff; J. Winter, *Sites of Memory, Sites of Mourning: The Great War in European Cultural History* (Cambridge, 1995), p. 102.

21. D. Young, 'East-End Street Names and British Imperialism', *The Local Historian* (1992), pp. 84–8; K. Jeffery, 'Introduction' in Jeffery (ed.), *An Irish Empire? Aspects of Ireland and the British Empire* (Manchester, 1996), p. 18.

22. R. Aldrich, 'Putting the Colonies on the Map: Colonial Names in Paris Streets' in T. Chafer and A. Sackur (eds), *Promoting the Colonial Idea: Propaganda and Visions of Empire in France* (Basingstoke, 2002), pp. 211–23 [quote from p. 213].

23. Port, *Imperial London*, p. 274.

24. F. Driver and D. Gilbert, 'Imperial Cities: Overlapping Territories, Intertwined Histories' in Driver and Gilbert (eds), *Imperial Cities: Landscape, Display and Identity* (Manchester, 1999), pp. 3, 6.

25. J. Musgrove (ed.), *Sir Banister Fletcher's History of Architecture* (19th edn, 1987), p. 1096.

26. J. Morris, *Pax Britannica: The Climax of an Empire* (1979, Penguin edn), pp. 454–5.

27. S. Daniels, *Fields of Vision: Landscape, Imagery and National Identity in England and the United States* (Cambridge, 1993), p. 5.

28. P. Conner, *Oriental Architecture in the West* (1979), pp. 121–5.

29. J. Morris, *Stones of Empire: The Buildings of the Raj* (Oxford, 1983), pp. 223–4; T. Metcalf, *An Imperial Vision: Indian Architecture and Britain's Raj* (Oxford, 2002, paperback edn), p. 18.

30. R. Wilson and A. Mackley, *Creating Paradise: The Building of the English Country House, 1660–1880* (2001), pp. 322–31.

31. D. Arnold, *Re-Presenting the Metropolis: Architecture, Urban Experience and Social Life in London 1800–1840* (Ashgate, 2000), pp. 25–6; J. Franklin, *The Gentleman's Country House and its Plan, 1835–1914* (1981), pp. 6–8.

32. The first bungalow to be built and named such was in 1869 on the north Kent coast, and the first development of bungalows was in the same area

in the early 1870s. Little was then heard of the bungalow until the late 1890s when it moved inland: see A. O. King, *The Bungalow: The Production of a Global Culture* (1984), pp. 65, 72–4, 89.

33. P. Inskip, *Edwin Lutyens* (1979), pp. 9–12; A. Service, *London 1900* (St Albans, 1979), p. 13.

34. Another index of the 'imperialisation' of British architecture would be the extent of its dependence on colonial commissions. This would repay further investigation, though the list of architects and their work compiled by Charles Marriott suggests that commissions were mostly domestic: *Modern English Architecture* (1924), pp. 227–54.

35. Lord Hardinge, *My Indian Years, 1910–16* (1948), p. 96; C. Hussey, *The Life of Sir Edwin Lutyens* (1950), pp. 259–60.

36. J. Ridley, *The Architect and his Wife: A Life of Edwin Lutyens* (2002), pp. 216, 223–4; M. Lutyens, *Edwin Lutyens by his Daughter* (1980), pp. 103–4.

37. Morris, *Stones of Empire*, p. 25.

38. Lutyens, *Edwin Lutyens*, pp. 113–14.

39. R. Gradidge, *Edwin Lutyens: Architect Laureate* (1981), pp. 70–1; Hussey, *The Life of Sir Edwin Lutyens*, p. 297.

40. Metcalf, *An Imperial Vision*, p. 238.

41. Ibid., p. 236; Morris, *Stones of Empire*, p. 32.

42. H. Baker, *Architecture and Personalities* (1944), pp. 24–5, 30–2, 39–41, 49–50; D. E. Greig, *Herbert Baker in South Africa* (Cape Town, 1970), pp. 37, 57, 100–2.

43. S. Dubow, 'Imagining the New South Africa in the Era of Reconstruction' in Omissi and Thompson (eds), *The Impact of the South African War*, pp. 85–6.

44. Metcalf, *An Imperial Vision*, pp. 222–3.

45. Baker, *Architecture and Personalities*, pp. 124–7; N. Jackson, *F. W. Troup: Architect, 1859–1941* (1985), pp. 51–74; Report of H. Baker to the Bank of England Rebuilding Committee, 12/12/1921, Bank of England Archives. I am grateful to Sarah Crellin for supplying this reference. The only notable exception was the Empire Clock above the chimney place in the Bank's Court Room – a 24-hour dial revolved around a 12-hour clock, with symbols marking the time-zones of the dominions and important colonies. Significantly, the Bank's Rebuilding Committee had first rejected the idea because it was felt to be of little use to the institution.

46. C. Wheeler, *High Relief* (Feltham, 1968), pp. 43–6, 55–9.

47. Watkin, *English Architecture*, p. 188.

48. Gradidge, *Edwin Lutyens*, p. 68.

49. Hussey, *The Life of Sir Edwin Lutyens*, p. 247.

50. J. Morris, 'In Quest of an Imperial Style' in R. Fermor-Hesketh (ed.), *Architecture of the British Empire* (1986), pp. 10–31.

51. Ridley, *An Architect and his Wife*, p. 224.   [325]

52. D. Watkin, *English Architecture: A Concise History* (revised edn, 2001), pp. 189–90. In this case, Lutyens's design was never built.

53. C. H. Reilly, 'The Architectural Scene, 1901–34', *Architectural Review* (1934), pp. 172, 174.

54. Ibid., p. 175; D. Wardleworth, *Building the Modern Corporation: Corporate Art Patronage in Inter-War Britain*, Southampton Institute Ph.D. (2002).

55. M. Crinson, *Empire Building: Orientalism and Victorian Architecture* (1996), pp. 1–2.

56. Watkin, *English Architecture*, pp. 192–3.

57. Mackenzie, *Propaganda and Empire*, p. 122.

58. T. Smith, ' "A grand work of noble conception": The Victoria Memorial and Imperial London' in Driver and Gilbert (eds), *Imperial Cities*, pp. 21–39.

59. E. Rappaport, 'Art, Commerce or Empire? The Rebuilding of Regent Street, 1880–1927', *HWJ* (2002), pp. 95–117.

60. E. B. Chancellor, *Liberty and Regent Street* (1926), p. 16.

61. *Selfridge's Decorations for the Coronation Souvenir Brochure* (1937); G. Honeycombe, *Selfridge's: Seventy-Five Years: The Story of the Store, 1909–84* (1984), p. 96. Selfridge's had long been regarded as London's most imperial commercial building – it carried flags of the dominions every day.

62. The subtitle of the display ('Let peace prevail'), and the fact that the historical pageant ended with the Armistice, were also significant, however.

63. J. Whitaker, *The Best: A History of H. H. Martyn & Co* (Cheltenham, 1985), p. 74.

64. H. Jennings and C. Madge (eds), *May the Twelfth: Mass-Observation Day-Surveys by Over Two Hundred Observers, 1937* (reprint Chatham, 1987, paperback edn), pp. 24–5, 149–50; R. Pound, *Selfridge* (1960), pp. 238–40.

65. Weight, *Patriots*, p. 7.

66. R. A. Huttenback, *Racism and Empire: White Settlers and Coloured Immigrants in the British Self-Governing Colonies, 1830–1910* (Ithaca, 1976), pp. 17–18; M. Morgan, *National Identities and Travel in Victorian Britain* (Basingstoke, 2001), pp. 92–4.

67. A. Summers, *Ranji: Maharajah of Connemara* (Dublin, 2002), pp. 16, 22–3, 30.

68. K. A. Sandiford, *Cricket and the Victorians* (Aldershot, 1994), pp. 153–5.

69. R. Broome, *Aboriginal Australians: Black Response to White Dominance, 1788–1980* (1983), pp. 69–71; D. J. Mulvaney, *Cricket Walkabout* (Melbourne, 1967). I have also drawn on one of my own students' survey of the provincial and sporting press: M. Jenkins, *British Reaction to the 1868 Australian Aboriginal Cricket Tour* (BA Thesis, University of Leeds, 2003).

[326]   70. They had only one win in the first seven games, but had achieved an equal number of victories and defeats by the end of the tour.

71. For a discussion of the players' 'native' and European names, see Mulvaney, *Cricket Walkabout*, pp. 38–9, 98–9.

72. See, especially, N. Parsons, *King Khama, Emperor Joe and the Great White Queen: Victorian Britain through the African Eyes* (Chicago, 1998) and 'British Press and Public Responses to the Visits of Southern African Royalty and Envoys to London, 1882–94', paper presented at the British World Conference, University of Cape Town, Jan. 2001. For an attempt to set the Southern African case in a broader imperial context, see Thompson, 'The Languages of Loyalism', pp. 683–4.

73. My account is partly based on Ellis Ashmead-Bartlett's papers in the Institute of Commonwealth Studies, University of London, which include extensive press cuttings of Bartlett's public speeches on behalf of the Swazis. See also P. L. Bonner, *Kings, Commoners and Concessionaires: The Evolution and Dissolution of the Nineteenth Century Swazi State* (Cambridge, 1983); H. Kuper, *The Swazi: A South African Kingdom* (New York, 1986); B. Nyeko, 'Pre-Nationalist Resistance to Colonial Rule: Swaziland on the Eve of the Imposition of British Administration, 1890–1902', *TransAfrican Journal of History* (1976), pp. 66–83; Parsons, 'British Press and Public Responses', pp. 11–13.

74. Press Cuttings, (1891–5), Ellis Ashmead-Bartlett Papers, E/1.

75. Flora Shaw, a friend of Rhodes, may have been behind its condemnatory editorials and letters.

76. In the short term the mission failed. However, after the Boer War, Swaziland was annexed by Britain and subsequently made a High Commission territory outside the Union (1910).

77. P. Maylam, *Rhodes, the Tswana and the British* (1980) and Parsons, *King Khama*.

78. Parsons, 'British Press and Public Responses', p. 16.

79. Parsons, *King Khama*, p. 248.

80. A. Lester, 'British Settler Discourse and the Circuits of Empire', *HWJ* (2002), pp. 25–44 [quote from p. 44] and *Imperial Networks and the Cape Eastern Frontier* (2001), pp. 189–92.

81. K. L. Little, *Negroes in Britain: A Study of Racial Relations in English Society* (1948), pp. 186–7; D. Killingray, 'Africans in the United Kingdom: An Introduction', *Immigrants and Minorities* (1993), pp. 7–8.

82. H. Adi, 'West African Students in Britain, 1900–60: The Politics of Exile', *Immigrants and Minorities* (1993), p. 107.

83. Possibly more so for men than women, however. See, for example, the experiences of the Indian social reformer Pandita Ramabai at Cheltenham Ladies College: A. Burton, *Heart of Empire: Indians and the Colonial Encounter*

in Late-Victorian Britain (Berkeley, 1998), ch. 2 and I. Grewal, *Home and Harem: Nation, Gender, Empire and the Cultures of Travel* (Durham, NC, 1996), pp. 189–97.   [327]

84. They were blamed for violence and disorder in Britain, and seen as carriers of sedition back home: see, especially, S. Lahiri, *Indians in Britain: Anglo-Indian Encounters, Race and Identity, 1880–1930* (2000).

85. A. Burton, 'Making a Spectacle of Empire: Indian Travellers in Fin-de-Siècle London', *HWJ* (1996), pp. 130–1.

86. P. Panyani, *Racial Violence in Britain, 1840–1950* (Leicester, 1993), p. 3.

87. J. Green, *Black Edwardians: Black People in Britain, 1901–14* (1998), pp. 147–58.

88. For the argument that British society was not monolithically racist, see R. Visram, *Asians in Britain: 400 Years of History* (2002), p. 356.

89. Walton, 'Britishness', pp. 518–21.

90. D. Cannadine, 'The Context, Performance and Meaning of Ritual: The British Monarchy and the "Invention of Tradition", *c.* 1820–1977' in E. J. Hobsbawm and T. Ranger (eds), *The Invention of Tradition* (Cambridge, 1983), pp. 120–1, 124–5, 134–5; B. Harrison, *Transformation of British Politics, 1860–1995* (Oxford, 1996), ch. 12; F. Prochaska, *Royal Bounty: The Making of a Welfare Monarchy* (New Haven, 1995), p. 163.

91. P. Fraser, *Lord Esher: A Political Biography* (1973), pp. 13, 69–70; Viscount Esher, 'The Ideals of the Masses' in *To-Day and Tomorrow and Other Essays* (1910), pp. 229–30.

92. J. Mackenzie (ed.), *The Victorian Vision: Inventing New Britain* (2001), p. 19; Thompson, *Imperial Britain*, p. 16.

93. The Queen ensured that the initials RI – Regina Imperatrix – appeared on coins, medals and seals, asked for a native Indian bodyguard in 1883, took lessons in Hindustani in 1887, employed Indian servants in her household, and opened the Indian and Colonial Exhibition in 1886. See also M. Homans, *Royal Representations: Queen Victoria and British Culture, 1837–1876* (Chicago, 1998), pp. xxii–xxv, 229–44.

94. V. Smith, *Constructing Victoria: The Representation of Queen Victoria in England, India and Canada, 1897–1914*, University of Rutgers Ph.D. (1998), pp. 378–9; R. Williams, *The Contentious Crown: Public Discussion of the British Monarchy in the Reign of Queen Victoria* (Aldershot, 1997), pp. 177–8.

95. Thompson, 'The Languages of Imperialism', p. 155.

96. P. Buckner, 'The Royal Tour of 1901 and the Construction of an Imperial Identity in South Africa', *SAHJ* (1999), pp. 324–48 and 'Casting Daylight upon Magic: Deconstructing the Royal Tour of 1901 to Canada', *JICH* (2003), pp. 158–89.

[328]   97. J. M. Golby and A. W. Purdue, *The Monarchy and the British People* (1988), pp. 92–4.

98. Harrison, *The Transformation of British Politics*, p. 320.

99. S. Schama, *A History of Britain: At the Edge of the World? 3000BC–AD1603* (2000), pp. 10–11.

100. Quoted in P. Hansen, 'Coronation Everest: The Empire and Commonwealth in the "Second Elizabethan Age"' in S. Ward (ed.), *British Culture and the End of Empire* (Manchester, 2001), p. 69.

101. B. Conekin, *The Autobiography of a Nation: The 1951 Festival of Britain* (Manchester, 2003), p. 183.

102. S. O. Rose, 'Race, Empire and British Wartime National Identity, 1939–45', *BIHR* (2001), pp. 220–1. It was at this time that Harold Moody's League of Coloured Peoples (1931) began to lose faith in fighting racial discrimination on the basis of a shared imperial British identity which gave rights of citizenship to blacks as well as whites: A. S. Rush, 'Imperial Identity in Colonial Minds: Harold Moody and the League of Coloured Peoples, 1931–50', *TCBH* (2002), pp. 381–3.

103. Conekin, *The Autobiography of a Nation*, pp. 184, 197–8.

104. The Royal Air Force is not discussed here, but for the importance of colonial air policing in providing it with a peacetime role, see D. Omissi, *Air Power and Colonial Control: The Royal Air Force, 1919–39* (Manchester, 1990); J. Cox, 'A Splendid Training Ground: The Importance to the Royal Air Force of its Role in Iraq, 1919–32', *JICH* (1985), pp. 157–84; J. Sweetman, 'Crucial Months for Survival: The Royal Air Force, 1918–19', *JCH* (1984), pp. 529–47.

105. N. d'Ombrain, *War Machinery and High Policy: Defence Administration in Peacetime Britain* (1973), pp. 225–31; J. Kendle, *The Colonial and Imperial Conferences, 1887–1911: A Study in Imperial Organisation* (1967), ch. 4.

106. J. Gooch, *The Plans of War: The General Staff and British Military Strategy, c. 1900–1916* (1974), chs 1, 5.

107. I. F. W. Beckett, 'Edward Stanhope at the War Office, 1887–1902', *JSS* (1982), pp. 278–307. For a copy, see Lord Carver, *Britain's Army in the Twentieth Century* (1998), pp. 8–9.

108. H. Bailes, 'Patterns of Thought in the Late Victorian Army', *JSS* (1981), pp. 29–45.

109. D. Schurman, *The Education of a Navy: The Development of British Naval Strategic Thought, 1867–1914* (1965), ch. 1.

110. J. Tomes, *Balfour and Foreign Policy: The International Thought of a Conservative Statesman* (Cambridge, 1997), p. 55.

111. D. Curtin, *Death by Migration: Europe's Encounter with the Tropical World in the Nineteenth Century* (Cambridge, 1989).

112. W. S. Hamer, *The British Army: Civil-Military Relations, 1885–1905* (Oxford, 1970), chs 3–6. [329]

113. E. Spiers, *The Army and Society, 1815–1914* (1980), p. 199.

114. Skelley, *The Victorian Army at Home: The Recruitment and Terms and Conditions of the British Regular, 1859–99* (1977), p. 254; B. Bond, *British Military Policy Between the Two World Wars* (Oxford, 1980), pp. 100–1.

115. D. French, 'The British Armed Forces, 1900–1939' in Wrigley (ed.), *A Companion to Early Twentieth Century Britain*, p. 177.

116. The figure for Britain includes Northern Ireland.

117. Bond, *British Military Policy*, pp. 118–19.

118. Spiers, *The Army and Society*, p. 206 and *The Late-Victorian Army*, p. 272.

119. Porter, *Atlas of British Overseas Expansion*, p. 118; J. Fortescue, *The Empire and the British Army* (1928), pp. 254–5; Spiers, *The Army and Society*, p. 209.

120. Bond, *British Military Policy*, pp. 16, 22; K. Jeffery, *The British Army and the Crisis of Empire, 1918–22* (Manchester, 1984), p. 149.

121. Carver, *Britain's Army*, p. 17; Skelley, *The Victorian Army at Home*, pp. 17–18.

122. J. Keegan, 'Regimental Ideology' in G. Best and A. Wheatcroft (eds), *War, Economy and the Military Mind* (1976), p. 15. See also B. Farewell, *Queen Victoria's Little Wars* (1973), p. 361: 'each [Scottish] regiment was a movable parish . . . returning to their Highlands after years in India, Afghanistan and Africa untouched by pagan customs or foreign ways to take their place by the peat fires in their cottages almost as if they had never left them.' For a different view, however, see T. A. Heathcote, *The Military in British India: The Development of British Land Forces in South Asia, 1600–1947* (Manchester, 1995), pp. 127–8: 'without its Indian experience the British army's institutional development would have taken other directions'.

123. See Chapter 1, pp. 21–2.

124. M. Lieven, 'The British Soldiery and the Ideology of Empire: Letters from Zululand', *Journal of the Society for Army Historical Research* (2002), p. 130.

125. Clayton, 'Imperial Defence and Security', p. 286; Spiers, *The Late-Victorian Army*, pp. 272, 277–8.

126. Spiers, *The Late-Victorian Army*, p. 300 and *The Army and Society*, pp. 209–10; Carver, *Britain's Army*, p. 157; Macksey, *The History of the Royal Armoured Corps*, pp. 45, 53.

127. Skelley, *The Victorian Army at Home*, p. 28; Spiers, *The Late-Victorian Army*, p. 275; I. F. W. Beckett, 'Military High Command in South Africa, 1854–1914' in P. B. Boyden, A. Guy and M. Harding (eds), *'Ashes and Blood': The British Army in South Africa, 1795–1914* (1999), pp. 75–6. See also A. Swinson and D. Scott (eds), *The Memoirs of Private Waterfield, Soldier in Her Majesty's 32nd Regiment of Foot, 1842–57* (1968), p. 152. Waterfield saw ten and a half years' service in India and four years at home.

[330]   128. F. Richards, *Old Soldier-Sahib* (1965), pp. 337–8. Richards was a private in the 2nd Battalion of the Royal Welch Fusiliers.

129. Ibid., pp. 192–3.

130. J. Mackenzie (ed.), *Popular Imperialism and the Military, 1850–1950* (Manchester, 1992), pp. 1–24.

131. Lieven, 'The British Soldiery', pp. 128–43 and E. Spiers, *The Victorian Soldier in Africa* (Manchester, 2004). I am grateful to Edward Spiers and David Omissi for their guidance on this issue.

132. Lieven, 'The British Soldiery', p. 130.

133. P. S. Thompson, *The Natal Native Contingent in the Anglo-Zulu War, 1879* (1997), pp. 121, 165, 186–7, 215–17.

134. E. Spiers, 'Campaigning under Kitchener' in Spiers (ed.), *Sudan: The Reconquest Reappraised* (1998), p. 60.

135. G. Dominy, 'The Making of the Rough and the Respectable: The Imperial Garrison and the Wider Society in Colonial Natal', *SAHJ* (1997), pp. 48–65.

136. Ibid., p. 61.

137. Richards, *Old Soldier-Sahib*, p. 143.

138. B. Farewell, *Armies of the Raj: From the Mutiny to Independence, 1858–1947* (1989), p. 59.

139. Richards, *Old Soldier-Sahib*, pp. 339–41.

140. Lieven, 'The British Soldiery', pp. 133, 135–7, 139, 143; F. Emery, *The Red Soldier: The Zulu War 1879* (Johannesburg, 1977), pp. 24, 169–75.

141. J. Mackenzie, 'Essay and Reflection: On Scotland and the Empire', *IHR* (1993), pp. 714–39; M. Fry, *The Scottish Empire* (East Linton, 2001); C. Harvie, *Scotland and Nationalism: Scottish Society and Politics, 1707–1977* (1977), pp. 90–110; A. Bielenberg, 'Irish Emigration to the British Empire, 1700–1914' in Bielenberg (ed.), *The Irish Diaspora* (Harlow, 2000), pp. 215–34; D. Fitzpatrick, 'Ireland and Empire', Vol. 3 *OHBE* (1999), pp. 494–521; Jeffery (ed.), *An Irish Empire?*; A. Jones and B. Jones, 'The Welsh World and the British Empire, c. 1851–1939: An Exploration', *JICH* (2003), pp. 57–81.

142. P. Cadett, 'Irish Soldiers in India', *The Irish Sword*, Vol. I (1950–1), pp. 77–9; K. Jeffery, 'The Irish Soldier in the Boer War' and E. Spiers, 'The Scottish Soldier in the Boer War' in J. Gooch (ed.), *The Boer War: Direction, Experience and Image* (2000), pp. 141–51 and 152–65 respectively; N. Holme, *The Noble 24th: Biographical Records of the 24th Regiment in the Zulu War and the South African Campaigns of 1877–1879* (Savannnah, 1999), pp. v, 1–5.

143. J. Ellis, 'Reconciling the Celt: British National Identity, Empire, and the 1911 Investiture of the Prince of Wales', *JBS* (1998), pp. 391–418; Jones and Jones, 'The Welsh World', pp. 59–60; K. Cardell, C. Cumming,

P. Griffiths and B. Jones, 'Welsh Identity on the Victorian Goldfields in the Nineteenth Century' in Cardell and Cumming (eds), *A World Turned Upside Down: Cultural Change on Victoria's Goldfields 1851–2001* (Canberra, 2001), pp. 25–60; G. A. Williams, *The Welsh in their History* (1982), pp. 175, 178, 183–5.

144. K. Robbins, *Nineteenth Century Britain: Integration and Diversity* (Oxford, 1995, paperback edn), pp. 18–28, 183–5.

145. Mackenzie, 'Empire and National Identities', p. 231.

146. D. G. Boyce, *Decolonisation and the British Empire, 1775–1997* (Basingstoke, 1999), pp. 258–9; K. Lunn, 'Reconsidering "Britishness": The Construction and Significance of National Identity in Twentieth Century Britain' in B. Jenkins and S. A. Sofos (eds), *Nationhood and Identity in Contemporary Europe* (1996), p. 87. See also John Kendle's explanation as to why the English willingly experimented with the federal idea in the empire but not at home: attached to the idea of undiluted sovereignty, they were determined that the British state would be English led: *Federal Britain: A History* (1997), pp. ix–xiii.

147. Thompson, *Imperial Britain*, pp. 30–2.

148. J. Clark, 'Not Fading Away Yet: How British Identity Survived the Declinist Intelligentsia', *TLS*, 7/6/2002, p. 4.

149. Kumar, *The Making of English National Identity*, pp. 188–96 [quotes from pp. 193, 96].

150. Robbins, *Nineteenth Century Britain*, pp. 182–3; P. Joyce, *Visions of the People* (Cambridge, 1991), pp. 279–92; E. Evans, 'Englishness and Britishness: National Identities, c. 1790–1870' in A. Grant and K. J. Stringer, *Uniting the Kingdom? The Making of British History* (1995), pp. 233–4.

151. Thompson, 'The Languages of Loyalism', pp. 629–30.

152. I am grateful to Donal Lowry for guiding me through the complexities of the Irish case, and for providing me with helpful bibliographical references.

153. C. Falls, *The Birth of Ulster* (1996 edn), pp. 230–54.

154. D. Lowry, 'Ulster Resistance and Loyalist Rebellion in the Empire' in Jeffery (ed.), *'An Irish Empire'?*, pp. 191–215.

155. M. Ignatieff, *Blood and Belonging: Journeys Into the New Nationalism* (1993), ch. 6.

156. This remark is truer of Ulster Presbyterians than Protestant Episcopalians. The latter regarded themselves as leaders of the country, and tried to bridge British and Irish identities. They also probably felt more Irish because (a) they had inherited a long Anglo-Irish tradition of identifying with Irish institutions, not least the all-Ireland organisation of the Anglican church, and (b) they were less doctrinaire and thus less likely to be alarmed by Catholicism.

[332]   157.   J. Loughlin, 'Imagining "Ulster": The North of Ireland and British National Identity, 1880–1921' in S. J. Connolly (ed.), *Kingdoms United? Great Britain and Ireland: Integration and Diversity since 1500* (Dublin, 1999), p. 112.

158.   P. Clayton, *Enemies and Passing Friends: Settler Ideologies in Twentieth Century Ulster* (1996), pp. 5–6.

159.   J. Todd, 'Unionist Political Thought, 1920–72' in D. G. Boyce, R. Eccleshall and V. Geoghegan (eds), *Political Thought in Ireland Since the Seventeenth Century* (1993), p. 192.

160.   A. Jackson, 'Irish Unionists and the Empire, 1880–1920: Classes and Masses' in Jeffery (ed.), *'An Irish Empire?'*, pp. 124–30.

161.   Fitzpatrick, 'Ireland and the Empire', p. 508; T. Hennessey, 'Ulster Unionist Territorial and National Identities, 1886–1893: Province, Island, Kingdom and Empire', *Irish Political Studies* (1993), pp. 30, 32–3.

162.   W. Jenkins, 'Negotiating Irishness and Britishness in Toronto in the Nineteenth and Twentieth Centuries', unpublished paper given to the British World Conference, University of Calgary, Canada, July 2003.

163.   Jackson, 'Irish Unionists and the Empire', pp. 131–7; J. Loughlin, *Ulster Unionism and British National Identity since 1885* (1995), p. 32.

164.   Bielenberg, 'Irish Emigration to the British Empire', p. 228.

165.   J. Lawrence, 'The Politics of Place and the Politics of Nation', *TCBH* (2000), p. 83.

166.   Ibid., p. 93. See also the different twentieth-century retellings of the legends of King Arthur and Robin Hood, the former subscribing to the imperial ideal, the latter critical of foreign adventurism: S. L. Barczewski, *Myth and National Identity in Nineteenth-Century Britain: The Legends of King Arthur and Robin Hood* (Oxford, 2000), pp. 201, 229–30, 242.

167.   P. A. Buckner and C. Bridge, 'Reinventing the British World', *The Round Table* (2003), pp. 79–80.

168.   For the argument that identities do not result from elite imposition only, see R. Colls, *Identity of England* (Oxford, 2002), pp. 3–4 and K. Kumar, *The Making of English National Identity* (Cambridge, 2003), p. 34.

169.   Compare the discussion of elites in Chapter 1 with organised labour in Chapter 3 and middle- and upper-class women in Chapters 5 and 6.

170.   G. Orwell, 'The Lion and the Unicorn: Socialism and the English Genius' (published Feb. 1941) in S. Orwell and I. Angus (eds), *The Collected Essays, Journalism and Letters of George Orwell. Vol. II: My Country Right or Left, 1940–3* (1968), p. 65.

171.   Weight, *Patriots*, p. 286.

172.   K. Robbins, '"This grubby wreck of old glories": The United Kingdom and the End of the British Empire', *JCH* (1980), pp. 81–95 [my italics].

173.   Clark, 'Not Fading Away Yet', p. 4.

Chapter 9 After-Effects [333]

1. J. Darwin, *The End of the British Empire: The Historical Debate* (Oxford, 1991), p. 118.

2. S. Howe, 'Labour Patriotism, 1939–83' in R. Samuel (ed.), *Patriotism: The Making and Unmaking of a British National Identity. Vol. 1: History and Politics* (1989), pp. 135–7.

3. A. Nandy, *The Intimate Enemy: Loss and Recovery of Self under Colonialism* (Delhi, 1988), pp. 31–5.

4. T. Benn, 'Britain as a Colony' in C. Mullin (ed.), *Arguments for Democracy* (1981), pp. 3–17.

5. P. Calvocoressi, *The British Experience, 1945–75* (1978), p. 245.

6. B. Porter, *The Lion's Share: A Short History of British Imperialism, 1850–1995* (Harlow, 3rd edn, 1996), p. 369.

7. R. Weight, *Patriots: National Identity in Britain, 1940–2000* (Basingstoke, 2002), pp. 63–6, 286–93.

8. R. Colls, *The Identity of England* (Oxford, 2002), pp. 4–5.

9. See, for example, K. Gardner and A. Shukur, '"I'm Bengali, I'm Asian, and I'm living here": The Changing Identity of British Bengalis' in R. Ballard (ed.), *Desh Pradesh: The South Asian Presence in Britain* (1994), pp. 154–4; J. Rex, *Colonial Immigrants in a British City: A Class Analysis* (1979), pp. 289–91; A. Shaw, *A Pakistani Community in Britain* (Oxford, 1988), p. 140.

10. J. Randle, *Understanding Britain: A History of the British People and Their Culture* (Oxford, 1981), p. 121.

11. D. Marquand, 'How United is the Modern United Kingdom?' in A. Grant and K. J. Stringer (eds), *Uniting the Kingdom: The Making of British History* (1995), p. 288.

12. D. Sanders, *Losing an Empire, Finding a Role: An Introduction to British Foreign Policy Since 1945* (New York, 1995), p. 290.

13. Ibid., p. 8.

14. R. Ovendale, 'The End of Empire' in R. English and M. Kenny (eds), *Rethinking British Decline* (2000), p. 274.

15. C. H. Feinstein, 'The End of Empire and the Golden Age' in P. Clarke and C. Trebilcock (eds), *Understanding Decline: Perceptions and Realities of British Economic Performance* (Cambridge, 1997), p. 228.

16. A. G. Hopkins, 'Macmillan's Audit of Empire, 1957', in Clarke and Trebilock (eds), *Understanding Decline*, p. 248.

17. J. Amery, 'The Suez Group: A Retrospective on Suez' in S. I. Troen and M. Shemesh (eds), *The Suez Sinai Crisis, 1956: Retrospective and Reappraisal* (1990), pp. 110–26; D. G. Boyce, *Decolonisation and the British Empire,*

1775–1997 (Basingstoke, 1999), p. 177; D.Goldsworthy, *Colonial Issues in British Politics, 1945–1961* (Oxford, 1971), pp. 295–300.

18. For the debate over withdrawal, see S. Onslow, *Backbench Debate Within the Conservative Party and Its Influence on British Foreign Policy 1948–57* (Basingstoke, 1997), ch. 9.

19. Ibid., p. 232; D. R. Thorpe, *Eden: The Life and Times of Anthony Eden, First Earl of Avon, 1897–1977* (2003), pp. 420–1, 542–3; J. Pearson, *Sir Anthony Eden and the Suez Crisis: Reluctant Gamble* (Basingstoke, 2003). During the crisis, Macmillan reported Eden's observation that 'It was 1938 all over again': P. Caterall (ed.), *The Macmillan Diaries: The Cabinet Years, 1950–1957* (2003).

20. Her own memoirs gave at least three, namely, the importance of standing up to aggressors; the need for Britain to display greater self-confidence in international affairs; and the right of the Falkland Islanders to remain British if they so desired: *The Downing Street Years* (1993), pp. 173–5.

21. 'Future Policy Study, 1960–1970', 24/2/1960, PRO, CAB 134/1929.

22. Similar remarks were made by leaders of the Labour party: see Denis Healey, *The Time of My Life* (1989), p. 281: 'Moreover, it [USA] had at last come to realise that Britain had an experience and understanding of the Third World, which it did not possess itself.'

23. Darwin, *End of Empire*, pp. 17–25.

24. There were 397 respondents. Report File 1158, 'Feelings About the British Empire', M-O panel, MO Directives and Replies (1939–51), M-O archive, University of Sussex.

25. The report was to help plan a series of radio programmes on the empire. There were 895 correspondents, 286 of whom offered their own opinions. 'Some Aspects of Public Opinion on the British Empire, and in particular, the Colonial Empire', BBC Listener Research Report, LR/1588, Audience Research Special Reports, 22/2/1943, File R9/9/7, BBC Written Archive Centre, Caversham, Reading. I am grateful to Sian Nicholas for supplying me with a copy of this report.

26. It was based on a national sample of 2,078 interviewees. File Report 3046, Survey Conducted by MO for Kemsley Newspapers Ltd, M-O archive.

27. It was based on a sample of 1,921 adults, aged 16 and above, drawn from all over the country and from all walks of society: File Report 3010, 'The Social Survey: Public Opinion on Colonial Affairs' (G. K. Evans), May–June 1948, M-O archive.

28. It was based on a sample of 2,078 people from England, Scotland and Wales: 'Report on the British Commonwealth and Empire', completed 6/10/1948, published 3/11/1948, Topic Collection, 25/17/K (Political Attitudes), M-O archive.

29. This prompted the Central Office of Information to embark on a national education programme in 1949, the main feature of which was 'Colonial

Month'. See M. Garlake, *New Art, New World: British Art in Postwar Society*   [335]
(New Haven, 1998), pp. 53–4.

30. The terms themselves are counter intuitive: 'dominion' describes a territory
in which there is extensive settlement, and 'colony' one where there is not,
despite the fact that 'colony' literally means settlement or settlers, derived
from the Latin 'colere', to cultivate or inhabit. The term 'colony' is still frequently used to mean any part of the empire outside the United Kingdom.

31. Interestingly, two of the surveys (*Daily Graphic*, Colonial Office) concluded
that the younger age brackets (16–29 and 25–44) were on the whole
better informed about the empire than the over-45s. Neither offered any
explanation as to why.

32. M. Havinden and D. Meredith, *Colonialism and Development: Britain and its
Tropical Colonies, 1850–1960* (1993), pp. 276–83.

33. I am grateful to Gordon Forster for drawing this to my attention. He shared
his vivid recollections of these music hall songs.

34. Havinden and Meredith, *Colonialism and Development*, pp. 212, 220, 225.

35. See, for example, A. Warren, *Singapore, 1942: Britain's Greatest Defeat* (2003),
p. 295.

36. A year later, 83% of the BBC's respondents said that they felt that Britain's
colonial record was mixed, though, of these, a majority of 7 to 1 felt that
the good exceeded the bad.

37. J. MacKenzie, 'The Persistence of Empire in Metropolitan Culture' in Ward
(ed.), *British Culture and the End of Empire*, pp. 28ff.

38. BBC Radio 4 interview with Sir James Spicer, 17/10/2002: 'Start the Week'
programme.

39. K. Miller, *730 Days Until Demob! National Service and the Post-1945 British Army!*
(2003), pp. 40–1; Weight, *Patriots*, p. 288.

40. For a survey of public opinion and the polls, see L. D. Epstein, *British Politics
in the Suez Crisis* (1964), pp. 141–70.

41. *Gallup*, Vol. 1, pp. 383–402, 432.

42. T. Shaw, *Eden, Suez and the Mass Media: Propaganda and Persuasion during the
Suez Crisis* (1996), p. 75.

43. Ibid., pp. 194–5.

44. Ibid., pp. 37, 52–4, 92, 128; Epstein, *British Politics in the Suez Crisis*,
pp. 158–9.

45. Sanders, *Losing an Empire*, p. 102; P. Murphy, *Party Politics and Decolonisation:
The Conservative Party and British Colonial Policy in Tropical Africa, 1951–64*
(Oxford, 1995), p. 4.

46. Sanders, *Losing an Empire*, pp. 112–20.

47. For the Wilson administration's ongoing evaluation of Britain's world role,
and its search for a more economical means of maintaining it, see especially

S. Dockrill, *Britain's Retreat from East of Suez: The Choice between Europe and the World?* (Basingstoke, 2002).

48. More than a half of these people favoured accelerating the existing timetable.

49. To quote a friend of my father's, who rose from a student mining engineer to become deputy director of the north Nottinghamshire area of British coal: 'it never stirred my blood'. However, other men that I spoke to from Midland and northern engineering firms said that they had not been nearly so eager to see Britain relinquish its overseas commitments. In the absence of polling data, this totally unscientific way of proceeding had to suffice.

50. It was under the Conservative governments of Macmillan and Douglas-Home that Britain's world role came under closer scrutiny, and was increasingly constrained by the control of defence expenditure: see Dockrill, *Britain's Retreat from East of Suez*.

51. 'Homage to a Government', 10/1/1969, *High Windows*, in A. Thwaite (ed.), *Philip Larkin: Collected Poems* (1988), p. 171.

52. Healey, *The Time of My Life*, pp. 278–300 and *A Labour Britain and the World* (Fabian Society Tract 352, 1964).

53. The Mau Mau were a secret society that emerged from the Kikuyu, and aimed to expel European settlers and to end British rule in Kenya.

54. S. L. Carruthers, *Winning Hearts and Minds: British Governments, the Media and Colonial Counter-insurgency, 1944–60* (Leicester, 1995), p. 267. Even two of the three independent feature films made about Kenya (*Simba*, 1954; *Something of Value*, 1957) expressed concern about the morality of Britain's African empire: D. M. Anderson, 'Mau Mau at the Movies: Contemporary Perceptions of an Anti-Colonial War', *SAHJ* (2003), pp. 71–89.

55. Murphy, *Party Politics and Decolonisation*, pp. 219–20.

56. Here I differ from R. Mackenzie and A. Silver, *Angels in Marble: Working Class Conservatives in Urban England* (1968), pp. 152–3, 281 – who (unintentionally) framed their questions in such a way as to prejudice the response. For the difficulty of framing a 'neutral' question on this subject see also Butler and Stokes, *Political Change in Britain: The Evolution of Electoral Choice* (1974), p. 464.

57. Murphy, *Party Politics and Decolonisation*, p. 9.

58. S. J. Ball, 'Macmillan, the Second World War and the Empire' in R. Aldous and S. Lee (eds), *Harold Macmillan: Aspects of a Political Life* (Basingstoke, 1999), pp. 170–1. For an amusing description of their lifestyle, see E. Waugh, 'Globe-Trotting in 1931' in *When the Going was Good* (1946), pp. 170–1.

59. 'Decolonisation: Changing Attitudes to a Post-War Empire', Centre for the Study of Cartoons and Caricature, University of Kent (1982), pp. 4–7.

60. D. Horowitz, 'The British Conservatives and the Racial Issue in the Debate on Decolonisation', *Race* (1971), pp. 181–3; P. Lynch, *The Politics of Nationhood: Sovereignty, Britishness and Conservative Politics* (Basingstoke, 1999),

pp. 22–4, 45–7; Onslow, *Backbench Debate Within the Conservative Party*,   [337]
p. 231.

61. *Gallup*, Vol. 2, pp. 834, 838. The horror of the Sharpeville massacre in South Africa in March 1960 provoked strong criticism in the British press. Whether the police shootings were regarded as an indictment of white South Africa or of Afrikaner nationalist rule is less clear: R. Hyam and P. Henshaw, *The Lion and the Springbok: Britain and South Africa since the Boer War* (Cambridge, 2003), pp. 317–9, 340.

62. D. Russell, '"The Jolly Old Empire": Labour, the Commonwealth and Europe, 1945–51' in A. May (ed.), *Britain, the Commonwealth and Europe: The Commonwealth and Britain's Applications to join the European Communities* (Basingstoke, 2001), pp. 9–29.

63. R. Samuel, 'Introduction: Exciting to be English' in Samuel (ed.), *Patriotism*, p. xxviii.

64. D. Judd, *Empire: The British Imperial Experience from 1765 to the Present* (1996), pp. 366–7.

65. R. Bothwell, I. Drummond and J. English, *Canada since 1945: Power, Politics and Provincialism* (Toronto, 1981), pp. 142–4, 277 [quote from p. 277]; J. English, *The Worldly Years: The Life of Lester Pearson. Volume II: 1949–72* (Toronto, 1992), pp. 127–45; L. B. Pearson, *Memoirs. Volume 2: 1948–1957. The International Years* (1974), pp. 225–73.

66. J. Nehru, *India's Foreign Policy: Selected Speeches, September 1946 April 1961* (Bombay, 1961), pp. 534–5.

67. Hyam and Henshaw, *The Lion and the Springbok*, pp. 308–11, 318–19.

68. Ibid., p. 340.

69. Young, *This Blessed Plot*, pp. 139, 156.

70. Equally, it should be noted how, during the 1950s and 1960s, the foreign and strategic policy of the dominions – Australia, in particular – was becoming more independent of an imperial framework; co-operation with Britain remained important, but the pull of the USA was increasingly strong. See, especially, D. Goldsworthy, *Losing the Blanket: Australia and the End of Britain's Empire* (Carlton South, Victoria, 2002).

71. Quote, ibid., p. 139. See also Aldous and Lee (eds), *Harold Macmillan and Britain's World Role*, p. 156; May, *Britain, the Commonwealth and Europe*, p. x. When Britain applied for membership in the summer of 1961, it was hoped that its influence in Washington would not be damaged, and that its ability to lead the Commonwealth might even be strengthened. However, negotiations made it clear that 'before it could succeed, Britain would have to become as parochial as the European Community' and abandon any hope of 'particular intimacy with the Commonwealth': see A. S. Milward, *The UK and the European Community. Vol. 1: The Rise and Fall of a National Strategy, 1945–63* (2002), pp. 310–11, 350–1, 369–70, 386–7, 415, 420.

[338]   72. Aldous and Lee (eds), *Harold Macmillan and Britain's World Role*, pp. 4–5.

73. Harrison, *The Transformation of British Politics*, p. 390.

74. David Marquand interviewed by English and Kenny in *Rethinking British Decline*, pp. 126–7.

75. J. Stephenson, 'Britain and Europe in the Later Twentieth Century: Identity, Sovereignty, Peculiarity' in M. Fulbrook (ed.), *National Histories and European History* (1993), pp. 230–54.

76. P. Marshall, 'Imperial Britain' in Marshall (ed.), *Cambridge Illustrated History of the British Empire* (Cambridge, 1996), p. 336.

77. A. Gamble, 'The European Issue in British Politics' in D. Baker and D. Seawright (eds), *Britain For and Against Europe: British Politics and the Question of European Integration* (Oxford, 1988), pp. 11–30.

78. For official thinking, see Young, *This Blessed Plot*, pp. 124–5, 138–9.

79. C. Schenk, *Britain and the Sterling Area: From Devaluation to Convertibility in the 1950s* (1994).

80. Feinstein, 'The End of Empire and the Golden Age', pp. 229–30.

81. G. Magee, 'Imperial Sentiment and the Growth of British Exports to the Empire, 1870–1960', *University of Melbourne Economics Working Paper* (2004).

82. D. Watt, 'Introduction: The Anglo-American Relationship' in W. Roger Louis and H. Bull (eds), *The 'Special Relationship': Anglo-American Relations Since 1945* (Oxford, 1986), p. 12.

83. J. Tomlinson, 'The Decline of the Empire and Economic Decline of Britain', *TCBH* (2003), pp. 201–21.

84. Procida, *Married to the Empire*, pp. 218–19.

85. See R. Scruton, *England: An Elegy* (2000), pp. 27–42, for a sensitive portrayal of a colonial official who returned to a job in teaching [quote from p. 27].

86. E. Wilson, *Mirror Writing: An Autobiography* (1982), pp. 1–12.

87. The Act divided British citizenship into two categories: 'UK and Colonies', and 'independent Commonwealth countries' – this allowed Indian nationals to retain their status as British subjects even after India became a republic.

88. Many were Jamaican but all of the main islands were represented including Barbados, Trinidad and Tobago, St Lucia and Antigua. See C. Peach, *West Indian Migration to Britain: A Social Geography* (1968), pp. 106–7.

89. Ballard, 'The Emergence of *Desh Pardesh*', p. 7.

90. That said, Gujarati settlers in Britain include a significant Muslim minority; as many as a quarter of Punjabis may be Hindus; and there is a small Christian minority among those from Pakistan. See R. Desai, *Indian Immigrants in Britain* (Oxford, 1963), p. 13.

91. J. Walvin, *Passage to Britain: Immigration in British History and Politics* (Harmondsworth, 1984), pp. 105–6.

92. Estimates vary, depending on whether one is measuring migration or ethnic [339] origin: see Kearney, *The British Isles*, p. 211; Walvin, *A Passage to Britain*, p. 106 and Tables 12–13.

93. A. Porter and A. J. Stockwell, *British Imperial Policy and Decolonisation, 1938–64. Vol. II: 1951–64* (Basingstoke, 1989), p. 76. For official perceptions, see D. Goldsworthy (ed.), *The Conservative Government and the End of Empire, 1951–1957*, Vol. 3 (1994), pp. 394–402.

94. R. Kelly, 'The Party Conferences' in A. Seldon and S. Ball (eds), *Conservative Century: The Conservative Party since 1900* (Oxford, 1994), pp. 248–9.

95. G. L. Bernstein, *The Myth of Decline: The Rise of Britain since 1945* (2004), pp. 289–90; M. Pugh, *State and Society: A Social and Political History of Britain, 1870–1997* (1999, 2nd edn), pp. 308–9. See also the (weighted) polls: Butler and Stokes, *Political Change in Britain*, p. 303: 'Do you think that too many immigrants have been let into this country or not' (81–84% answered 'yes').

96. Porter, *The Lion's Share*, p. 346.

97. See the recollections of members of the 'white, elderly middle-class' in E. Cashmore, *The Logic of Racism* (1987), pp. 166–8.

98. There is a fierce debate about the impetus for restrictive immigration legislation, and the question of whether it was racist in design. See, especially, R. Hansen, *Citizenship and Immigration in Post-War Britain* (Oxford, 2000) and K. Paul, *Whitewashing Britain: Race and Citizenship in the Postwar Era* (Ithaca, 1997).

99. The free flow of immigrants to Britain was limited by the employment voucher scheme introduced by the 1962 Commonwealth Immigrants Act; by annual quotas on East African Asians; by the notion of a 'patrial' (a person born in the UK, or with at least one UK-born grandparent, granted the right of abode; the vast majority, of course, were white) introduced by the 1968 Commonwealth Immigrants Act; by the abolition of the special quotas and other advantages enjoyed by non-patrial Commonwealth citizens by the 1971 Immigration Act (like any other 'alien', they now had to apply for work permits, rather than employment vouchers); and by the creation of 'Citizens of British Dependent Territories' and 'British Overseas Citizens' (neither of which had a right of abode in the UK), under the 1981 British Nationality Act. For further discussion, see I. Spencer, *British Immigration Policy since 1939: The Making of a Multi-Racial Britain* (1997).

100. We still lack a comprehensive social history of Commonwealth immigrants – why they came here, how (far) they have integrated into society and what they feel toward Britain. Dilip Hiro's *Black British, White British* (1971) comes closest. In addition to sociological studies from the 1960s and 1970s, and oral history of the last two decades, my analysis draws on A. S. Thompson with R. Begum, *Asian 'Britishness': A Study of First Generation Asian Migrants in Greater Manchester*, Asylum and Migration Working Paper Series, Institute of Public Policy Research (2004).

[340]   101.   This discussion of new Commonwealth migrants focuses on what they held in common. However, only up to a point did the three main movements – West Indian, South Asian, and East African – share the same motivations and mechanisms. If 'pull' factors in Britain were generally more important than 'push' factors, there is a notable exception in the case of the 27,000 Asian refugees from Kenya, Uganda and Malawi. Another difference would be the demand for labour in Britain. This seems to have been most significant for Caribbean migrants, who were acutely aware of the state of the employment market in Britain; the relationship is less clear in the case of Indians and Pakistanis.

102.   This was during the debate on the Commonwealth Immigrants Bill: *House of Commons Debates, 5th Series,* Vol. 649 (1961–2), col. 800.

103.   See also M. Collins, 'Pride and Prejudice: West Indian Men in Mid-Twentieth Century Britain', *JBS* (2001), p. 417; D. Lawrence, *Black Migrants; White Natives: A Study of Race Relations in Nottingham* (1974), pp. 39–42; E. J. B. Rose, *Colour and Citizenship, A Report on British Race Relations* (1969), pp. 419–22.

104.   Carey, *Colonial Students,* p. 162; PEP, *Colonial Students in Britain,* p. 141.

105.   Acc No. C0130, recorded on 4/11/1987, Heritage Recording Unit, Bradford Central Library.

106.   J. Stanley, 'Mangoes to Moss Side: Caribbean Migration to Manchester in the 1950s and 1960s', *Manchester Region History Review* (2002–3), p. 43. I am grateful to Gordon Forster for this reference.

107.   Walvin, *Passage to Britain,* p. 148.

108.   W. James, 'Migration, Racism and Identity: The Caribbean Experience in Britain', *New Left Review* (1992), p. 29.

109.   Hiro, *Black British, White British,* pp. 10–13, 106–7, 113–14, 155–6.

110.   See Rose, *Colour and Citizenship,* pp. 440–52 [quote from p. 440].

111.   M. Anwar, *The Myth of Return: Pakistanis in Britain* (1979), pp. 214–20; Thompson with Begum, *Asian 'Britishness'.*

112.   G. S. Aurora, *The New Frontiersman: A Sociological Study of Indian Immigrants in the United Kingdom* (Bombay, 1967), ch. 4. Similar claims have been made for West Indian migrants: Chamberlain, 'Family and Identity', pp. 122–3 and 'Gender and the Narratives of Migration', *HWJ* (1997), pp. 88, 91; S. B. Philpott, *West Indian Migration: The Montserrat Case* (1973), pp. 32–3, 178–9, 188–9.

113.   As late as the 1990s as many as half of Pakistani men may have belonged to funeral associations that would help pay the expenses to send the dead back to the ancestral village for burial: D. Joly, *Britannia's Crescent: Making a Place for Muslims in British Society* (Avebury, 1995), p. 53.

114.   Shaw, *A Pakistani Community in Britain,* pp. 49–50.

115. This was certainly a key finding of the interviews we conducted among thirty first-generation Asian migrants in Tameside: see Thompson with Begum, *Asian 'Britishness'*.

116. T. Modood and R. Berthoud *et al.*, *Ethnic Minorities in Britain: Diversity and Disadvantage* (1997); Thompson with Begum, *Asian 'Britishness'*.

117. B. Schwarz, '"The only white man in there": The Re-Racialisation of England, 1956–1968', *Race & Class* (1996), pp. 65–6; Walvin, *Passage to Britain*, pp. 44–7, 127.

118. Collins, 'Pride and Prejudice', p. 417.

119. Rex and Tomlinson, *Colonial Immigrants in a British City*, pp. 12–13, 91–2, 286–94.

120. Lawrence, *Black Migrants, White Natives*, pp. 54–5.

121. Marshall, 'Imperial Britain', pp. 332–3.

122. P. Panayi, 'Anti-Immigrant Riots in Nineteenth and Twentieth Century Britain' in Panayi (ed.), *Racial Violence in Britain, 1840–1950* (Leicester, 1993), pp. 1–25.

123. S. Hall, 'Racism and Reaction' in *Five Views of Multi-Racial Britain: Talks on Race Relations Broadcast by BBC TV* (1978), pp. 23–35 [quote from p. 26].

124. Hall, 'Racism and Reaction', p. 26; J. Solomos, B. Findlay, S. Jones and P. Gilroy, 'The Organic Crisis of British Capitalism and Race: The Experience of the Seventies' in *The Empire Strikes Back: Race and Racism in 70s Britain* (1982), pp. 9–46. See also Raphael Samuel's remark that the racial language of white supremacy is better understood not as 'the residues of imperial sentiment' but as 'a defensive hysteria . . . in which the indigenous population is pictured as an endangered species': *Patriotism*, Vol. 1, p. xxxiv.

125. Layton-Henry, *The Politics of Immigration*, p. 9; Holmes, *John Bull's Island*, pp. 243–4.

126. S. Rushdie, 'The New Empire Within Britain' in *Imaginary Homelands: Essays and Criticism, 1981–1991* (1991), p. 130.

127. W. H. Israel, *Colour and Community: A Study of Coloured Immigrants and Race Relations in an Industrial Town* (Slough, 1994), p. 74.

128. D. Feldman, 'Migrants, Immigrants and Welfare Reform from the Old Poor Law to the Welfare State', *TRHS* (2003), pp. 98–104 [quote from p. 100].

129. For immigrants and the labour market, see R. Miles and A. Phizacklea, *The TUC, Black Workers and New Commonwealth Immigration, 1954–1973*, Working Papers on Ethnic Relations, No. 6 (Bristol, 1977) and *White Man's Country: Racism in British Politics* (1984), ch. 1; S. Joshi and B. Carter, 'The Role of Labour in the Creation of a Racist Britain', *Race & Class* (1984), pp. 53–70; S. Patterson, *Immigration and Race Relations in Britain, 1960–1967* (Oxford, 1969), pp. 173–81.

130. Language barriers, different diets and the very size of the Indian workforce could be a hindrance to social intercourse, while the perception among white

[342]   workers that coloured workers were resistant to trade unionism and willing to work for lower wages further impeded integration. See Aurora, *The New Frontiersman*, ch. 8.

131. Such social problems could, of course, have been constructed in terms of the stereotypical 'colonial' immigrant – 'undisciplined', 'childishly excitable', 'lascivious', and a threat to orderly English life. For media representations, see W. Webster, '"There'll Always Be An England": Representations of Colonial Wars and Immigration, 1948–68', *JBS* (2001), pp. 557–84. For continuing prejudices toward colonial subjects in political discourse, see M. Francis, 'Tears, Tantrums, and Bared Teeth: The Emotional Economy of Three Conservative Prime Ministers, 1951–63', *JBS* (2002), pp. 363–4.

132. C. Dustman and I. Preston, 'Racial and Economic Factors in Attitudes to Immigration'. Copy kindly supplied by Dr Dustman, University College, London.

133. See, in particular, the account of the BNP in R. Eatwell, 'The Extreme Right in Britain: The Long Road to "Modernisation"' in Eatwell and C. Mudde (eds), *Western Democracies and the New Extreme Right Challenge* (2004), pp. 62–79.

134. 51% of respondents to a recent Guardian/ICM poll on asylum and migration said that they were content to see the door open to both the unskilled and skilled economic migrant: 'Special Report: Refugees in Britain', *Guardian*, 21/5/2001; 86% of respondents to a Mori poll for the Commission for Racial Equality believed it was right to respect the rights of minorities, and thought that British people should do more to learn about other cultures in this country: 'At Ease With Our Diversity', *The Guardian*, 13/5/2002.

135. Hall, *Civilising Subjects*, pp. 1–22 and 'Roundtable', *JBS* (2003), pp. 534–5.

136. For the trans-national linkages of Britain's South Asian immigrants, and the extent of their involvement with their communities of origin, see R. Ballard, 'The South Asian Presence in Britain and its Transnational Connections' in H. Singh and S. Vertovec (eds), *Culture and Economy in the Indian Diaspora* (2002).

137. For the accuracy of the comparison, see P. Weil and J. Crowley, 'Integration in Theory and Practice: A Comparison of France and Britain' in M. Baldwin-Edwards and M. A. Schain (eds), *The Politics of Immigration in Western Europe* (1994), pp. 110–26.

138. Ward, 'Introduction' in *British Culture and the End of Empire*, pp. 11–12.

139. See p. 203 above.

140. Onslow, *Backbench Debate Within the Conservative Party*, p. 235.

141. A. Forster, *Euroscepticism in Contemporary British Politics: Opposition to Europe in the British Conservative and Labour Parties since 1945* (2002), esp. pp. 135–8.

142. S. Bruce, *The Edge of the Union: The Ulster Loyalist Political Vision* (Oxford, 1994), pp. 129–30.

143. S. Howe, *Ireland and Empire: Colonial Legacies in Irish History and Culture* [343] (Oxford, 2000), pp. 232-3.

144. Ibid., pp. 215-16; P. Clayton, *Enemies and Passing Friends: Settler Ideologies in Twentieth Century Ulster* (1996), p. 122.

145. YouGov poll for *Daily Telegraph*, 25/08/03, p. 3.

146. International Association for the Evaluation of Educational Achievement, reported in the *Sunday Times*, 8/12/2002, p. 11.

147. *Great Britons: The Top Hundred*, BBC2 20/10/2002, BBC website and *The Times*, 22/2/2002, p. 11: Lord Baden-Powell, Winston Churchill, T. E. Lawrence, David Livingstone, Florence Nightingale and Queen Victoria.

148. YouGov poll for *Daily Telegraph*, 26/8/2002, pp. 9, 19. Meanwhile, in Australia, it has recently been ruled by the Canberra High Court that British residents who commit a crime can be deported back to their homeland, and are to be treated like the citizens of any other country for immigration purposes. The decision affects approximately 350,000 Britons who live in Australia but have never taken out dual citizenship: 'Australia to send convicts back to Britain', *The Times*, 11/12/2003, p. 15.

149. I. F. W. Beckett, *The Victorians at War* (2003), pp. xiii–xiv, 13.

150. Chauhuri and Strobel (eds), *Western Women and Imperialism*, p. 1; Rushdie, 'Outside the Whale' in *Imaginary Homelands*, pp. 87–101.

151. J. Hill, *British Cinema in the 1980s: Issues and Themes* (Oxford, 1999), ch. 5.

152. A slang term for the Bombay-based Hindi film industry.

153. Indian and Pakistani films had begun to be shown to Asian people in Britain by the mid-1950s. By the end of that decade an estimated two hundred cinemas were showing films to an audience of approximately 100,000 people: see Hiro, *Black British, White British*, p. 122.

154. The film received much praise from the mainstream and movie press, and was recognised to have broken barriers in terms of cross-cultural viewing. Information kindly supplied in September 2003 by Priti Peshawaria, Marketing Executive, Sony Films.

155. For two enjoyable travelogues, which criticise Britain for their neglect, see H. Ritchie, *The Last Pink Bits* (1997) and S. Winchester, *Outposts* (Sevenoaks, 1985).

156. Anguilla, Bermuda, the Virgin Islands, and the Turks and Caicos Islands.

157. The Cayman and Channel Islands, Gibraltar, and the Isle of Man.

158. Gibraltar, and the British Indian Ocean Territory, the main island of which is Diego Garcia.

159. The Falkland Islands, Pitcairn Islands, St Helena, Ascension Island and Tristan da Cunha.

160. R. Aldrich and J. Connell, *The Last Colonies* (Cambridge, 1998).

161. Ibid., pp. 244-51.

[344] 162. G. M. F. Drower, *Britain's Dependent Territories* (Aldershot, 1992), pp. xii–xiii, xvii, 227–8; M. Parsons, 'Some Far Corner: The Last Vestiges of Empire and Traditional Values' in *Revue française de civilisation britannique* Vol. XII, No. 4, pp. 163–74.

163. R. Moore, 'The Debris of Empire: The 1981 Nationality Act and the Oceanic Dependent Territories', *Immigrants and Minorities* (2000), pp. 1–24. Only in 2002 was full British citizenship restored to all 150,000 inhabitants of the remaining thirteen overseas British territories; an injustice belatedly recognised after the six million inhabitants of Hong Kong had been safely handed over to China – the fear of them moving to Britain had been the real impetus for the 1981 Act. See also P. Dennis, *Gibraltar and Its People* (1990), pp. 152–3, 160–1.

164. See also K. Dodds, *Pink Ice: Britain and the South Atlantic Empire* (2002), pp. 137, 166–7. Not everyone was persuaded that this was so: see A. Chancellor, 'Notebook' in P. Marsden-Smedley (ed.), *Britain in the Eighties: The Spectator's View of the Thatcher Decade* (1989), p. 44 – 'What is in question is not their desire to remain British, but the quality of that desire. They would not, on the face of it, appear to be the most passionate of patriots. They lead strange, lonely lives many thousands of miles away from the mother country . . . It is possible to imagine that, at the end of the day, they would value more highly the right to carry on their chosen way of life in security and tranquillity than the Britishness of the Falklands administration.'

165. A. Barnett, 'Thatcher's Armada, Parliament's War', *New Left Review* (1982) and *Iron Britannia* (1982).

166. For the polls, see A. King (ed.), *British Political Opinion, 1937–2000* (2001), pp. 323–36.

167. A. Bartlett, *Iron Britannia*, pp. 89–90.

168. Dodds, *Pink Ice*, pp. 137, 166–7.

169. D. E. Morrison, *Journalists at War: The Dynamics of News Reporting during the Falklands Conflict* (1988), pp. 286–300: a survey conducted by the author suggested that 50% of the population considered the Argentines to have some right to the Falklands, notwithstanding the fact that they were recognised to be a British possession.

170. G. M. Dillon, *The Falklands, Politics and War* (Basingstoke, 1989), pp. 112–21.

171. 'The last hurrah for a symbol of empire', *Guardian*, 24/6/1997, p. 1.

172. 'A last hurrah and an empire closes down', *Guardian*, 1/7/1997, p. 1.

173. 'Final farewell to Hong Kong', *The Times*, 1/7/1997, p. 1.

174. A. Marshall, 'End of empire for Perfidious Albion', *Independent*, 30/6/1997, p. 13. To my mind, the most perceptive account of the British reaction to the transfer.

175. J. Darwin, 'Hong Kong in British Decolonisation' in J. M. Brown and R. Foot (eds), *Hong Kong's Transitions, 1842–1997* (Basingstoke, 1997), p. 17.

176. B. Lowe, 'Pomp and Pathos: Through the Lens of British TV' in A. Knight and Y. Nakano (eds), *Reporting Hong Kong: Foreign Media and the Handover* (Richmond, 1999), p. 99.

177. Healey, *The Time of My Life*, p. 294.

178. Lowe, 'Pomp and Pathos', pp. 102–3, 106–9.

179. R. Hodder, 'The Glory That Was Empire?', *Salisbury Review* (Winter 1997), p. 8

180. J. Halliday, 'Hong Kong: Britain's Chinese Colony', *New Left Review* (1974), pp. 91–113. On the weakness of Hong Kong trade unionism, see H. A. Turner (ed.), *The Last Colony: But Whose? A Study of the Labour Movement, Labour Market and Labour Relations in Hong Kong* (Cambridge, 1980).

181. When asked whether they took personal pride in the fact that Britain once had a great empire, 70% answered 'yes', 28% 'no' and 2% 'don't know': *Daily Telegraph*, 26/8/1997, p. 4.

182. Porter, *The Lion's Share*, p. 368.

183. For key works, see the Archives Committee of the Anti-Apartheid Movement, *The Anti-Apartheid Movement: A Forty Year Perspective* (2000); R. Davenport and C. Saunders, *South Africa: A Modern History* (Houndmills, Basingstoke, 2000), pp. 533–40; R. Fieldhouse, *A History of the British Anti-Apartheid Movement* (2004); Hyam and Henshaw, *The Lion and the Springbok*, pp. 320–42.

184. He was born Harry Penrith, but in the late 1970s changed his name to Burnum Burnum (the name of his great-great-grandfather was Burnum Burnum McCrae, a 'Great Warrior' of the Wurundjeri people). For the full story, see M. J. Norst, *A Warrior for Peace: Burnum Burnum* (East Roseville, NSW, 1999).

185. *Cultural Property: Return and Illicit Trade. 7th Report of the Select Committee of the House of Commons on Culture, Media and Sport* (2000), paragraphs 112–66, and principal recommendations set out in paragraph 199.

186. *Report of Working Group on Human Remains in Museum Collections (HRWG)* (Nov. 2003). This can be downloaded from the website of the Department of Culture, Media and Sport at http://www.culture.gov.uk/cultural_property/wg_human_remains/default.htm.

187. Nor are indigenous peoples the only beneficiaries of repatriation. In Nov. 2003, the residents of a Fiji village apologised to the family of an English missionary, the Reverend Thomas Baker, who was killed by islanders in 1867, some eight years before Fiji was annexed by Britain. In Baker's case, however, there were no remains to be returned; he and his followers had been clubbed to death by the people of Navosa, cooked and then eaten. Apparently, all that was left were his boots, the desiccated remains of which had been returned to Fiji's Methodist Church in 1993. See 'Fijians

apologise for ancestral cannibalism in bid to lift curse', *Independent*, 13/11/2003, p. 18; '136 years on, Fiji says sorry for its cannibal past', *The Times*, 15/10/2003, p. 3.

188. P. Bean and J. Melville, *Lost Children of the Empire: The Untold Story of Britain's Child Migrants* (1989); S. Constantine, 'The British Government, Child Welfare, and Child Migration to Australia after 1945', *JICH* (2002), pp. 99–132; A. Gill, *Orphans of the Empire: The Shocking Story of Child Migration to Australia* (NSW, 1997); M. Humphreys, *Empty Cradles* (1994). A note of caution is worth sounding here: there is a tendency for migration historians to latch onto hard cases: the 'successes' are less well documented in the archives; moreover, when one does come across positive experiences, they are perhaps too easily dismissed as propaganda.

189. Broadcast weekly on Radio 4 from 15/9/2003 to 6/10/2003.

190. *The Welfare of Former British Child Migrants: Government Response to the Third Report from the Health Committee, Session 1997–8* (1998), and available at http://www.archive.official-documents.co.uk/document/cm41/4182/4182.htm.

191. In August 2001, an Australian Senate Inquiry reported on this 'very sorry chapter' in the country's history, and offered a reparation package of £1.38 million, though no formal apology – that was left to the Catholic Church, and the state governments of Queensland and Western Australia.

192. For the work of the Child Migrants Trust today, see

http://www2.nottscc.gov.uk/child_migrants/Cmt.HTM. By the end of 1992, the Trust had received more than 20,000 enquiries.

193. They were, of course, extensively memorialised outside the UK, not least by the India Gate in New Delhi.

194. I interviewed Baroness Flather on 19/1/04, in the House of Lords, and am very grateful to her for speaking about the project so fully and frankly. See also S. Singh, 'Forgetting the saga of sacrifice', *Tribune*, 28/11/1998; 'India did a lot for Britain', *Times of India*, 26/4/2001.

195. H. Suroor, 'A British memorial to forgotten "natives"', *The Hindu*, 7/11/2002.

196. J. C. D. Clark, 'National Identity: State Formation and Patriotism: The Role of History in the Public Mind', *HWJ* (1990), pp. 100–1.

197. A. Hochschild, *King Leopold's Ghost: A Story of Greed, Terror and Heroism in Colonial Africa* (Boston, 1998), ch. 19.

198. A. Raybaud, 'Deuil sans travail, travail sans deuil: la France a-t-elle une memoire coloniale?', *Dedale* (1997), pp. 87–104.

199. See, in particular, the torture of Algerian prisoners at the hands of French soldiers, and the fate of the *harkis* (loyal Algerian troops) who were abandoned during the French retreat, or parked in refugee camps in France.

200. My survey of museums comprises the National Portrait Gallery, 'The Raj: India and the British 1600–1947' (Oct. 1990–Mar. 1991) and the National

Gallery, 'An Indian Encounter' (Nov. 2002–Jan. 2003); the National Maritime Museum, 'Trade and Empire Gallery' (opened 1999); the Merseyside Maritime Museum, 'Transatlantic Slavery Gallery' (opened 1994); the British Library, 'Trading Places: the East India Company and Asia, 1600–1834' (May–Sept. 2002); and the British Empire and Commonwealth Museum in Bristol (fully opened in Sept. 2002). I was fortunate to be able to interview the following on the telephone: Dr Robert J. Blyth (Curator of Imperial and Maritime History) and Dr Nigel Rigby (previously Head of the Gallery) on 11 and 15 Sept. 2003 respectively; Mr Anthony Tibbles (Curator of Maritime History) on 30 Sept. 2003. I also consulted press scrapbooks for the Raj exhibition in the Heinz Archive, National Portrait Gallery, 4 vols, 29-A-Z, and for Bristol's Empire and Commonwealth Museum, provided by Liz Boyce, Education Administrator. I am grateful to all concerned.

201. G. Ramnarayan, 'Comprehensive view of the British Raj', *The Hindu*, 1/2/1991. See also C. A. Bayly (ed.), *The Raj: India and the British, 1600–1947* (1990).

202. A. Tibbles, 'Against Human Dignity: the Development of the Transatlantic Slavery Gallery at the MMM', p. 101 and 'Comments on the Transatlantic Slavery Gallery', 1/2/1995. Copies supplied by the author.

203. Interview with R. J. Blyth; J. Ezard, 'Britannia rules are waived. Makeover for imperial exhibition', *Guardian*, 7/8/2000, p. 9.

204. Information supplied by Catriona Finlayson, Senior Press Officer, British Library, 25/9/2003.

205. Information supplied by Alison Bomford, Communications and Media, The National Gallery, 12/9/2003.

206. See, for example, Homi Bhaba's comments on the NPG exhibition, 'Still Sparkling Jewel', *THES*, 2/11/1990, which argued that what really needed to be addressed was the 'inward influence wrought by the experience of the *Raj* upon the mind and heart of "native" England'.

207. A. Sivanandan, editor of *Race & Class*, led the way here: see N. Murray, 'Apprehending Reality: *Race & Class* as an Anti-Imperialist Journal', *Race & Class* (1999), pp. 74–5, 80–1.

208. See, for example, the remarks of the Black historian, Ben Bousquet, who felt that the Bristol Empire and Commonwealth Museum would help Britain's migrant communities come to terms with their own history, quoted by P. Fray, 'The sun hasn't quite set on the real Britannia', *Sydney Morning Herald*, 5/10/2002.

209. And it is beginning to be recognised in general histories of post-war Britain: see, for example, G. L. Bernstein's remarks on 'immigrant cultures' in *The Myth of Decline: The Rise of Britain since 1945* (2004), pp. 427–36.

210. S. Mathur, *An Indian Encounter: Portraits for Queen Victoria* (2003), pp. 26–7.

[348] 211. A. Farrington, *Trading Places: The East India Company and Asia, 1600–1834* (2002), pp. 108–25.

212. There are some signs that this is about to change: see, especially, http://www.britishbornchinese.org.uk, and the essay on this website by Graham Chan, 'The Chinese in Britain'.

213. 'Empire gallery is a disgrace', *Daily Telegraph*, 18/8/1999; T. Pocock, 'Was Britain's Empire so evil?', *Mail on Sunday*, 29/8/1999, pp. 54–5.

214. For an example, see P. Reginier, 'Tempest in a tea cup. The English flooded China with opium. Does the British Library get the story right?', *Time*, 17/6/2002, p. 67.

215. N. Ferguson, 'Let's stop saying sorry for the Empire', *BBC History* (Feb. 2000), p. 34 and 'Egypt 1882: a fine template for running Baghdad today', *Sunday Times*, 1/6/2003, p. 8.

216. N. Ferguson, *Empire: How Britain Made the Modern World* (2003), pp. 367–70 and *Colossus: The Rise and Fall of the American Empire* (2004).

217. S. Feeley, 'Hundreds attend major US debate', *Evening Post*, 24/1/2004, p. 2.

218. Speaking to Nigel Rigby and Robert Blyth brought this point home very forcefully. See also Gary Younge, 'Distant voices, still lives', *Guardian*, 2/11/02: 'Caught between those who wished to romanticise the past and those who sought to forget it, there has been limited space to chart a path from our imperial past to our multicultural present.'

219. R. Duthy, 'The Art of Fairly Modern India' (review of NPG 'Raj' exhibition), *The Field* (Oct. 1990), p. 18.

220. A. Marr, *The Day Britain Died* (2000), pp. 25–9.

221. B. Macintyre, 'If a politician turns to the past, he's probably pulling that old trick', *The Times*, 3/1/04, p. 24.

222. D. Gadher, 'Asian pop musician turns down MBE from "colonialist" Britain', *Sunday Times*, 30/6/2002, p. 3; B. Zephaniah, 'It's got to be wrong to accept a gong', *Sunday Times*, 30/11/03, p. 17.

223. M. Kite and J. Sherman, 'Call for end of empire in new-look honours', *The Times*, 16/12/03, p. 2; P. French, 'Nothing political about it, I had to turn down an OBE', *The Times*, 21/12/03, p. 4; 'A matter of honour', *Guardian*, 28/11/03, p. 29.

224. 'Prized prizes. The honours system needs reform', *The Times*, 31/12/2003, p. 19.

225. For a brief but thought-provoking discussion of the cultural function of today's museums, see A. S. Ahmed, 'Understanding People: The Exhibition as Teacher', *Anthropology Today* (Oct. 1991).

226. Much of the favourable comment toward the NPG exhibition on the *Raj* praised the way in which Indian and British (if not Pakistani and Bangla-

deshi) views were equally depicted; Bristol's Empire and Commonwealth   [349]
Museum has also been complimented on its even-handed approach.

227. Y. Alibhai-Brown, 'Personally, I'm all for a museum of the Empire', *Independent*, 17/6/2002, p. 15.

228. G. Eley, *The Future of the Past* (Cambridge, 1966), p. 22 and *The History of England* (1984), p. 28.

229. J. McEwen, 'Not a tiger-skin to be seen', *Daily Telegraph*, 28/10/1990.

230. The 'democracy walls' at the NMM, MMM and Bristol's Empire and Commonwealth Museum, upon which visitors record their reactions, have been particularly instructive here.

231. A remark made about the history of 'punishment' and its many meanings: see F. Nietzsche, *On the Genealogy of Morality and Other Writings*, ed. K. Ansell-Pearson, trans. C. Diethe (Cambridge, 1994), p. 57.

232. For the multiplicity of its meanings in the wider public domain, see J. Wilson, 'Niall Ferguson's Imperial Passion', *HWJ* (2003), pp. 181–2.

Afterword

1. Much of the research undertaken for this project has accordingly focused on these areas, and some of it will continue to be developed in further publications on the British 'imperial economy' and on the attitudes of Asian migrants to Britain. See, especially, G. Magee and A. S. Thompson, 'Imperial Globalisation? A Cultural Economy of the British Empire, *c*. 1860–1914' (forthcoming) and A. Thompson with R. Begum, 'Asian "Britishness": A Study of First Generation Asian Migrants in Greater Manchester', *Asylum and Migration Working Paper Series*, Institute of Public Policy Research (2004).

2. This distinction originates with J. H. Hexter's famous essay criticising Christopher Hill: 'The Burden of Proof', *TLS*, 24/10/1975, pp. 1250–2. It was drawn to my attention by Peter Marshall at the *Studies in Imperialism after 20 Years: A Colloquium*, University of Southampton, 16 Apr. 2004.

3. D. Goodhart, 'Is Britain becoming too diverse to sustain the mutual obligations that underpin a good society and a generous welfare state?', *Prospect* (Feb. 2004), pp. 30–7.

4. D. Omissi, *Indian Voices of the Great War: Soldiers' Letters, 1914–18* (Basingstoke, 1999) and 'Europe Through Indian Eyes: Indian Soldiers in England and France, 1914–18', *EHR* (forthcoming). See also pp. 232–3.

5. C. Gluck, 'Past Obsessions: War and Memory in the 20th Century', Lecture given at the University of Leeds, 15 Mar. 2004.

SELECT BIBLIOGRAPHY

Place of publication is London unless otherwise stated.

A1. Primary Sources, Unpublished

(i) Personal Papers

Ellis Ashmead-Bartlett papers, Institute of Commonwealth Studies, University of London.
J. B. Glasier papers, Sydney Jones Library, University of Liverpool.
Tom Mann papers, Modern Records Centre, University of Warwick.
Horatio Gilbert Parker papers, Special Collections, Brotherton Library, University of Leeds.

(ii) Organisational Archives

Heinz Archive, National Portrait Gallery.
Listener Research Reports, LR/1558, BBC Written Archive Centre, Caversham, Reading.
Post Office Archives, Post 27 and 92, Farringdon Road, London.
London Typographical Society, Modern Records Centre, University of Warwick.
Amalgamated Society of Engineers, Modern Records Centre, University of Warwick.
Association of Boilermakers, Modern Records Centre, University of Warwick.
Board of Trade Library, Modern Records Centre, University of Warwick.
Hong Kong and Shanghai Bank (HSBC), Canary Wharf, London.

(iii) Oral History and Social Survey Archives

Edwardians On-Line, 'Family Life and Work Experience Summaries before 1918', Albert Sloman Library, University of Essex.
Heritage Recording Unit, Bradford Central Library.

Mantle Collection, East Midlands Oral History Archive, Centre for Urban History, [351]
    University of Leicester.
Topic Collections (Children & Education; Political Attitudes), Mass Observation
    Archive, University of Sussex.
North-West Sound Archive, Clitheroe Castle, Clitheroe, Lancashire, BB7 1AZ.

(iv) Other Archival Material

Notebooks of Newspaper Editors, Elites Survey Records, copy supplied by Profes-
    sor W. D. Rubinstein, Department of History, University of Aberystwyth.
John Johnson Collection of Printed Ephemera, Bodleian Library, University of
    Oxford.
Interview transcripts of first-generation Asian migrants in Greater Manchester,
    Institute of Public Policy Research.

(v) Interviews

Dr Robert Blyth, National Maritime Museum, London, 11/9/2003.
Baroness Shreela Flather, House of Lords, London, 19/1/2004.
Dr Gareth Griffiths, Empire and Commonwealth Museum, Bristol, 19/5/2004.
Dr Nigel Rigby, National Maritime Museum, London, 15/9/2003.
Mr Anthony Tibbles, Merseyside Maritime Museum, Liverpool, 30/9/2003.
[All interviews, except that with Baroness Flather, were by telephone.]

A2. Published Primary Sources

(i) Parliamentary Command Papers and Other Official Reports

Annual Reports of the Postmaster General (1859–1914).
*Board of Education, Suggestions for the Consideration of Teachers and Others Concerned in
    the Work of Public Elementary Schools* (HMSO, 1905, 1914, 1923, 1927, 1937).
*Cultural Property. Return and Illicit Trade. 7th Report of the Select Committee of the House
    of Commons on Culture, Media and Sport* (2000).
Distribution of Regimental Establishments, Army Estimates for the Year ending March 1926
    (1926), Cmd. 16203.
General Annual Return of the British Army for the Year 1895 (1896), Cmd. 8225.
General Annual Report on the British Army for the Year ending September 1905 (1906),
    Cmd. 2696.
*Report by the Central British Red Cross Committee on Voluntary Organisations in Aid of the
    Sick and Wounded during the South African War* (1902).
Report of a Committee on the Appointment in the Colonial Office and the Colonial Services
    (April 1930) Cmd. 3554.
Report of the Working Group on Human Remains in Museum Collections (November 2003).

[352] *The Welfare of Former British Child Migrants. Government Response to the Third Report from the Health Committee, Session 1997–8* (1988).

(ii) Newspapers and Periodicals

Architectural Review
Ballarat Courier
Clitheroe Advertiser and Times
Cotton Factory Times
Daily Express
Daily Mail
Darwen News
India's Women and China's Daughters (CEZMS Magazine)
Journal of the Royal Statistical Society
Labour Leader
Library
Macmillan's Magazine
Movie
The British Quarterly Review
The Daily Telegraph
The Economic Review
The Independent
The Manchester Guardian
The Nineteenth Century
The Salisbury Review
The Times
The Westminster Review
TUC Annual Reports
Women's Penny Paper

(iii) Essays, Poems, Speeches, Letters and Diaries

Austin, A. G. (ed.), *The Webbs' Australian Diary, 1898* (Melbourne, 1965).
Dupree, M. (ed.), *Lancashire and Whitehall: The Diary of Raymond Street, 1931–39* (Manchester, 1987).
Esher, Viscount, *To-day and Tomorrow and Other Essays* (1910).
Gandhi, M. K., *The Collected Works of Mahatma Gandhi, XL VIII* (Delhi, 1971).
Gordon, P. (ed.), *Politics and Society: The Journals of Lady Knightley of Fawsley, 1885–1913* (Northampton, 1999).
Guedalla, P., *The Queen and Mr Gladstone, 1880–1898* (1933).
Hamer, D. A., *The Webbs in New Zealand, 1898: Beatrice Webb's Diary with Entries by Sidney Webb* (Wellington, 1974).
Howard, A., *The Crossman Diaries: Selections from the Diaries of a Cabinet Minister, 1964–70* (1979).

Lowe, R., *Speeches and Letters on Reform* (1867).

Nehru, J., *India's Foreign Policy: Selected Speeches, 1946–1961* (Bombay, 1961).

Orwell, S., and Angus, I., *The Collected Essays, Journalism and Letters of George Orwell. Vol. II: My Country Right or Left, 1940–3* (1968).

Piercy, G., *Love for China: Exemplified in the Memorials of Mary Gunson, the First Female Teacher in Connection with the Wesleyan Methodist Mission at Canton* (1865).

Rankin, R., *A Subaltern's Letters to His Wife* (1901).

Rushdie, S., *Imaginary Homelands: Essays and Criticism, 1981–1991* (1991).

Stanley, H. M., 'Central Africa and the Congo Basin: Or, the Importance of the Scientific Study of Geography', *Journal of the Manchester Geographical Society* (1885).

Thwaite, A. (ed.), *Philip Larkin: Collected Poems* (1988).

Walrond, T., *Letters and Journals of James, Eighth Earl of Elgin* (1872).

(iv) Memoirs and Travelogues

Amery, L., *My Political Life. Vol. 1: England before the Storm, 1896–1914* and *Vol. 2: War and Peace, 1914–29* (1953).

Andrews, C. S., *Dublin Made Me: An Autobiography* (Dublin, 1979).

Attlee, C., *Empire into Commonwealth* (1961).

Baker, H., *Architecture and Personalities* (1944).

Barnes, I., *Behind the Great Wall: The Story of the CEZMS' Work and Workers in China* (1896).

Barnes, I., *Behind the Pardah: The Story of the CEZMS' Work in India* (1897).

Bremner, C. S., *A Month in a Dandi: A Woman's Wanderings in Northern India* (1891).

Brunton, J., *John Brunton's Book: Being the Memories of John Brunton* (Cambridge, 1939).

Chancellor, E. B., *Liberty and Regent Street* (1926).

Cromer, Earl, *Modern Egypt* (1911).

Duncan, A. N., *The City of Springs or Mission Work in Chinchew* (1902).

Fessnden, R., *The Founding of Empire Day* (Bermuda, c. 1930).

Foakes, G., *Between High Walls: A London Childhood* (1972).

Foley, A., *A Bolton Childhood* (Manchester, 1973).

Froude, J. A., *Oceana or England and her Colonies* (1886).

Furse, R., *Aucuparius: Recollections of a Recruiting Officer* (1962).

Gitsham, E., and Trembath, J. F., *A First Account of Labour Organisation in South Africa* (Durban, 1926).

Hardinge, Lord, *My Indian Years, 1910–16* (1948).

Healey, D., *The Time of My Life* (1989).

Humphreys, M., *Empty Cradles* (1994).

Jones, K., *Fleet Street and Downing Street* (1919).

Lawrence, D. H., *Kangaroo* (first published 1923; 1966 Heinemann reprint). [Strictly speaking, this is not a travelogue but a predominantly fictional account based on Lawrence's experiences of Australia in 1922.]

Llewellyn Smith, H., and Nash, V., *The Story of the Dockers' Strike: Told by Two East Londoners* (1889; 1970 reprint, Portway, Bath).

[354] Lutyens, M., *Edwin Lutyens by his Daughter* (1980).

Mackay, C., *Forty Years' Recollections of Life, Literature and Politics: From 1830 to 1870*, 2 vols (1877).

Mackay, C., *Through the Long Day: Memorials of a Literary Life During Half a Century*, 2 vols (1887).

Mosley, O., *My Life* (1968).

Orpen, J. M., *Reminiscences of Life in South Africa from 1846 to the Present Day*, 2 vols (Cape Town, 1964).

Parkinson, C., *The Colonial Office from Within, 1909–45* (1947).

Parks, F., *Wanderings of a Pilgrim in Search of the Picturesque during Four-and-Twenty Years in the East: With Revelations of Life in the Zenana*, 2 vols (1850).

Pascoe, C. F., *Two Hundred Years of the SPG: An Historical Account of the Society for the Propagation of the Gospel in Foreign Parts, 1701–1900* (1901).

Pearson, L. B., *Memoirs. Vol. 2: 1948–1957: The International Years* (1974).

Richards, F., *Old Soldier-Sahib* (1936).

Rowse, A. L., *All Souls in My Time* (1993).

Snowden, P., *An Autobiography* (1934).

Swinson, A., and Scott, D. (eds), *The Memoirs of Private Waterfield, Soldier in Her Majesty's 32nd Regiment of Foot, 1842–57* (1968).

Taylor, M. G., *The Story of the China Inland Mission* (2nd edn, 1893–4).

Thatcher, M., *The Downing Street Years* (1993).

Tillett, B., *Memories and Reflections* (1931).

Waugh, E., *When the Going Was Good* (1946).

Wheeler, C., *High Relief* (Feltham, 1968).

Wilson, E., *Mirror Writing: An Autobiography* (1982).

(v) Contemporary Social and Economic Surveys

Bowker, B., *Lancashire Under the Hammer* (1928).

Burnett-Hurst, A. R., 'Lancashire and the Indian Market', *Journal of the Royal Statistical Society* (1932).

Clow, A. G., *The State and Industry: A Narrative of Indian Government Policy and Action in Relation to Industry under the Reformed Constitution* (Calcutta, 1928).

Coghlan, T. A., *Labour and Industry in Australia, from the First Settlement in 1788 to the Establishment of the Commonwealth in 1901* (1918).

Dennis, J. S., *Christian Missions and Social Progress: A Sociological Study of Foreign Missions* (1899).

Dennis, J. S., *Centennial Survey of Foreign Mission* (New York, 1902).

Engels, F., *The Condition of the Working-Class in England in 1844* (1892 edn.).

Esquiros, A., *The English at Home, translated and edited by L. Wraxall*, 2 vols (1861).

Gitsham, E., and Trembath, J. F., *A First Account of Labour Organisation in South Africa* (Durban, 1926).

Haslam, J., *The Press and the People: An Estimate of Reading in Working-Class Districts, Reprinted from the Manchester City News* (Manchester, 1906).

Jennings, H., and Madge, C. (eds), *May the Twelfth: Mass-Observation Day-Surveys by* [355]
   Over Two Hundred Observers, 1937 (reprint Chatham, 1987, paperback edn).
Leavis, Q. D., *Fiction and the Reading Public* (1932).
Mayhew, H., *The Morning Chronicle Survey of Labour and the Poor: The Metropolitan
   Districts, 1850* (Horsham, 1982).
Oliphant, Mrs., *et al.*, *Women Novelists of Queen Victoria's Reign* (1897).
Paul, E. T. (Lieut.-Colonel), *The Imperial Army of India* (Calcutta, 1902).
Pavy, F. W., *A Treatise on Food and Dietetics: Physiology and Therapeutically Considered*
   (1874).
Russell, C. E., *Manchester Boys: Sketches of Manchester Lads at Work and Play* (Man-
   chester, 1905).
Salmon, E., *Juvenile Literature As It Is* (1888).
Shaw, T., *Report of Investigations into the Conditions of Indian Textile Workers* (1927).
Spalding, T. A., *The Work of the London School Board* (1900).
Taylor, M. G., *The Story of the China Inland Mission*, 2 vols (2nd edn, 1893–4).
Thorp, M. F., *America at the Movies* (1946).
Tooley, S., *The History of Nursing in the British Empire* (1906).

(vi) Exhibition Catalogues and Guides

Babbage, C., *The Exposition of 1851* (1851).
Cox, I., *The South Bank Exhibition* (1951).
Gaspey, W., *Tallis's Illustrated London: In Commemoration of the Great Exhibition of 1851*,
   6 vols (1851).
*Hunt's Hand-Book to the Official Catalogues: An Explanatory Guide to the Natural Produc-
   tions and Manufacturers of the Great Exhibition of the Industry of All Nations*, 2 vols
   (1851).
Ismay, Lord, *The Story of the Festival of Britain, 1951* (1951).
Official Catalogue of the Great Exhibition of the Workers of Industry of All Nations, 1851
   (1851).
Phillips, S., *A Guide to the Palace and Park* (1856).
Selfridge's Decorations for the Coronation Souvenir Brochure (1937).
*Tallis's History and Description of the Crystal Palace, and the Exhibition of the World's
   Industry in 1851* (1851).
The Crystal Palace Exhibition Illustrated Catalogue. London, 1851 (1970 Dover reprint,
   New York).
The Story of the Festival of Britain, 1951 (1952).

(vii) On-line Primary Sources

Bodleian Library Broadside Ballads, University of Oxford:
   http://www.bodley.ox.ac.uk/ballads
http://www.britishbornchinese.org.uk
http://www2.nottscc.gov/child_migrants/Cmt.htm

[356] B. Secondary Sources

My criteria for the inclusion of secondary sources in this bibliography were: (a) works cited frequently in the notes; (b) works central to the development of my own thinking about 'imperial Britain'; (c) organisational histories (which have proved key works of reference for this study).

(i) Books

Ackrill, M., and Hannah, L., *Barclays: The Business of Banking, 1690–1996* (Cambridge, 2000).

Appleyard, R., *The History of the Institution of Electrical Engineers, 1871–1931* (1939).

Ballard, R. (ed.), *Desh Pardesh: The South Asian Presence in Britain* (1994).

Bird, P., *The First Food Empire: A History of J. Lyons & Co* (Chichester, 2000).

Bridge, C., and Fedorowich, K. (eds), *The British World: Diaspora, Culture and Identity* (2003).

Brown, J., and Louis, W. R. (eds), *The Oxford History of the British Empire. Vol. 4: The Twentieth Century* (Oxford, 1999).

Burton, A., *Burdens of History: British Feminists, Indian Women and Imperial Culture, 1865–1914* (Chapel Hill, 1994).

Cain, P. J., *Hobson and Imperialism: Radicalism, New Liberalism and Finance, 1887–1938* (Oxford, 2002).

Cain, P. J., and Hopkins, A. G., *British Imperialism, 1688–2000* (Harlow, 2002).

Cannadine, D., *Ornamentalism: How the British Saw Their Empire* (New York, 2001).

Chaudhuri, N., and Strobel, M. (eds), *Western Women and Imperialism: Complicity and Resistance* (Bloomington, 1992).

Corley, T. B. A., *Quaker Enterprise in Biscuits: Huntley and Palmers of Reading, 1822–1972* (1972).

Cox, J., *Take a Cold Tub, Sir! The Story of the Boys' Own Paper* (Guildford, 1982).

Crossley, J., and Blandford, J., *The DCO Story: A History of Banking in Many Countries, 1925–71* (1975).

Daunton, M., *Royal Mail: The Post Office since 1840* (1985).

Daunton, M., *Trusting Leviathan: The Politics of Taxation in Britain, 1799–1914* (Cambridge, 2001).

Davis, L. E., and Huttenback, R. A., *Mammon and the Pursuit of Empire: The Economics of British Imperialism* (Cambridge, 1988).

Dellheim, C., 'The Creation of a Company Culture: *Cadburys, 1861–1931*', *AHR* (1987).

Drayton, R., *Nature's Government: Science, Imperial Britain, and the 'Improvement' of the World* (New Haven, 2000).

Driver, F., and Gilbert, D. (eds), *Imperial Cities: Landscape, Display and Identity* (Manchester, 1999).

Edelstein, M., *Overseas Investment in the Age of High Imperialism: The United Kingdom, 1850–1914* (1982).

English, R., and Kenny, M. (eds), *Rethinking British Decline* (Houndmills, 2000).　　[357]

Fairburn, M., *An Ideal Society and Its Enemies: The Foundations of Modern New Zealand Society, 1850–1900* (Auckland, 1989).

Ferguson, N., *Empire: How Britain Made the Modern World* (2003).

Fitzgerald, R., *Rowntree and the Marketing Revolution, 1862–99* (Cambridge, 1995).

Forrester, W., *Great Grandma's Weekly: A Celebration of the Girls' Own Paper, 1880–1901* (Guildford, 1980).

Gallagher, J., *The Decline, Revival and Fall of the British Empire: The Ford Lectures and Other Essays*, edited by A. Seal (Cambridge, 1982).

Ghose, I., *Memsahibs Abroad: Writings by Women Travellers in Nineteenth Century India* (Delhi, 1998).

Grant, A., and Stringer, K. J. (eds), *United the Kingdom: The Making of British History* (1995).

Green, E. H. H., *The Crisis of Conservatism: The Politics, Economics and Ideology of the British Conservative Party, 1880–1914* (1995).

Green, S. J. D., *Religion in the Age of Decline: Organisation and Experience in Industrial Yorkshire, 1870–1920* (Cambridge, 1996).

Hadley, P., *The History of Bovril Advertising* (1972).

Hall, C., *Civilising Subjects: Metropole and Colony in the English Imagination, 1830–67* (Oxford, 2002).

Harbin, V., *The RKO Story* (1982).

Harris, J., *Private Lives, Public Spirit: A Social History of Britain, 1870–1914* (Oxford, 1993).

Harrison, B. H., *The Transformation of British Politics, 1860–1995* (Oxford, 1996).

Havinden, M., and Meredith, D., *Colonialism and Development: Britain and its Tropical Colonies, 1850–1960* (1993).

Heathorn, S., *For Home, Country and Race: Constructing Gender, Class and Englishness in the Elementary School, 1880–1914* (Toronto, 2000).

Hiro, D., *Black British, White British* (1971).

Hobson, J. A., *Imperialism: A Study* (3rd revised edn, 1938).

Honeycombe, G., *Selfridge's: Seventy-Five Years: The Story of the Store, 1909–84* (1984).

Hoppen, K. T., *The Mid-Victorian Generation, 1846–86* (Oxford, 1998).

Howe, S., *Anti-Colonialism in British Politics: The Left and the End of Empire, 1918–64* (Oxford, 1993).

Humphries, S., *Hooligans or Rebels? An Oral History of Working-Class Childhood, 1889–1939* (Oxford, 1981).

Jeffery, K. (ed.), *An Irish Empire? Aspects of Ireland and the British Empire* (Manchester, 1996).

Kumar, K., *The Making of English National Identity* (Cambridge, 2003).

Lester, A., *Imperial Networks: Creating Identities in Nineteenth-Century South Africa and Britain* (2001).

McAleer, J., *Popular Reading and Publishing in Britain, 1914–50* (Oxford, 1992).

Mackenzie, J. M., *Propaganda and Empire: The Manipulation of British Public Opinion, 1880–1960* (Manchester, 1986).

[358]   Mackenzie, J. M. (ed.), *Imperialism and Popular Culture* (Manchester, 1986).

McKibbin, R., *Classes and Cultures: England, 1918–51* (Oxford, 1998).

Marsden, W. E., *Educating the Respectable: A Study of Fleet Road Board School, Hampstead, 1879–1903* (1991).

Midgely, C. (ed.), *Gender and Imperialism* (Manchester, 1998).

Mintz, S., *Sweetness and Power: The Place of Sugar in Modern History* (New York, 1984).

Mortimer, J. E., *History of the Boilermakers' Society. Vol. 2: 1906–39* (1982).

Moss, M., *Standard Life, 1825–2000: The Building of Europe's Largest Mutual Life Company* (Edinburgh, 2000).

Mowat, C. L., *The Charity Organisation Society, 1869–1913: Its Ideas and Work* (1961).

Musson, A. E., *The Typographical Association: Origins and History up to 1949* (1954).

Nandy, A., *The Intimate Enemy: Loss and Recovery of Self Under Colonialism* (Delhi, 1988).

Nicholson, M., *The TUC Overseas: The Roots of Policy* (1986).

Payton, P., *The Cornish Overseas* (Fowey, 1999).

Peach, C., *West Indian Migration to Britain: A Social Geography* (1968).

Perkin, H., *The Rise of Professional Society: England since 1880* (1990, paperback edn).

Perry, C. R., *The Victorian Post Office: The Growth of a Bureaucracy* (Woodbridge, 1992).

Peterson, J. M., *The Medical Profession in Mid-Victorian London* (Berkeley, 1978).

Porter, A. N. (ed.), *The Oxford History of the British Empire. Vol. 3: The Nineteenth Century* (Oxford, 1999).

Porter, B., *The Lion's Share: A Short History of British Imperialism, 1850–1995* (Harlow, 3rd edn, 1996).

Price, R., *An Imperial War and the British Working Class: Working Class Attitudes and Reactions to the Boer War, 1899–1902* (1972).

Procida, M. A., *Married to the Empire: Gender, Politics and Imperialism in India, 1883–1947* (Manchester, 2002).

Richards, J., *Films and British National Identity: From Dickens to Dad's Army* (Manchester, 1997).

Robbins, K., *Nineteenth Century Britain: Integration and Diversity* (Oxford, 1995, paperback edn).

Robinson, H., *The British Post Office: A History* (Princeton, 1948).

Rose, J., *The Intellectual Life of the British Working Classes* (New Haven, 2002).

Said, E., *Culture and Imperialism* (1993).

Samuel, R. (ed.), *Patriotism: The Making and Unmaking of a British National Identity*, 3 vols (1989).

Stewart, G., *Jute and Empire: The Calcutta Jute Wallahs and the Landscapes of Empire* (Manchester, 1998).

Thompson, A. S., *Imperial Britain: The Empire in British Politics, c. 1880–1932* (Harlow, 2000).

Thorne, S., *Congregational Missions and the Making of an Imperial Culture in C19th England* (Stanford, 1999).

Vizram, R., *Asians in Britain: 400 Years of History* (2002).

Walvin, J., *Passage to Britain: Immigration in British History and Politics* (Harmondsworth, 1984).

Weight, R., *Patriots: National Identity in Britain, 1940–2000* (Basingstoke, 2003).

Williams, I., *The Firm of Cadbury, 1831–1931* (1931).

Young, H., *This Blessed Plot: Britain and Europe from Churchill to Blair* (Basingstoke, 1998).

(ii) Articles and Chapters in Books

Cain, P. J., 'The Economic Philosophy of Constructive Imperialism', in C. Navari (ed.), *British Politics and the Spirit of the Age* (Keele, 1996).

Cain, P. J., 'Economics and Empire: The Metropolitan Context', Vol. 3 *OHBE* (1999).

Chaudhuri, N., 'Memsahibs and their Servants in Nineteenth-Century India', *WHR* (1994).

Colley, L., 'Britishness and Otherness', *JBS* (1992).

Constantine, S., 'Migrants and Settlers', Vol. 4 *OHBE* (1999).

Darwin, J., 'The Fear of Falling: British Politics and Imperial Decline since 1900', *TRHS* (1986).

Darwin, J., 'Imperialism and the Victorians', *EHR* (1997).

Darwin J., 'A Third British Empire? The Dominion Idea in Imperial Politics', Vol. 4 *OHBE* (1999).

Davin, A., 'Imperialism and Motherhood', *HWJ* (1978).

Dubow, S., 'Colonial Nationalism, the Milner Kindergarten and the Rise of "South Africanism", 1902–10', *HWJ* (1997).

Feinstein, C., 'The End of Empire and the Golden Age', in P. Clarke and C. Trebilcock (eds), *Understanding Decline: Perceptions and Realities of British Economic Performance* (Cambridge, 1997).

Fieldhouse, D., 'The Metropolitan Economics of Empire', Vol. 4 *OHBE* (1999).

Harper, M., 'British Migration and the Peopling of the Empire', Vol. 3 *OHBE* (1999).

Hopkins, A. G., 'Back to the Future: From National History to Imperial History', *P&P* (1999).

Howe, S., 'The Slow Death and Strange Rebirths of Imperial History', *JICH* (2001).

Hyslop, J., 'The Imperial Working Class Makes Itself "White": White Labourism in Britain, Australia and South Africa before the First World War', *Journal of Historical Sociology* (1999).

James, W., 'Migration, Racism and Identity: The Caribbean Experience in Britain', *New Left Review* (1992).

Kennedy, D., 'Review Article: The Boundaries of Oxford's Empire', *IHR* (2001).

Kiernan, V., 'Working Class and Nation in Nineteenth-Century Britain', in M. Cornforth (ed.), *Rebels and Their Causes* (1978).

Mackenzie, J. M., 'Empire and National Identities: The Case of Scotland', *TRHS* (1998).

Mackenzie, J. M., 'The Persistence of Empire in Metropolitan Culture', in S. Ward (ed.), *British Culture and the End of Empire* (Manchester, 2001).

[360] Marks, S., 'History, the Nation and Empire: Sniping from the Periphery', *HWJ* (1990).

Marshall, P., 'No Fatal Impact? The Elusive History of Imperial Britain', *TLS*, 12/3/1993.

Marshall, P., 'Imperial Britain', *JICH* (1995).

Marshall, P., 'Imperial Britain', in P. Marshall (ed.), *The Cambridge Illustrated History of the British Empire* (Cambridge, 1996).

Offer, A., 'The British Empire, 1870–1914: A Waste of Money?', *EcHR* (1993).

Pocock, J. G. A., 'The Limits and Division of British History: In Search of the Unknown Subject', *AHR* (1982).

Porter, A. N., 'London and the British Empire, c. 1815–1914', in H. Diederiks and D. Reeder (eds), *Cities of Finance* (Amsterdam, 1996).

Porter, A. N., 'Religion, Missionary Enthusiasm and Empire', Vol. 3 *OHBE* (1999).

Smith, P., 'Refuge for Aristocracy', *LRB*, 21/6/2001.

Taylor, M., 'Imperium et Libertas? Rethinking the Radical Critique of Imperialism during the Nineteenth Century', *JICH* (1991).

Taylor, M., 'The 1848 Revolutions and the British Empire', *P&P* (2000).

Thompson, A. S., 'The Languages of Imperialism and the Meanings of Empire: Imperial Discourse in British Politics, 1895–1914', *JBS* (1997).

Thompson, A. S., 'Publicity, Philanthropy and Commemoration: British Society and the War', in D. Omissi and A. S. Thompson (eds), *The Impact of the South African War, 1899–1902* (Basingstoke, 2002).

Thompson, A. S., and Magee, G., 'A Soft Touch? British Industry, Empire Markets and the Self-Governing Dominions, 1870–1914', *EcHR* (2003).

Thompson, A. S., with Begum, R., 'Asian "Britishness": A Study of First Generation Asian Migrants in Greater Manchester', Asylum and Migration Working Paper Series, *Institute of Public Policy Research* (2004).

Thompson, F. M. L., 'Social Control in Victorian Britain', *EcHR* (1981).

Tomlinson, B. R., 'The British Economy and the Empire', in C. Wrigley (ed.), *A Companion to Early Twentieth Century Britain* (Oxford, 2003).

(iii) Unpublished Theses

Berridge, V. S., *Popular Journalism and Working Class Attitudes, 1854–86: A Study of Reynolds' Newspaper, Lloyd's Weekly Newspaper and the Weekly Times*, University of London Ph.D. (1976).

Buettner, E., *Families, Children and Memories: Britons in India, 1857–1947*, University of Michigan Ph.D. (1998).

Bradlow, E., *Immigration into the Union, 1910–48: Policies and Attitudes*, University of Cape Town (1978).

Elliott, B. J., *The Development of History Teaching in England for Pupils Aged 11–18 Years, 1918–39*, University of Sheffield Ph.D. (1975).

Ewing, H. A., *The Indian Civil Service, 1919–42: Some Aspects of Control in India*, University of Cambridge Ph.D. (1980).

Friend, E. A., *Professional Women and the British Empire, 1880–1939*, University of Lancaster Ph.D. (1998).

Gardiner, N., *Sentinels of Empire: The British Colonial Administrative Service, 1919–54*, University of Yale Ph.D. (1998).

Glendenning, F., *The Evolution of History Teaching in British and French Schools in the Nineteenth and Twentieth Centuries with Special Reference to Attitudes to Race and Colonial History in History Schoolbooks*, University of Keele Ph.D. (1971).

Lloyd D., *Tourism, Pilgrimage and the Commemoration of the Great War in Britain, Australia and Canada, 1919–39*, University of Cambridge Ph.D. (1994).

Maughan, S. S., *Regions Beyond and the National Church: Domestic Support for the Foreign Missions of the Church of England in the High Imperial Age, 1870–1914*, University of Harvard Ph.D. (1995).

Morgan, J., *The Work of the Leeds School Board, 1870–1903*, University of Leeds MA thesis (1986).

Morrow, M., *The Origins and Early Years of the BCINC, 1885–1907*, University of London Ph.D. (1977).

Omissi, D., *The Mills and Boon Memsahibs: Women's Romantic Indian Fiction, 1877–1947*, University of Lancaster Ph.D. (1995).

Potter, S. C., *The Social Origins and Recruitment of English Protestant Missionaries in the Nineteenth Century*, University of London Ph.D. (1974).

Pymer, S., *An Imperial Philanthropist? The Earl of Meath and the Empire Day Movement, c. 1900–29*, University of Leeds MA thesis (2001).

Reidi, E., *Imperialist Women in Edwardian Britain: The Victoria League, 1899–1914*, University of St Andrews Ph.D. (1998).

Ryan, D. S., *The Daily Mail Ideal Home Exhibition and Suburban Modernity, 1908–51*, University of East London Ph.D. (1995).

Smith, V., *Constructing Victoria: The Representations of Queen Victoria in England, India and Canada, 1897–1914*, University of Rutgers Ph.D. (1998).

Steele, I. J., *A Study of the Formative Years of the Development of the History Curriculum in English Schools, 1833–1901*, University of Sheffield Ph.D. (1974).

Thompson, A. S., *Thinking Imperially? Imperial Pressure Groups and the Idea of Empire in Late-Victorian and Edwardian Britain*, University of Oxford D.Phil. (1994) [cited as Thompson, *Thesis*].

Wardleworth, D., *Building the Modern Corporation: Corporate Art Patronage in Inter-War Britain*, Southampton Institute Ph.D. (2002).

Worboys, M., *Science and British Colonial Imperialism, 1895–1940*, University of Sussex Ph.D. (1979).

Workman, G. B., *The Reactions of Nineteenth-Century English Literary Men to the Governor Eyre Controversy*, University of Leeds Ph.D. (1973).

INDEX

The Empire Strikes Back?